River Restoration

SELECTED EXTRACTS FROM

THE RIVERS HANDBOOK

EDITED BY

GEOFFREY PETTS

Environmental Research and Management
The University of Birmingham
Edgbaston, Birmingham

AND

PETER CALOW

Department of Animal and Plant Sciences
University of Sheffield, Sheffield

b

**Blackwell
Science**

© 1996 by
Blackwell Science Ltd
Editorial Offices:
Osney Mead, Oxford OX2 0EL
25 John Street, London WC1N 2BL
23 Ainslie Place, Edinburgh EH3 6AJ
238 Main Street, Cambridge
    Massachusetts 02142, USA
54 University Street, Carlton
    Victoria 3053, Australia

Other Editorial Offices:
Arnette Blackwell SA
    224, Boulevard Saint Germain,
    75007 Paris, France

Blackwell Wissenschafts-Verlag GmbH
    Kurfürstendamm 57
    10707 Berlin, Germany

    Zehetnergasse 6
    A-1140 Wien
    Austria

First published 1996
Set by Setrite Typesetters, Hong Kong
Printed and bound in Great Britain
at the Alden Press Limited,
Oxford and Northampton

The Blackwell Science logo is a
trade mark of Blackwell Science Ltd,
registered at the United Kingdom
Trade Marks Registry

DISTRIBUTORS

    Marston Book Services Ltd
    PO Box 269
    Abingdon
    Oxon OX14 4YN
    (Orders: Tel: 01235 465500
             Fax: 01235 465555)
USA
    Blackwell Science, Inc.
    238 Main Street
    Cambridge, MA 02142
    (Orders: Tel: 800 215-1000
             617 876-7000
             Fax: 617 492-5263)

Canada
    Copp Clark, Ltd
    2775 Matheson Blvd East
    Mississauga, Ontario
    Canada, L4W 4P7
    (Orders: Tel: 800 263-4374
             905 238-6074)

Australia
    Blackwell Science Pty Ltd
    54 University Street
    Carlton, Victoria 3053
    (Orders: Tel: 03 9347 0300
             Fax: 03 9349 3016)

A catalogue record for this title
is available from the British Library

ISBN 0-86542-919-7

Library of Congress
Cataloging-in-Publication Data

Rivers handbook. Selections
    River restoration: selected extracts
from the Rivers handbook/
edited by Geoffrey Petts and Peter Calow.
        p.   cm.
    Includes bibliographical references
    and index.
    ISBN 0-86542-919-7
    1. River engineering.
    I. Petts, Geoffrey E.
II. Calow, Peter. III. Title.
TC405.R59 1996
    628.1'12 — dc20
                                96-11447
                                CIP

Contents

Colour plate falls between pp. 112 and 113

List of Contributors

P. CALOW *Department of Animal and Plant Sciences, University of Sheffield, PO Box 601, Sheffield S10 2UQ, UK*

A. J. DOBBS *WRc plc, Henley Road, Medmenham, Marlow, Buckinghamshire SL7 2HD, UK*

D. P. DODGE *Ontario Ministry of Natural Resources, Great Lakes Branch, PO Box 5000, Maple, Toronto, Ontario L6A 1S9, Canada*

R. D. HEY *School of Environmental Sciences, University of East Anglia, Norwich, Norfolk NR4 7TJ, UK*

A. R. G. LARGE *Department of Geography, University of Technology, Loughborough, Leicestershire LE11 3TU, UK*

P. LARSEN *Institute of Hydraulic Structures and Agricultural Engineering, University of Karlsruhe, Kaiserstrasse 12, D-76128 Karlsruhe, Germany*

C. C. MACK *Ontario Ministry of Natural Resources, Great Lakes Branch, PO Box 5000, Maple, Ontario LGA 1S9, Canada*

I. MADDOCK *Department of Geography, University of Technology, Loughborough, Leicestershire LE11 3TU, UK*

J. L. METCALFE-SMITH *Rivers Research Branch, National Water Research Institute, PO Box 5050, 867 Lakeshore Road, Burlington, Ontario L7R 4A6, Canada*

A. M. MILNER *Environmental Sciences, University of Birmingham, Edgbaston, Birmingham B15 2TT, UK*

G. E. PETTS *Environmental Research and Management, University of Birmingham, Edgbaston, Birmingham B15 2TT, UK*

R. A. SWEETING *National Rivers Authority Thames Region, 6th Floor, Reading Bridge House, Reading Bridge, Reading RG1 8DQ, UK*

A. J. UNDERWOOD *Institute of Marine Ecology, Zoology Building A08, University of Sydney, New South Wales 2006, Australia*

P. M. WADE *International Centre of Landscape Ecology, Department of Geography, University of Technology, Loughborough, Leicestershire LE11 3TU, UK*

T. F. ZABEL *WRC plc, Henley Road, Medmenham, Marlow, Buckinghamshire SL7 2HD, UK*

Preface

If the extent to which books are 'borrowed' from libraries is a measure of their success, then personal experience with the extent to which *The Rivers Handbook* volumes have gone missing from our own shelves has to be encouraging! Another factor is, of course, price; and we have been very much aware that the *Handbook* in its original form was not affordable for most students. So following some encouragement we have decided to produce less expensive versions. In doing this we could have simply published softback editions of the originals. But, again following encouragement, we opted instead to take a selection of chapters from the *Handbooks* and reorganize these into three groupings intended to be especially helpful for supporting course work (for undergraduate and postgraduate programmes) in river ecology. The result has been the development of three books: *River Biota; River Flows and Channel Forms* and *River Restoration* of which this is one.

Each book opens with a completely new chapter, presenting general principles and indicating how the rest of the book is structured around these. All the other chapters are taken, with some updating, from the parent *Handbooks*. Our hope, therefore, is that the repackaging brings benefits in terms of both availability and convenience for a broader readership and we would welcome feedback on this. As ever, we are grateful to authors of individual chapters for their co-operation in compiling the reorganized versions and especially to the Publishers for their encouragement and support in this venture.

Geoffrey E. Petts
Peter Calow

1: The Nature of Rivers

G. E. PETTS AND P. CALOW

1.1 INTRODUCTION

River systems have been dramatically altered by dams and reservoirs, channelization, and landuse developments throughout their drainage basins (e.g. Petts *et al* 1989). Some species of flora and fauna have disappeared; exotic species have invaded; the functional characteristics of the river systems have been disrupted; and there has been a reduction in landscape quality and loss of wilderness areas. The need to develop rivers and their water resources continues to intensify, especially in developing countries because of their existing needs for hydro-electric energy and irrigation, the increasing needs of rapidly growing populations, and their likely increase in per capita resource demands. However, there is arising a strong concern for ecosystem sustainability in the face of both socio-economic development and climatic change. Over the past two decades, attempts have been made to restore damaged systems (e.g. Gore 1985; NRC 1992) and to improve watershed management (Naiman 1992).

Increasingly, efforts have been directed to the application of scientific principles to the development of environmentally sensitive approaches for managing rivers. The restoration of rivers degraded by past urban, industrial and agricultural developments is now a priority for the developed nations. The following chapters in this volume provide critical state-of-the-art reviews of the approaches currently available to diagnose and mitigate problems, and to rehabilitate damaged systems. The following sections of this chapter summarize the key points that underpin approaches for developing environmentally sensitive water projects. A more detailed treatment of some of these issues is presented in companion volumes: *The Textbook of River Hydrology* (Petts & Calow 1996a), *The Textbook of River Biota* (Petts & Calow 1996b). A more expansive treatment of all these issues, including case studies, is presented in the parent volumes: *The Rivers Handbook* volume 1 (Calow & Petts 1992), on the basic scientific principles, and volume 2 (Calow & Petts 1994) on applied aspects.

1.2 DIFFERENT TYPES OF RIVERS

From a biological point of view, flowing water has a number of advantages over still water, despite the stress exerted on biota: it is constantly mixed by turbulence providing nutrients, exchange of respiratory gases, and removal of wastes. Some species of aquatic macrophyte, for example, are highly adapted to the improved metabolic conditions of flowing water. Producers and consumers must be efficient at nutrient uptake, especially the sessile biota which cannot pursue their food items, because of the rapid downstream transport of nutrients. Flowing water is also fundamental for the downstream and lateral dispersal of attached and suspended algae, macrophytes and invertebrates, despite the high mortality caused by mechanical stress. Floods cause hydraulic disturbance but this is important in determining the composition of biotic communities within the channel, the riparian zone and the floodplain.

The principal components of the abiotic milieu of river ecosystems — hydrology, temperature and channel morphology — reflect regional-scale climate and geology. Thus, regional water resource and fisheries management in the United States has utilized an 'ecoregion' approach to delineate large areas (greater than $1000\,km^2$) based upon climate, physiography, and vegetation (Rohm *et al* 1987). However, in practice, the analysis of river systems and their evaluation for purposes of restoration, requires a recognition of the influence of spatial scale.

A useful way to approach studies of individual rivers is to utilize a hierarchical classification incorporating spatially nested levels of resolution, such as that proposed by Frissell *et al* (1986), (Fig. 1.1). A river may be viewed as a series of reaches or sectors each receiving and discharging water, sediments, organic matter and nutrients. Individual sectors may be defined by tributary confluences, by changes of valley and channel morphology, or by changes of riparian vegetation; surrogate variables providing an indication of hydrology, water-quality and disturbance. Habitats include pools and riffles and backwater, marginal and main flow sites. Microhabitats relate, for example, to different hydraulic or substrate characteristics.

At the scale of the drainage basin, the physical, chemical and biological characteristics of a river are seen to vary from headwaters to mouth. Most ecological studies have employed stream ordering techniques as an objective, and widely applicable, classification system to account for this longitudinal pattern. The most commonly used system is that proposed by Strahler (1952). This convention (see Fig. 1.2) designates all headwater streams, terminated by the first confluence, as first-order streams; two first-order streams join to form a second-order stream, the confluence of two second-order streams produces a third-order river, and so on. Ordering forms the basis of the River Continuum Concept (Fig. 1.3; Vannote *et al* 1980).

The traditional view of a river is as a *longitudinal* gradient or sequence of interlinked zones. The classic high-gradient upland stream with small channel, cold temperatures and highly oxygenated water, dominated by fastwater habitats, contrasts with low-gradient sectors of large floodplain rivers with a diversity of channel forms and floodplain water bodies. In general, large rivers tend to be characterized by more regular and predictable variations of the abiotic variables than headwater streams and the greater range of habitats and food sources is associated with greater fish diversity and a wide range of trophic adaptations.

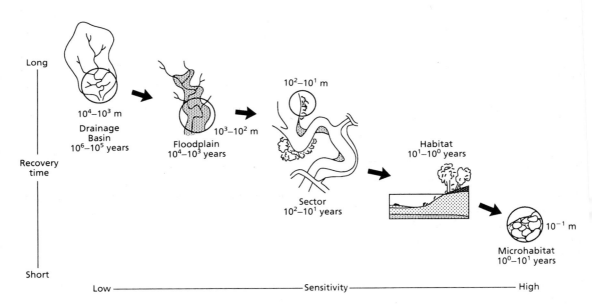

Fig. 1.1 Hierarchical organization of a river system in relation to sensitivity to disturbance and recovery time (after Frissell *et al* 1986).

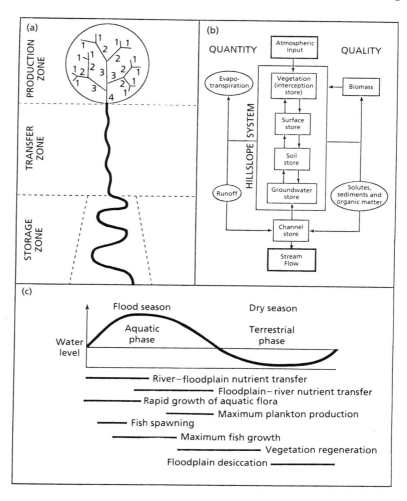

Fig. 1.2 Land-water interactions within fluvial hydrosystems. (a) The three primary zones (after Schumm 1977). (b) Hillslope controls on flow quantity and quality within headwater streams. (c) The influence of the floodpulse within the storage zone (based on Ward 1989).

The River Continuum Concept (Vannote *et al* 1980) describes the change in relative abundance of invertebrate functional groups along a river from headwater to mouth (Fig. 1.3). Three types of channel are defined: litter-dominated, usually, headwater channels characterized by shredders and collectors; relatively wide and shallow mid sectors where light and nutrients favour benthic algae production, characterized by scrapers; and lower sectors where high levels of fine particulate organic matter from upstream or from floodplain inputs favour collectors. Predators tend to have similar relative abundances in all sectors.

1.3 KEY PROCESSES

Throughout fluvial hydrosystems important interactions take place across the land-water boundary (Fig. 1.2b,c). These interactions are manifest in a number of ways: organic matter inputs; nutrient fluxes; predation by terrestrial birds and mammals etc. In the production zone, channel processes are closely tied to hillslope processes. In floodplain rivers, the ecological integrity of the system is dependent upon the strength of connectivity between the channel and the floodplain. This has been described as the 'flood pulse' concept (Junk *et al* 1989). It emphasizes the importance of flood regime upon the ecological dynamics of aquatic

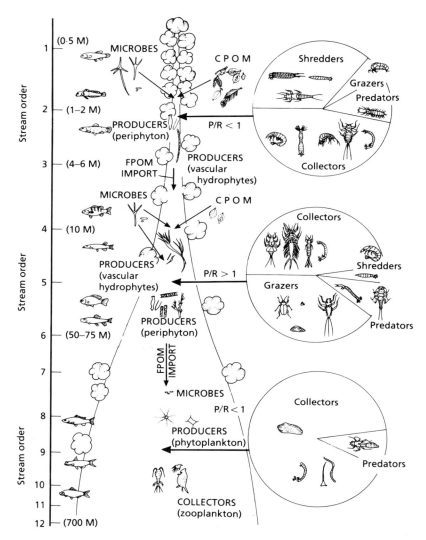

Fig. 1.3 A generalized model of the shifts in the relative abundances of invertebrate functional groups along a river tributary system from headwaters to mouth as predicted by the river continuum concept (RCC; e.g. Vannote *et al* 1980). The river system is shown as a single stem of increasing stream order and width. The headwaters (orders 1−3) are depicted as dominated by riparian shading and litter inputs resulting in heterotrophic $P/R < 1$. The invertebrates are dominated by shredders which utilize riparian litter as their food resource once it has been appropriately conditioned by aquatic micro-organisms (especially aquatic hyphomycete fungi) and collectors that feed on fine particulate organic matter (FPOM). The mid-reaches (orders 4−6) are less dependent upon direct riparian litter input and with increased width and reduced canopy shading they are autotrophic with a $P/R > 1$. The shredders are reduced and the scrapers are relatively more important as attached microalgae become more abundant. The larger rivers are dominated by FPOM (and therefore collectors), and the increased transport load of this material together with the increased depth results in reduced light penetration, and the system is again characterized by a $P/R < 1$ (after Cummins 1975).

and terrestrial biota and on carbon and nutrient spirals.

Within river channels habitats are in large part determined by a range of hydraulic and morphological variables: flow depth, velocity, shear stress; and channel width, depth, slope, pattern and substrate characteristics. At any point along a river, the channel morphology is adjusted to the supplies of water and sediment from upstream, modified by local conditions. Relationships between channel form dimensions and discharge provide scale frameworks for ecological analyses.

Flowing water provides a wide variety of habitats reflecting the channel planform and cross-sectional variation of hydraulic conditions. The pattern of velocity variation in space and time has a strong influence on biota, especially benthic invertebrates and algae. Three general velocity zones may be defined: near the bed over riffles, pools, and channel margins. For many species survival of some life stage, at least, is assisted by the presence of refuges along the channel margins; one widespread human impact has been to simplify the structure of the river margin and to eliminate these refuges. In reality, a natural reach of river is characterized by a diversity of hydraulic patches. The importance of channel morphology and local hydraulic variations for biota have been elaborated by Statzner and Higler (1986) and Statzner et al (1988).

Within this physical context, river ecosystems are structured by food webs. The role of food webs is a key topic because of the importance of river communities in both environmental management and assessment. Food web structure obviously relates to the nature of biological interactions such as competition and predation but they too, also relate to environmental characteristics. Habitat diversity, especially the complexity of refugia along the channel margins and on, and within, the channel bed have an important influence on the shape of the food web.

Primary production can be important in most running waters, including small, shaded streams. However, it is the detritus from both allochthonous (wood, leaves etc.) and autochthonous (dead aquatic animals and plants) sources that is quantitatively the most important fuel for running water food webs. The importance of detritus is

that it comprises not only decomposing organic matter but also an assemblage of living organisms, such as fungi, bacteria, microinvertebrates and algal cells. Micro-organisms play the pivotal role in stream ecosystem dynamics but invertebrates have received most attention not least because they link the micro-organisms that dominate nutrient cycling on the one hand and fish, often the focus of interest in river management, on the other.

Disturbances such as floods or erosion play a critical role in organizing communities and ecosystems (Townsend 1989; Reice et al 1990) and this has important management implications, especially with regard to the long-term effects of human impacts. For example, the diversity of vegetation patches on floodplains is related to the rejuvenation of successions associated with channel erosion and deposition so that the patch mosaic reflects age structure and patch type (see Plate 7.1).

1.4 MANAGEMENT PERSPECTIVE

All levels of conservation require management; controls — and the administration of these controls — on the wide range of human activities that influence river ecosystems. These include:
1 Point-source pollution controls (especially implementation of effluent discharge standards).
2 Landuse regulation (include the definition of 'protection zones' for groundwater and the use of buffer zones to minimize diffuse-source pollution).
3 Water allocation to meet seasonally-variable instream and riparian flow needs.
4 Channel and floodplain management to sustain morphological diversity.
5 Controls on human use of a river for fishing, recreation etc.
6 Controls on biota to prevent overpopulation of certain species, including deliberate or accidental introductions and biological invasions.

These management options may be organized in a decision-making framework that focuses on achieving maximum resource development while providing for ecological conservation (Petts 1989). At the first level, options for modifying river projects (ideally but not exclusively at the design stage) should be considered with the specific aim of maintaining the natural structural and biological dynamics of the affected fluvial hydrosystem. Water-quality control, flow manipulation and channel management are key concerns. The economic and environmental effectiveness of first-order management proposals should then be evaluated in relation to second-order options (direct controls on biota and on human uses).

1.5 THE STRUCTURE OF THE BOOK

This book presents the fundamental building blocks for developing restoration programmes or to mitigate impacts. The first part of the book focuses on the water-quality: on river pollution (Chapter 2), biological monitoring of water quality (Chapter 3), and water quality control (Chapter 4). The book then develops the basis for allocating water to meet ecological needs (Chapter 5). This leads into a discussion of the physical structure of the river corridor, focusing on environmentally-sensitive channel engineering (Chapter 6), the role of river margins (Chapter 7), and the restoration of river corridors (Chapter 8). In artificially-influenced systems, populations of fauna and flora often must be controlled directly and these options are evaluated in Chapters 9 (macrophytes) and 10 (fish). Finally, the volume ends with two chapters that provide the theoretical framework for designing schemes to evaluate the ecology of a disturbance and appraise the success or failure of restoration schemes. These concluding chapters examine the principles of environmental monitoring (Chapter 11) and system recovery (Chapter 12).

REFERENCES

Calow P, Petts GE. (1992) *The Rivers Handbook*, Vol 1. Blackwell Scientific Publications, Oxford. [1.1]

Calow P, Petts GE. (1994) *The Rivers Handbook*, Vol 2. Blackwell Scientific Publications, Oxford. [1.1]

Cummins KW. (1975) The ecology of running waters; theory and practice. In: Baker DB, Jackson WB, Prater BL (eds) *Proceedings of the Sandusky River Basin Symposium, International Joint Commission, Great Lakes Pollution*, pp. 227–93. Environmental Protection Agency, Washington DC. [1.2]

Frissell CA, Wiss WJ, Warren CE, Huxley MD. (1986) A hierarchical framework for stream classification: viewing streams in a watershed context. *Environmental Management* **10**: 199–214. [1.2]

Gore JA. (ed) (1985) *The Restoration of Rivers and Streams*. Butterworth Publishers, Boston. [1.1]

Junk WJ, Bayley PB, Sparks RE. (1989) The flood-pulse concept in river-floodplain systems. In: Dodge DP (ed) *Proceedings of the International Large River Symposium (LARS)*, pp. 110–27. Canadian Special Publication of Fisheries and Aquatic Sciences 106. [1.3]

Naiman RJ. (ed) (1992) *Watershed Management*. Springer-Verlag, New York. [1.1]

NRC. (1992) *Restoration of Aquatic Ecosystems*. National Academy Press, Washington.

Petts GE. (1989) Perspectives for ecological management of regulated rivers. In: Gore JA, Petts GE (eds) *Alternatives in Regulated River Management*, pp. 3–24. CRC Press, Boca Raton, Florida. [1.4]

Petts GE, Calow P. (1996a) *River Flows and Channel Forms*. Blackwell Scientific Publications, Oxford. [1.1]

Petts GE, Calow P. (1996b) *River Biota: Diversity and Dynamics*. Blackwell Scientific Publications, Oxford. [1.1]

Petts GE, Moller H, Roux AL. (eds) (1989) *Historical Changes of Large Alluvial Rivers*. John Wiley and Sons, Chichester.

Reice SR, Wissmar RC, Naiman RJ. (1990) Disturbance regimes, resilience, and recovery of animal communities and habitats in lotic ecosystems. *Environmental Management* **14**: 647–60. [1.3]

Rohm CM, Giese JW, Bennett CG. (1987) Evaluation of an aquatic ecoregion classification of streams in Arkansas. *Journal of Freshwater Ecology* **4**: 127–39. [1.2]

Schumm SA. (1977) *The Fluvial System*. John Wiley, New York, pp. 338. [1.2, 1.3]

Statzner B, Higler B. (1986) Stream hydraulics as a major determinant of benthic invertebrate zonation patterns. *Freshwater Biology* **16**: 127–39. [1.3]

Statzner B, Gore JA, Resh VH. (1988) Hydraulic stream ecology: observed patterns and potential applications. *Journal of the North American Benthological Society* **7**: 307–60. [1.3]

Strahler AN. (1952) Quantitative analysis of watershed geomorphology. *American Geophysical Union Transactions* **38**: 913–20. [1.2]

Townsend CR. (1989) The patch dynamics concept of stream community ecology. *Journal of the North American Benthological Society* **8**: 36–50. [1.3]

Vannote RL, Minshall GW, Cummins KW, Sedell JR, Cushing CE. (1980) The river continuum concept. *Canadian Journal of Fisheries and Aquatic Sciences* **37**: 130–7. [1.2]

Ward JV. (1989) The four-dimensional nature of lotic ecosystems. *Journal of the North American Benthological Society* **8**: 2–8. [1.2]

2: River Pollution

R. A. SWEETING

Filthy river, filthy river,
Foul from London to the Nore,
What art thou but one vast gutter,
One tremendous common shore!
All beside thy sludgy waters,
All beside thy reeking ooze,
Christian folk inhale mephitis,
Which thy bubbly bosom brews.

Punch (1858) vol. xv, p161.

THE "SILENT HIGHWAY"-MAN.
"Your MONEY or your LIFE!"

2.1 THE NATURE OF POLLUTION

Pollution is a term applied to any environmental state or manifestation which is harmful or unpleasant to life, resulting from failure to achieve or maintain control over the chemical, physical or biological consequences or side-effects of human scientific, industrial and social habits (Collocott & Dobson 1974). Since the advent of our industrial society we have regarded it as our prerogative to pollute the environment, whether aquatic, aerial or terrestrial. Historically, pollution of the aquatic environment was recognized in Biblical times. In Great Britain it was regarded as an environmental problem as long ago as the 13th century, when laws were passed prohibiting the charcoal burners of Staines in Middlesex from washing their charcoal in the River Thames for fear of befouling the river downstream. Many of the major rivers of Europe, such as the Elbe, Rhine and Danube, and of the USA, including the Ohio, Connecticut, and the Hudson, experienced marked pollution problems in the late 19th and early 20th centuries.

These problems were originally those of gross contamination and subsequent deoxygenation by untreated sewage. High organic suspended solids and high ammonia levels, with high biochemical oxygen demand (BOD) were characteristic of such problems. Reduction in fish species, invertebrate species and macrophyte species was followed by a total disappearance of fish, survival of two or three pollution-tolerant invertebrate groups and massive encroachment by one or two species of emergent macrophytes, or dense algal blooms (Klein 1962).

The problems were gross, the solutions were essentially simple. In the UK they were solved, in theory if not in practice, by the resolution of a series of Royal Commissions on Pollution. Royal Commissions in the UK had their equivalents in other developed countries with the result that most developed countries today have in place effluent controls for sewage-based discharges.

River uses

One of the major corollaries of effluent control policies is that acceptance by society that rivers are suitable environments for getting rid of wastes. The fact that they flow downstream means that, unlike still freshwaters and, to a lesser extent, coastal waters, any pollutant entering them is washed away from its point of entry. When humans were ecological rather than global creatures and lived in relatively small numbers in small communities, rivers were able to cope with the biological loads that were discharged into them. Increasingly large communities, increasing densities of populations and increasing use of resources by developed countries have meant that not only are effluent controls necessary, but effluent treatment to limit the effects of discharges is also accepted as a necessity to maintain a reasonable water quality. A reasonable water quality is important in order that we can benefit from the rivers by a series of 'uses'. In the UK a set of uses have been proposed (Department of the Environment 1992) as follows.

1 Fisheries Ecosystem: six classes suggested from salmonid to no fish.

2 Abstraction for Drinking Water Supply: related to EC directives.

3 Agricultural Abstraction: sets of standards for livestock watering and for irrigation.

4 Industrial Abstraction: suitable standards are being considered.

5 Special Ecosystem: for sites where unusual fauna and/or flora are present.

6 Watersports: chemical and bacteriological standards related to human health risk.

Each of these 'uses' influences the quality of the river water. A complex series of rules, laws and directives in the UK and Europe attempts to control the effects of these uses (Haigh 1987). At present, rivers (and other waters) are an indispensable receptacle for wastes, but this 'use' differs from those listed above in that quality criteria are applied to the effluents, so that the final quality of the receiving river enables it to be suitable for specific purposes. In reality the balance between effluent quality, quantity and river use has been achieved by a combination of historic precedents and economic constraints. The 'use'-related quality objective system is an attempt to plan this process.

Chemical measurements

Pollutants can be measured in two ways: firstly by chemical analysis, and secondly by their effect on the biota present in and around the river. This dichotomy of approach has been one of the greatest strengths and simultaneously one of the greatest weaknesses in the assessment of pollution. Measurement by chemical analysis is the most obvious method of assessing pollution and has the great advantage that it can be applied directly to effluents. It can be applied to simple chemicals such as metals, salts and dissolved gases as well as complex organic compounds such as chlorinated hydrocarbons (Meybeck et al 1989). Measurements of some other parameters can also be carried out on effluents relatively easily, e.g. temperature, turbidity, colour and pH. Controls of discharges are relatively simple to operate when applied to these parameters.

However, knowing the nature of a pollutant in an effluent is only the first of a series of requirements. Measurement of the amount of effluent entering a river provides a total loading of that material. Most effluents vary in quantity as well as quality so total load may be very different at different times of the day, of the week or seasons of the year. The river flow will also vary throughout the year: in a chalk stream it may vary by up to 10 times between the smallest (September) and largest flows (March); clay catchments and upland catchments may have variations of flow of the order of 2000-fold over a year. Calculation of dilution factors is rendered more complex by such variation and often the worst situation is used to define consent limits, i.e. maximum effluent concentration and maximum permitted effluent quantity under dry weather flow conditions of the river.

Variations in quantities of chemicals in effluents may create difficulties in assessing pollutant loading of rivers. This is particularly important when dealing with substances which bioaccumulate, as sampling programmes have to be designed to determine total input over defined time periods. Many discharges to rivers are intermittent (e.g. storm overflows) and produce peaks of chemical concentration in the river downstream. As the chemical moves downstream the short burst becomes attenuated, so that a lower, but longer-lasting presence is detected. The concentrations of pollutants in the river will be lower the further downstream it is sampled away from the discharge. Consequently the sensitivity of the analytical technique needs to be much greater with river water than with effluents. The presence of a particular pollutant in a river indicates an input upstream, but does not pinpoint its source.

The consent limit therefore provides the ceiling level of pollutant (concentration multiplied by quantity of effluent) allowed into a river by the regulatory authority. It does not necessarily equate with a 'no observable effect concentration' (NOEC) in the receiving river.

Ecotoxicological effects

Historically, traditional chemical analyses have enabled the recognition and measurement of relatively large amounts of relatively few substances. Over the last 50 years analytical techniques have improved in sensitivity and now can be used to detect thousands of polluting substances. Modern technology uses tens of thousands of different compounds, most of which find their way to the local river via sewage works, industrial discharge or diffuse input (e.g. agriculture). It is not possible to have analytical suites to monitor for the presence of all of these materials, so their effect on biological systems is often used. This is particularly helpful in assessing the toxicity of complex effluents where many similar organic compounds may be released into the discharge. Simple toxicity tests involve the addition of an effluent to certain volumes of water to produce a series of dilutions to which fish, invertebrates or bacteria are introduced. Until recently the end-point of toxicity tests was death of the test organisms (Cairns & Dickson 1973). Over the last 10 years progress has been made towards measurement of sublethal end-points. These can be used for effluents, diluted effluents or riverwaters and whereas previously they were all carried out in the laboratory, increasingly the tests are carried out *in situ* (i.e. in the receiving river). The use of rainbow trout (*Oncorhynchus mykiss*) in water intakes is a good illustration of this at the vertebrate level. Monitoring is carried out on respiratory rhythm and heart beat. A pronounced change in either, or both, of these activity patterns elicits an alarm system and further investigations, both biological and chemical (Cairns *et al* 1976).

Invertebrate toxicity tests using the crustaceans *Daphnia magna* or *Gammarus pulex* are frequently used, the former for lethality or oxygen consumption, the latter in a 'scope for growth' situation. 'Scope for growth' involves the calculation of an organism's available resources for growth under specified circumstances. It can be represented by the equation:

$$P = C - F - U - R$$

where P = scope for growth, C = energy consumed, F = energy lost as faeces, U = energy excreted and R = energy metabolized.

The amount of energy available for growth (and reproduction) after all metabolic requirements have been met, will decrease as environmental stressors (e.g. pollution concentrations) increase (Crane & Maltby 1991). This effect on an individual organism, whether eukaryote or prokaryote, mirrors the effects on individuals in the field. Different individuals will react slightly differently to a particular level of pollutants, so that in any population there will be variation (usually normally distributed) in effect. Different species will respond both at a different level of pollutant and in a different way. This is described below.

2.2 ECOLOGICAL IMPACTS OF POLLUTANTS

In a population subjected to a pollutant challenge, there will be intrinsic factors that determine the severity of damage to individuals within it. Age, sex, general condition and sexual condition will influence the capacity of the individual to avoid or cope with the pollutant. In the case of mobile organisms it may involve swimming down a concentration gradient, slowing feeding or moving into the flow and increasing its rate of drift. In non-mobile organisms the production of detoxifying enzymes may be increased (Beverley et al 1991) or, as in bacteria, alternative metabolic pathways may be used (Stewart 1990).

A riverine community, because of the different niches occupied by component organisms, will be disproportionately damaged in some areas by extrinsic factors as well. For example, with benthic macroinvertebrate communities, competition between individuals in populations may force the smaller or less fit members into the substrate. In the event of pollution of the river, these individuals may survive to recolonize the more favourable parts of the substrate, replacing those organisms lost. Enhanced detachment and increased drift can occur as a result of pesticide application to streams, resulting in changes in insect distribution (Muirhead-Thomson 1987).

The immediate environment of organisms in the water flow also influences their survival and here the influence of dead zones becomes apparent. These zones of relatively static water within rivers may have retention times many times greater than that of the main river. Their stability depends on the nature of the river bed and banks, and the speed of flow. In low-flow summer conditions retention times of water in these dead zones can be up to several weeks. Absorption of pollutants is slower, but so is release downstream. Fish and macroinvertebrates may use them as refuges from chemical assaults under certain conditions of flow. Impaired flows at the edges of rivers will act in similar ways and enable some organisms to escape from high concentrations of toxic materials flowing downstream.

There is a large element of chance in pollution incidents in that at any one time a different group of organisms may be affected. For example, low dissolved oxygen is the most common cause of fish mortality in rivers. It can result from a large number of organic materials entering rivers (e.g. pulp, sewage, silage, milk, urea, ammonia) and depressing the available oxygen. If it coincides with migratory fish presence in that section of the river, then considerable inroads can be made into those populations. The same occurrence days or weeks later may have little effect on those populations. At other times, coarse fish fry or eggs may be severely affected. Such intermittent pollution episodes result in biological communities of an apparently unbalanced nature being present for significant periods of time. The ecological picture presented as a result of intermittent discharges is consequently different from that presented by continuous discharges.

Physical effects

The chemical composition of polluting materials has been the subject of many investigations over the last 150 years. Less attention has been paid to physical pollution studies. Studies in this area have concentrated on temperature, pressure or the nature of suspended or settleable solids.

In the UK, the number of thermal discharges to rivers is over 2000. Thermal discharges (e.g. power station effluents, cooling waters from chemicals manufacture) have direct and indirect effects. The direct temperature effect of increased productivity as a result of raised metabolic rates is illustrated in the middle sections of the River Trent in Nottinghamshire with its numerous coal-fired power-station effluents. Less well documented are temperature influences in the lower River Thames as a result of major sewage works inputs. For organisms well within their thermal range, minor temperature changes are relatively unimportant, but for organisms at the edge of their range this additional environmental stress may decide between species survival or extinction. The return of salmon to the River Thames may be jeopardized by relatively small increases in temperature. In historic times the burbot (*Lota lota*) disappeared from the UK. The gradual warming of Northern Europe over the last 500 years meant that the low temperatures required for incubation of burbot eggs was no longer guaranteed at the edges of its range (which included the UK). Conversely thermal inputs to the St Helen's Canal in Merseyside ensured survival of a population of introduced guppies for several decades. Rapid changes in temperature are not tolerated by poikilotherms as their isoenzyme complement at any one temperature will need to be replaced as variation of more than a few degrees centigrade occurs, a process which may take several days or even weeks.

Indirect temperature effects are well documented in relation to dissolved oxygen content of water and ammonia toxicity. Pressure effects associated with dams, pumped water and changes in air pressure have been the subject of considerable work in the USA. Rapid changes in concentrations of nitrogen (producing symptoms similar to divers' 'bends') with major haemorrhaging of the systemic circulation are indicated by bleeding from the gills and fins. Seismic surveying in lowland Britain in the 1980s produced several instances of swimbladder implosion in communities of freshwater fish: such instances indicate the need to consider pollution in a much broader sense than convention indicates.

Suspended solids are referred to frequently in pollution investigations and yet the majority of problems arise from settleable solids. They are all included in the effects of 'suspended solids'. A major component of sewage is suspended solids with an organic fraction onto which bacteria are attached. The turbidity introduced by these solids prohibits photosynthesis, as does their deposition on the leaves of aquatic macrophytes and on benthic algae. For filter-feeders in the water column and on the substrate the solids may, depending on their size and composition, act as food or interfere with the filtration process. Some solids clog gills of fish and invertebrates leading to asphyxiation. Deposition of silt on gravel can smother diatoms, benthic algae, macroinvertebrates and fish eggs. If the deposits are large then the macrophyte assemblages may be radically altered. In the USA fishery scientists classify their waters as turbid ($>100 \, mg \, l^{-1}$ solids), intermediate ($25-100 \, mg \, l^{-1}$ solids) or clear ($<25 \, mg \, l^{-1}$ solids) according to the mean value of suspended solids. Although a crude classification, it enables distinctions to be made in the predicted faunal composition both in the water column and on the substrate.

The nature of the suspended solids is also important in determining damage. Angular, inorganic material (from shotblasting, chinaclay mining, stone-working) produces physical abrasion besides inducing clogging-effects (Alabaster & Lloyd 1980). Formerly sediments were thought to be of minor importance, but investigations into sediment-associated phosphorus in eutrophication indicates that they are of major importance in determining nutrient availability in the water column. Other pollutants are also known to become readily associated with sediments, and as the physical and chemical changes take place in sedimented particles, degradation, solubilization and release of toxic materials to the aqueous phase can occur (Dickson *et al* 1987).

Physical characteristics of effluents other than those described above are also of fundamental importance. Many materials are suspended or dissolved in organic solvents. The nature of these organic solvents is normally lipophilic, i.e. cell-membrane-dissolving or exoskeleton-affecting. Damage caused by such solvents, because of their detergent effect, is irreversible and often greater than the solute or suspension that they carry.

Pesticide applications and veterinary treatments are often geared to most effective contact with the target organisms. By their very design they may specifically affect the aquatic flora or fauna (e.g. high adsorbed particulate suspension or finely divided emulsion).

Biological pollutants

Pollution studies have been centred on chemical analysis and biological effects. The major contributor to river pollution in most developed countries is still the domestic component of sewage. There is a scientific discipline geared to measuring BOD, dissolved oxygen and ammonia in all its forms. Statistical derivations and algorithms to determine percentile concentrations on any number of samples analysed are available in order to help the discharge consent setting process.

The bacterial component of effluents like sewage (and silage) is considerable and normally expressed as coliforms, *Escherichia coli* or faecal *Streptococcus* numbers per 100 ml of receiving water. In Europe the methodology is standardized (Department of Environment 1983) and geared towards two major European Directives – the Drinking Water Quality Directive and the Bathing Beach Directive. Neither of these reports considers the effects on the environment of a massive influx of foreign bacteria other than from a human-use point of view. Coliforms are primarily Gram-negative non-sporing bacteria of the family Enterobacteriaceae. Their importance is that many of them are natural inhabitants of the gut of mammals (and birds, reptiles, amphibians and fish), some are parasitic and several are markedly pathogenic, so that their presence in water indicates a potential risk to human health. *Escherichia coli* (*E. coli*) and *Streptococcus faecalis* (faecal *Streptococcus*) are two of the most common of these coliforms in human and mammalian guts and faeces. Coliforms derived from mammals normally die at temperatures less than 37°C and their rate of death depends on a series of physical and chemical environmental factors (e.g. light intensity, temperature, organic material present). However, many coliforms, although capable of survival in conditions simulating mammalian intestinal conditions, derive from plant material (e.g. *Erwinia*, *Proteus*, *Leuconostoc*). Their presence in large numbers (crude sewage may contain 10^6-10^8 coliforms per ml) influences the microbial ecology of the receiving water, so much so that heterotrophic, sewage-derived bacteria far outnumber the indigenous autotrophic–heterotrophic mix of the riverine flora. In more eutrophic waters the natural balance would favour heterotrophs; in mesotrophic and oligotrophic environments, autotrophs would predominate. The influence of this bacterial input to riverine ecology is both fundamental and massive and yet it remains one of the least investigated components of sewage pollution.

The input of viruses derived from human and domestic animal and plant sources is largely unknown. The Bathing Waters Directive refers to the presence of viruses to provide a legislative framework for immersion sports, but other implications of viral ecology as a result of organic inputs are poorly understood.

In recent years, following outbreaks of giardiasis and cryptosporidiosis in human populations using surface waters as their potable water source, there has been considerable interest in protozoan pathogens (cf. the Badenoch Report; Badenoch 1990). With these parasites, as with viruses and bacteria, there is considerable debate as to whether they should be treated as environmental contaminants and removed from any discharge to the environment or whether they should be regarded as part of the normal riverine biota and eliminated during the process of treatment for drinking-water purposes. There are cost implications for both routes, but the latter provides no environmental benefit.

Pollutant pathways

There are three major routes by which pollutants can enter living organisms – with their food, via their respiration and by contact. The major route of entry depends on the physical and chemical characteristics of the pollutant and the level of organization of the assaulted animal or plant. Some materials have immediate effect on the individual while others bioaccumulate and their effects may not be realized for a considerable time. Chlorine is a good example of the former: in water it can exist as free chlorine or combined with ammoniacal compounds as chloramines. The proportion of combined chlorine depends on the concentration of ammonia in the receiving water. Free chlorine, acting as an oxidizing agent, will kill fish such as rainbow trout in 24 hours at 12°C and at concentrations of $0.3\,\mathrm{mg\,l^{-1}}$ (Alabaster & Lloyd 1980). Similar concentrations of the chloramines kill trout over several days. Temperature and pH have little effect on this toxicity. Once contact with the fish epithelium has been achieved, a marked pathology results which is irreversible. Acute poisoning with metals such as copper, zinc and cadmium and with phenols is seen to have similar, direct, rapid effects.

Some compounds are absorbed directly from the water and accumulated. Again metals are good examples of these. Zinc is accumulated in gills, liver, kidney and bone of fish and elevated levels produce a reduction in egg numbers. However, mechanisms exist in the fish whereby zinc can be lost through the gills, in the faeces and via deposition with eggs. Zinc is a trace-element essential for life (being involved in the manufacture of the enzyme carbonic anhydrase) but occurs naturally in some geological formations at levels which initially may seem detrimental to fish. However, under such circumstances fish become acclimated to these levels and have an enhanced detoxification capacity. Absorption of zinc from the surrounding water is influenced by pH and water hardness: calcium competes with zinc for binding sites on the epithelial cells (Lloyd 1992). It is also influenced by the form the metal takes in the water – simple salts will be readily absorbed whereas complexes containing zinc may not be bioavailable, but may eventually become locked up in sediments. Copper is similar in many respects to zinc in its toxicity for fish, but has traditionally been used as a molluscicide, bactericide, algicide and general herbicide. Copper serves as a good illustration of obvious multiple environmental effects with both immediate, direct and long-term effects.

Many synthetic compounds are accumulated by living organisms, e.g. organochlorines, polychlorinated biphenyls (PCBs), organotin compounds. Here the mechanism of toxicity may be different, longer-term and bear little relationship to the acute toxicity data produced for that compound. Because these synthetic compounds are long-lasting there is the opportunity for them to be reworked in the food web and reach concentration factors of several hundred thousand near the top end of the trophic chain. Little is known about their accumulation, degradation mechanism or rate of movement through the various trophic levels. Concern over synthetic compounds is so great in areas like the lower Rhine that programmes of sediment removal have been embarked upon on a major scale. Polychlorinated biphenyls form a major part of the argument for this work, because of their persistence and extreme toxicity under some circumstances. They are a group of 209 related compounds which accumulate in fatty tissues and which were manufactured between 1929 and 1971. Their primary use was in electrical transformers and condensers, but also in paints, printing inks and oils. About 2 million tons have been produced worldwide. It is estimated that 30% of this is cycling through the biota, mainly freshwater. Elevated levels in fish, like eels, with a high fat content present a problem for predators such as herons, otters and humans, where the accumulation will continue. Fish-eating mammals are particularly at risk as during the production of milk by the mother, high PCB concentrations fed to the offspring are undiluted by other food.

During the metabolism of pollutants by the aquatic fauna and flora some degradation to other compounds takes place, or a change in the physical characteristics of the original material may result. Under some circumstances these changes may compound the toxic effect. The use of lead shot by anglers in the UK was for many years suspected as the cause of lead poisoning in swans. Lead as metal lumps is not available for biological uptake. However, as the swans used shot along with gravel from the river bed to help grind up food in their gizzards, metallic lead was ground down. This resulted in significant solubilization which took place in the acid part of the gut. The lead was then absorbed. Following the cessation of use of lead shot by anglers the population of swans on rivers in southern England increased dramatically over 2 years (Lievesley & Perrins 1991).

Such transformations of apparently innocuous materials, whether by physical, chemical or biological mechanisms, render suspect the 'no effect' level proposed in some pollution control policies.

Eutrophication

A whole series of human activities has resulted in the enrichment of rivers in many parts of the world. In the UK, particularly in the south and east, various activities have accelerated eutrophication. Changes in the physical environment such as widening and dredging with consequent slowing of flow and the elimination of bankside trees in order to provide access for leisure activities, commercial activities or river maintenance are predisposing factors in the encouragement of eutrophication. Canalized or 'improved' rivers allow greater light input to the river surface and riverside environment. The very act of canalization increases the available river surface area, thereby increasing light availability further. Eutrophication and the opposite process, oligotrophication, are naturally occurring processes with a long time-scale. The accelerated eutrophication caused by human activity is a rapid process seen over the last 50 years.

Sewage effluent, industrial discharges, farm slurries and agricultural run-off are all major sources of plant nutrients, notably nitrates and phosphates. In rivers in their natural state the limiting factors to plant growth vary according to topography, geology and geography (Haslam 1990). There is consequently a natural variation in plant community composition throughout the rivers of the UK. By increasing light, increasing nitrate, but primarily by addition of phosphate an enhanced plant growth results. This growth may be of relatively small numbers of submerged or emergent macrophytes (*Elodea canadensis*, *Potamogeton crispus*, *Nuphar lutea*), floating-leaved plants (*Lemna minor*), or diatoms (*Stephanodiscus hantzschii*, *Asterionella formosa*) green algae (*Ankistrodesmus*) or blue-green algae (*Microcystis*). The particular species that predominate will depend on the original diversity present, but essentially the effect is one of species impoverishment with a large biomass of very few species. Habitat provision afforded by plant communities is a major influence on the diversity of macroinvertebrates, so that enriched rivers become impoverished in their macroinvertebrate fauna, not only because of direct influences of water quality, but also by indirect influences. Such changes inevitably control the composition of the fish community, which tends towards the limited, cyprinid-dominated coarse fisheries of lowland Britain where two or three species – roach (*Rutilus rutilus*), bream (*Abramis brama*) and dace (*Leuciscus leuciscus*) – make up over 60% of the fish biomass. The appearance of blue-green algal blooms is of major importance

in still waters, where their presence may preclude some of the uses referred to in Section 2.1, but the appearance of *Aphanizomenon* in bloom proportions in the lower Thames in late 1990 is of potentially greater significance. As water is abstracted for London's drinking water from the lower Thames, this use may create the requirement to reverse eutrophication.

Algal communities in many nutrient-enriched lowland rivers extend through the whole water column and are only limited by their own competition for light. Very few submerged macrophytes can withstand this shading (the exception being *Nuphar lutea*), so the impoverishment of the riverine ecosystem is magnified. Changes can be observed both in the water column and in the benthic communities: these are sequential so that methods of assessment of eutrophication using algae or diatoms have been developed by aquatic biologists (Whitton *et al* 1991).

Acidification

In the context of aquatic pollution, the decrease in pH of freshwaters in Europe and North America in recent historic times is encompassed by the term acidification. Simple chemistry informs us that it is a shift to the right of the following equation:

$$[H_2O] \leftrightharpoons [H^+] + [OH^-]$$

with pH being defined as $-\log_{10}[H^+]$. Naturally there is variation in the pH of freshwaters depending on the geological influences that can buffer the acidity of natural rainfall (pH of 5.5). The dissolution of calcium carbonate in areas of chalk, limestone, calciferous sandstone and calcium-rich alluvia produces waters of neutral or slightly alkaline pH, which, because of their buffering, are also pH-stable. The pH values of freshwaters in geologically-older and other non-calcium-bearing areas are acid and far more liable to be changed by other factors: the acidification produced by respiration and decomposition of plant material in already slightly acid waters contrasts with the increase in pH that accompanies active photosynthesis as carbon dioxide is absorbed from the water. Faunal and floral communities in both terrestrial and aquatic environments have evolved to cope with local levels of acidity and in more acid areas with the pH variation that naturally occurs.

In the last 150 years, human activity has produced a marked change in many of these poorly buffered waters, primarily by the production of acid rain, a term first coined by Smith in 1872. Rain becomes acid rain by the addition of the products of combustion of fossil fuels – primarily the anions of sulphate, nitrate, ammonia and other micropollutants of organic origin. Immediately a climatological factor has to be incorporated into acid rain – if hilly areas of high rainfall, mountainous and/or more northerly areas of high snowfall, or areas susceptible to extensive fogs and mists coincide with calcium-poor geology, then acidification results. However, according to NERC (1984), dry deposition accounts for two-thirds of the total acid load in the UK, so the formerly simple acid rain theory is not quite as simple as earlier theorists believed. Other causes of acidification in freshwaters are upland coniferous afforestation (Nillson *et al.* 1982) heathland regeneration (Rosenquist 1978), open-cast mining as well as post-glacial natural acidification (Pennington 1984).

An increase in acidity produces a change in the solubility of all ionic materials and may, by chemical reaction, induce a change in the solubility of many non-ionic or weakly ionic materials. One of the major effects of the acidity increase is the dissolution of metal ions. Lentic environments are affected more readily than lotic environments by acidification, because of the more finite resources that they possess to counteract the acidification process.

The effects of acidification are the gradual removal of fish species until only the most tolerant are left, the elimination of the crustaceans and the disappearance of molluscs. Depending on the original fauna, the change may be slight or catastrophic. The floral composition is also markedly altered and many macrophytes will disappear altogether, being deleteriously affected by the acidity or by the increasing concentration of metal ions in the water. The metals most commonly affected by pH changes from 7 down to 4 are aluminium, copper, mercury, lead and iron, all of which show significant speciation over this range. With aluminium, for example, the most toxic forms to fish are found in the pH range 5.2–5.8.

Attempts have been made in acid-stressed waters to counteract the increase in acidity by the addition of lime, chalk or limestone. For fisheries, the recovery is apparent within a few years but for large parts of the biota the change to a calcium-rich environment precludes their recolonization. The only effective long-term solution to freshwater acidification is the reduction in emissions of fossil fuel gases, primarily oxides of sulphur and nitrogen. Industrialized countries in the northern hemisphere have agreed to this over the next decade. Changes in forestry practice are available to forestry managers which would decrease the acid enhancement due to these activities. There is some concern that the use of fertilizers on agricultural land also leads to a more acid agricultural run-off directly to watercourses or indirectly via ammonia volatilization – major changes in intensive agriculture are required before this is counteracted.

2.3 PROSPECT

The pollution that characterized the 19th and first half of the 20th centuries was essentially sewage or heavy-industry related. The technology and controls available in the second half of the 20th century are sufficient to check the worst excesses of these effluents. However, the proportion of our rivers that are effluent-derived continues to increase as does the number and complexity of compounds disgorged by our society. Our understanding of riverine ecology has moved from almost nothing to simple cognisance at the same time. So now we are able to demonstrate the complexity of the ecosystem and see the ecological ripples that result from dropping an organochlorine or nutrient stone. The complexity of legislation required to cope with this situation has created a subject in itself. Inevitably emission standards will get stricter and major polluters will have to shoulder an ever-increasing financial penalty. In the 21st century the axiom that effluent discharge to rivers is an inevitable consequence of society may be seriously challenged. The technology that enables us to take suspended solids, micropollutants and bacteria out of effluents is already past the drawing board, so that we may be in sight of having cleaner rivers than for 500 years.

REFERENCES

Alabaster JS, Lloyd R. (1980) *Water Quality Criteria for Freshwater Fish*. Butterworths, London. [2.2]

Badenoch, J. (1990) *Report of the Group of Experts on Cryptosporidium in Water Supplies*. HMSO, London. [2.2]

Beverley M, Garrood AC, Craven M, Johnson I. (1991) Elevation of glutathione S transferase in response to xenobiotic and general stress in molluscs. SETAC-Europe Proceedings. Inaugural meeting, University of Sheffield (unpublished). [2.2]

Cairns J, Dickson KL. (eds) (1973) *Biological Methods for the Assessment of Water Quality*. American Society for Testing and Materials, Philadelphia. [2.1]

Cairns J, Dickson KL, Westlake GL. (eds) (1976) *Biological Monitoring of Water and Effluent Quality*. American Society for Testing and Materials, Philadelphia. [2.1]

Collocott TC, Dobson AB. (eds) (1974) *Chambers Science and Technology Dictionary*. Chambers, Edinburgh. [2.1]

Crane M, Maltby L. (1991) The lethal and sublethal responses of *Gammarus pulex* to stress: sensitivity and sources of variation in an *in situ* bioassay. *Environmental Toxicology and Chemistry*. **10**: 1331–9. [2.1]

Department of Environment. (1983) *Reports on Public Health and Medical Subjects No. 71: The Bacteriological Examination of Drinking Water Supplies 1982*. HMSO, London. [2.2]

Department of Environment. (1992) *River Quality*. HMSO, London. [2.1]

Dickson KL, Maki AW, Brungs WA. (eds) (1987) *Fate and Effects of Sediment Bound Chemicals in Aquatic System*. SETAC Special Publications Series. Pergamon Press, Oxford. [2.2]

Haigh N. (1987) *EEC Environmental Policy and Britain*, 2nd edn. Longman, Harlow, Essex. [2.1]

Haslam SM. (1990) *River Pollution – An Ecological Perspective*. Belhaven Press, London. [2.2]

Klein L. (1962) *River Pollution 2. Causes and Effects*. Butterworths, London. [2.1]

Lievesley P, Perrins CM. (1991) *Swans and Lead Poisoning. Report for the year 1990*. Edward Grey Institute, Oxford. [2.2]

Lloyd R. (1992) *Pollution and Freshwater Fish*. Fishing News Books, Oxford. [2.2]

Meybeck M, Chapman DV, Helmer R. (1989) *Global Freshwater Quality*. Blackwell Publishers, Oxford. [2.1]

Muirhead-Thomson RC. (1987) *Pesticide Impact on Stream Fauna with Special Reference to Macroinvertebrates*. Cambridge University Press. [2.2]

NERC (Natural Environment Research Council) (1984) *Acid Rain*. The Environment Committee: House of Commons. [2.2]

Nillson ST, Miller HG, Miller JD. (1982) Forest growth as a possible cause of soil and water acidification: An examination of the concepts. *Oikos* **39**: 40–9. [2.2]

Pennington WR. (1984) Long term natural acidification of upland sites in Cumbria. *Report Freshwater Biological Association* **52**: 28–46. [2.2]

Rosenquist IT. (1978) Acid precipitation and other possible sources for acidification of rivers and lakes. *Science of the Total Environment* **10**: 39–49. [2.2]

Stewart GSAB. (1990) *In vivo* bioluminescence: New potentials for microbiology. *Letters in Applied Microbiology* **10**: 1–8. [2.2]

Whitton BA, Rott E, Friedrich G. (eds) (1991) *Use of Algae for Monitoring Rivers. Proceedings of an International Symposium, Düsseldorf, 1991*. University of Innsbruck. [2.2]

3: Biological Water-quality Assessment of Rivers: Use of Macroinvertebrate Communities

J. L. METCALFE-SMITH

3.1 INTRODUCTION

At present, the monitoring, assessment and regulation of aquatic ecosystems is largely based on chemical measures of water quality. Yet, chemical parameters alone do not provide adequate information for sound management of aquatic resources because they tell us little of the effects of pollution on living organisms.

Direct biological assessments of the health of biotic communities in receiving waters offer several important advantages over chemical-based approaches. For example, organisms integrate environmental conditions over time, whereas chemical data are instantaneous in nature and require large numbers of measurements for an accurate assessment (De Pauw & Vanhooren 1983). Biological communities also integrate the effects of multiple stresses and demonstrate cumulative impact (Plafkin *et al* 1989). Biological studies can serve an early warning function by detecting intermittent pollution and subtle disruptions which would likely be missed by conventional chemical surveys (Howmiller & Scott 1977; Reynoldson 1984). Because chemical monitoring programmes are usually menu-driven, the possibility exists that the pollutants or factors responsible for environmental degradation will be excluded from consideration. Finally, it must be recognized that not all impacts are chemical in nature; biological assessments may also be able to detect the impact of flow alterations, habitat destruction, overharvesting of biological resources, etc. (Karr 1991).

At it is obviously impractical to conduct bioassessments on entire aquatic ecosystems, most workers have focused on a particular component.

Hellawell (1977) and Reynoldson (1984) tabulated the advantages and disadvantages of all major groups, and a clear preference for using macroinvertebrates emerged. Benefits of using benthos include the following.

1 Macroinvertebrate communities are differentially sensitive to pollutants of various types and react to them quickly (Cook 1976), and are capable of a graded response (Pratt & Coler 1976).

2 Macroinvertebrates are present in most aquatic habitats, especially flowing water systems (Reynoldson 1984), and are abundant and relatively easy and inexpensive to collect (Plafkin *et al* 1989). Furthermore, their taxonomy is well established, although admittedly difficult at the species level for some groups (Reynoldson 1984).

3 Benthic invertebrates are relatively sedentary, and are therefore representative of local conditions (Cook 1976).

4 They have lifespans long enough to provide a record of environmental quality (Pratt & Coler 1976).

5 Finally, macroinvertebrate communities are very heterogeneous, with numerous phyla and trophic levels represented. The probability that at least some of these organisms will react to a particular change in environmental conditions is, therefore, high (France 1990).

The use of macrobenthos in bioassessment has three major disadvantages.

1 They respond to seemingly minor changes in substrate particle size, organic content and even texture. As a result, discrimination between the effects of pollution and other environmental factors is often difficult (France 1990).

2 Their life histories are complex and the results

17

of bioassessments can vary with season (Hellawell 1977).

3 Spatial heterogeneity is high, requiring considerable replication (Reynoldson 1984).

This chapter is largely based on an earlier review of bioassessment techniques developed and applied in Europe (Metcalfe 1989). The information has been updated and expanded to include the North American literature as well as several new and alternative approaches. Sampling design and methodology will not be specifically addressed, as these topics have been adequately covered elsewhere (e.g. Voshell *et al* 1989; Klemm *et al* 1990).

3.2 TRADITIONAL APPROACHES TO BIOASSESSMENT

The saprobic system

The term 'saprobia' refers to the dependence of an organism on decomposing substances as a food source (Persoone & De Pauw 1979). Early research efforts of two German scientists, R.W. Kolkwitz and M. Marsson, led to the classic Saprobic System, best known through the saprobic index (Pantle & Buck 1955). This is based on the presence of indicator species (mainly bacteria, algae, protozoans and rotifers, but also some benthic invertebrates and fish) which have been assigned saprobic values based on their pollution tolerance. Values range from 0 to 8; the higher the value the more tolerant the organism. Pollution tolerances of individual species are determined by observations on their relative occurrence under specifically-defined conditions of water quality. According to the saprobic system, water quality is classified into one of ten categories ranging from the purest groundwater to anaerobic sewage and industrial wastes (see Table 1 in Metcalfe 1989). No single indicator species will be representative of only one saprobic zone; rather, its distribution will follow a normal curve over a range of zones reflecting its tolerance. The shape and area of this distribution curve defines the saprobic 'valency' of the species (Zelinka & Marvan 1961), and the position of the apex is its saprobic value (Sladecek 1979). Various lists of

saprobic values have been published, all for European species. Most notable is that of Sladecek (1973), which contains information for aproximately 2000 species.

Briefly, the Saprobic Index is calculated as follows:

$$S = \frac{\Sigma (s.h)}{\Sigma h}$$

where S = Saprobic Index for the site, s = saprobic value for each indicator species, h = frequency of occurrence of each species (rare, $h = 1$; frequent, $h = 3$; abundant, $h = 5$). The value of S will normally range from 1 to 4 for ambient waters.

Major criticisms of saprobic systems are:

1 The taxonomy is not far enough advanced for some groups and too controversial for others; intensive sampling is required; species lists and saprobic values will not be applicable to other geographical locations; and the system cannot be confidently applied to other types of pollution (Persoone & De Pauw 1979).

2 The pollution tolerances of species are very subjective, as they are based on observational rather than experimental data (Slooff 1983).

3 Each taxon is considered as a separate entity, therefore no information on the community as a whole is provided (Jones *et al* 1981).

Two saprobic-based systems are currently in use: the Biologically Effective Organic Loading (BEOL) method in West Germany (Persoone & De Pauw 1979) and the Quality-index, or K-index, in The Netherlands (Woodiwiss 1980). The K-index is calculated as follows. Approximately 60 indicator taxa are arranged in five groups, each of which is assigned a pollution factor (see Table 2 in Metcalfe 1989). The percentage of the total number of animals in the sample belonging to each group is then multiplied by the appropriate factor, and the group values are summed into an index value ranging from 100 (very heavily polluted) to 500 (not polluted), as follows:

$$
\begin{aligned}
K_{135} = & (\% \ Eristalis + Chironomus\text{-group}) \times 1 \\
& + (\% \ \text{Hirudinea-group}) \times 3 \\
& + (\% \ Gammarus + Calopteryx\text{-group}) \\
& \times 5
\end{aligned}
$$

In 1980, the Limburg Water Pollution Control Authority began to develop a biological classification system for rivers and streams in the province of Limburg, The Netherlands. Their purposes were to determine the extent of pollution by organic wastes, evaluate the effectiveness of enforced measures to reduce pollution, and define reference communities for different types of streams which could be used as water quality objectives. To select the most appropriate bioassessment method, Tolkamp (1985a,b) applied a variety of biotic and saprobic indices to a large data set from the drainage basin of the River Geul. None performed as well as the K-index, which was more sensitive to smaller changes in the middle range of the pollution scale. Most other indices underestimated water quality because they included indicator organisms which do not normally occur in these lowland streams. Vandelannoote *et al* (1981) reported similar results for lowland streams in Belgium. The majority of biotic indices available were developed for small upland streams, and the assessment of lowland streams and rivers has generally been neglected.

Diversity indices

Diversity indices are mathematical expressions which use three components of community structure, namely *richness* (number of species present), *evenness* (uniformity in the distribution of individuals among the species) and *abundance* (total number of organisms present), to describe the response of a community to the quality of its environment. Undisturbed environments are characterized by high diversity or richness, an even distribution of individuals among the species, and moderate to high counts of individuals (Ghetti & Bonazzi 1977; Mason *et al* 1985). Organic pollution causes a decrease in diversity as sensitive organisms are lost, an increase in the abundance of tolerant organisms due to nutrient enrichment, and a decrease in evenness. In contrast, toxic or acidic pollution may cause a decrease in both diversity and abundance as sensitive organisms are eliminated and there is no additional food source for the remaining tolerant forms, and an increase in evenness (Kovalak 1981).

By far the most widely used diversity index is the Shannon–Wiener index (H′), because it is stable in any spatial distribution and insensitive to rare species (Cairns & Pratt 1986). Its formula is as follows (after Wilhm & Dorris 1968):

$$H' = -\sum \frac{Ni}{N} \log_2 \frac{Ni}{N}$$

where H′ = index value, N = total number of individuals of all species collected, and Ni = number of individuals belonging to the ith species. The higher the value of H′, the greater the diversity and, supposedly, the cleaner the environment. The reader is referred to Washington (1984) for a critical review of the many diversity indices which have been applied to aquatic ecosystems.

Diversity indices are considered to have the following advantages:
1 They are strictly quantitative, dimensionless, and lend themselves to statistical (Cook 1976).
2 Most are relatively independent of sample size (Wilhm & Dorris 1968).
3 No assumptions are made about the relative tolerances of individual species, assumptions which may be very subjective (Pinder *et al* 1987).

France (1990) notes that 'few subjects in applied ecology are as controversial as the use (and misuse) of diversity indices'. Many criticisms have been levelled at diversity indices, and only the major ones will be identified here. Their most serious problem is that they reduce individual species to anonymous numbers which disregard their environmental adaptations. This could result in equating, theoretically, a pollution-tolerant oligochaete/chironomid community with a pollution-sensitive mayfly/amphipod community (France 1990). Secondly, not all undisturbed communities have inherently high diversity and, consequently, it is not always possible to correlate certain values with ecological damage (Jones *et al* 1981). For example, the oligotrophic offshore areas of large lakes (Howmiller & Scott 1977) and the headwaters of streams fed by nutrient-poor groundwater (Pinder & Farr 1987a) are naturally low in productivity. Because wide variations in diversity index values have been reported for unpolluted conditions (Cook 1976), standards set for the interpretation of values are not universally applicable.

Thirdly, diversity indices may generate 'false negatives' under certain circumstances. Moderate pollution can cause an increase in abundance without excluding species, with the result that the index value actually goes up (Cook 1976). Because H' is more sensitive to changes in evenness than diversity, its value may be high at sites heavily contaminated by toxic chemicals (Kovalak 1981).

Finally, many studies have shown that diversity indices are insensitive and give poor site discrimination, particularly over the moderate range of various types of pollution including nutrients (Jones *et al* 1981), metals (Perkins 1983) and pesticides (Webber *et al* 1989). It is this last characteristic that limits the usefulness of diversity indices to assessing the impact of gross point source pollution of known chemical composition on relatively simple systems. They are of little use in complex systems affected by multiple and diverse stresses and/or basin-wide non-point source pollution. Some developing countries (e.g. Jhingran *et al* 1989) continue to rely on diversity indices for assessing severe sewage pollution.

Biotic indices

The biotic approach to bioassessment, as defined by Tolkamp (1985b), is one which combines diversity on the basis of certain taxonomic groups with the pollution indication of individual species or higher taxa or groups into a single index or score. Numerous biotic index and score systems have been developed, most of them in Europe and the UK. The major indices and their relationships are illustrated in Fig. 3.1. Only the most widely used systems and their recent modifications will be described. The reader is referred to Metcalfe (1989) and Washington (1984) for information on other biotic indices.

Trent Biotic Index

The Trent Biotic Index (TBI) was originally devised for use in the Trent River Authority area in England, but has since been adapted for use in many other countries and appears to form the basis for most modern biotic indices and scores (Persoone & De Pauw 1979). Organisms are collected from all available habitats by means of a kicknet, then identified to family, genus or species depending on the type of organism, but they are not enumerated. The index is based on the sensitivity of key groups to pollution and on the number of component groups in a sample. Clean streams are given an index value of 10, and this value decreases with increasing pollution. The TBI was later extended to cover a wider range of water qualities (0 to 15 instead of 0 to 10) to improve sensitivity. This version, called the Extended Biotic Index (EBI), is shown in Table 3.1. One major drawback of these indices is that

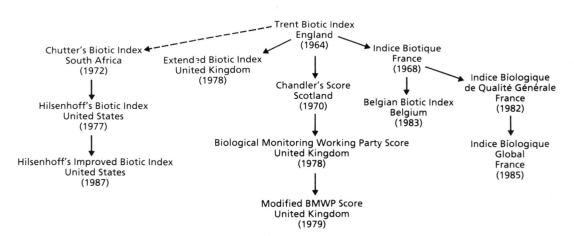

Fig. 3.1 Development of the most widely used biotic index and score systems (after Metcalfe 1989, with permission).

Table 3.1 Extended Biotic Index (from Persoone & De Pauw 1979, with permission)

Extended Biotic Index — Total number of groups present

Trent Biotic Index — Total number of groups present

Biotic indices

Organisms in order of tendency to disappear as degree of pollution increases

		0–1 (0–1)	2–5 (2–5)	6–10 (6–10)	11–15 (11–15)	16–20 (16+)	21–25	26–30	31–35	36–40	41–55
Clean											
Plecoptera nymphs present	More than one species	–	7	8	9	10	11	12	13	14	15
	One species only	–	6	7	8	9	10	11	12	13	14
Ephemeroptera nymphs present (excluding *Baetis rhodani*)	More than one species	–	6	7	8	9	10	11	12	13	14
	One species only	–	5	6	7	8	9	10	11	12	13
Trichoptera larvae or *Baetis rhodani* present	More than one species	–	5	6	7	8	9	10	11	12	13
	One species only	4	4	5	6	7	8	9	10	11	12
Gammarus present	All above species absent	3	4	5	6	7	8	9	10	11	12
Asellus present	All above species absent	2	3	4	5	6	7	8	9	10	11
Tubificid worms and/or red chironomid larvae present	All above species absent	1	2	3	4	5	6	7	8	9	10
Polluted											
All above species absent	Some organisms such as *Eristalis tenax* not requiring dissolved oxygen may be present	0	1	2	–	–	–	–	–	–	–

abundance is ignored. Therefore, the accidental presence of an organism in a sample (due to drift, for example), could drastically alter the value of the index (Cook 1976).

Chandler's Score system

This system was developed for upland rivers in Scotland (Cook 1976). Chandler's Score is theoretically an improvement over the TBI because it includes an abundance factor and incorporates a more detailed list of macroinvertebrates. The Score is determined by identifying the organisms present, determining the abundance classification for each group, then selecting the appropriate points for that group (see Table 5 in Metcalfe 1989). The points for all groups are added to give a site Score. Points scored increase with increasing abundance for sensitive groups and decrease with increasing abundance for tolerant groups, and the value of the site Score is unending. Criticisms of this system are that it is too complicated, the level of taxonomic identification is not uniform for all groups and also that it is geographically restricted due to the number of indicators identified to genus. However, Cook (1976) found that modifications aimed at adapting Chandler's Score to local conditions did not significantly improve the performance of the system in a New York stream. The Score was superior to the diversity index H' in grading sections of a mildly polluted stream according to water quality. Armitage (1980) applied Chandler's Score to a zinc-contaminated river in northern England and found that Score values were lowest at sites affected by high zinc levels, suggesting that it may be adaptable to other types of pollution.

Biological Monitoring Working Party Score system

The Biological Monitoring Working Party (BMWP) was set up in 1976 to develop a standardized system for assessing the biological quality of rivers in Great Britain. Its terms of reference were 'to provide an overall view of the condition of rivers and canals and of the discharges to them and to show the effectiveness of pollution control policies' (ISO 1984). They

developed a standardized score system which was a simplification of Chandler's Score, where all organisms were identified to family for uniformity, families with similar pollution tolerances were grouped together, and the abundance factor was eliminated because it was time-consuming and had only a small effect on score value. The method for scoring is as follows, using Table 3.2: list the families present in the sample, ascribe the score for each family, then add the scores together to arrive at a site score.

The 'average score per taxon' (ASPT) computation, which simply refers to dividing the total score by the number of scoring taxa, has frequently been applied to both the Chandler and BMWP Scores because it is independent of the number of taxa counted. Murphy (1978) compared the performance of Chandler's Score and ASPT, the TBI and several diversity indices over a range of polluted and unpolluted sites in Welsh rivers. The Chandler ASPT showed the least temporal variability, thus allowing the best spatial discrimination. While Chandler's Score and TBI values were depressed at headwater sites, probably reflecting physical habitat properties, ASPT values were high, reflecting good water quality. Armitage *et al* (1983) evaluated the BMWP Score vs. ASPT for classifying unpolluted sites with different physical and chemical characteristics. The results showed a steady decline in ASPT values from the upland to the lowland range of environmental features, while Score values varied. Predictive equations based on multiple regressions using physical and chemical parameters explained 65% of the variance in ASPT values as opposed to only 22% for BMWP Score values.

The performance of the Chandler and BMWP Scores and their ASPT versions were compared in a three-part study on a chalk stream in southern England (Pinder *et al* 1987; Pinder & Farr 1987a,b). They found that the BMWP Score stabilized after fewer replicates than Chandler's Score, and that the ASPT versions of both were much less affected by sample size, season and habitat. The BMWP-ASPT was most sensitive to slight changes in pollution status, ranked sites similarly to both Scores and several diversity indices, and was also best correlated with direct chemical measures of water quality. In contrast, the Chandler–

Table 3.2 The modified BMWP Score system (from Armitage *et al* 1983, with permission)

Families	Score
Siphlonuridae, Heptageniidae, Leptophlebiidae, Ephermerellidae Potamanthidae, Ephemeridae Taeniopterygidae, Leutridae, Capniidae, Perlodidae, Perlidae Chloroperlidae Aphelocheiridae Phryganeidae, Molannidae, Beraeidae, Odontoceridae Leptoceridae, Goeridae, Lepidostomatidae, Brachycentridae Sericostomatidae	10
Astacidae Lestidae, Agriidae, Gomphidae, Cordulegasteridae, Aeshnidae Corduliidae, Libellulidae Psychomyiidae, Philopotamidae	8
Caenidae Nemouridae Rhyacophilidae, Polycentropodidae, Limnephilidae	7
Neritidae, Viviparidae, Ancylidae Hydroptilidae Unionidae Corophiidae, Gammaridae Platycnemididae, Coenagriidae	6
Mesoveliidae, Hydrometridae, Gerridae, Nepidae, Naucoridae Notonectidae, Pleidae, Corixidae Haliplidae, Hygrobiidae, Dytiscidae, Gyrinidae Hydrophilidae, Clambidae, Helodidae, Dryopidae, Eliminthidae Chrysomelidae, Curculionidae Hydropsychidae Tipulidae, Simuliidae Planariidae, Dendrocoelidae	5
Baetidae Sialidae Piscicolidae	4
Valvatidae, Hydrobiidae, Lymnaeidae, Physidae, Planorbidae Sphaeriidae Glossiphoniidae, Hirudidae, Eropobdellidae Asellidae	3
Chironomidae	2
Oligochaeta (whole class)	1

ASPT consistently failed to agree with other indices. Pinder and Farr (1987b) concluded that the BMWP-ASPT was the best biotic index available, although they recommended eliminating the Chironomidae (except *Chironomus riparius*) and Oligochaeta from the scoring system. Since both of these groups include many species which are tolerant of pollution and many which are sensitive, their inclusion without further discrimination had the effect of depressing the ASPT while contributing nothing to the score. After eliminating these groups from their calculations, Pinder and Farr (1987b) achieved better site discrimination.

The Belgian Biotic Index method

The Belgian Biotic Index (BBI) method is derived from the French Indice Biotique (IB), which in turn is a modification of the Trent Biotic Index. The IB differs from the TBI in that it includes a greater number of indicator taxa (Persoone & De Pauw 1979), separates the Ecdyonuridae from other Ephemeroptera and divides the Trichoptera into species with and without cases (De Pauw & Vanhooren 1983), does not separate *Nais* from other Naididae and *Baetis* from other Ephemeroptera (Ghetti & Bonazzi 1977), and does not consider a systematic unit represented by a single individual since its occurrence may be accidental. Also, the TBI specifies that a handnet be used for sampling all habitats, while the IB calls for lentic and lotic habitats to be sampled separately and for indices from both habitats to be used in interpreting water quality (Persoone & De Pauw 1979). De Pauw and Vanhooren (1983) adapted the IB for use in Belgium, with the following modifications: sampling would be by handnet only, as this technique explores a larger array of habitats than other samplers; nematodes would be excluded from consideration, as most would not be caught in a 300–500 μm mesh handnet; the Chironomidae were divided into two systematic units, those belonging to the *thummi-plumosus* group and those not; level of taxonomic identification would generally be set at a higher level (genus or family) to avoid erroneous interpretations due to misidentification.

The BBI is calculated using Table 3.3 which has

Table 3.3 Standard table to determine the Belgian Biotic Index (from De Pauw & Vanhooren 1983, with permission)

	Total number of systematic units present				
Faunistic groups	0–1	2–5	6–10	11–15	16 and more
	Biotic Index				
1 Plecoptera or Ecdyonuridae (=Heptageniidae)					
Several SU*	–	7	8	9	10
Only one SU	5	6	7	8	9
2 Cased Trichoptera					
Several SU	–	6	7	8	9
Only one SU	5	5	6	7	8
3 Ancylidae or Ephemeroptera except Ecdyonuridae					
More than two SU	–	5	6	7	8
Two or less SU	3	4	5	6	7
4 *Aphelocheirus* or Odonata or Gammaridae or Mollusca (except Sphaeridae)					
All SU mentioned above are absent	3	4	5	6	7
5 *Asellus* or Hirudinea or Sphaeridae or Hemiptera (except *Aphelocheirus*)					
All SU mentioned above are absent	2	3	4	5	–
6 Tubificidae or Chironomidae of the *thummi-plumosus* group					
All SU mentioned above are absent	1	2	3	–	–
7 Eristalinae (=Syrphidae)					
All SU mentioned above are absent	0	1	1	–	–

* SU: systematic units observed of this faunistic group.

both rows and columns representing faunistic groups and systematic units (SUs), respectively. The seven faunistic groups are ranked in order of increasing tolerance to pollution. For groups 1–3, it is necessary to know whether there are one, two or more SUs present. The row chosen from the table is the one corresponding to the presence of the most sensitive faunistic group in the sample. The column chosen depends on the number of systematic units present in the sample.

The intersection of the appropriate row and column gives the index value for the site.

The surface water quality of Belgian rivers has been routinely surveyed by the BBI since 1978, and by 1985 over 30 000 km of watercourses had been surveyed and mapped using the BBI. The programme is sponsored by the National Institute for Hygiene and Epidemiology in Brussels and is driven by the urgent need for a coordinated policy in the field of surface water sanitation and management (De Pauw & Vanhooren 1983). Goals of the programme are to obtain better insight into the self-purification of rivers and streams and to assist decision-makers in selecting sites for water purification plants and surface water reservoirs. Belgium requires a method which is equally applicable in fast-flowing shallow streams and slow-running deep lowland rivers and canals. The BBI has been declared highly successful (De Pauw & Vanhooren 1983) for this application. Identification keys and handnet specifications have been standardized, and intercalibration exercises with respect to sampling and identification gave satisfactory results. Results are reproducible over long periods of time in areas where no changes in pollution status occur, and seasonal changes are minor. A single sampling in either early summer or autumn is sufficient for a proper assessment. Artificial substrates were found to be a valid alternative for deep, lowland rivers where handnet sampling was difficult. De Pauw *et al* (1986) found that three pooled replicates of a 2250–4500 cm³ sampler yielded BBI values equivalent to those generated by handnet collections.

De Pauw and Roels (1988) investigated the relationship between the BBI and various common chemical indicators of pollution, using data from a wide variety of polluted and unpolluted sites in Belgium, Italy, Portugal and the UK. They found that correlations between chemical variables and the BBI were consistently positive (dissolved oxygen) or negative (BOD, COD, NH_4, PO_4), but that the slopes of the regression lines varied considerably among watersheds. This indicated that the degree of stress associated with a particular chemical factor in one river was not necessarily of the same magnitude in another. They suggested, therefore, that 'biological assessments should be used as an early warning system and be the precursor of extensive chemical analyses, identifying the causes of biological stress.' The BBI has recently been shown to be applicable in other countries, including Spain, Algeria, Luxemburg, Portugal and Canada (De Pauw *et al* 1986).

Bervoets *et al* (1989) proposed several modifications to the BBI to improve reliability, save time and provide better correlation with water chemistry. BBI values were found to be higher if samples were sorted live, instead of preserved in formalin and washed through a series of sieves, and if SUs consisting of only one individual were included in the calculation of the index. With respect to sample replication, polluted sites could be accurately characterized in only two subsamples, whereas new single-individual SUs were often found in the 10th subsample from unpolluted brooks. They strongly recommended that sampling effort be standardized for area sampled rather than time, because the specified 5-minute period was insufficient for finding rarer individuals in the cleanest streams. Their modification was also more efficient, allowing more samples to be processed within a given time period.

The Indice Biologique Global is the standard method presently used in France (AFNOR 1985). It is also derived from the IB, and its application appears to be restricted to that country. Further details on the development of the French indices are presented in Metcalfe (1989).

Chutter's Biotic Index

A biotic index for South African streams and rivers was developed by Chutter (1972). European indices such as the TBI could not be readily applied, because some of the key indicators were absent (e.g. *Gammarus, Asellus*) or of very restricted occurrence (Plecoptera) in South African rivers, while the Baetidae fauna was much richer. Chutter assigned Quality (tolerance) values of 1(clean)–10(polluted) to all taxa collected, based on the literature. All 'pristine' species were assigned a value of 0. Each organism found in the sample was recorded at its quality value, then the values were summed for all taxa and divided by the total number of individuals. Because some taxa were extremely abundant, he included a 'sliding scale' of quality values which takes into account the abundance and diversity of these dominant taxa. Because of the instability of flows river beds in the rainy season in South Africa, the index was not reliable in recently flooded areas. Although loosely based on the TBI, this approach is unique in that every individual organism contributes to the index value. According to Washington (1984), Hilsenhoff is the only worker to consider Chutter's index and adapt it for use in another country.

Hilsenhoff's Biotic Index

In 1977, Hilsenhoff introduced a biotic index (BI) for evaluating organic pollution in Wisconsin streams based on riffle-dwelling arthropod fauna (Hilsenhoff 1987). To determine the index value for a given site, a sample of 100 or more arthropods was collected by means of a handnet and the organisms identified to genus or species. Each taxon was assigned a tolerance value ranging from 0 (most sensitive) to 5 (most tolerant) based on information from 53 streams. As per Chutter's index, the average of the tolerance values for all individuals constituted the site index value. Hilsenhoff's Biotic Index was extensively tested by the Wisconsin Department of Natural Resources and the data generated were used to improve the index. Tolerance values were revised by comparing the original tolerance value assigned to a species with the average biotic index value of streams in which it most commonly occurred. To provide greater precision, the scale was expanded from 0 to 10. To date, tolerance values have been assigned to some 400 species or genera, and these are listed in Hilsenhoff (1987). The influence of current, temperature and seasonal factors on BI values have also been evaluated (Hilsenhoff 1988b). BI values were found to be erroneously high in summer, when many sensitive species are in diapause, and in currents of less than $0.30 \, \text{m s}^{-1}$. Table 3.4 is a guide to the water quality of streams based on this index.

Hilsenhoff (1988a) also adapted his index for a rapid assessment by providing tolerance values for families. Because family tolerance values are averages, they are lower than the tolerance values for some species in the family and higher than the values for other species. The result should be a dampening effect on the performance of the index. This was confirmed in testing on second- and third-order Wisconsin streams, where the family-level biotic index (FBI) tended to be higher than the BI at unpolluted sites and lower at polluted sites. The FBI was also more variable. However, an average of only 23 minutes was required to sample, sort and calculate an FBI in the field, as compared with at least 85 minutes to calculate a BI. Hilsenhoff (1988a) recommended using the FBI only for rapid assessment of the general status of organic pollution in streams, in essence as a screening tool to identify problem areas. He noted that if all organisms were preserved, the BI could always be calculated later if needed.

Despite all the effort which has gone into the development of biotic indices, they have serious limitations as bioassessment tools. First of all, 'they set the same target for all sites when it is clear that different physical and chemical regimes of fast-flowing mountain streams and slow-flowing lowland rivers will support totally different faunal communities' (Armitage *et al* 1990). Secondly, a primary weakness of biotic indices is the subjective approach which is often used to classify organism tolerance. Herricks and Cairns (1982) suggest that only where a long record of study is available (e.g. Sladecek 1973;

Table 3.4 Evaluation of water quality using biotic index values of samples collected in March, April, May, September and early October (from Hilsenhoff 1987, with permission)

Biotic index	Water quality	Degree of organic pollution
0.00–3.50	Excellent	No apparent organic pollution
3.51–4.50	Very good	Possible slight organic pollution
4.51–5.50	Good	Some organic pollution
5.51–6.50	Fair	Fairly significant organic pollution
6.51–7.50	Fairly poor	Significant organic pollution
7.51–8.50	Poor	Very significant organic pollution
8.51–10.00	Very poor	Severe organic pollution

Hilsenhoff 1987) is reliability high. They recommend replacing 'subjective tolerance estimates' with 'quantitative tolerance determinations', which require extensive correlations between species presence and water quality. Thirdly, biotic indices apply only to organic pollution, and their application to other types of pollution or perturbation is questionable at best and erroneous at worst. Clearly, a more diagnostic approach is needed.

Community comparison indices

Community comparison indices (CCIs), which measure the similarity of the structure of two communities, have mostly been developed for use in terrestrial ecology and have not been extensively applied to aquatic ecosystems (Washington 1984). CCIs require a clean water station for comparison, and have therefore mainly been used for upstream–downstream contrasts of the response to point source pollution. Like diversity indices, they are strictly quantitative and therefore provide no information about the actual composition of communities. Unlike biotic indices, they will respond to any perturbation that affects benthic communities, not just organic pollution. There is some evidence that CCIs may be more sensitive to subtle changes in community structure than diversity indices. For example, Perkins (1983) found that CCIs demonstrated a consistent decrease in similarity among benthic communities exposed to increasing concentrations of copper, while the diversity index H' gave false negatives for the lower concentrations. Washington (1984) called for further evaluation of CCIs, specifically for comparisons with both diversity and biotic indices. Hellawell (1986) assessed the relative performances of many of the older 'pollution' (i.e. saprobic and biotic), diversity and community comparison indices and provided a summary of the preferred methods. He concluded that no single index would satisfy all requirements and recommended that several types of index should always be used.

A wide range of CCIs are currently available, each having somewhat different mathematical and ecological properties. To add to the confusion, some measure similarity and others dissimilarity.

Because of their differing properties, various indices generate somewhat different results when applied to the same data set. Most require both validation under controlled conditions and careful consideration of their intrinsic properties to determine which index is most suited to the objectives of a particular study and the type of data available. Formulae for an exhaustive list of indices are presented in Perkins (1983) and Washington (1984). One example of the application of CCIs will be presented here.

Brock (1977) used the indices P_{sc} and B to evaluate the effects of thermal effluents on zooplankton communities in a reservoir in central Texas. The formulae are as follows:

$$P_{sc} = 100 - 0.5 \sum_{}^{k} |a - b|$$

where a and b are, for a given species, percentages of the total samples A and B which that species represents. The absolute value of their difference is summed over all species, k.

$$B = \frac{1}{k} \sum_{}^{k} \frac{\min (Xia, Xib)}{\max (Xia, Xib)}$$

where Xia and Xib = abundances of species i at stations A and B, the smaller number being divided by the larger number for each species, and k = total number of species observed between the two stations.

P_{sc} is based on relative abundance while B is based on actual abundance, therefore the two indices respond differently to certain changes in community structure. Brock (1977) found that sites with very similar proportions of taxa but very different total abundances registered a high degree of similarity according to P_{sc} and less similarity according to B. The removal of a few rare species from a data set for two stations hardly affected the value for P_{sc}, whereas B indicated a definite change. Conversely, B was insensitive to the addition of a substantial number of individuals to a dominant taxon. Brock (1977) concluded that if B overemphasizes shifts in rare taxa and de-emphasizes changes among dominant species, then it is too sensitive to normal sampling error. It could, however, have an important application where the loss of rare or endangered species is of interest.

Camargo (1990) recently developed a new 'ecotoxicological index' for assessing the impact of a regulated and industrial area on the Duraton River in Spain. This index combines a measure of the percentage difference between the number of species occurring above and below a disturbance point,

$$\left[(A - B) \times \frac{100}{A} \right]$$

with a measure of the species substitution between the two sites,

$$\left[(A - C) \times \frac{100}{A} \right]$$

where A = number of species occurring upstream, B = number of species downstream and C = number of species common to both sites, into a single index:

$$EI = \frac{(2A - B - C) \times 50}{A}$$

The values of the ecotoxicological index, or EI, range from 0 (no impact) to 100 (maximum impact). He reported that the new EI was significantly correlated (but inversely, due to their inverted scales) with H' and Margalef's diversity index. However, the range of values was much greater for the EI than for H', suggesting that the EI may be more sensitive to subtle changes. Interestingly, Margalef's index gave better site discrimination than H', a finding which was also reported by Wilhm (1967).

3.3 ALTERNATIVE APPROACHES

Functional feeding groups

According to the River Continuum Concept (RCC: Vannote *et al* 1980; Minshall *et al* 1985), drainage networks form a predictable continuum of increasing channel size and associated biological characteristics. Stream morphology, current velocity, substrate composition, temperature and allochthonous vs. autochthonous food sources all interact to influence food availability to invertebrates, and these interactions vary systematically with stream order thereby regulating distribution patterns of invertebrate functional

feeding groups (Hawkins & Sedell 1981). These feeding groups are referred to as the scrapers, collector–filterers, collector–gatherers, predators and shredders (Cummins 1974). Under unperturbed conditions, headwater areas are normally dominated by shredders and collectors due to the mainly allochthonous energy source; mid-sized streams are autotrophically driven and dominated by scrapers and collector–filterers; and communities in large rivers are mainly composed of collector–gatherers due to the accumulation of fine sediment from upstream (Rabeni *et al* 1985; Cummins 1988).

Although this general pattern appears to hold worldwide, the exact nature and rate of change will vary from river to river depending on catchment characteristics and water chemistry at the origin (Ormerod & Edwards 1987) and on the efficiency of retention of sediments and organic matter (Cummins 1988). Cushing *et al* (1983) verified the changes in functional feeding groups predicted by the RCC in a study of 16 streams in Oregon, Idaho, Michigan and Pennsylvania. An important finding was that rates of change varied regionally, such that first-order streams in Pennsylvania and Michigan were more like third-order than first-order streams in Oregon. Because the RCC was developed in North America, rivers on other continents may show considerable divergence from the original model (e.g. Winterbourn *et al* 1981 and Marchant *et al* 1985, for New Zealand and Australia).

Cummins and others (e.g. Cummins 1974; Cummins & Klug 1979; Merritt & Cummins 1984; Cummins 1988) have developed a functional classification of stream invertebrates over the last 15 years in response to the inadequacies of systematic and trophic analyses; i.e. identification to the species level is still difficult and gut content analyses reveal that all invertebrates are omnivores. According to Cummins (1988), the functional view permits 'clustering of genetically and taxonomically diverse entities into groups, or guilds, which share fundamental properties — such as invertebrates having the same morphological-behavioural mechanisms of food acquisition'. Hawkins and Sedell (1981) point out that such a system reduces the variability associated with taxonomic complexity, allowing trends to be more easily recognized. This approach is also more universally applicable because local taxonomic differences do not seriously affect it. The only drawback to the functional feeding group (FFG) approach is that it is based on nutrient dynamics and can therefore only be used to assess the effects of organic enrichment.

Thus, Rabeni *et al* (1985) assessed changes in benthic community structure and function in the Penobscot River, Maine, before and after pollution abatement technology had been implemented at all of the major point sources of organic enrichment, including pulp mills and municipal sewage treatment plants. Characteristics of the study area, including the stream order, water clarity and general erosional substrate, classified the river as autotrophically-driven under the RCC scheme. At unperturbed sites, densities of scrapers exceeded those of collector–filterers and collector–gatherers combined, reflecting the normal autotrophic nature. As water quality degraded, the functional groups responded in a manner predicted by the RCC (e.g. the percentage density of scrapers decreased from a high of 45% to less than 1% at the most polluted sites) and the system became heterotrophic. This change occurred in the absence of any longitudinal gradient, suggesting that organic pollution can 'reset' the normal sequence of feeding group shifts and convert an autotrophic system into a heterotrophic state that would normally be found farther downstream in a much larger river. As water quality improved due to pollution abatement, the ratio of collector–filterers and scrapers to collector–gatherers increased, indicating that the river was returning to its normal condition. Rabeni *et al* (1985) concluded that the FFG approach is promising because it 'may reflect more ecologically significant attributes of streams and rivers than do structurally-based water-quality systems'.

Reduced assemblages

Most macroinvertebrate bioassessment techniques are based on the response of the entire benthic community to pollution. However, focusing on a single component of the community (generally an order or family) has several attractive benefits. It can simplify the collection, sorting and identification of benthic samples, thereby reducing time and effort. Selective sampling techniques can be employed which provide more precise estimates of the diversity and abundance of the organisms under consideration. The resources saved by limiting the investigation to one group can then be redirected into more intensive or extensive studies and species-level taxonomic identification. The latter is an extremely important consideration. Indices which use species-level identification have better potential for site discrimination (Hilsenhoff 1988a; Furse *et al* 1984), since species have more precise environmental requirements than families and species belonging to a single group may have a wide range of susceptibilities to various pollutants (Slooff 1983). Working at the species level also allows the identification of indicator species for certain types of perturbations. Observational data can then be verified by laboratory toxicity tests on these species, such as those conducted by Chapman *et al* (1982a,b), in order to establish cause/effect links.

For a group to be a candidate for the reduced assemblage approach, it must be capable of representing the response of the community as a whole. Therefore, it must be a prominent group comprising a large proportion of the fauna; it must contain many ecologically different species; and individual species within the group must have a broad range of tolerances for different types of pollution. The groups which have been most successfully exploited are the oligochaetes, chironomids and caddisflies.

Oligochaetes have mainly been used in lakes because of their prominence in soft sediment communities. They have been used both for trophic classification (e.g. Saether 1979, for nearctic and palaearctic lakes; Howmiller & Scott 1977 and Lauritsen *et al* 1985, for the Laurentian Great Lakes) and for indicating different types and degrees of pollution (e.g. Lang & Lang-Dobler 1979, for eutrophication and heavy metal pollution in Lake Geneva). Saether (1979) felt that oligochaete communities could not provide as distinct a classification system as chironomid communities because their environmental requirements are less restricted. However, Chapman *et al* (1982a,b) have since demonstrated that oligochaete species have a broad range of tolerances to organic pollution and specific chemicals. Recently, there have been several studies on oligochaetes in lotic environments. Smith *et al* (1990) observed changes in species composition and dominance in oligochaete assemblages in low-order woodland streams in the Adirondack Mountains of New York, in response to the degree of acid pollution. Barton and Metcalfe-Smith (1991) found that variations in oligochaete densities in both the soft sediments and riffles in an agriculturally-polluted watershed in Quebec gave excellent site discrimination, were highly correlated with other indices and were temporally stable. It appears that oligochaetes deserve further consideration for river and stream applications. They may be particularly suitable for assessing sediment quality in large rivers. As Barton (1989) points out, a drawback to using oligochaetes is that they can only be identified if they are sexually mature, whereas chironomids, for example, can be identified at any stage of maturity after the first instar.

Chironomids are an extremely diverse group of insects, frequently accounting for 50% of the total species diversity in benthic communities (Merritt & Cummins 1984). They occur in a wide range of freshwater habitats, have representatives in all trophic groups (predators, herbivores, detritivores) and are important food items for fish (Rosenberg *et al* 1986). They have been successfully used in lake classification (e.g. Saether 1979; Johnson 1989, for Swedish Lakes), although Johnson (1989) commented that many genera and species have wide tolerance ranges and are therefore poor indicators of lake type. He recommended identifying and focusing on indicator species. In a study on the Scioto River basin in Ohio, Rae (1989) found that several groups of common chironomid genera were indicative of certain chemical conditions. *Stictochironomus* was an indicator of hard, clean, unpolluted water, while *Pentaneura*, *Cricotopus* and *Tanytarsus* were characteristic of sewage pollution (phosphates, low oxygen), *Ablabesmyia* and *Tribelos* were associated with soft water and general or-

ganic pollution, and *Procladius* and *Dicrotendipes* indicated moderate hardness and high agricultural runoff (nitrates and turbidity due to fertilizers and siltation, respectively). Thus, Rae (1989) succeeded in isolating indicator taxa which were extremely tolerant or intolerant of certain types of pollution. He makes a strong case for focusing on indicator taxa rather than studying the entire benthic community, by pointing out that little information is gained by examining the distributions of facultative organisms.

Trichoptera are also a very diverse group of insects, occupying a wide variety of habitats and trophic levels. Caddisflies are also well represented in all functional feeding groups (Cummins & Klug 1979). Basaguren and Orive (1990) investigated Trichoptera as indicators of water quality in the River Cadagua basin in Spain. They identified 33 taxa from 12 families within the basin and observed a succession of species from the headwaters to the lowland reaches in relation to selected physico-chemical features. This succession was particularly evident in the family Hydropsychidae among species of the genus *Hydropsyche*. In organically-polluted river sections, species substitutions occurred which deviated from those in unpolluted sections with the same habitat.

In an earlier study on a nearby pristine river, the River Lea, Basaguren and Orive (1989) had identified 47 taxa from 14 families and 32 genera and described, using ordination techniques, zones characterized by different communities of caddisflies. The headwaters of the main river were distinct from those of the tributaries and a downstream sequence was indicated in the main river. The main river had a more diverse fauna, and diversity increased in a downstream direction with increasing river width, water level and substrate diversity. Although this is a characteristic pattern for unpolluted rivers, it is rarely observed today due to the counter-effects of cumulative pollution.

Basaguren and Orive (1989) worked largely at the species level, and were able to describe a very detailed continuum of caddisflies in this system which should be extremely useful for assessments of similar systems in the Basque country. Higler and Tolkamp (1983) also found the

Hydropsychidae to be useful for classifying water-courses in The Netherlands. Based on historical data, the distributions of 10 native species in small streams to large rivers throughout The Netherlands were determined. A succession was again identified, and deviations from the expected pattern for a given area could be attributed to pollution sources. Although several species of Hydropsychidae were found to be tolerant of organic pollution, even these species were eliminated by severe agricultural runoff.

Ratio indices

Ratio indices express the dominance of one group of organisms over another and have been used in conjunction with both taxonomic and functional feeding group data. They are simple to determine, but can be fairly specific and therefore useful in certain situations. Thus Saether (1979) found that an increasing ratio of oligochaetes to chironomids was a good indicator of eutrophication in lakes. Winner *et al* (1980) demonstrated that the ratio of chironomids to total insects was related to the degree of metal contamination (Cu, Cr, Zn).

Several ratio indices have been incorporated into the US EPA's Rapid Bioassessment Protocols for river assessment (Plafkin *et al* 1989), which will be discussed in more detail in the next section. For example, a decrease in the ratio of scrapers to filtering collectors is used to indicate degradation from an abundance of diatoms (which are the primary food source for scrapers) to an abundance of filamentous algae and aquatic mosses (which provide attachment sites for filterers and accumulations of the fine particulate matter on which they feed). Also, communities having an even distribution of organisms among four key insect groups – the mayflies, stoneflies, caddisflies and chironomids – are considered healthy, while those skewed towards a disproportionate number of chironomids indicate environmental stress.

Whitehurst and Lindsey (1990) compared the performance of a *Gammarus*:*Asellus* ratio index with traditional biotic indices (Chandler's Score, Extended Biotic Index, BMWP Score) for assessing mild sewage pollution in the River Adur in Sussex, England. *Gammarus* is more sensitive to

organic pollution than *Asellus*. Since these taxa are direct niche competitors, a reduction in the abundance of *Gammarus* due to pollution will result in a corresponding increase in the abundance of *Asellus*, thereby altering the ratio. Whitehurst and Lindsey (1990) found this ratio index to be more sensitive to mild organic pollution than the biotic indices. The reason for this may be that if an impact is subtle and affects only certain organisms in the community, then the appropriate ratio index should provide good site discrimination. However, a biotic index could mask this response because it includes information on other organisms which are not affected by the impact. In a similar study using a variety of diversity, biotic and ratio indices, Olive *et al* (1988) found that different indices did not always agree in the classification of sites, usually due to the confounding effects of habitat. They caution against using indices of community response interchangeably or relying on only one type of index for assessing the effects of pollution, and conclude that ratio indices may be most useful when combined with other indices.

3.4 RECENT DEVELOPMENTS

The purpose of biomonitoring and assessment is to distinguish degraded sites from healthy ones, identify the cause of the impact, then monitor the response of the system to remedial action. The situation is rarely simple. Rather, multiple stresses, which originate from both point and non-point sources and can be chemical or physical in nature, generally act in a cumulative manner on aquatic systems. Traditional approaches to bioassessment have been unsatisfactory for a variety of reasons. Diversity and community comparison indices respond to all types of perturbations and the normal range of environmental factors, so that except in clear-cut situations they cannot be easily interpreted. On the other hand, biotic and saprobic indices only respond to organic pollution and are geographically restricted.

Probably the major obstacle to incorporating bioassessments into water management policies has been the lack of realistic targets with which to compare index values and to serve as water quality criteria. There has been a general recognition on both sides of the Atlantic of the need for identifying and characterizing reference sites in unimpaired locations in order to define attainable water quality objectives. The UK and the USA have addressed this problem differently, but both countries have succeeded in incorporating macroinvertebrate community assessments into the water resource management process.

The multivariate approach – UK

In the early 1980s, the Freshwater Biological Association (FBA) began to explore the relationships between environmental parameters and macroinvertebrate communities using multivariate analysis techniques. The goal of this 'River Communities Project' was to prepare a biological classification of all running-waters in Great Britain. The work was conducted in three phases, the results of which have appeared in a series of papers published over the last 10 years. A good overview is presented by Wright *et al* (1989).

Armitage *et al* (1983) examined the possibility of predicting 'expected' communities from physical and chemical variables unrelated to pollution, using data collected from 268 sites on 41 unpolluted rivers. Multiple linear regressions were computed using BMWP Score or ASPT as the dependent variable and various physical and chemical parameters as the independent variables. The predictive equations for ASPT were superior; as previously noted, ASPT is less sensitive to sampling effort and seasonal change than is the Score. Approximately 70% of the variability was explained using both physical and chemical data, and 60% by physical data alone.

Wright *et al* (1984), in perhaps the 'keystone' paper of the series, then used the same data set to develop a classification of running-water sites based on all macroinvertebrate taxa (not just BMWP Scores) and to predict community type from environmental data. Using ordination (detrended correspondence analysis) and a hierarchical clustering technique called TWINSPAN (two-way indicator species analysis), the sites were classified into 16 groupings using species lists generated from three seasons of sampling. Multiple discriminant analysis was then used to correlate the groupings with 28 physical and chemical variables (Table 3.5). Using environmental data, 76.1% of the sites were predicted to the correct grouping. For a further 15.3% of the sites, the correct grouping was the second most probable.

The influence of season and level of taxonomic identification on the performance of this system was tested (Furse *et al* 1984). Qualitative species-

Table 3.5 Various environmental factors considered in the ordination and classification of running-water sites in Great Britain, and the prediction of community type (after Wright *et al* 1984, and others)

Physical variables	Chemical variables
Distance from source*	pH
Slope*	Dissolved oxygen
Altitude*	Total oxidized nitrogen*
Discharge	Chloride*
Mean channel width*	Dissolved orthophosphate
Mean channel depth*	Total alkalinity*
Surface velocity (max., min., median/mode)	
Mean substratum size*	
Dominant particle size (max., min., median/mode)	
Substratum heterogeneity	
% macrophyte cover (max., min., mean)	
Air temp. range*	
Mean air temp.*	

* Used in latest version of RIVPACS (Wright *et al* 1989; see text).

level data were found to give more reliable classifications and predictions than either quantitative or qualitative family-level data, because of the greater number of taxa and because individual species have more precise environmental requirements than families. The greatest accuracy was achieved by combining the results from all three seasons, because species which were absent from one season's data due to life cycle, drought, etc., had a good chance of being captured in another season.

Although the prediction of site groupings is useful for classification, it is only a step towards the prediction of species occurrence at sites with know environmental characteristics (Wright *et al* 1985). Thus Moss *et al* (1987) conducted field trials to test the accuracy of classification and prediction of 21 new unpolluted sites and to determine the probability that a certain species would occur at a given site. Reducing the number of environmental variables was shown to result in very little loss of predictive accuracy. For example, of all taxa predicted as having a >75% chance of occurring at a given site, using suites ranging from five physical features to 28 physical and chemical features, 87.0–89.7% actually did occur.

Moss *et al* (1987) stated that the major use of their system would be to provide a 'target' community to be used as a standard for a given site when it is unpolluted. The magnitude of the difference between the expected and observed fauna gives a measure of the loss of biological quality due to pollution or other perturbations. Subsequently, RIVPACS (River InVertebrate Prediction and Classification System) software was developed (Wright *et al* 1989) to analyse combined three-seasons data obtained by standard procedures (Furse *et al* 1981; Wright *et al* 1984). The program permits the prediction of fauna at one or all of the following taxonomic levels: species (qualitative), all families (logarithm of categories of abundance), all families (qualitative), and the more restricted listing of BMWP families (qualitative) using various combinations of environmental variables. The system also allows for determination of the BMWP score or ASPT, which is widely used for rapid site appraisal.

The predictive equations were revised after the database was expanded to 370 sites on 61 rivers, including more small streams and lowland river sites.

The latest (Phase III) version of RIVPACS is based on 438 sites from 80 rivers, and permits a classification to either 10 or 25 TWINSPAN groups. Each group contains at least six reference sites, ensuring reliability of the system. It is more flexible in that data from one, several or all three seasons can be imported, and predictions of ASPT, BMWP score and number of scoring taxa can be obtained. However, for the purpose of

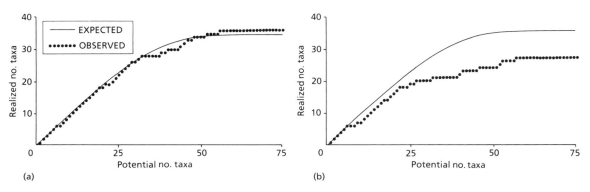

Fig. 3.2 Observed and expected BMWP family accretion curves for an upstream control site (a) and an impact site (b) which receives paper-mill effluent. 'Expected' curve accumulates the probabilities of occurrence of 75 BMWP families using the sequence given in the prediction. 'Observed' curve accumulates the number of families captured, based on the same sequence of taxa (from Wright *et al* 1988, with permission).

River : LOURO   Site : 5 EIDOS

Environmental data used :

    Substratum composition
        Boulders+cobbles (%)   0.00
        Pebbles+gravel (%)   50.00
        Sand (%)   30.00
        Silt+clay (%)   20.00
    Mean substratum (phi)   0.57
    Dist. from source (km)   18.70
    Total oxidised N (ppm)   1.51
    Alkalinity (ppm CaCO3)   31.42
    Chloride (ppm)   28.95

Groups predicted from MDA with 5 physical and chemical variables

42 42.2%   23 28.5%   41 8.8%   44 5.1%   37 5.0%
38 3.3%   40 3.1%

Predicted taxa, in decreasing order of probability

99.7% Oligochaeta √	48.9% Psychomyiidae	
99.7% Chironomidae √	48.2% Goeridae	
99.7% Elminthidae √	27.2% Planorbidae √	
99.3% Baetidae	24.9% Brachycentridae	
99.2% Simuliidae	23.9% Aphelocheiridae	
98.7% Ephemerellidae √	22.2% Coenagriidae	
96.9% Tipulidae	21.5% Odontoceridae	
96.7% Leuctridae	21.1% Perlidae	
95.4% Sphaeriidae √	18.0% Cordulegasteridae √	
94.2% Gammaridae	17.1% Gerridae	
93.9% Hydropsychidae	12.9% Beraeidae	
93.9% Limnephilidae	12.3% Helodidae	
93.1% Perlodidae	11.9% Piscicolidae	
90.4% Dytiscidae	11.3% Dryopidae	
90.1% Polycentropodidae √	8.4% Physidae √	
89.8% Heptageniidae	7.3% Neritidae	
89.8% Hydrobiidae √	6.2% Capniidae	
87.7% Erpobdellidae √	5.9% Phryganeidae	
87.6% Rhyacophilidae	5.7% Hydrometridae	
86.2% Leptoceridae	4.7% Nepidae	
86.2% Nemouridae	4.7% Siphlonuridae	
85.6% Sericostomatidae	3.7% Dendrocoelidae	
84.8% Lymnaeidae	3.6% Philopotamidae	A) Predicted number of families to 50% = 33.2
84.6% Gyrinidae	3.4% Valvatidae	B) Observed number of families to 50% = 11
80.7% Ancylidae	2.1% Astacidae	C) Total observed families = 14
78.8% Hydrophilidae	1.1% Molannidae	D) Observed BMWP score = 66
78.4% Caenidae	0.7% Unionidae	E) Observed ASPT = 4.714
77.4% Glossiphoniidae √	0.4% Hirudidae	F) Faunal index 11/33.2
76.7% Ephemeridae	0.3% Viviparidae	G) BMWP score index 66/234
75.3% Leptophlebiidae √	0.2% Notonectidae	H) ASPT index 4.714/5.827
73.3% Hydroptilidae	0.0% Platycnemididae	
73.0% Planariidae	0.0% Aeshnidae	
72.3% Chloroperlidae	0.0% Libellulidae	
65.0% Sialidae	0.0% Corophiidae	
62.6% Lepidostomatidae	0.0% Pleidae	
58.6% Corixidae √		
56.7% Asellidae	Expected taxa with P >=.75 = 26.9. with P >= .5 = 33.2	
56.5% Haliplidae	Predicted BMWP score = 234	
56.3% Taeniopterygidae	Predicted average BMWP score per taxon = 5.827	
51.9% Agriidae		

Fig. 3.3 Example of a printout showing predicted families with their probability of capture for site 5-Eidos, on the Rio Louro. Taxa actually observed at the site are indicated with a √ (from Armitage *et al* 1990, with permission).

standardization, a single group of 11 physical and chemical variables is used (Table 3.5). Testing has now begun in polluted systems to demonstrate the utility of the prediction technique. Wright *et al* (1988) compared the observed vs. expected occurrence of 75 BMWP families at sites above and below the input of a paper-mill effluent on a river in southwest England. As illustrated in Fig. 3.2, the under-representation of families at the impact site compared to the control site is clearly evident.

The application of the BMWP score system and RIVPACS to the biological assessment of Spanish rivers is also currently being evaluated. Armitage *et al* (1990) applied the Phase II version of RIVPACS to the assessment of 18 sites in two Galician rivers in northwest Spain, one receiving minor organic pollution and one unpolluted. An example printout is shown in Fig. 3.3. At this particular site, Plecoptera were conspicuously absent and this was attributed to low dissolved oxygen (DO) and an unsuitable substratum. Although this study indicated that RIVPACS could be successfully applied in Spain, the most efficient application of the system will require the acquisition of a national or regional database similar to that available in Great Britain.

EPA approach – USA

The quality and quantity of water resources in the USA continue to decline despite massive regulatory efforts (Karr 1991). For example, 602 stream and river segments in the northwest USA are water-quality limited due to chemical contamination, and 56% of degraded segments nationwide have reduced fishery potential due to pollution. Hunsaker and Carpenter (1990) state that 27% of the fish fauna of the USA are endangered, threatened or of special concern, over 50% of the mollusc species of the Tennessee River system are either extinct or endangered, and 38 states reported fisheries closures, restrictions or advisories in 1985. Serious and widespread biological impairment is apparent, clearly indicating that existing monitoring and assessment programmes, which are based on chemical criteria, are inadequate.

Under the most recent amendment (1987) of the Clean Water Act, the US EPA is required

to develop programmes to 'evaluate, restore and maintain the chemical, physical and biological integrity of the Nation's waters' (US EPA 1990). The inclusion of biological integrity as a goal on equal footing with chemical water quality is a major step forward. For a review of the arduous process leading up to this legislation, see Karr (1991). Biological criteria based on structural and functional attributes of resident fish and benthic invertebrate communities are currently being developed and integrated with chemical-specific criteria and whole-effluent toxicity evaluations for a more holistic approach to water management.

Under Section 303 of the Act, individual states will be required to develop narrative biological criteria by 1993, with numerical criteria to follow. Biocriteria will be used to improve water quality standards, identify impairment of beneficial uses, assist in setting programme priorities and detect problems which might otherwise be missed or underestimated. Biological criteria are especially suited for the detection of non-point source, cumulative and episodic pollution, as well as physical changes such as habitat deterioration, none of which would be detected using traditional chemical assessment methods. It has also been demonstrated that biocriteria are more sensitive than chemical criteria; in Ohio, an evaluation of instream biota indicated that 36% of biologically impaired sites had not been identified using chemical criteria (Ohio EPA 1987).

Twenty states now use some form of biological assessment and five (Florida, Arkansas, North Carolina, Maine, Ohio) are currently using biological criteria to define aquatic life use classifications and enforce water-quality standards (US EPA 1990). The application of biocriteria differs somewhat among the various states. Florida has a legal criterion based on macroinvertebrate diversity whereby impact is defined as a reduction of more than 75% below established reference values. Maine uses macroinvertebrate community data to assess attainment or non-attainment of standards for designated water uses (e.g. drinking-water supply, fish and wildlife habitat, recreational use, agriculture, industrial use). Oklahoma uses biotic information to assess long-term trends in water quality.

Ohio's programme is the furthest advanced,

and serves as an example of the successful incorporation of biological criteria in water quality regulations. Biological criteria were developed for Ohio rivers and streams using the 'ecoregion' approach, which has been adopted nationwide as a framework for defining attainable water quality objectives. An ecoregion is 'a relatively homogeneous area defined by similarity of geography, hydrology, land use, or other ecologically relevant variable' (US EPA 1990). Sites within a given ecoregion have similar ecological potentials, and 'attainable quality is then based on assessment of conditions in minimally impacted reference sites that characterize the region' (Hughes & Larsen 1988). In Ohio, parts of five ecoregions occur, these being the Eastern Corn Belt Plains, the Huron/Erie Lake Plain, the Erie/Ontario Lake Plain, the Western Allegheny Plateau and the Interior Plateau (Ohio EPA 1987).

The Ohio EPA has used biological criteria based on fish and macroinvertebrates for quantitatively determining attainment/non-attainment of designated aquatic life uses (warmwater habitat, exceptional warmwater habitat, coldwater habitat, seasonal salmonid habitat and limited resource waters) since 1980. For invertebrates, early criteria were narrative and based on simple structural measures of diversity, abundance and biomass. These have recently been replaced by the Invertebrate Community Index (ICI).

The ICI is derived from the IBI (Index of Biotic Integrity), which is based on attributes of fish communities and is described in detail in Karr (1991). The ICI consists of 10 essentially structural community metrics (Table 3.6), each with four scoring categories of 6, 4, 2 and 0 points which correspond to exceptional, good, fair and poor community condition. The scoring categories were calibrated using data from 232 reference sites in the five ecoregions. Individual metric scores are summed to generate a site ICI score which could theoretically range from 0 to 60. Quantitative sampling is conducted using multiple-plate artificial substrate samplers. However, additional qualitative sampling of the natural fauna from all available habitat types is also conducted. Metrics 1–9 are based on artificial substrate samples, while metric 10 is based on the natural fauna. Attainable values for the ICI were determined for each of the five

Table 3.6 Metrics for calculating the Invertebrate Community Index (ICI) (after Ohio EPA 1987)

1 Total number of taxa
2 Total number of mayfly taxa
3 Total number of caddisfly taxa
4 Total number of dipteran taxa
5 Percent mayfly composition
6 Percent caddisfly composition
7 Percent tribe Tanytarsini midge composition
8 Percent other dipteran and non-insect composition
9 Percent of tolerant organisms (oligochaetes and selected midges, limpets and pond snails)
10 Total number of qualitative EPT (Ephemeroptera, Plecoptera, Trichoptera) taxa

ecoregions based on median values for the reference sites in these regions. Within each ecoregion, the lower (25%) and upper (75%) percentile values are used to determine attainment or non-attainment of criteria for warmwater habitat and exceptional warmwater habitat, respectively.

To determine the performance of the ICI, index values were determined for 431 sites sampled between 1981 and 1984, including 279 which had been classified as 'good', 76 'fair' and 76 'poor' quality sites based on best professional judgement. The results indicated a wide segregation of the good and excellent sites from the fair sites and the poor sites. It was concluded that the ICI provides an 'objective, quantifiable, and standardized means of evaluating biological integrity' (Ohio EPA 1987).

The US EPA has also supported the development of a hierarchy of methods for biological monitoring which is referred to as the Rapid Bioassessment Protocols (Plafkin *et al* 1989). The document presents a tiered approach to using fish and macroinvertebrate communities in biological assessment. Three protocols are present for invertebrates, each one progressively more intensive and rigorous than the previous one. Protocol III is similar to the ICI, but includes some functional metrics (Table 3.7). It was intended for riffle/run habitats in wadable streams. The original protocols were designed as inexpensive screening tools for determining if a stream is supporting or not supporting a designated aquatic life use. However, they were also found to be useful for discovering and determining the cause and severity

Table 3.7 Rapid Bioassessment Protocol III (after Plafkin *et al* 1989)

1 Taxon richness
2 Hilsenhoff's Family Biotic Index
3 Ratio of scrapers to filtering collectors
4 Ratio of EPT and chironomid abundances
5 Percentage contribution of dominant family
6 EPT index
7 Community similarity index
8 Ratio of shredders: total organisms

EPT = Ephemeroptera/Plecoptera/Trichoptera.

of impairment, evaluating the effectiveness of control actions, determining attainability of aquatic life uses and trend monitoring.

3.5 NEW DIRECTIONS

Because biological systems are complex and the causes of degradation in rivers and streams are multiple, not all measures of community structure or function will be useful under all circumstances. Instead of rejecting the more specific approaches because they cannot be generalized, Karr (1991) favours integration of the various indices and metrics to create a more robust approach to biological monitoring and assessment. What is needed most now is information on the differential responses of benthic communities to the wide range of polluted conditions and physical perturbations which occur. To date, only the responses to organic pollution (mainly domestic sewage) have been adequately documented.

It is unlikely that indices developed for assessing organic pollution will be useful for detecting toxic pollution or habitat alterations, because organisms do not respond in the same way to different stresses. For example, Chapman *et al* (1982a) exposed nine species of freshwater oligochaetes to selected chemical pollutants under bioassay conditions. They observed that eutrophic species were, as expected, the most tolerant of sewage and anoxia. However, when specific pulp-mill constituents, heavy metals and pentachlorophenol were tested, the relative tolerances of the various species were found to be pollutant-specific. This suggests that assemblages used to indicate organic enrichment are not appropriate for indicating other types of pollution. Similarly, Slooff (1983) compared the relative tolerances of 12 invertebrates from various taxonomic groups to 15 chemicals as well as surface-water concentrates from the Rhine River in The Netherlands. His most interesting finding was that organisms considered to be intolerant of organic pollution in general were sometimes very tolerant to specific toxicants, and vice versa.

Although much of the information is scattered at present, it may soon be possible to describe macroinvertebrate assemblages which are characteristic of broad categories of impacts, such as agricultural activities, heavy metals, acidic pollution and river regulation. Acidic pollution will be discussed as an example.

Several independent studies have collectively provided a profile of the characteristic responses of benthic communities to acid pollution. As previously noted (see Section 3.2), communities affected by toxic or acidic pollution are typically depauperate in comparison with those influenced by organic pollution. Reash *et al* (1988) described the benthos of a stream draining a coal strip-mining area (pH 4.5) in southern Ohio as characterized by oligochaetes, Odonata (*Pantala, Ishcura*), Heteroptera (*Trichocorixa, Notonecta*), the alderfly *Sialis*, the diving beetle *Laccophilus*, the mosquito *Anopheles* and chironomids, all in relatively low numbers. *Sialis* and the odonates were absent from the most impacted site. Tomkiewicz and Dunson (1977) investigated a tributary of the West Branch of the Susquehanna River in Pennsylvania, which was also polluted by acid strip-mine drainage. The normal pH of the system was 6.0, that of the acid feeder stream was 3.2, and that of the stream below the feeder was 4.7, recovering to 5.0. Only a chironomid, *Sialis* and the caddisfly *Ptilostomis* inhabited the acid feeder. Populations of Coleoptera, Ephemeroptera and Trichoptera showed little or no recovery as the acid pollution abated over three downstream sites. Heptageniid mayflies, and baetid mayflies, and pteronarcyid and peltoperlid stoneflies, which were present at the control site, did not re-occur. However, Diptera and leutrid and nemourid stoneflies showed a decided recovery at pH 5.0.

Peterson and van Eeckhaute (1990) determined

the distributions of 30 stonefly and 100 caddis-fly species in relation to stream acidity in the Maritime provinces of Canada. Stonefly taxa most sensitive to acidic conditions were primarily the large Perlidae, but also the Chloroperlidae, Pteronarcidae and Perlodidae. Least sensitive were the Nemouridae, Leutridae and Capniidae. The Trichoptera were more difficult to categorize because several families contained both sensitive and tolerant species. The Hydropsychidae in particular had representative species in all categories (sensitive, tolerant, ubiquitous), confirming other reports of the utility of this group for pollution assessment (e.g. Higler & Tolkamp 1983; Basaguren & Orive 1990). Like Tomkiewicz and Dunson (1977), Peterson and van Eeckhaute (1990) also found the presence of *Ptilostomis* to be indicative of acid pollution.

While such descriptive studies are informative, a more precise and quantitative method for defining characteristic communities is needed. Smith *et al* (1990) employed multiple regression models to determine the response of benthic communities to acidity in low-order woodland streams in the Adirondack Mountains in New York. The findings of this study were generally in agreement with those described earlier, but the data analysis technique permitted a more precise definition of the environmental requirements of the indicator species. For example, *Cynigmula* (Heptageniidae), *Baetis* (Baetidae), Elmidae (Coleoptera) and Perlidae occurred at pH 6.2, but not at pH 5.8; mayfly densities increased steadily from pH 4.9 to pH 6.2; *Ephemerella* was excluded at pH 4.9, but not at pH 5.3; nemourid and leutrid stoneflies were found at sites ranging from pH 4.9 to 6.2. It is worth noting that the indicator value of the mayfly *Baetis* with respect to acidity is exactly the opposite of its value as an indicator of organic pollution. This genus features largely in almost all biotic indices due to its extreme tolerance of organic pollution, yet it is very sensitive to low pH. It is abundantly clear that the application of traditional biotic indices to acidic pollution would give completely erroneous assessments.

Reynoldson and Zarull (1989) demonstrated that combined analysis of physical, chemical and biological data could be used to link cause and effect between sediment-associated contaminants and benthic communities in a study on the heavily industrialized Detroit River in Canada. Using clustering techniques applied to benthic community data, five distinct benthic communities were defined, mainly based on densities of tubificids, mayflies and amphipods. These five groups were correlated individually against 18 chemical and physical characteristics of the sediment in which they live. Site groups were found to be highly correlated with Hg, Cr, Zn, Ni, hexachlorobenzene and phosphorus and also significantly correlated with five other factors, including concentrations of Pb, Cd and Cu. Multiple discriminant analysis was then used to determine the ability of these physico-chemical factors to predict benthic community structure. When all 11 environmental variables were included, every site was assigned to its correct group. Using this integrated strategy, Reynoldson and Zarull (1989) were able to associate concentrations of contaminants with specific levels of biological impact. The main variables responsible for degradation of the system were identified and could be singled out for remedial action. The method also defined a site-specific target (the cleanest group) to be used as an objective for cleanup.

This approach would be particularly suitable for large lowland rivers with significant accumulations of fine sediment, where sediment toxicity is probably more significant and limiting than water quality.

Rutt *et al* (1990) developed a similar system for assessing acid streams in upland Britain. Multiple discriminant analysis revealed that stream pH, aluminium concentration and total hardness were the major variables discriminating among groups of streams with different benthic faunas. They felt that their model could be used to forecast the effects of management decisions concerning acidifying influences such as sulphur emissions and conifer forestry.

The incorporation of pollution variables into multivariate analyses to determine the cause of community change could lead to a useful development of RIVPACS. At present, RIVPACS can predict the expected community at a given location in the absence of pollution and provide a measure of the *degree* of impact (i.e. deviation from normal). However, it cannot determine the *type* of impact.

More studies on relatively simple systems with well-known specific impacts are needed in order to define the characteristic responses of benthic communities to different types of pollution and habitat alterations. These community profiles or 'fingerprints' could then be included in models such as RIVPACS for comparison with observed communities, in order to identify the probable cause of deviation from normal conditions. The information could also be used to develop new biotic indices which respond to polluted conditions other than enrichment and for the development of new specific metrics for inclusion in the ICI or RBPs (rapid bioassessment protocols). Furthermore, characteristic community profiles could be used to identify the 'worst offender' in multiple stress situations.

It will probably not be feasible to develop biotic indices suitable for large-scale application. This task would require the generation of extensive databases on species occurrences and tolerances, such as those prepared by Sladecek (1973) and Hilsenhoff (1987), which would still be geographically restricted in their application. However, specialized biotic indices could be very useful for managing systems at the local level. For example, Rabeni *et al* (1985) developed a biotic index which was specific to the Penobscot River in Maine. Tolerance values were assigned by direct observation of the species occurring in the system, and best achievable communities were defined as those occurring at the cleanest sites. As they state, the index was 'specific for the watershed, and specific in response to pulp and paper mill effluents and municipal sewage, and therefore sensitive to improvements in water quality.'

It is perhaps too early to suggest improvements to the ICI and RBPs, since they (particularly the latter) have not been extensively tested. However, Karr (1991) maintains that the goals for the future should be to develop suites of metrics that integrate taxa (fish, invertebrates, diatoms, microorganisms) and consider biological responses to stress at all levels of organization (individual, population, community, ecosystem).

Many different approaches to bioassessment have been presented and compared in this chapter. Because the most recent systems have not yet been directly compared, it is difficult to determine whether sophisticated multivariate techniques or suites of simple, yet specific, metrics are the way of the future for large-scale monitoring and assessment applications.

REFERENCES

AFNOR (Association Française de Normalisation). (1985) Essais des eaux. Determination de l'indice biologique global (IBG). AFNOR T90-350, Paris. [3.2]

Armitage PD. (1980) The effects of mine drainage and organic enrichment on benthos in the River Nent system, Northern Pennines. *Hydrobiologia* **74**: 119–28. [3.2]

Armitage PD, Moss D, Wright JF *et al.* (1983) The performance of a new biological water quality score system based on macroinvertebrates over a wide range of polluted running-water sites. *Water Research* **17**: 333–47. [3.2, 3.4]

Armitage PD, Pardo I, Furse MT *et al.* (1990) Assessment and prediction of biological quality. A demonstration of a British macroinvertebrate-based method in two Spanish rivers. *Limnetica* **6**: 147–56. [3.2, 3.4]

Barton DR. (1989) Some problems affecting the assessment of Great Lakes water quality using benthic invertebrates. *Journal of Great Lakes Research* **15**: 611–22. [3.3]

Barton DR, Metcalfe-Smith JL. (1991) A comparison of sampling techniques and summary indices for assessment of water quality in the Yamaska River, Quebec, based on benthic macroinvertebrates. *Environmental Monitoring and Assessment* **21**: 225–44. [3.3]

Basaguren A, Orive E. (1989) Spatio-temporal changes in the caddisfly (Trichoptera) communities of the river Lea basin (Basque Country, North Spain). *Annals of Limnology* **25**: 61–8. [3.3]

Basaguren A, Orive E. (1990) The relationship between water quality and caddisfly assemblage structure in fast-running rivers. The River Cadagua basin. *Environmental Monitoring and Assessment* **15**: 35–48. [3.3, 3.5]

Bervoets L, Bruylants B, Marquet P *et al.* (1989) A proposal for modification of the Belgian biotic index method. *Hydrobiologia* **179**: 223–8. [3.2]

Brock DA. (1977) Comparison of community similarity indexes. *Journal of the Water Pollution Control Federation* **49**: 2488–94. [3.2]

Cairns J Jr, Pratt JR. (1986) Developing a sampling strategy. In: Isom BG (ed) *Rationale for Sampling and Interpretation of Ecological Data in the Assessment of Freshwater Ecosystems*, pp. 168–86. American Society for Testing and Materials, Philadelphia. [3.2]

Camargo JA. (1990) Performance of a new ecotoxicological index to assess environmental impacts on freshwater communities. *Bulletin of Environmental Contamination and Toxicology* **44**: 529–34. [3.2]

Chapman PM, Farrell MA, Brinkhurst RO. (1982a) Relative tolerances of selected aquatic oligochaetes to individual pollutants and environmental factors. *Aquatic Toxicology* **2**: 47–67. [3.3, 3.5]

Chapman PM, Farrell MA, Brinkhurst RO. (1982b) Relative tolerances of selected aquatic oligochaetes to combinations of pollutants and environmental factors. *Aquatic Toxicology* **2**: 69–78. [3.3]

Chutter FM. (1972) An empirical biotic index of the quality of water in South African streams and rivers. *Water Research* **6**: 19–30. [3.2]

Cook SEK. (1976) Quest for an index of community structure sensitive to water pollution. *Environmental Pollution* **11**: 269–88. [3.1, 3.2]

Cummins KW. (1974) Structure and function of stream ecosystems. *Bioscience* **24**: 631–41. [3.3]

Cummins KW. (1988) The study of stream ecosystems: A functional view. In: Pomeroy LR, Alberts JJ (eds) *Concepts of Ecosystem Ecology*, pp. 247–62. Springer-Verlag, New York. [3.3]

Cummins KW, Klug MJ. (1979) Feeding ecology of stream invertebrates. *Annual Review of Ecology & Systematics* **10**: 147–72. [3.3]

Cushing CE, McIntire CD, Cummins KW *et al.* (1983) Relationships among chemical, physical, and biological indices along river continua based on multivariate analyses. *Archiv für Hydrobiologie* **98**: 317–26. [3.3]

De Pauw N, Roels D. (1988) Relationship between biological and chemical indicators of surface water quality. *Verhandlungen Internationale Vereinigung für theoretische und angewandte Limnologie* **23**: 1553–8. [3.2]

De Pauw N, Vanhooren G. (1983) Method for biological quality assessment of watercourses in Belgium. *Hydrobiologia* **100**: 153–68. [3.1, 3.2]

De Pauw N, Roels D, Fontoura AP. (1986) Use of artificial substrates for standardized sampling of macroinvertebrates in the assessment of water quality by the Belgian Biotic Index. *Hydrobiologia* **133**: 237–58. [3.2]

France RL. (1990) Theoretical framework for developing and operationalizing an index of zoobenthos community integrity: Application to biomonitoring with zoobenthos communities in the Great Lakes. In: Edwards CJ, Regier HA (eds) *An Ecosystem Approach to the Integrity of the Great Lakes in Turbulent Times*, pp. 169–93. Great Lakes Fishery Commission Special Publication, Ann Arbor, MI. [3.1, 3.2]

Furse MT, Wright JF, Armitage PD *et al.* (1981) An appraisal of pond-net samples for biological monitoring of lotic macro-invertebrates. *Water Research* **15**: 679–89. [3.4]

Furse MT, Moss D, Wright JF *et al.* (1984) The influence of seasonal and taxonomic factors on the ordination and classification of running water-sites in Great Britain and on the prediction of their macroinvertebrate communities. *Freshwater Biology* **14**: 257–80. [3.3, 3.4]

Ghetti PF, Bonazzi G. (1977) A comparison between various criteria for the interpretation of biological data in the analysis of the quality of running water. *Water Research* **11**: 819–31. [3.2]

Hawkins CP, Sedell JR. (1981) Longitudinal and seasonal changes in functional organization of macroinvertebrate communities in four Oregon streams. *Ecology* **62**: 387–97. [3.3]

Hellawell J. (1977) Biological surveillance and water quality monitoring. In: Alabaster JS (ed) *Biological Monitoring of Inland Fisheries*, pp. 69–88. Applied Science Publishers, London. [3.1]

Hellawell JM. (1986) *Biological Indicators of Freshwater Pollution and Environmental Management*. Elsevier, London. [3.2]

Herricks EE, Cairns J Jr. (1982) Biological monitoring part III — receiving system methodology based on community structure. *Water Research* **16**: 141–53. [3.2]

Higler LWG, Tolkamp HH. (1983) Hydropsychidae as bioindicators. *Environmental Monitoring Assessment* **3**: 331–41. [3.3, 3.5]

Hilsenhoff WL. (1987) An improved biotic index of organic stream pollution. *The Great Lakes Entomologist* **20**: 31–9. [3.2, 3.5]

Hilsenhoff WL. (1988a) Rapid field assessment of organic pollution with a family-level biotic index. *Journal of the North American Benthological Society* **7**: 65–8. [3.2, 3.3]

Hilsenhoff WL. (1988b) Seasonal correction factors for the biotic index. *The Great Lakes Entomologist* **21**: 9–13. [3.2]

Howmiller RP, Scott MA. (1977) An environmental index based on relative abundance of oligochaete species. *Journal of the Water Pollution Control Federation* **49**: 809–15. [3.1, 3.2, 3.3]

Hughes RM, Larsen DP. (1988) Ecoregions: An approach to surface water protection. *Journal of the Water Pollution Control Federation* **60**: 486–93. [3.4]

Hunsaker CT, Carpenter DE (eds). (1990) *Ecological Indicators for the Environmental Monitoring and Assessment Program*. United States Environmental Protection Agency, EPA 600/3-90/060, Office of Research and Development, Research Triangle Park, N.C. [3.4]

ISO (International Organization for Standardization). (1984) Assessment of the water and habitat quality of rivers by a macroinvertebrate 'score'. *ISO/TC* 147/SC 5/WG 6 N 40. British Standards Institution, London. [3.2]

Jhingran VG, Ahmad SH, Singh AK. (1989) Application of Shannon–Wiener Index as a measure of pollution of river Ganga at Patna, Bihar, India. *Current Science* 58: 717–20. [3.2]

Johnson RK. (1989) Classification of profundal chironomid communities in oligotrophic/humic lakes of Sweden using environmental data. *Acta Biologica Debrecina Oecologia Hungarica* 3: 167–75. [3.3]

Jones JR, Tracy BH, Sebaugh JL et al. (1981) Biotic index tested for ability to assess water quality of Missouri Ozark streams. *Transactions of the American Fisheries Society* 110: 627–37. [3.2]

Karr JR. (1991) Biological integrity: A long-neglected aspect of water resource management. *Ecological Applications* 1: 66–84. [3.1, 3.4, 3.5]

Klemm DJ, Lewis PA, Fulk F et al. (1990) *Macroinvertebrate Field and Laboratory Methods for Evaluating the Biological Integrity of Surface Waters.* United States Environmental Protection Agency, EPA/600/4-90/030, Washington, DC. [3.1]

Kovalak WP. (1981) Assessment and prediction of impacts of effluents on communities of benthic stream macroinvertebrates. In: Bates JM, Weber CI (eds) *Ecological Assessments of Effluent Impacts on Communities of Indigenous Aquatic Organisms*, pp. 255–63. American Society for Testing and Materials, Philadelphia. [3.2]

Lang C, Lang-Dobler B. (1979) The chemical environment of tubificid and lumbriculid worms according to the pollution level of the sediment. *Hydrobiologia* 65: 273–82. [3.3]

Lauritsen DD, Mozley SC, White DS. (1985) Distribution of oligochaetes in Lake Michigan and comments on their use as indices of pollution. *Journal of Great Lakes Research* 11: 67–76. [3.3]

Marchant R, Metzeling L, Graesser A et al. (1985) The organization of macroinvertebrate communities in the major tributaries of the LaTrobe River, Victoria, Australia. *Freshwater Biology* 15: 315–31. [3.3]

Mason WT Jr, Lewis PA, Weber CI. (1985) An evaluation of benthic macroinvertebrate biomass methodology. *Environmental Monitoring & Assessment* 5: 399–422. [3.2]

Merritt RW, Cummins KW. (1984) *An Introduction to the Aquatic Insects of North America*, 2nd edn. Kendall/Hunt Publishing, Dubuque, Iowa. [3.3]

Metcalfe JL. (1989) Biological water quality assessment of running waters based on macroinvertebrate communities: History and present status in Europe. *Environmental Pollution* 60: 101–39. [3.1, 3.2]

Minshall GW, Cummins KW, Petersen RC et al. (1985) Developments in stream ecosystem theory. *Canadian Journal of Fisheries and Aquatic Sciences* 42: 1045–55. [3.3]

Moss D, Furse MT, Wright JF et al. (1987) The prediction of the macro-invertebrate fauna of unpolluted running-water sites in Great Britain using environmental data. *Freshwater Biology* 17: 41–52. [3.4]

Murphy PM. (1978) The temporal variability in biotic indices. *Environmental Pollution* 17: 227–36. [3.2]

Ohio Environmental Protection Agency. (1987) *Biological Criteria for the Protection of Aquatic Life: Vol. I. The Role of Biological Data in Water Quality Assessment.* Division of Water Quality Monitoring and Assessment, Surface Water Section, Columbus, Ohio. [3.4]

Olive JH, Jackson JL, Bass J et al. (1988) Benthic macroinvertebrates as indexes of water quality in the upper Cuyahoga River. *The Ohio Journal of Science* 88: 91–8. [3.3]

Ormerod SJ, Edwards RW. (1987) The ordination and classification of macroinvertebrate assemblages in the catchment of *Freshwater Biology* 17: 533–46. [3.3]

Pantle R, Buck H. (1955) Die biologische Überwachung der Gewässer und die Darstellung der Ergebnisse. *Gas Wasserfach* 96: 604. [3.2]

Perkins JL. (1983) Bioassay evaluation of diversity and community comparison indexes. *Journal of the Water Pollution Control Federation* 55: 522–30. [3.2]

Persoone G, De Pauw N. (1979) Systems of biological indicators for water quality assessment. In: Ravera O (ed) *Biological Aspects of Freshwater Pollution*, pp. 39–75. Pergamon Press, Oxford. [3.2]

Peterson RH, van Eeckhaute L. (1990) Distributions of stonefly (Plecoptera) and caddisfly (Trichoptera) species in three stream systems in New Brunswick and Nova Scotia, Canada, with reference to stream acidity. *Canadian Technical Report of Fisheries & Aquatic Sciences* No. 1720. [3.5]

Pinder LCV, Farr IS. (1987a) Biological surveillance of water quality – 2. Temporal and spatial variation in the macroinvertebrate fauna of the River Frome, a Dorset chalk stream. *Archiv für Hydrobiologie* 109: 321–31. [3.2]

Pinder LCV, Farr IS. (1987b) Biological surveillance of water quality – 3. The influence of organic enrichment on the macroinvertebrate fauna of small chalk streams. *Archiv für Hydrobiologie* 109: 619–37. [3.2]

Pinder LCV, Ladle M, Gledhill T et al. (1987) Biological surveillance of water quality – 1. A comparison of macroinvertebrate surveillance methods in relation to assessment of water quality, in a chalk stream. *Archiv für Hydrobiologie* 109: 207–26. [3.2]

Plafkin JL, Barbour MT, Porter KD et al. (1989) *Rapid Bioassessment Protocols for Use in Streams and Rivers: Benthic Macroinvertebrate and Fish.* United States Environmental Protection Agency, EPA/444/4-89-001, Washington, DC. [3.1, 3.3, 3.4]

Pratt JM, Coler RA. (1976) A procedure for the routine biological evaluation of urban runoff in small rivers. *Water Research* 10: 1019–25. [3.1]

Rabeni CF, Davies SP, Gibbs KE. (1985) Benthic invertebrate response to pollution abatement: Structural changes and functional implications. *Water Resources Bulletin* **21**: 489–97. [3.3, 3.5]

Rae JG. (1989) Chironomid midges as indicators of organic pollution in the Scioto River Basin, Ohio. *The Ohio Journal of Science* **89**: 5–9. [3.3]

Reash RJ, Van Hassel JH, Wood KV. (1988) Ecology of a southern Ohio stream receiving fly ash pond discharge: Changes from acid mine drainage conditions. *Archives of Environmental Contamination and Toxicology* **17**: 543–54. [3.5]

Reynoldson TB. (1984) The utility of benthic invertebrates in water quality monitoring. *Water Quality Bulletin* **10**: 21–8. [3.1]

Reynoldson TB, Zarull MA. (1989) The biological assessment of contaminated sediments – the Detroit River example. *Hydrobiologia* **188/189**: 463–76. [3.5]

Rosenberg DM, Danks HV, Lehmkuhl DM. (1986) Importance of insects in environmental impact assessment. *Environmental Management* **10**: 773–83. [3.3]

Rutt GP, Weatherley NS, Ormerod SJ. (1990) Relationships between the physicochemistry and macroinvertebrates of British upland streams: the development of modelling and indicator systems for predicting fauna and detecting acidity. *Freshwater Biology* **24**: 463–80. [3.5]

Saether OA. (1979) Chironomid communities as water quality indicators. *Holarctic Ecology* **2**: 65–74. [3.3]

Sladecek V. (1973) System of water Quality from the biological point of view. *Archiv für Hydrobiologie Beiheft Ergebnisse der Limnologie* 7: 1–218. [3.2, 3.5]

Sladecek V. (1979) Continental systems for the assessment of river water quality. In: James A, Evison L (eds) *Biological Indicators of Water Quality*, pp. 3-1 to 3-32. John Wiley & Sons, Chichester. [3.2]

Slooff W. (1983) Benthic macroinvertebrates and water quality assessment: Some toxicological considerations. *Aquatic Toxicology* **4**: 73–82. [3.2, 3.3, 3.5]

Smith ME, Wyskowski BJ, Brooks CM *et al.* (1990) Relationships between acidity and benthic invertebrates of low-order woodland streams in the Adirondack Mountains, New York. *Canadian Journal of Fisheries and Aquatic Sciences* **47**: 1318–29. [3.3, 3.5]

Tolkamp HH. (1985a) Using several indices for biological assessment of water quality in running water. *Verhandlungen Internationale Vereinigung für theoretische und angewandte Limnologie* **22**: 2281–6. [3.2]

Tolkamp HH. (1985b) Biological assessment of water quality in running water using macroinvertebrates: A case study for Limburg, The Netherlands. *Water Science and Technology* **17**: 867–78. [3.2]

Tomkiewicz SM, Dunson WA. (1977) Aquatic insect diversity and biomass in a stream marginally polluted by acid strip mine drainage. *Water Research* **11**: 397–402. [3.5]

US EPA (United States Environmental Protection Agency). (1990) *Biological Criteria: National Program Guidance for Surface Waters*. United States Environmental Protection Agency, EPA-440/5-90-004. [3.4]

Vandelannoote A, De Gueldre G, Bruylants B. (1981) Ecological assessment of water quality: Comparison of biological–ecological procedures in a rain-fed lowland waterway (Kleine Nete, N. Belgium). *Hydrobiological Bulletin* **15**: 161–4. [3.2]

Vannote RL, Minshall GW, Cummins KW *et al.* (1980) The river continuum concept. *Canadian Journal of Fisheries and Aquatic Sciences* **37**: 130–7. [3.3]

Voshell JR Jr, Layton RJ, Hiner SW. (1989) Field techniques for determining the effects of toxic substances on benthic macroinvertebrates in rocky-bottomed streams. *Aquatic Toxicology and Hazard Assessment* **12**: 134–55. [3.1]

Washington HG. (1984) Diversity, biotic and similarity indices. A review with special relevance to aquatic ecosystems. *Water Research* **18**: 653–94. [3.2]

Webber CE, Bayne DR, Seesock WC. (1989) Macroinvertebrate communities in Wheeler Reservoir (Alabama) tributaries after prolonged exposure to DDT contamination. *Hydrobiologia* **183**: 141–55. [3.2]

Whitehurst IT, Lindsey BI. (1990) The impact of organic enrichment on the benthic macroinvertebrate communities of a lowland river. *Water Research* **24**: 625–30. [3.3]

Wilhm JL. (1967) Comparison of some diversity indices applied to populations of benthic macroinvertebrates in a stream receiving organic waste. *Journal of the Water Pollution Control Federation* **39**: 1673–83. [3.2]

Wilhm JL, Dorris TC. (1968) Biological parameters for water quality criteria. *Bio Science* **18**: 477–81. [3.2]

Winner RW, Boesel MW, Farrell MP. (1980) Insect community structure as an index of heavy-metal pollution in lotic ecosystems. *Canadian Journal of Fisheries and Aquatic Sciences* **37**: 647–55. [3.3]

Winterbourn MJ, Rounick JS, Cowie B. (1981) Are New Zealand stream ecosystems really different? *New Zealand Journal of Marine & Freshwater Research* **15**: 321–8. [3.3]

Woodiwiss FS. (1980) *Biological Monitoring of Surface Water Quality. Summary Report*. Commission of the European Communities, Environment and Consumer Protection Service, No. ENV/223/74-EN, Nottingham. [3.2]

Wright JF, Moss D, Armitage PD *et al.* (1984) A preliminary classification of running-water sites in Great Britain based on macro-invertebrate species and the prediction of community type using environmental data. *Freshwater Biology* **14**: 221–56. [3.4]

Wright JF, Armitage PD, Furse MT *et al.* (1985) The classification and prediction of macroinvertebrate communities in British rivers. *Annual Report of the Freshwater Biological Association* **53**: 80–93. [3.4]

Wright JF, Armitage PD, Furse MT *et al.* (1988) A new approach to the biological surveillance of river quality using macroinvertebrates. *Verhandlungen Internationale Vereinigung für Theoretische und angewandte Limnologie* **23**: 1548–52. [3.4]

Wright JF, Armitage PD, Furse MT *et al.* (1989) Prediction of invertebrate communities using stream measurements. *Regulated Rivers: Research and Management* **4**: 147–55. [3.4]

Zelinka M, Marvan P. (1961) Zur prazisierung der biologischen klassifikation der reinheit fliessender gewasser. *Archiv für Hydrobiologie* **57**: 389–407. [3.2]

4: Water-quality Control

A. J. DOBBS AND T. F. ZABEL

4.1 INTRODUCTION

Traditionally, control of the chemical and biological quality of waters in rivers to protect different uses has been considered adequate to provide full environmental protection. This can be achieved by control of point and diffuse discharges using a variety of measures. However, a profound change is occurring whereby water-quality control is considered as a necessary but not sufficient condition to protect the ecological quality of rivers and other water bodies (Newman et al 1992). Consideration of sediment quality and protection of riparian habitat in addition to water-quality control are now seen as requirements for full environmental protection. Doubtless this wider aspect of river-quality control will assume more importance in the future (Royal Commission on Environmental Pollution 1992), but this chapter concentrates solely on aspects of the control of river water quality itself. Such control is effected (i) by regulation of the entry or discharge of contaminated or polluted waters into the river and (ii) by control of the flow regime. The effects of abstractions and other aspects of flow regime control will not be discussed in this chapter, but it is important to emphasize that effective river management requires that control of abstractions and discharges are inextricably linked.

In the past there were considered to be two fundamentally different approaches to pollution control: the 'quality objective approach' traditionally used in the UK, which took into account the dilution capacity of the receiving waters, and the 'uniform emission standard approach' favoured elsewhere in Europe, which applied the same concentration and load conditions to discharges from the same industrial sector. Currently, these two approaches are being seen as complementary and are being applied together.

As indicated above, river water-quality control is concerned with the control of pollution which can be defined in the widest sense with reference to European Community legislation as 'the discharge by man, directly or indirectly of substances or energy into the environment, the results of which are such as to cause hazards to human health, harm to living resources and to ecosystems, damage to amenities or interference with other legitimate uses of water'. Thus any control strategy adopted must not only control those activities likely to cause pollution in the aquatic environment, but must also protect humans from exposure to pollutants. The selection of the most appropriate control strategy to minimize the effects of the discharge of pollutants will depend on the type of pollutant, its source and the nature and use of the receiving water.

The following sections summarize the different approaches which may be taken to control the entry of pollutants to surface waters. We then discuss some river engineering approaches that are used for ameliorating the effects of pollution in rivers and finally discuss some potential future developments. Before discussing the control options it is useful to consider the nature and sources of pollutants.

4.2 TYPE OF POLLUTANTS

Pollutants can be classified in a variety of different ways. Holdgate (1979) lists several of these and gives advantages and disadvantages of the alternatives. EC Directives tend to divide substances in terms of the significance of their effects into List I (black) and List II (grey) substances, based on their toxicity, persistence, bioaccumulation, carcinogenicity, teratogenicity and mutagenicity. However, little guidance is provided in the Directives on the precise means to be adopted for the selection of specific List I and List II substances. Various selection schemes have therefore been developed to identify List I substances by assigning threshold values to the appropriate parameters and estimating likely concentrations in the environment based on production and physico-chemical data. A community selection scheme is currently being developed by the EC Commission.

An alternative approach is to divide substances into those causing direct toxic effects and those resulting in indirect effects.

1 Pollutants causing direct toxic effects: most of the List I and List II substances may be classified under this heading and may include heavy metals (e.g. cadmium) organometallics (e.g. organotins), other inorganics (e.g. ammonia), persistent organic compounds (e.g. pesticides) or volatile organic compounds (e.g. industrial solvents).

2 Pollutants causing indirect adverse effects: gross pollutants causing oxygen depletion and/or sulphide formation (e.g. farm waste, sewage effluent) or those causing eutrophication (nutrients) fall into this category. Aesthetic parameters such as foaming (presence of detergents), colour, litter and oil, which although not toxic at the concentrations present, may also affect the use of the water. Bacteria and viruses may also be considered as causing indirect effects by, for instance, reducing the tolerance of animals to the effect of other pollutants present. However, they can also cause direct effects (e.g. illness in bathers).

The way in which contaminants cause effects and thereby become pollutants varies widely. For instance, the organotins are toxic at very low concentrations to mollusc species but fish are more tolerant. In contrast, DDT's main effect occurs via the food chain, because of its high bioaccumulation potential, leading to problems in higher animals, for instance the thinning of egg shells in birds of prey. In practice almost any chemical or contaminant can become a pollutant if it is present in high enough concentration, and the main value of pollutant classification is to focus pollution control activity on the most hazardous.

4.3 SOURCES OF POLLUTANTS

Whilst the distinction is not very precise it is often useful to distinguish between point and diffuse pollution sources because different pollution control strategies are required in each case. Point sources are best thought of as discharges from fixed sites, such as a factory or sewage treatment plant, which if the process involved was stopped so would the discharge. Generally speaking a modification to the nature of the process or treatment of the discharge will change the composition of a point discharge. Diffuse imputs on the other hand result from no particular process but originate from the widespread use of the substance. Using this approach, for example, agricultural run-off would be considered a diffuse source. Phosphates used in detergents would probably also be best considered as a diffuse input, at least to the sewerage system. However, the aggregate phosphate discharged from a sewage treatment plant can be considered as a point source. It is monitored in this way and is capable of reduction by tertiary treatment.

In addition to consideration of the nature of the sources, point or diffuse, which as we have just seen depends to some extent on the point in the system where the pollutant is being considered, the temporal variability of discharges needs to be considered. In general three classes of discharge can be distinguished.

1 Continuous – a discharge whose composition and flow may fluctuate but which effectively happens all the time. A sewage treatment works effluent or a cooling water discharge from a power station are good examples.

2 Intermittent – as the name implies these do not discharge all the time and they may or may not discharge regularly but their location can be identified and the discharge is to some degree predictable in terms of composition and flow. Probably the best example is a storm sewer overflow; during rain events of a given severity such overflows will produce a discharge.

3 Incidents – the location, nature and timing of these is unpredictable. Examples are transport accidents and fires.

Each of these have their own range of control measures. Most pollutants will arrive in rivers from a variety of sources, and control requires an understanding of all the routes if it is to be effective and efficient.

4.4 CONTROL OPTIONS

For most substances, particularly those which occur naturally, it is unrealistic to expect zero discharge to the environment. Control must be exercised and whatever control option is used, the end result must be to protect the vulnerable targets, i.e. humans and human food sources, or other living organisms at the different levels. Thus for most substances it is generally accepted (GESAMP 1986):

- that there is a minimum acceptable concentration which does not produce unacceptable effects on the target;
- the environment therefore has a certain capacity to assimilate pollutants;
- the capacity can be quantified.

This line of thought requires evidence of harm to justify controls. However, in recent years pressure has grown to move away from the system where evidence of harm is required to a precautionary approach where proof of safety is needed. In principle such a precautionary approach is sound, but in practice it is difficult to apply. In particular proof of safety is impossible; effectively you are trying to prove a negative. Also the relative safety of one substance in comparison with another is extremely difficult to quantify because it often requires the comparison of a poorly defined risk in one area with another poorly defined risk in a different area. For example, evidence to suggest a certain carcinogenicity risk may have to be compared with long environmental persistence. In the extreme the precautionary approach can lead to a requirement for zero emission of a particular substance. While this is conceivable as a *target* for particularly dangerous substances, because continued reduction can be charted, it is not a

Table 4.1 Limits for metals (from Miller 1991)

Metal	Standards ($\mu g\,l^{-1}$)		
	Drinking water MAC*	Freshwater EQS†	Seawater EQS†
Copper	3000	1–28	5
Zinc	5000	8–125	40
Nickel	50	50–200	30
Lead	50	4–20	25
Mercury	1	1	0.3
Cadmium	5	5	2.5
Chromium	50	5–50	15
Arsenic	50	50	25

* Maximum admissible concentration – absolute – total.
† Environmental quality standard – annual average – dissolved/total; EC/UK EQS values.

feasible *requirement* because it is simply technically impossible to show a zero concentration of anything in anything. For most substances it seems discharges will have to occur and for these a reference concentration will be needed to ensure that the selected control option is sufficient to protect humans and the environment.

These reference values are likely to vary depending on the use of the water to be protected. For example, the standards required for metals to protect the ecosystem are often more stringent than those required for the protection of humans directly (Table 4.1), although it has to be noted that the limits are expressed in different ways (Miller 1991).

In some countries reference values are chosen on a non-environmental risk basis, e.g. expressed as a percentage of the background concentration. However, background levels can vary widely depending on the origin of the water. For instance, for metals, streams originating from a mineral-rich area will have much higher background concentrations than those from mineral-poor areas.

It is important that the reference values are based on scientific evidence and that these values are reviewed periodically in the light of new scientific evidence. Otherwise the use of the substance may be so restricted that its use is economically unattractive, leading to substitution by other substances which have different, but maybe unknown, effects on the environment. A typical example is the replacement of phosphate in detergents by alternative substances for which some of the effects are only now emerging (Dwyer *et al* 1990).

A number of different options are available to control pollutants entering the aquatic environment, which include the establishment of standards relating to different aspects of the overall production/use/disposal cycle (Holdgate 1979):

- process standards;
- product standards;
- exposure standards;
- biological standards;
- environmental quality standards;
- emission standards.

Besides these standards, two further control options need to be considered (Haigh 1985):

- preventative controls, e.g. total prohibition on the use of a substance;
- standards for total emissions for a given area, e.g. whole catchment area of a river system.

Most of these different control options have been utilized either individually or in different combinations in current EC* and national legislation. Obviously the effectiveness of the options depends critically on the enforcement.

Process standards

The process standard approach specifies the process to be used to ensure that the required quality is achieved. As such it is not really directly relevant to the process of the control of river water quality. However, the process control aspects of integrated pollution control and waste minimization are becoming increasingly important and these will have important implications for river water quality. For example, the mothproofing industry is experiencing increasing difficulties meeting the tightening consent conditions. Processes are therefore being developed to move

from aqueous to solvent-based processes for the application of mothproofing chemicals to minimize their release to the aquatic environment. This could lead to the adoption of a process standard requiring solvent-based application of mothproofing agents.

Product standards

Product standards are widely used in Europe in both EC and national legislation to control the release of certain substances to the aquatic environment. One of the first examples was the EC Detergent Directive (73/404/EEC) (CEC 1973). This was introduced to prevent foaming in rivers caused by detergent residues which resisted biodegradation in sewage treatment works. The Directive requires that the detergents satisfy certain biodegradation criteria established in the form of test protocols. A more recent example is the restriction imposed on the use of tributyltin compounds in antifouling paints used on boats. This bans the use of tributyltin compounds in paints used on small boats.

Product standards are particularly useful for substances entering the aquatic environment from diffuse sources. For example restrictions on lead in petrol, Directive 85/210/EEC (CEC 1985), has resulted in reduced emissions of lead to the air which, via reductions in atmospheric deposition and run-off, has reduced the amounts of lead entering the aquatic environment.

Exposure standards

Exposure standards may be defined as primary protection standards for the target, which can be either humans or aquatic organisms. The standards laid down in the EC Directive on the Quality of Water Intended for Human Consumption (80/778/EEC) (CEC 1980a) can be considered as exposure standards. The Directive provides maximum admissible concentrations for certain parameters, taking into account exposures from other sources such as air and food.

Applying exposure standards, for instance maximum admissible concentration in drinking water, could, in the extreme, require that discharges to receiving water used for the abstraction

---

* European Community legislation (EC Directives) is not in itself legally enforceable in Member States. However, adoption of EC Directives by the Council of Ministers requires Member States to ensure that the national legislation includes measures no less stringent than those agreed in the Directives.

of drinking water may have to meet those exposure standards if insufficient dilution is available in the receiving water and the water-treatment plant is not equipped for the removal of the particular substance. Alternatively the treatment plant would need to be improved. This dilemma lies at the heart of the current problems with pesticides in Europe. A uniform non-toxicologically derived exposure standard of $0.1 \, \mu g \, l^{-1}$ has been set in the Drinking Water Directive yet agricultural use frequently gives rise to run-off waters with pesticide concentrations considerably higher than this value.

The standards laid down in EC Directives on the quality of live bivalve molluscs to be placed on the market (91/492/EEC) (CEC 1991b), may be considered a further example of an exposure standard. If the standards for bacteria are exceeded, which can lead to illness in people consuming the bivalves, the bivalves must either be treated in special purification plants to reduce the levels of bacteria prior to sale, or the water quality must be improved to ensure that the standards in the bivalves are not exceeded. This particular case is more complicated though because a clear relationship between levels of bacteria in the water column and in the bivalve have so far not been established. The relationship may depend on the age of the animal, the availability of food and environmental conditions such as temperature and salinity.

Biological standards

Not many biological standards have been set so far. However, most of the daughter Directives of the EC Dangerous Substances Directive (76/464/EEC) (CEC 1976b), which lay down standards for individual List I substances, contain the statement that the concentration of the particular substances in shellfish and/or fish must not increase significantly with time, the so-called 'standstill' provision. Only the EC Directive on limit values and quality objectives for mercury discharges by the chlor-alkali electrolysis industry (82/779/EEC) (CEC 1982) contains besides the 'standstill' provision for shellfish, also a numerical standard for mercury of $0.3 \, mgHg \, kg^{-1}$ wet flesh in representative samples of fish flesh chosen as an indicator.

The EC Shellfish (79/923/EEC) and the EC Freshwater Fish (78/659/EEC) Directives also contain the general requirement that the concentration of identified substances in the flesh must be so limited that there is no effect on the quality of shellfish and fish products, respectively (CEC 1979a, 1978). However, no numerical values are laid down for individual substances.

The advantage of using biological assessments related to accumulation of the substance in tissue or blood is that it provides an indication of total exposure from all sources whether point or diffuse or from intermittent events such as storm overflows. The effect of intermittent events is particularly difficult to assess by the usually employed periodic spot-sampling methods and even diffuse inputs can vary substantially depending on the use pattern of the substances and the meteorological conditions.

The difficulties in applying biological standards are in relating tissue or blood levels to concentrations in the water or sediment, to actual effects on the ecosystem or harm to higher organisms and in obtaining representative samples for analysis from 'vulnerable' areas.

Preventative controls

Preventative controls can include a total prohibition on the use of a particular substance or partial prohibition for a particular purpose or in a designated 'protection zone'. This control can be similar to the product standard approach, as with the example of tributyltin compounds discussed above. Preventative controls can also relate to the location of a plant or the requirement that emergency plans are produced or particular storage facilities used to minimize any accidental release that could occur.

For particularly dangerous substances, total prohibition on their use may be the most appropriate control strategy. However, for other less dangerous substances partial prohibition of use may be sufficient if the permitted uses do not cause unacceptable effects and particularly if no equally effective and economical alternatives are available.

The ban on the use of certain pesticides in groundwater protection zones in Germany may be considered as an example of this approach. The ban relates to those pesticides which may reach concentrations in the groundwater above the maximum admissible concentration of $0.1 \, \mu g \, l^{-1}$ for individual pesticides in the EC Drinking Water Directive (80/778/EEC) (CEC 1980a).

The various amendments of the EC Directive 76/769/EEC on the approximation of the laws, regulations and administrative provisions of the Member States relating to restrictions on the marketing and use of certain dangerous substances and preparations (CEC 1976c) prohibit the use of certain products within the EC, such as the use of mercury-containing pesticides and the use of cadmium for pigmentation in a range of products and as a stabilizer in certain plastics and surface treatments. Another example of EC legislation applying preventative control is the Directive prohibiting the placing on the market and use of plant protection products containing certain active ingredients (79/117/EEC) (CEC 1979b). For instance, the fourth amendment (90/335/EEC) (CEC 1990) bans the use of endrin, aldrin and alkyl mercury compounds.

Although preventative controls can be applied to point sources of pollution they are most appropriate for the control of substances originating from diffuse sources.

Environmental Quality Standards

The EC has adopted several use-related directives laying down standards for individual parameters which must be met in order that the water is suitable for the particular use. The use-related directives are:

1 Directive concerning the quality required of surface water intended for the abstraction of drinking water in the Member States (75/440/EEC) (Surface Water Directive) (CEC 1975).
2 Directive concerning the quality of bathing water (76/160/EEC) (Bathing Water Directive) (CEC 1976a).
3 Directive on the quality of freshwaters needing protection or improvement in order to support fish life (78/659/EEC) (Freshwater Fish Directive) (CEC 1978).
4 Directive on the quality required of shellfish waters (79/923/EEC) (Shellfish Directive) (CEC 1979a).
5 Directive on the protection of groundwater

against pollution caused by certain dangerous substances (80/68/EEC) (Groundwater Directive) (CEC 1980b).
These directives apply only to designated waters.

In the EC Dangerous Substances Directive (76/464/EEC) (CEC 1976b) Environmental Quality Standards (EQSs) are provided but the use-related concept has not been adopted and a distinction is only made for discharges to fresh waters, estuaries and coastal waters. The EC Dangerous Substances Directive also allows control of individual substances by Uniform Emission Standards (UES) (see below).

Confusion has arisen in the EC Member Countries relating to the definition of the term 'Environmental Quality Objective' (EQO). In the UK the EQOs laid down by the EC are used as operational standards (EQSs) for the setting of consents for discharges and the control of diffuse inputs. In most of the other EC countries the EQOs are interpreted as long-term aims to be achieved in the future. Thus, for many EC countries, particularly the Netherlands and Germany, the EQOs laid down by the EC are not sufficiently stringent because the long-term aim of these countries is to achieve 'background concentrations' in all surface waters. This has discredited the use of EQSs for the control of direct discharges, which in most other EC countries are controlled by technology-based 'uniform emission standards' (UESs).

The application of EQSs requires control over the whole catchment area of the receiving water. In the UK the National Rivers Authority (now part of the UK Environmental Agency) in England and Wales and the River Purification Boards in Scotland, have responsibility for whole catchments. The EQS approach is less attractive in the other European countries which have to share the catchments of their surface waters with other countries and therefore do not have effective control over the incoming river quality at national borders. In these circumstances demands for treatment by 'best available technology' or for contaminants to be reduced to levels 'as low as reasonably (or technically) achievable', seems more reasonable.

Nevertheless, as discussed above, the application of technology-based effluent standards requires reference values to assess that the controls implemented are sufficient to ensure that the target species are protected. Similarly the application of EQSs requires the setting of consents for discharges to ensure that the EQS values are not exceeded.

The EQO/EQS approach

The Environmental Quality Objective (EQO)/ Environmental Quality Standard (EQS) approach is based on the premise that a minimum acceptable concentration of a pollutant can be defined which does not interfere with the use of the water. A distinction has therefore to be made between the EQO,[*] which defines the use for which the water is intended (e.g. abstraction for drinking water), and the EQS,[†] which specifies the concentration of the substance which should not be exceeded to ensure that the water is suitable for the particular designated use. For example, for the abstraction of drinking water (the EQO), the EQS for nitrate is $50\,mg\,l^{-1}$.

Thus to apply the EQO/EQS approach, the different uses of the water need to be defined, and standards, in terms of the maximum acceptable concentration of the particular pollutant to protect the different uses, must be derived. These standards must be sufficiently low to protect vulnerable targets implied or specified in the objective, including humans, human food sources or other living organisms. The standards can then be used to set consents for individual discharges, taking into account the dilution in the receiving water, but also the concentration of the pollutant already present in the receiving water from other sources. The EQO/EQS approach can therefore also deal with diffuse inputs and can be used to control multiple point sources.

In the UK the common uses of both fresh and saline surface waters have been defined for the derivation of EQS values for List II substances.

---

[*] Environmental Quality Objective (EQO) is defined as the level of water quality that a body of water should achieve in order to be suitable for its agreed use (NRA 1991).
[†]Environmental Quality Standard (EQS) is defined as that concentration of a substance which must not be exceeded if a specified use of the environment is to be maintained.

Table 4.2 Designated uses of water for derivation of EQS values

Use	Fresh water	Saline water
For direct abstraction to potable supply	✓	−[*]
For abstraction into impoundment prior to potable supply	✓	−[*]
As a source of food for human consumption	✓	✓
Protection of fish and shellfish	✓	✓
Protection of other aquatic life and dependent non-aquatic organisms	✓	✓
Irrigation of crops	✓	−[*]
Watering of livestock	✓	−[*]
Industrial abstraction	✓	✓
Bathing and water-contact sports	✓	✓
Aesthetic considerations	✓	✓

[*] Not applicable.

These take into account the use-related directives adopted by the EC listed above in Table 4.2.

The provisions of the UK's 1989 Water Act, now incorporated into the 1991 Water Resources Act, enable a scheme of statutory water-quality objectives to be developed and used. Under the 1991 Act the Secretary of State for the Environment has the duty to set Water Quality Objectives (WQO) taking advice from the National Rivers Authority (NRA). The Secretary of State and the NRA then have a duty to ensure WQOs are met with the usual UK statutory proviso 'as far as is reasonably practical'. This scheme now seems likely to start in 1993. In response to this requirement, proposals for Statutory Water Quality Objectives have recently been published by the NRA (1991) with reference to specific water uses.[‡]

Derivation of EQSs

The approach adopted in the UK for the derivation of EQSs is illustrated in Fig. 4.1. Available data on the toxic effects, both from laboratory studies and field observations, are critically assessed.

[‡] Recent developments with Statutory Water Quality Objectives, since this chapter was written are reviewed by Seager (1993).

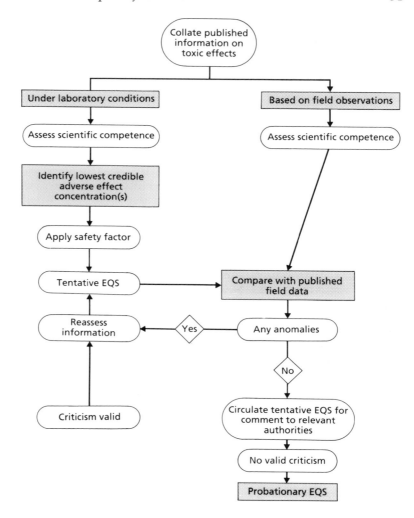

Fig. 4.1 Schematic flow chart for the derivation of environmental quality standards.

Particular attention is paid to the experimental test method used. The lowest credible adverse effect concentration is derived from the available toxicity data. Particular emphasis is placed on chronic effects and effects on sensitive life stages of the target species. A safety factor is then applied to obtain a tentative EQS. The magnitude of the safety factor depends on the quality and extent of the available toxicity data. If only acute (short-term) LC_{50} values are available, an arbitrary safety factor of 100 is usually applied. This factor tends to be reduced to 10 if chronic LC_{50} data are available for sensitive species.

For some substances 'no observable effects con-centrations' (NOEC) are reported for long-term chronic studies. Despite concerns over the value of the NOEC concept these values may be used as tentative standards without applying a safety factor, provided the test design is acceptable, and provided they refer to relevant species and are supported by the other data available.

The tentative EQS derived from the laboratory toxicity data is verified by comparison with the available field toxicity data, taking care to distinguish between the effects of the particular compound and those of other toxic compounds present. It is important to compare the tentative EQS with the highest observed concentration which has no effect on the ecosystem, rather than with the lowest concentration which does have an effect. Any discrepancies between the field data and the tentative EQS require the reassessment of the available field and laboratory data and, if necessary, the application of a different safety factor.

It is important that EQS values are frequently reviewed to take account of new laboratory or field toxicity data. The response of ecosystems to pollutants is extremely complex and until we have a much better understanding of the mechanisms of ecosystem response to pollutants EQS values need to be continually reviewed.

The safety factor applied obviously has a crucial impact on the final EQS proposed. For instance, the German proposals for the derivation of Water Quality Objectives involve larger safety factors (Federal Government 1989) with the following values:

1 10 if NOEC values are available for each of the four trophic levels (bacteria, *Pseudomonas putida*, the alga *Scenedesmus subspicatus*, *Daphnia magna* and a fish species in chronic studies).

2 100 if NOEC values of at least two of the above trophic levels are available and if in addition a wide range of aquatic toxicity data is available.

3 An additional safety factor of 10 can be applied, e.g, if:

(a) data are available for organisms of ecological importance which are lower than the NOEC values obtained using the standard test methods;

(b) the substance is persistent in the aquatic environment;

(c) the substance can change into a dangerous substance in the environment.

However, the German EQS values are intended as long-term 'quality-aim' (*Qualitätsziel*) values to be achieved in the future. These values have therefore an additional built-in precautionary safety factor compared to the UK EQS values which are used for the control of discharges.

In the USA, Water Quality Criteria have been derived by the Environmental Protection Agency (EPA) for a number of substances. EPA standards are derived from acute and chronic toxicity studies with species from three trophic levels (algae,

crustacea and fish), using 'uncertainty factors' to account for missing toxicity data. The values of these factors are (EPA 1984) as follow.

1 1: to data from field studies (e.g. artificial streams) as long as one/some of the most sensitive species are included.

2 10: to the lowest chronic values derived from partial or whole life-cycle studies, where the uncertainty factor allows for additional stress in the environment compared to laboratory conditions, existence of more sensitive species, other toxins in the environment and for extrapolation from partial to whole life cycles.

3 100: to the lowest acute values of the three trophic levels (based on an acute/chronic ratio of 10 and the existence of more sensitive life stages than those tested, but can be increased if acute/chronic ratio is large).

4 1000: to a single acute LC_{50} – but this is rarely used as QSAR (Quantity Structure–Activity Relation) studies are carried out to generate further data.

The EPA criteria are intended as reference values to ensure that the technology-based standards are sufficient to protect the environment.

The recently published Netherlands Environmental Water Quality Objectives 2000 are based on the NOECs from standard chronic toxicity tests with aquatic species but also include an allowance for the equilibrium partitioning of the substance between the dissolved fraction in water and the fraction adsorbed on suspended solids or sediment, the joint toxic action of related substances in aquatic species and the impact of persistent, bioaccumulating chemicals on predator species feeding on the aquatic environment (van der Gaag *et al* 1991). This approach leads to even lower concentrations as quality standards.

When setting EQSs, it is important to define explicitly the form of the chemical, e.g. as total concentration or dissolved fraction or, as in the case of ammonia, the un-ionized species. A decision has also to be made on the degree of compliance required for the standard to protect the use (100, 95, 90 or 50% compliance). This decision will have to take into account the sources of the substance and the difference between acute and chronic toxicities and the practical constraints imposed by sampling and analysis.

Although the EC has recently favoured the technology-based fixed emission approach, e.g. with the adoption of the EC Urban Waste Water Directive (91/271/EEC) (CEC 1991a) the proposals for a Minimum Ecological Quality Directive will be based on the quality standards approach and will most likely include chemical and biological standards.

Emission standards

The EC Dangerous Substances Directive (76/464/ EEC) (CEC 1976b) allows Member States to opt either for the Environmental Quality Standards (EQSs) or the Uniform Emission Standards (UESs) or limit value approach, for the control of List I or Black List substances. Most EC countries have favoured the UES approach. Standards are laid down in terms of permitted concentration of the substance in the effluent and the maximum load which may be discharged expressed in terms of load per unit of production for the different types of activities discharging the substance. Thus larger production facilities can discharge larger loads and different activities may discharge different loads.

However, the trend in Europe and the USA is to move away from controlling individual substances towards the control of effluents from industrial sectors, setting limit values for all important substances which may be present in the effluent from that particular industry. For the control of complex effluents the use of aggregate parameters such as AOX (adsorbable organic halogen) in Germany and toxicity-based consents in the UK and USA (see below) are being promoted.

Only two industrial sector EC Directives have been adopted so far. These concern the titanium dioxide industry (CEC 1989) and the treatment of urban waste water (91/271/EEC) (CEC 1991a). The Urban Waste Water Directive sets limits for biological oxygen demand (BOD), for chemical oxygen demand (COD), suspended solids (SS), total phosphorus (P) and total nitrogen (N). The values are partly related to the size of the treatment plant, but also to the sensitivity to eutrophication of the receiving water.

The most extensive industry sector-based controls are practised in Germany and the USA, whereas, for instance, France and The Netherlands have issued guidelines for only some branches of industry. Germany has adopted industry-specific standards for 52 branches of industry which include chemical standards, but also limits effluent toxicity (based on fish tests) for some branches of industry. The standards laid down are applied as minimum standards and, if the effluent contains dangerous substances, are applicable independently whether the effluent is discharged to sewer or to surface waters (Cartwright *et al* 1991).

In the UK under the Integrated Pollution Control legislation (see below) industry sector-based guidance notes are currently being issued for different industrial activities based on 'best available techniques not entailing excessive costs' (BATNEEC). These notes contain standards for emissions to water, air and in waste.

In the USA the control of discharges to surface waters is also based on 'uniform emission standards' for industrial sectors, but more stringent standards can be set if the water-quality criteria for the receiving water are not met. Under the Clean Water Act 1977 three programmes for the control of discharges have been established.

1 The National Protection Programme (NPP) which requires industry to pretreat its effluent to a technology-based standard before discharge to the sewer.

2 The National Pollutant Discharge Elimination System (NPDES) Program which provides technology and water-quality-based effluent standards that dischargers of effluents to surface waters must meet.

3 Water-quality-based effluent standards to ensure that State requirements for water quality and pollutant loading are met.

The NPDES and NPP programmes operate on the basis of 'categorical standards' (uniform emission standards) which are applied to all industries in a given category uniformly across the country. A general listing of the main industrial branches is given in Table 4.3. However, most industrial sectors are further subdivided and other industries not covered are regulated on a case-by-case basis with reference to statutory guidelines. These 'uniform emission standards' are also assessed in

Table 4.3 Industrial sectors with Uniform Emission Standards

Adhesives and sealants
Aluminium forming
Coal mining
Coil coating
Copper forming
Electroplating
Foundries
Inorganic chemicals
Iron and steel manufacturing
Leather tanning and finishing
Finishing/mechanical products
Non-ferrous metals manufacturing
Ore mining and dressing
Organic chemicals, plastics and synthetic materials
Pesticides, chemicals
Petroleum refining
Pharmaceutical manufacturing
Plastics and synthetics
Porcelain enamelling
Pulp, paper and paperboard
Steam electric power generation
Textile industry
Timber products

relation to local or State water quality criteria, which may result in more stringent discharge limits at a specific site.

The pretreatment standards are based on BAT – best available technology economically achievable – for the 126 toxic substances listed in the Clean Water Act, whereas BCT – best conventional pollutant control technology – is applied for the control of conventional parameters such as pH, BOD, COD, oil and grease, etc. Depending on the industry sector for new discharges more stringent pretreatment standards may be laid down than for existing discharges.

The emission standards approach is of course only applicable to the control of point sources. Strict implementation of emission standards may lead to the introduction of clean technology, particularly if the cost of complying with the standards is very high.

Combining the EQS and UES approaches

The protracted debate about the relative merits of the EQS and UES approaches for controlling dis-charges to surface waters has obscured the fact that neither method, in isolation, is fully effective for operational purposes. For receiving waters with a large dilution capacity the UES approach will lead to more stringent requirements whereas the EQS approach will lead to more stringent effluent consents for discharges to surface waters with a small dilution capacity.

As outlined above, reference values (EQS) are required to ensure that the technology-based standards are sufficiently stringent to protect the environment. Similarly, sufficiently stringent effluent standards have to be set to ensure that the EQS values in the receiving waters are met.

At the second Ministerial Conference on the Protection of the North Sea, the UK committed itself to apply a dual approach to the control of certain particularly dangerous substances, The

Table 4.4 The UK Red List substances (DoE 1989)

Substance	EC Directive adopted (List I status)
Mercury	+
Cadmium	+
Gamma-hexachlorocyclohexane (lindane)*	+
DDT*	+
Pentachlorophenol (PCP)*	+
Hexachlorobenzene (HCB)	+
Hexachlorobutadiene (HCBD)	+
Aldrin*	+
Dieldrin*	+
Endrin*	+
PCB (polychlorinated biphenyls)*	
Tributyltin compounds*	
Triphenyltin compounds*	
Dichlorvos*	
Trifluralin*	
1,2-Dichloroethane	+
Trichlorobenzene	+
Azinphos-methyl*	
Fenitrothion*	
Malathion*	
Endosulfan*	
Atrazine*	
Simazine*	

* Substances which enter the environment predominantly by indirect routes.

Red List (Table 4.4). There are also indications that some EC Member States who claim to use the UES approach are adopting a mixed system of control which takes account of the quality of the receiving water and allows the setting of stricter limit values. The system in the USA, although technology-based, also allows stricter standards to meet water-quality standards if local conditions warrant it.

Toxicity-based control

The chemical-specific approach is generally used for the control of point discharges to surface waters. However, there is increased interest in the USA and Europe in the application of toxicity-based consents (TBCs) for complex effluents, particularly those of variable nature but also for effluents containing substances for which analytical methods or toxicity data (to derive safe discharge concentrations) are not available. Using a toxicity-based consent procedure also provides some protection against possible synergistic or additive toxicological effects of the substances present and the contribution to toxicity from impurities and degradation products. The application of this approach may require that either the diluted (with receiving water) or the undiluted effluent is non-toxic to specified organisms, e.g. bacteria, *Daphnia* or fish, and that there is no evidence of chronic toxic effects. In practice the application of toxicity-based consents should be supported by chemical-specific controls wherever appropriate.

Integrated pollution control

In the UK the adoption of the Environmental Protection Act 1990 introduced the concept of integrated pollution control (IPC) for the control of the 'most polluting' (prescribed) processes. Only one process authorization for the disposal of waste to air, water and land will be required. 'Best available technology not entailing excessive costs' (BATNEEC) will have to be applied for the control of discharges and an assessment of the 'best practicable environmental option' (BPEO) will have to be carried out to avoid damaging transfer of pollution from one environmental compart-ment to another. In theory the need to achieve BPEO will dictate BATNEEC and what is BATNEEC for BPEO will prevail over what is BATNEEC for releases into individual media (Priest *et al* 1991).

The authorization conditions obtained by applying IPC must also be assessed to ensure that they are sufficiently stringent to meet the EQS values in the receiving water. This assessment may lead to tighter limits than those given by BATNEEC. There are also indications that the EC is moving away from controlling individual substances towards an integrated permitting system.

Effluent charges

Several EC Member States (Germany, The Netherlands, France) are operating effluent charging systems. Charges are levied at levels which depend on the pollution load discharged. Although these charges have no legal force to improve the quality of the effluent they neverthe-less can provide an incentive to improve the quality of the effluent especially if the charges are sufficiently high or, as practised in Germany, if much lower charges are levied if certain effluent standards are met. It has been claimed that the introduction of effluent charges in Germany has provided an incentive to improve effluent qualities more rapidly for existing plants, which are normally allowed an extended implemen-tation period (up to 10 years) for new legislation (Cartwright *et al* 1991).

In the UK charges for the monitoring of dis-charges have been introduced enabling NRA to recover the costs for processing applications and monitoring consents. The charges depend on the volume of the discharge, the substances present in the discharge and the type of receiving water of the effluent. This may incidentally also provide an incentive to improve the quality of the effluent especially as the monitoring charges for the par-ticularly dangerous substances (UK Red List) present are quite high, reflecting the analytical costs involved. However, the Water Resources Act 1991 only allows such a cost recovery charging scheme and any move to a true pollu-tion tax or incentive charging scheme would require new legislation.

4.5 ENGINEERING CONTROLS OF WATER QUALITY

In some cases the kinds of discharge control philosophy discussed above are insufficient. Catchments in old industrialized areas are polluted as a result of historic pollution and inadequate storm-water provisions; river water quality is often poor, in particular if the flow in the river is comprised mainly of sewage effluent. In such cases 'purification lakes' can alleviate the pollution load carried by the rivers and lead to improvements in downstream water quality. A good example is the River Tame reclamation lakes situated near Birmingham in the UK. The Upper Tame catchment above the lakes includes one of the largest urban conurbations in the UK; approximately 20% of the catchment is impermeable and run-off is rapid carrying a high polluting load into the river. The area was also highly industrialized during the 19th century, which has left a heritage of contaminated land. The first reclamation lake was completed in 1983 and a second one was brought into use in 1987. These lakes have led to significant improvements in downstream water quality as a result of reductions in the suspended solid and to a lesser extent BOD load, but at the considerable cost of some £1 million per year, most of which results from the continuous process of removal and disposal of the contaminated sediment (Hellawell & Green 1986).

Another example of an engineering solution is the artificial introduction of oxygen into river waters. Such an approach has been successfully used to minimize the impact of pollution events such as that involving a spillage of sugar. It is also used on the River Thames in the UK to minimize the impact of oxygen depletion in the estuary resulting from storm discharges. The 'Thames Bubbler' can move up and down the estuary and inject up to 30 tonnes per day of oxygen into the water (Adams 1992).

Such engineering solutions ameliorate the effects of inadequate historic pollution control practices. They are best viewed as expedients until the origins of the pollution are identified and more effective control measures introduced.

4.6 RIVER-QUALITY CONTROL IN THE FUTURE

The technology and philosophy of point discharge control is now well advanced although at times leading to increased loads to other environmental compartments (land, air). While improvements in efficiency are to be expected in the future, improved control is largely a matter of resources and priorities. It is a sign of the state of technology and knowledge that some industrial companies can set themselves targets of zero discharge notwithstanding the technical problems posed by the term. The issues of the future are how to define river water quality; how to monitor and control it most effectively; and how to identify and control diffuse sources of pollution? With regard to the last, the use of buffer zones is attracting increasing attention (see Large & Petts 1994).

Progress on the definition of water quality is being assisted by the recognition that both biological measures (species diversity and numbers) and chemical measures are useful and complementary. The quality objectives proposals by the NRA in the UK recognizes three main elements to the quality objectives for surface waters.

1 A 'use' category defining what the community expects to use the river for, e.g. basic amenity, cyprinoid fishery, etc. (see Section 4.4).

2 A 'regulatory' category linked to relevant EC Directives, e.g. the Dangerous Substances Directive mentioned above.

3 A classification category defined by reference to chemical water quality and the biological state of the water, based on species present.

There is possibly some value in considering extending the use classification by taking a functional view of river systems. Consideration of the basic functions that rivers have to perform may lead to new procedures to assess and monitor the overall 'health' of a river system. Such functions could include the ability to assimilate waste material at a given rate, an ability to support a population of primary producer organisms, etc. Monitoring procedures applied to such biological functions might prove to be more robust than simple species-occurrence monitoring approaches.

In monitoring chemical water quality there appears to be considerable scope for improvements both in the determinands selected and the way monitoring and classification is conceived and organized. The conventional river water quality determinands are dissolved oxygen (DO), biochemical oxygen demand (BOD) and ammonia. Dissolved oxygen is clearly of key importance for the aesthetics of water quality and aquatic species survival. Ammonia is a toxicant occurring widely so is of direct environmental relevance. However, BOD is merely a measure of oxygen depletion potential, interesting, but as long as DO is sufficiently high, of no direct biological relevance. More profound consideration of BOD use in this way seems long overdue. The requirement to measure nutrient concentrations is also likely in coming years.

Chemical monitoring in the conventional way usually involves spot sampling. This approach, while valuable, suffers from two fundamental weaknesses. The first is the low probability of detecting pollution events and the second is that the determinands selected for analysis may not include the important ones. Two developments are providing remedies for this weakness: one is the increasing use and improved basis for biological monitoring; the other is the advance in technology enabling more use of continuous chemical monitoring.

Biological monitoring, which usually involves the study of species diversity and abundance, solves these problems by integrating the effects of all pollutants and all sources whether continuous or one-off pollution events. Alternative approaches based on body burdens, physiology and biochemical changes are also starting to show promise but are not currently routinely used. Biological monitoring offers clear advantages in being capable of responding to episodic events and to unidentified pollutants and to mixtures. Its drawbacks are that causes are difficult to identify and when changes are found it can be too late.

One problem with species occurrence and diversity which has in the past limited its value is the difficulty of taking natural physical or chemical factors into account. Rivers with hard and soft water will clearly be expected to have different flora and fauna. If these natural factors could be taken into account it would be possible to attribute changes in natural population to those caused by pollution. Such an approach (RIVPACS – Wright *et al* 1989) has been developed for predicting benthic invertebrate communities. The NRA are proposing to use this approach in the future to provide an additional biological component to the conventional data used for water quality classification (NRA 1991).

Advances in technology have enabled continuous water monitoring to develop rapidly although there is still only a small number of determinands that can be measured reliably in this way. Whereas 20 or so years ago water quality in drinking-water treatment plants was monitored continuously for process control reasons, it is now fairly commonplace for raw water quality to be monitored often using broad-spectrum sensor systems such as fish monitors to detect pollution events (Evans & Wallwork 1988). These devices are really quality-assurance tools rather than quality control, but the development of relatively small portable devices with in-built communications offers possibilities of detecting and tracing the source of pollution events. One such device uses a Cellnet phone with a microcomputer and pH, turbidity and DO probes powered by an onboard power pack which can be moored in a river. When any of the probes registers a change outside a pre-set range a sequence of samples of water can be taken and someone alerted by phone (Adams *et al* 1992). Such developments in monitoring technology will doubtless continue and will be valuable operational tools, although by the time they register a problem it is often too late.

The process of setting quality objectives, determining action plans and monitoring trends to assess achievements is much like an industrial production process. If it is viewed in this way then river quality control can be considered to be a true quality control task much like any other. Monitoring can then be viewed as quality control sampling rather than a snapshot picture of water quality, and there is the prospect of added value and better control resulting. Such an approach has been proposed for groundwater monitoring at hazardous sites (Starks & Flatman 1991) but, not as far as we are aware, for river waters. The approach would need to take account of natural variability but this could be built into a model to underlie the quality-control approach.

REFERENCES

Adams IM. (1992) Management of River Thames. In: Newman PJ, Piavaux MA, Sweeting RA (eds) *River Water Quality – Ecological Assessment and Control*. EUR 14606 EN-FR, Office of Official Publications of European Communities, Luxembourg. [4.5]

Adams JRW, Dolby JC, Williams NP. (1992) National Rivers Authority initiatives in the development of portable monitoring equipment. *Journal of the Institution of Water and Environmental Management* **6**: 64–71. [4.6]

Cartwright NG, Rees YJ, Derick M, Zabel TF. (1991) *The Application of Limit Values in Three EC Member States*. National Rivers Authority R&D Note 30, Bristol. [4.4]

CEC (Council of the European Communities). (1973) Directive on detergents (73/404/EEC). *Official Journal L347* 22 November 1973. [4.4]

CEC (Council of the European Communities). (1975) Directive concerning the quality required of surface water intended for the abstraction of drinking water in the Member States (75/440/EEC). *Official Journal L194/39* 25 July 1975. [4.4]

CEC (Council of the European Communities). (1976a) Directive concerning the quality of bathing water (76/160/EEC). *Official Journal L31/1* 5 February 1976. [4.4]

CEC (Council of the European Communities). (1976b) Directive on pollution caused by certain dangerous substances discharged into the aquatic environment of the Community (76/464/EEC). *Official Journal L129/23* 18 May 1976. [4.4]

CEC (Council of European Communities). (1976c) Directive on the approximation of the laws, regulations and administrative provisions of the Member States relating to restrictions on the marketing and use of certain dangerous substances and preparations (76/769/EEC). *Official Journal L262* 27 September 1976. [4.4]

CEC (Council of the European Communities). (1978) Directive on the quality of fresh waters needing protection or improvement in order to support fish life (78/659/EEC). *Official Journal L222/1* 14 August 1978. [4.4]

CEC (Council of the European Communities). (1979a) Directive on the quality required of shellfish waters (79/923/EEC). *Official Journal L281/47* 10 November 1979. [4.4]

CEC (Council of the European Communities). (1979b) Directive prohibiting the placing on the market and use of plant protection products containing certain active substances (79/117/EEC). *Official Journal L33* 8 February 1979. [4.4]

CEC (Council of the European Communities). (1980a) Directive relating to the quality of water intended for human consumption (80/778/EEC). *Official Journal L229/11* 30 August 1980. [4.4]

CEC (Council of the European Communities). (1980b) Directive on the protection of groundwater against pollution caused by certain dangerous substances (80/68/EEC). *Official Journal L20/43* 26 January 1980. [4.4]

CEC (Council of the European Communities). (1982) Directive on limit values and quality objectives for mercury discharges by the chlor-alkali electrolysis industry (82/176/EEC). *Official Journal L81* 27 March 1982. [4.4]

CEC (Council of the European Communities). (1985) Directive on the approximation of the laws of the Member States concerning the lead content of petrol (85/210/EEC). *Official Journal L96* 3 April 1985. [4.4]

CEC (Council of the European Communities). (1989) Directive on procedures for harmonising the programme for the reduction and eventually elimination of pollution caused by waste from the titanium dioxide industry (89/428/EEC). *Official Journal L201* 14 July 1989. [4.4]

CEC (Council of the European Communities). (1990) Commission Directive amending for the fourth time the Annex to Council Directive 79/117/EEC prohibiting the placing on the market and the use of plant protection products containing certain active substances (90/335/EEC). *Official Journal L162* 28 June 1990. [4.4]

CEC (Council of the European Communities). (1991a) Directive concerning urban waste water treatment (91/271/EEC). *Official Journal L135/40* 30 May 1991. [4.4]

CEC (Council of the European Communities). (1991b) Directive laying down the health conditions for the production and the placing on the market of live bivalve molluscs (91/492/EEC). *Official Journal L268* 24 September 1991. [4.4]

Dwyer M, Yeoman S, Lester JW, Perry R. (1990) A review of proposed non-phosphate detergents builders utilisation and environmental assessment. In: *Environmental Technology* vol. II, pp. 263–94. [4.4]

DoE (Department of the Environment). (1989) Agreed 'Red list' of dangerous substances confirmed by the Minister of State (Lord Caithness). *News Release 194*, DoE, Marsham Street, London, 10 April 1989. [4.4]

EPA (Environmental Protection Agency). (1984) *Estimating Concern Levels for Concentrations of*

Chemical Substances in the Environment. Report of the EPA Environmental Effects Branch, Washington, DC. [4.4]

Evans GP, Wallwork JF. (1988) The WRc fish monitor and other biomonitoring methods. In: Gruber D & Diamond JM (eds) *Automated Biomonitoring*, pp. 75–90. Ellis Horwood, Chichester. [4.6]

Federal Government. (1989) Federal States Working Group 'Quality Objectives' (BLAK QZ) Concept for the Derivation of Quality Objectives for the Protection of Inland Surface Waters Against Dangerous Substances, 10 October 1989. [4.4]

GESAMP (Joint Group of Experts on the Scientific Aspects of Marine Pollution). (1986) *Environmental Capacity – An Approach to Marine Pollution.* [4.4]

Haigh N. (1985) The co-ordination of standards for chemicals in the environment. Paper presented at the European Environmental Bureau Seminar on: *A European Community Policy Concerning Existing Chemicals*, Brussels, 9–11 June 1985. [4.4]

Hellawell JM, Green MB. (1986) Performance of the Tame Purification Lake. In: Solbe JG (ed) *Effects of Land Use on Water Quality*. Ellis Horwood, Chichester. [4.5]

Holdgate MW. (1979) *A Perspective of Environmental Pollution*. Cambridge University Press, Cambridge. [4.2, 4.4]

Large ARG, Petts GE. (1994) Rehabilitation of river margins. In: Calow P, Petts GE (eds) *The Rivers Handbook*, Vol. 2, pp. 401–18. Blackwell Scientific Publications, Oxford. [4.6]

Miller DG. (1991) Environmental Issues and Concerns in Europe. Paper presented at the IWEM Scientific Section Seminar on Environmental Research In Europe, London, 24 April 1991. [4.4]

Newman PJ, Piavaux MA, Sweeting RA (eds). (1992) *River Water Quality – Ecological Assessment and Control*. EUR 14606 EN-FR, Office of Official Publications of European Communities, Luxembourg. [4.1]

NRA (National Rivers Authority). (1991) *Proposals for Statutory Water Quality Objectives*. Water Quality Series No. 5, December 1991. NRA, Bristol. [4.4, 4.6]

Priest W, Griffith R, Zabel TF. (1991) *Towards Integrated Pollution Control – BATNEEC and the Challenge for Industry*. Clifford Chance, Earnst & Young and WRc plc. [4.4]

Royal Commission on Environmental Pollution. (1992) *16th Report: Freshwater Quality*. HMSO, London. [4.1]

Seager J. (1993) Statutory Water Quality Objectives and river water quality. *Journal of the Institution of Water and Environmental Management* 7(5): 556–66. [4.4]

Starks TH, Flatman GT. (1991) RCRA groundwater monitoring decision procedures viewed as quality control schemes. *Environmental Monitoring and Assessment* 16: 19–37. [4.6]

van der Gaag M, Stortelder PBM, van de Kooij LA, Bruggeman WA. (1991) Setting Environmental Quality Criteria for water and sediment in the Netherlands: a pragmatic ecotoxicological approach. *European Water Pollution Control* 1(3). [4.4]

Wright JF, Armitage PD, Furse MT, Moss D. (1989) Prediction of invertebrate communities using stream measurements. *Regulated Rivers: Research and Management* 4: 147–55. [4.6]

5: Flow Allocation for In-river Needs

G. E. PETTS AND I. MADDOCK

5.1 INTRODUCTION

The structure and functioning of river systems has recently been synthesized as the 'fluvial hydrosystem' concept (Amoros & Petts 1993). A fluvial hydrosystem comprises the whole river corridor – the river channel, riparian zone, floodplain and alluvial aquifer – and is viewed as a four-dimensional system, being influenced not only by longitudinal processes but also by lateral and vertical fluxes, and strong temporal changes. Flow is important in three contexts. First, flow characteristics define the environmental domains within which biological communities develop. Secondly, the geomorphological effectiveness of flows of different magnitude – i.e. the amount of sediment transport, erosion and deposition – determines the channel and floodplain morphology, and the types and age structure of the different sediment-landform units that comprise the river corridor. Thirdly, the river and groundwater regimes determine the nature of vertical interactions within the hyporheic zone. Interactions between flow and biota are complex and highly sensitive to river regulation and abstraction.

With the increasing demands upon water resources and growing concern for environmental protection over the past decade, greater attention has been given to the allocation of water for in-river needs. Typically, this attention has been directed to maintaining habitat for a target species, usually a salmonid, during the summer, dry-weather period. However, the maintenance of minimum flow is only one of a range of considerations necessary for the protection or rehabilitation of fluvial hydrosystems. Hill *et al* (1991) argue that a holistic streamflow manage-

ment framework requires the integration of flow regimes to maintain four groups of biotic and abiotic resources: (i) overbank flows that inundate riparian and floodplain areas; (ii) floodflows that form floodplain and valley features; (iii) in-channel flows that sustain the functioning of the instream system; and (iv) in-channel flows that meet critical fish requirements. To this must be added a fifth: surface-water and groundwater regimes to sustain the functioning of the hyporheic system.

5.2 THE SCIENTIFIC BASIS

Quantitative and process-based research on rivers was founded during the 1950s and 1960s. A number of early works established relationships between flow (see Fraser 1972) and current velocity (see Statzner *et al* 1988) and salmonid fish, macroinvertebrates and macrophytes. Three of the first papers to emphasize the importance of flow as an ecological factor were Phillipson (1954), Wickett (1954) and Ambuhl (1959). However, the role of flow and its associated hydraulic characteristics in structuring river ecosystems received little development until the early 1980s (Newbury 1984; Nowell & Jumars 1984). Throughout the intervening period, stream ecologists focused on energy flows, carbon fluxes and macroinvertebrate life histories (Resh 1985).

Studies of biotic responses to flows and especially to changes of flows have gained considerable momentum over the past decade. The first important catalyst for linking flows and ecology was *River Ecology and Man*, edited by R.T. Oglesby, C.A. Carlson and J.A. McCann (Oglesby *et al* 1972). At the time, however, river management was an 'art' rather than a science. This is illustrated by Fraser's statement: 'Discharge recommendations are often based more on a biologist's or engineer's guess than on a quantified evaluation of the relationship between discharge and the ecology of the stream, its aesthetics and other in-place uses.'

During the late 1970s, a significant response to the intensifying need for an objective method to assess instream-flow allocations was the development of the Instream Flow Incremental Methodology (IFIM) by the US Fish and Wildlife Service Cooperative Instream Service Group. The methodology has become one of the most widely used methods in North America for estimating the effect of changes in flow on trout habitat (Conder & Annear 1987) and provides a useful guide for determining low-flow requirements, particularly in late summer and autumn (Hill *et al* 1991).

In the UK, advances in linking hydrology and ecology have lagged behind those in the USA. At a symposium held in 1970, on *Conservation and Productivity of Natural Waters* (Edwards & Garrod 1972), organized by the British Ecological Society and the Zoological Society of London, Morgan notes: 'In the long term it would be desirable to gain knowledge of the wider implications of the amounts of water let down rivers on the ecosystem as a whole.' Importantly, Morgan urged the focusing of efforts on the intricate relationships between animals and plants and their environment if better management is to be achieved. Significant advances were slow to be made although influential reviews were published by Brooker (1981), Milner *et al* (1981) and Petts (1984). Furthermore, despite detailed studies of the River Tees below Cow Green reservoir (see Armitage 1978; Crisp *et al* 1983), in a study of compensation flows in the UK Gustard *et al* (1987) concluded that the primary research need remained the development of quantitative relationships between freshwater biota and the physical and chemical variables at a scale appropriate to the river reach. A marked acceleration of research effort followed the Fourth International Symposium on Regulated Streams, held at Loughborough in 1988 (Petts & Wood 1988; Petts *et al* 1989). Subsequently, IFIM was introduced

(Bullock & Gustard 1992; Petts 1992) and progress made in addressing biological responses to water abstraction (Armitage & Petts 1992; Bickerton *et al* 1993).

Research directions

Four complementary lines of scientific research are of significance for linking hydrology and ecology: (i) the flood pulse concept; (ii) the channel-forming discharge; (iii) the concept of hydraulic stream ecology; and (iv) the demonstration of the ecological significance of the hyporheic zone.

The flood pulse concept

The river margin is a water-land ecotone (see Chapter 7). The downstream transport of organic matter derived from the headwaters and nutrient spiralling, the core of the 'river continuum concept' (Vannote *et al* 1980), have little significance for floodplain systems. Large floodplain rivers derive most of their animal biomass from within the floodplain; they are dominated by lateral exchanges between floodplain and river channel, and nutrient recycling within the floodplain. The 'flood pulse concept' (Junk *et al* 1989) proposes that the biota of large floodplain rivers is determined principally by the hydrological regime. The biota is adapted to the pronounced aquatic and terrestrial phases: aquatic organisms colonize the floodplain at rising and high water levels because of feeding and spawning opportunities; terrestrial organisms occupying non-flooded habitats along the borders are adapted to exploit the floodplain at low water levels.

Floodplains and floods are now regarded as essential components of fluvial systems (Sedell *et al* 1989). Without the 'flood pulse' (see Fig. 1.2), production within the fluvial hydrosystem is reduced, and community composition and energy pathways are radically changed. The 'flood pulse advantage' (Bayley 1991) describes the degree by which annual multispecies fish yield exceeds that from a system with constant water level (Fig. 5.1). An 'advantage' is also seen in the 'subsidy' to production of higher vegetation due to seasonal flooding of the riparian zone (e.g. Stromberg 1993). Vegetation decline consequent upon flow diver-

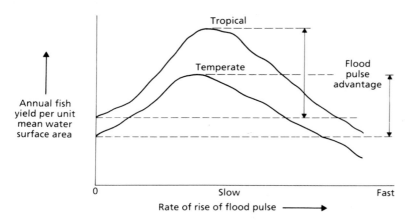

Fig. 5.1 The 'flood-pulse advantage' (after Bayley 1991). The relationship between mean water surface area of a floodplain and annual multispecies fish yield is shown to depend upon the flood pulse (no flood pulse is indicated by the abscissa = 0) and particularly the rate of hydrograph rise. The 'advantage' of the slow rise and long duration hydrograph contrasts with the 'disadvantage' associated with a flashy regime.

sion from semi-arid streams demonstrates the limiting conditions of water availability upon riparian vegetation in these environments (e.g. Smith *et al* 1991).

A key component of the flood pulse concept is the 'moving littoral', the inshore edge of the aquatic environment that traverses the floodplain. The effectiveness of the moving littoral relates to the rate of hydrograph rise (Fig. 5.1). A slow hydrograph rise allows sufficient time for *in situ* processes, mineralized products from any preceding aquatic cycle and the current terrestrial one being released into the water. In dry periods, oxygenation of sediments promotes processing of organic material; subsequent submergence recycles plant nutrients into the water, enhancing productivity. During the flood phase, food supply in fertile floodplains can be so abundant that individual growth and population density of fish and other aquatic animals are limited by factors other than food, such as dissolved oxygen levels, availability of spawning habitat, and predation. Thus, large rivers are characterized by terrestrial and aquatic organisms with anatomical, morphological, physiological and/or ethological adaptations to utilize the opportunities created by predictable and prolonged floodplain inundation the drying out.

The occurrences, life cycles and abundances of primary and secondary producers and decomposers are determined by duration, magnitude, frequency, timing and predictability of floods.

Timing and predictability may be key factors explaining differences between regions in terms of flood pulse effectiveness. Unpredictable floods include irregular events to which the biota is unable to develop profitable strategies for occupying the inundated riparian and floodplain areas, and disturbances – catastrophic events that periodically 'reset' the physical and biotic environment (see Chapters 11 and 12).

Junk *et al* (1989) stated that the effect of a flood on biota is principally hydrological. From a conceptual viewpoint, flood characteristics may be the driving variable over short time-scales (1–10 years) but over longer time-scales, geomorphological processes are seen to play an increasingly significant role. Floodplain morphology, sediment characteristics and disturbance regimes reflect the geomorphological setting as well as the flow regime (see Amoros & Petts 1993).

Hydraulic stream ecology

The concept of hydraulic stream ecology is founded on the basic ecological principle that the relative difference in speed between an organism and the medium in which it lives affects the energy budget of the organism (Statzner *et al* 1988). Current velocity influences respiration and other measures of metabolism in all major groups of organisms found in running waters. Velocity also affects the feeding biology and behavioural characteristics of lotic animals, including rheotaxis, locomotory activity, schooling and territoriality. Some species undergo progressive changes in body shape, and are able to exploit different hydraulic habitats at different stages of their life history.

The morphology of a stream channel is a key component for river management, influencing the productivity and biological quality of the in-stream habitat. The hydraulic conditions where organisms live arise from the interaction of flow and channel form: the shape of the channel in cross-section, especially its asymmetry; bedform, such as pool-riffle development; the heterogeneity of the channel margins; and planform (see Petts 1994). Stream power – the slope-discharge product – describes the rate of energy supply at the channel bed, relates to channel stability (Brookes 1988) and is especially useful for explaining differences between river sectors (upland/ lowland; meandering/braided; stable/unstable: see Petts 1994). However, at a smaller scale, velocity, depth and a range of complex hydraulic variables such as shear stress, Froude number and Reynolds number (Table 5.1) relate to the distribution of instream biota.

Gore (1994) and Brookes (1994) have demonstrated the effects of changes of channel hydraulics upon biota. In channelized streams, the reduction in abundance and diversity of fish species may result from the inability of some species to maintain physiological equilibrium in conditions where the 'hydraulic fitness' of their body shape is suboptimal. In natural channels, the heterogeneous flow environment supports a biota of comparatively greater variety and abundance, and hydraulic refugia play a major role in determining the impact of hydrological changes.

Habitat preference curves.

Different species of fish and macroinvertebrates select specific habitat types in terms of preferred water velocities, depths and substrates, and these may be defined as habitat suitability criteria. The use of habitat profiles and preference curves for target species (e.g. Fig. 5.2) has become established as a means of describing habitat requirements for both fish and invertebrates. In their

Table 5.1 Common complex hydraulic variables

Froude number	(Fr)	=	$V/(gd)^{0.5}$	Dimensionless
Reynolds number	(Re)	=	VR/v	Dimensionless
Shear stress	(r)	=	$pgSR$	dyne cm^{-2}
Manning's roughness	(n)	=	$R^{0.67}S^{0.5}/V$	Dimensionless
Bagnold power	(Ω)	=	$pgQS$	watts $(= J s^{-1})$

$\Omega = V$ = velocity; d = depth; R = hydraulic radius (cross-sectional area/wetted perimeter length; for wide shallow channels this approximates to the mean depth); power; Q = discharge; S = slope; p = water density; v = kinematic viscosity; and g = acceleration due to gravity.

simplest form, habitat criteria may be derived from life-history studies in the literature or from professional experience or judgement (e.g. Chaveroche & Sabaton 1989). Alternatively, detailed field observations enable the frequency analysis of microhabitat conditions utilized by different life stages and species. In this latter case, problems may arise where preferred habitat conditions are absent or limited at the time of observation.

A variety of techniques have been used to relate presence/absence or abundance data to hydraulic parameters. The binary format provides the simplest approach, establishing a suitable range of conditions for a hydraulic parameter as it pertains to a life stage of a species; conditions are either suitable (a rating of 1.0) or unsuitable (rating of 0.0). More complex methods include an incremental approach (Gore & Judy 1981), multiple regression (Morin *et al* 1986) and bivariate depth and velocity exponential polynomial models (Lambert & Hanson 1989).

The channel-forming discharges

Consideration of channel-forming flows is important if the diversity of instream, riparian and floodplain habitats is to be protected or restored. Channel and floodplain processes are intimately linked, although models to quantify these links remain in their infancy (Howard 1992). For management purposes, channel-forming flows may be viewed from three perspectives.

First, it is necessary to consider the *bankfull flow*. Although channel form is a function of the full range of discharges and sediment loads

Chapter 5

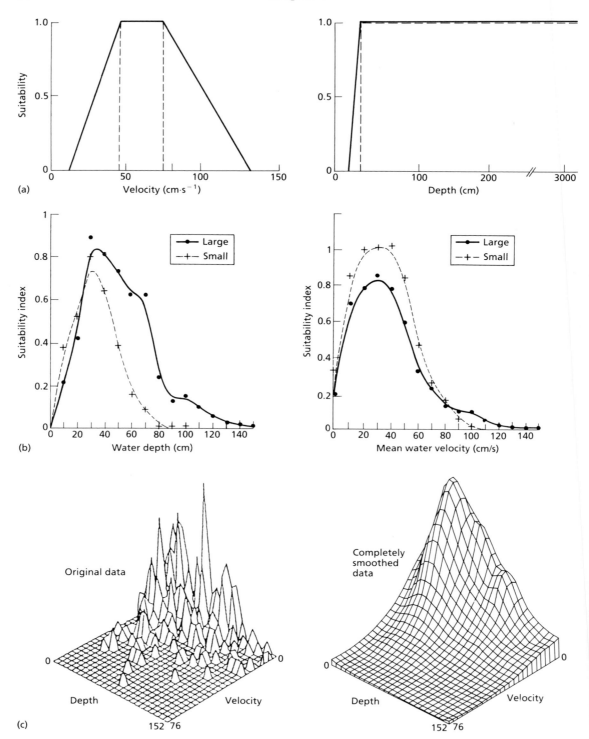

(a)

(b)

(c)

experienced, on many rivers the bankfull flow has been shown to approximate the most effective discharge for sediment transport and to re-form bar shape and orientation, re-order substrate size distribution in local areas, and maintain channel width. The bankfull discharge is perhaps best viewed as a hydrological benchmark (Hill *et al* 1991), representing the range of intermediate flows that determine the size and shape of many alluvial channels. For a range of rivers, the bankfull discharge has been shown to have a return period of between 1 and 3 years, with a modal value of about 1.5 years, using the annual series. However, Chorley *et al* (1984) for 36 active floodplain rivers, showed that bankfull recurrence interval varied between 1 and 32 years, differences that may reflect variations in sediment loads and flow regimes.

Secondly, *flushing flows* must be assessed. The channel substrate provides important habitat for a wide-ranging biota and in gravel-bed rivers is a composite feature that can be divided into four components.

1 The substrate framework of coarse particles (>2 mm).
2 The substrate matrix of fines (<2 mm).
3 The surface ('armour') layer of coarse gravel which is usually incomplete and of one grain thickness.
4 Surface deposits of fine gravel and sand or superficial fines that form more or less discontinuous patches on top of the armour layer.

Flushing flows are moderately high discharges required to maintain the quality of the substrate, preventing vegetation encroachment into the channel and removing superficial and interstitial accumulations of fine organic and inorganic sediments (Reiser *et al* 1989a).

Thirdly, it is important to consider *floodplain-maintenance flows*. Floodplains are formed by a suite of accretional and erosional processes and comprise a range of sedimentary facies reflected on the surface by the floristic mosaic (e.g. Salo 1990; see also Plate 7.1). Floods disrupt the floodplain system by lateral erosion, meander cut-off and channel avulsion, bar deposition, cut-off channel siltation, and overbank sedimentation. Such disturbance sustains habitats for pioneer species and lower successional stages, and the mosaic of landform-sediment-vegetation units reflects the channel stability: some channels maintain a stable course for long periods of time (>10^2 years) whereas at the other extreme channel migration by more than $1000\,\mathrm{m\,yr^{-1}}$ has been reported.

Very high floods cause disturbance which counteracts the advantage of the flood pulse in the short term but over longer time-scales such floodplain maintenance flows are important for maintaining habitat diversity. Thus, Stromberg (1993) demonstrated that in semi-arid basins, the greatest plant richness and abundance occurred along rivers with intermediate flood magnitudes (as indexed by the magnitude of the 50-year flood). Low vegetation diversity is associated with highly stable systems, as evidenced by a decline in diversity on regulated streams where flooding has been suppressed and the geomorphological dynamics reduced (see Chapter 7).

The hyporheic zone

The channel substrate provides important habitat for a wide range of invertebrates and fish, especially salmonid-spawning habitat. Once perceived as a stable environment, the subsurface zone along the river corridor is now recognized as an important and dynamic system that is largely determined by the hydrological conditions. Research on these subsurface systems – phreatobiology – has a long history (see Obrdlik *et al* 1992 for review) and many studies have focused

---

Fig. 5.2 (*Opposite.*) Examples of habitat suitability criteria curves. (a) Binary and simple continuous curves for Chinook salmon spawning (Raleigh *et al* 1986); (b) curves for Atlantic salmon parr showing variable preferences according to fish size (large parr and small parr or young-of-the-year) (Heggenes 1990); and (c) response surface plot for a depth and velocity relationship showing the raw data and completely smoothed data produced by application of an inverse distance squared smoothing algorithm (Lambert & Hanson 1989); various polynomial models were also used to establish bivariate response surfaces.

on the groundwater fauna of major alluvial plains along the Danube, Rhine and Rhône. However, most studies have involved taxonomic and biogeographic descriptions. Various species of the exclusively hypogeon-dwelling organisms (e.g. the amphipod group *Niphargopsis*) have been found throughout the alluvial plains of the three major European rivers. Particularly interesting groundwater faunas have been found associated with floodplain wetlands and springs.

During the 1980s a new research direction developed, considering the hyporheic zone as an ecotone between the surface water and groundwater (Gibert *et al* 1990). In many cases, the hyporheic zone is of limited extent bordering the channel but in some geomorphological settings, notably glacial troughs infilled with highly permeable gravels, the zone may be extensive. On the Flathead River, Montana, USA, the hyporheic zone extends 10 m vertically and about 1500 m laterally (Stanford & Ward 1988).

Gibert *et al* (1990) identify four unique features that distinguish groundwater ecotones. First, the ecotone is colonized by both epigeal and hypogeal organisms, and has a biodiversity intermediate between the rich surface-water assemblage and the low-diversity groundwater community. Secondly, the ecotone plays an important role in the connectivity and the exchange of organisms between landscape patches. Thirdly, the ecotone acts as a physical and biological filter for exchanges between surface and groundwater environments (Triska *et al* 1993). Finally, but most importantly from the perspective of determining instream flow needs, the dimensions of the ecotone vary strongly in space and time in relation to surface flow and groundwater levels.

Spatial variations occur both at the scale of an entire alluvial plain (Marmonier *et al* 1992), river reach (Creuze des Chatelliers & Reygrobellet 1990) and an individual riffle (Sterba *et al* 1992). Temporal variations relate to flow variations (Marmonier & Creuze des Chatelliers 1991); surface water infiltration during floods causes the active or passive movement of organisms within the sediments, displacing the limits of the ecotone. Two of the most important ecological factors, thermal gradients and oxygen profiles, are closely linked to the strength and direction of flow

lines within the hyporheic zone (White 1990). Thus, Shepherd *et al* (1986) suggested that the influence of flow on processes and biological communities within the hyporheic zone should be of concern to all those involved in fisheries research, benthic invertebrate studies and environmental impact assessments.

5.3 METHODS FOR DEFINING FLOWS

The effect of flow on instream biota is important but the effects may be masked by environmental factors that determine regional variations and downstream patterns of biota and biological processes within catchments (Armitage & Petts 1992). The location along the river continuum, water quality and channel morphology are used most frequently for habitat evaluation in river management (e.g. Milner *et al* 1985). Altitude and a measure of distance from source, such as stream order or drainage area, are important indices of position along the river continuum, providing surrogates for temperature and organic-matter sources as well as for discharge and channel form. Important water-quality indicators include pH, alkalinity and hardness. Typically, such indicators change from source to mouth along a river, reflecting the variable contributions of runoff from different sources. Channel morphology, usually indexed by width, depth, velocity and substrate size, relates not only to the downstream continuum but also to the historical legacy of channel change in relation to climate (over the Quaternary). Today, along many rivers, the spatial pattern of water-quality and channel-form variation reflect the historical legacy of human impacts. Thus, in order to elucidate the influence of flow patterns on biota it is necessary to classify sites at the appropriate scale, i.e. to match the geomorphological setting to the hydrological processes (Hill *et al* 1991) and to minimize the influence of the higher-level attributes to biological responses.

The general principles of classifying rivers for the purpose of assessing conservation potential have been reviewed by Naiman *et al* (1992). For the assessment of instream-flow needs, a three-level classification system is proposed. First, the river may be divided into *types* (e.g. upland, inter-mediate and lowland), reflecting position along the river. Secondly, each type may be divided into *sectors*. Within each sector, water quality, sediment load and hydrological regime are seen as invariant between sites. Thirdly, each sector is divided into *reaches* on the basis of local variations in channel morphology or river-margin vegetation. Along natural rivers, channel morphology often has the same general form throughout each sector.

Minimum acceptable flows

Three approaches are available for determining minimum acceptable flows: hydrological methods; river assessment methods; and PHABSIM (physical habitat simulation).

Hydrological approaches

Traditionally, minimum acceptable flows have been set using discharge-based methods. These express the instream flow as a hydrological statistic: commonly either as a flow duration statistic (such as the 95th percentile) or as a fixed percentage of the average daily flow (ADF). The classic example of the later is Tennant's (1976) Montana Method (Table 5.2). Orth and Leonard (1990) demonstrated that for streams in Virginia, USA: (i) 10% ADF correctly defines degraded or poor habitat conditions; (ii) 20% ADF provides an appropriate criterion for protecting aquatic ha-

Table 5.2 Examples of discharge methods based upon average daily flow (ADF)

	Percentage of ADF	
	Minimum	Maximum
Baxter (1961) flow for *Salmo salar*		
Juveniles in summer	20	25
Adult migration	30	70
Spawning	12.5	30
Incubation	10	17
Tennant (1976)		
Absolute minimum	10	
Good habitat	30	60
Optimum habitat	60	100
Flushing flow	200	

bitats; and (iii) 30% ADF defines near-optimum habitat in small streams.

In the UK water industry, two measures of the dry weather flow (DWF), the 95th percentile flow or the mean annual minimum 7-day flow frequency statistic, have been used most frequently to set prescribed flows. An alternative approach (Drake & Sheriff 1987) employs a proportion of the dry weather flow weighted according to a range of environmental characteristics and uses. Thus the prescribed flow is set at $1.0 \times \text{DWF}$ for the most sensitive rivers and at $0.5 \times \text{DWF}$ for the least sensitive.

The Northeast Region of the US Fish and Wildlife Service has established an aquatic baseflow (ABF), which defines the minimum acceptable flow as the median flow in the month during which low flow conditions typically result in the most metabolic stress to aquatic organisms (Kulik 1990). Stress was recognized as being exerted by high water temperature and diminished living space, dissolved oxygen and food supply.

The justification for a hydrological approach is that over the long term, stream flora and fauna have evolved to survive periodic adversities without major population changes. In natural systems, the effects of stress on the biological communities are seen to be balanced by recovery mechanisms. However, any human impact that reduces the effectiveness of these recovery mechanisms will clearly affect the level of flow required to meet the primary objective, namely 'to sustain and perpetuate indigenous aquatic fauna'. Relevant impacts include channelization that isolates a river from floodplain backwaters or reduces instream habitat diversity, and dams that create barriers to upstream and downstream migrations. Synergistic toxicity effects may also be significant because of the water-quality changes often associated with low-flow problems.

A major criticism of discharge methods is their exclusion of any explicit consideration of actual habitat requirements. A second concern arises from the complex array of processes, influenced by flow, that can affect biota. Consideration of discharge in isolation of other water-quality and geomorphological factors can provide only a very superficial understanding of potential impacts of flow regulation. Thus, attention has been directed towards a more scientific understanding of the response of species and biological communities to hydrological change.

River assessment techniques

Recent models for river assessment are based on flow–habitat relationships and make the assumption that habitat attributes provide an index of suitability for biota. The approach implicitly assumes that the abundance data for invertebrates or fish, for example derived from field survey, are maximum values appropriate to the habitat conditions at each site. In reality this 'maximum' is a theoretical concept; population levels are usually below the maximum because of (i) variation in biotic factors, such as predation, competition and recruitment; and (ii) disturbance, such as floods, and variable rates of population recovery.

Quantitative and semi-quantitative studies have often been employed to relate a biological criterion, such as fish abundance, to habitat attributes. Quantitative approaches require a detailed field survey of the habitat attributes, including measurements of depths, widths, velocities, substrate size, composition, etc. Semi-quantitative studies combine field transect measurements of physical attributes with subjective assessments of elements of habitat quality, such as fish cover. Whilst simple reconnaissance methods providing quick assessments have met with disapproval for ignoring the specific character of the stream, more sophisticated approaches have been criticized for the length of time required to obtain meaningful results.

Simple linear regression and multiple regression have often been used in habitat evaluation studies, for example by Binns and Eiserman (1979), Milner *et al* (1985) and Scarnecchia and Bergensen (1987). Many attributes are strongly interrelated and careful selection of habitat attributes is necessary to minimize the problem of autocorrelation between variables (Table 5.3). A second problem is the non-linearity between physical and biotic variables, a problem that is usually overcome by using a rating system, such as the five-point scores of Binns and Eiserman.

Thus, Maddock (1992) developed an empirical relationship between an invertebrate-based score,

Table 5.3 Attributes commonly used in habitat-fish abundance relationships

I Catchment	*III Flow regime*
Altitude	Average daily flow
Drainage area	Average seasonal flow
Stream order	Baseflow index
II Water quality	*IV Channel structure*
Maximum temperature	Average depth
pH	Maximum depth
Alkalinity	Width
Hardness	Velocity
Conductivity	% pool
Nitrate concentration	% riffle
	% cover
	Dominant substrate

the BMWP, and habitat variables. For 28 streams in East Anglia, UK, field data were obtained during summer low-flow at approximately 100 points from five transects within a reach defined as five channel widths or one riffle-pool sequence, whichever was the greater. All sites had long-term invertebrate records showing a stable BMWP and had good-quality flow-gauging data.

$$BMWP = a + CSb + Qc + Md + He \quad (r^2 = 0.88)$$

where CS is a chemical score based upon oxygen and ammonia levels; Q is Q_{95} divided by channel width; M is an index of instream cover; H is a hydraulic index; and a–e are regression coefficients. The relationship was validated for the River Glen, to which it was then applied to assess the improvement in BMWP with flow augmentation (Petts *et al* 1995).

Empirical relationships using physical habitat variables have successfully described variations of trout abundance within a uniform group of streams (>25 mg l^{-1} CaCO$_3$) in Wales (Milner *et al* 1985). Fish population estimates were obtained by electro-fishing. Average daily flow was significantly inversely related to the abundance of small trout (≤ 10 cm) but in this study, ADF may simply reflect stream size. Site attributes, such as average depth, percentage of reach with depth of 46–60 cm, depth variance, were significant in explaining the distribution of larger fish, yielding explained variances of more than 80%. Milner *et al* suggested that between- and within-site variability not accounted for by habitat models may be explained by randomly changing habitat attributes and biotic factors. Further, they proposed that the difficulty in establishing fish–habitat relationships in softwater streams may reflect their more unstable discharge regime introducing a stronger stochastic element in their overall carrying capacity.

PHABSIM

Physical HABitat SImulation (Bovee 1982) provides a methodology to integrate the changing hydraulic conditions with discharge and the habitat preferences of biota (Fig. 5.3). Detailed field-survey data are inputted to the simulation model, which relates changes in discharge or channel structure to changes in physical habitat availability for one or more chosen species. Habitat is defined as comprising two basic components: rigid structural characteristics (channel width, bed configuration and substrate composition, which are assumed to be constant over the range of flows of concern) and variable hydraulic conditions. The underlying principles of PHABSIM are:

1 the chosen species exhibits preferences within a range of habitat conditions that it can tolerate;
2 these ranges can be defined for each species;
3 the area of stream providing these conditions can be quantified as a function of discharge and channel structure.

PHABSIM can be applied in two situations: the investigation of either critical reaches which provide a particular type of habitat that is otherwise

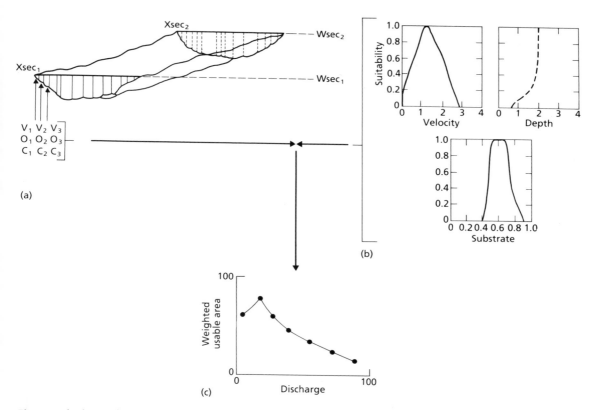

Fig. 5.3 The basis of PHABSIM (after Nestler *et al* 1989) showing the integration of hydraulic measurements and habitat suitability criteria to define the relationship between discharge and weighted usable area.

limited within the system, or representative reaches which are similar to any other reach within a sector and, ideally, contain all the habitat patches found within the entire sector. Hydraulic conditions are characterized usually at three known (calibration) streamflows from point measurements taken along transects within the reach. Transects are located so as to sample (i) all the hydraulic controls, i.e. physical aspects of the streambed that determine the height of the water surface upstream, and (ii) all habitat types that are represented along the reach. A typical reach for analysis using PHABSIM has a length of the order of 20 channel widths.

Hydraulic simulation models are used to estimate hydraulic conditions at unmeasured flows. Three types of approach are available for calculation of water surface elevation at unknown discharges: (i) the stage–discharge relationship; (ii) the use of Manning's equation; and (iii) the standard step backwater method. In many situations it may be necessary to use a mixture of models to simulate the hydraulic characteristics of the reach over the full range of flows. For instance, under low flows the stage–discharge relationship may simulate water-surface elevations and velocities most accurately whereas the standard step backwater method may be more suitable over the higher flows. The technique used for hydraulic simulation can have a significant impact on the habitat versus streamflow relationship; the correct choice of hydraulic model(s) as well as the proper calibration can be time consuming and may represent the most difficult step in the process of analysing streamflows.

Hydraulic simulation is then combined with habitat suitability curves for target organisms to define available habitat – the weighted usable area (WUA) – in the reach. PHABSIM contains a number of different programs that can be used for this purpose, each having specific conditions for their application. The most often used is the multiplicative composite suitability index:

$$WUAi = Ai \times f(v) \times f(d) \times f(s) \times f(c), \text{ etc.}$$

where the reach is divided into cells; Ai is the area of a cell (i) which is multiplied by all suitability indices used: velocity $(f(v))$, depth $(f(d))$, substrate $(f(s))$, cover $(f(s))$, etc. Effects of stream-

flow changes on the physical habitat available for the target organism can then be evaluated by changes in the amount of WUA. The approach may also be used to assess the habitat quality of reaches, and then sectors, where 'quality' is related to the configuration of the bed morphology. Thus, PHABSIM is able to present biological information in a format suitable for entry into the water resource planning process. The information is made explicitly in terms of changes to the physical properties of the aquatic habitat (i.e. velocity, depth and substrate) and does not predict changes in the biomass of organisms. The IFIM methodology has been applied in several countries outside the USA including Canada (Mathur *et al* 1985; Shirvell 1989), New Zealand (Scott & Shirvell 1988), Australia (Gan & McMahon 1990), Norway (Heggenes *et al* 1990), France (Chaveroche & Sabaton 1989; Courot 1989), South Africa (Gore *et al* 1992) and the UK (Bullock *et al* 1991; Bullock & Gustard 1992; Petts 1992, 1993).

Application

The results of applying the methods to define in-river needs may be illustrated by data for one reach on the River Babingley, a small but high-quality chalk stream in north Norfolk, UK, with a good stock of brown trout (*Salmo trutta*) (Petts 1993).

Long-term average monthly flows, based on the period 1976–87, compared to those experienced during subsequent years (Fig. 5.4) highlight the extent of the recent drought. Average monthly flows peak in March at a discharge of 0.770 cumecs falling to 0.339 cumecs in September. For PHABSIM, calibration flows corresponded to Q_{99}, Q_{96} and Q_{77} on the flow duration curve for the period 1963–92. Habitat suitability curves were taken from Armitage and Ladle (1991) for four life stages of brown trout (i.e. spawning, fry, juvenile and adult) and four species of aquatic invertebrates, one stonefly (*Leuctra fusca*), two caseless caddis (*Rhyacophila dorsalis* and *Polycentropus flavomaculatus*) and one pea mussel (*Sphaerium corneum*). Results of the different methods are given in Table 5.4.

An example of the discharge versus usable

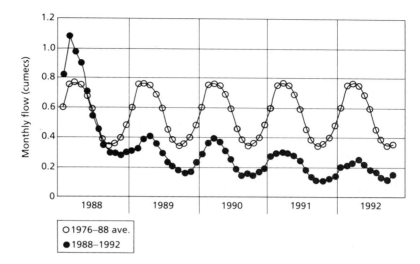

Fig. 5.4 Monthly flow data for the River Babingley contrasting the 1976–88 average data with the 1988–92 series.

○ 1976–88 ave.
● 1988–1992

Table 5.4 Recommendations for minimum flows (as gauged at Castle Rising)

Method	Record	Discharge (m³ s⁻¹)
95 percentile flow	1976–85	0.300
95 percentile flow	1963–92	0.157
30% of mean flow	1976–85	0.165
30% of mean flow	1963–92	0.136
Aquatic baseflow	1976–85	0.261
PHABSIM		
Trout		
Adult		0.280
Spawning		0.280
Juveniles		0.170
Fry		0.090
Invertebrates		0.127

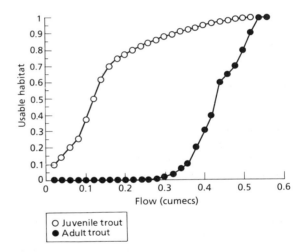

○ Juvenile trout
● Adult trout

Fig. 5.5 Examples of habitat–discharge relationships for the River Babingley, for brown trout adults and juveniles.

habitat relationship is given in Fig. 5.5, and clear reductions in usable habitat can be defined for each life stage when flows fall below critical levels (Table 5.4). The results of the discharge versus percent usable area relationships were combined with the actual discharges experienced during the drought to show the effect these reduced flows had on habitat area available for life stages of brown trout (e.g. Fig. 5.6). During 1988–92 little habitat was available for adults and suitable habitat was eliminated in mid-1991. For the juvenile life stage usable habitat was

consistently below average conditions but good quality habitat was sustained throughout the drought period.

One application of PHABSIM is to assess the impacts of alternative flow-management scenarios using habitat duration curves (Bovee 1982). For example, Fig. 5.7 shows two curves, one based on the flow duration statistics for the period 1963–92 and one based on a curve with similar

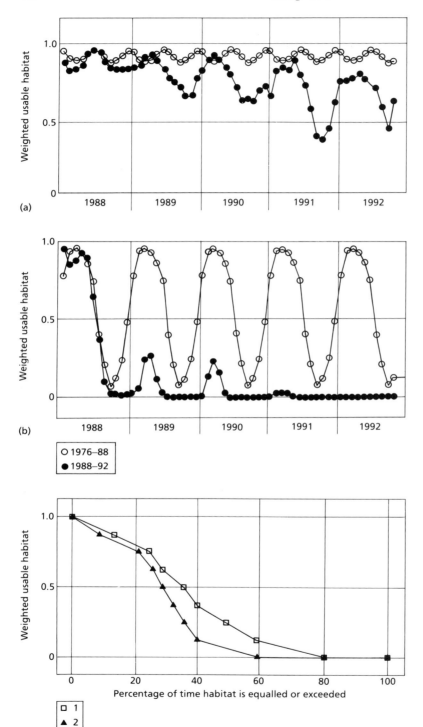

(a)

(b)

O 1976–88
● 1988–92

Fig. 5.6 Examples of habitat changes predicted by PHABSIM for the River Babingley, comparing the average usable habitat with that available during the 1988–92 drought for brown trout juveniles (a) and adults (b).

□ 1
▲ 2

Fig. 5.7 Examples of habitat duration curves for the River Babingley, showing brown trout habitat under (1) average flow conditions and (2) a hypothetical flow management scenario (mean daily flow reduced by 30% but no change in Q_{10} or Q_{95}).

Q_{10} and Q_{95} values but with mean daily flow reduced by 30%. In this case, the most critical change in habitat would be experienced by the adult life stage. Under reduced average daily flows, the median habitat value would be reduced by 75% and zero habitat would be experienced for approximately 42% of the time.

Analyses such as those illustrated above allow definition of a range of minimum flows. For example, a *desirable* minimum ecological flow could be defined as 0.28 cumecs – the minimum flow for adult trout – which approximates to the naturalized 95th percentile flow and to the median flow in the driest month, September. The results from this one reach also show that a flow of 0.13 cumecs should sustain habitat for invertebrates and juvenile trout, even though for the latter this will be only about 50% of the potential habitat. These results suggest that exceptionally, under severe natural drought conditions, flows could be reduced to this *emergency* minimum ecological flow. Although for the duration of the drought this flow would probably eliminate habitat for adult trout, habitat for juveniles and invertebrates would be sustained and evidence (e.g. Milner, Chapter 12; Petts *et al* 1995) suggests that the biota should recover rapidly once flows return to 'normal'.

High flows and the
minimum streamflow hydrograph

Determination of the minimum acceptable flow is only the first step in defining a minimum streamflow hydrograph for sustaining the ecological integrity of the fluvial hydrosystem. Flood flows of up to the 50-year event can be important for rejuvenating floodplain systems whilst the riparian system and the channel morphology will respond to changes of the dominant discharge, indexed by the 1.5-year flood. Ideally, the river corridor should be delineated as the historical geomorphologically-active floodplain defined from aerial photographs or satellite imagery, cartographic evidence and field survey.

Hill *et al* (1991) developed an annual hydrograph based upon mean monthly flows for the Whitebird reach of the Salmon River, Idaho, USA (Fig. 5.8a). The average annual hydrograph was examined to determine the timing of high and low flows, the slope of the rising hydrograph and the flow recession. Minimum instream flows to maintain habitat for fish were defined as the 7-day low flow with a 1.5-year return period; a hydraulic model (HEC-2) was used to estimate the bankfull discharge and the flows required to inundate areas of valley floor of different elevations. It was recommended that daily flow recession should not exceed 10% of the previous day's flow; in general, the slower the flow recession the greater the advantage for biota by protecting fauna from stranding and providing a longer period of high flows for vegetation seeding.

For the Yampa River in Dinosaur National Monument, Colorado, O'Brien (1987) defined a minimum streamflow hydrograph (Fig. 5.8b) to maintain existing aquatic habitat, especially for the endangered Colorado squawfish (*Ptchocheilus lucius*). The hydrograph was derived using the results of a 2-year field data collection programme, a physical model, laboratory simulation of flows on a cobble substrate and a mathematical model simulation of sediment transport. It included four components: the *baseflow*, defined as the mean baseflow for the period of record, to provide food supply during the low-flow period in the fall and winter; a gradual *rising limb* that would provide backwater habitat for shelter during high-flow periods; a *recessional limb* with sufficient flow over an extended period to remove any possible sand deposition in the spawning areas; and a *peak discharge* that would inundate the active channel area to eliminate any encroaching vegetation. The peak flow was defined as the effective discharge for sediment transport, based on a sediment discharge rating curve.

Pulse releases

Where rivers are regulated by dams, artificial flow variations – pulse releases – can stimulate biological functions and advantage instream habitats. The provision of artificial flow fluctuations becomes increasingly important as the level of regulation and abstraction intensifies, particularly important for salmonids to stimulate migration and to clean spawning grounds. In a classic paper, Hayes (1953) demonstrated that large natural

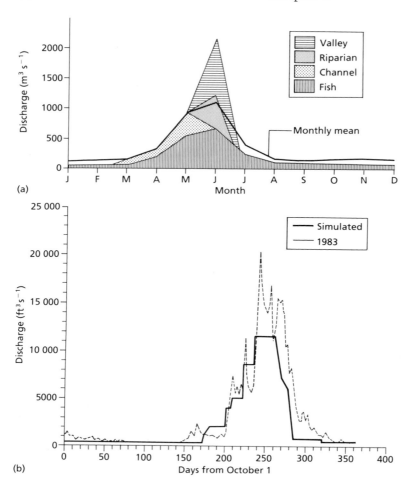

(a)

(b)

Fig. 5.8 Examples of minimum streamflow hydrographs: (a) for the Salmon River, Idaho, USA (from Hill *et al* 1991), and (b) for the Yampa River, Colorado (from O'Brien 1987).

freshets can be associated with a major run of fish into a river, as long as tides and winds are also favourable. Subsequent research has been inconclusive, but Alabaster (1970) suggested that short-term changes of flow together with accompanying changes in concentrations of dissolved substances, may stimulate entry of salmon into rivers and their upstream migration.

For channel maintenance, a general rule-of-thumb is that sediment within gravel-bed channels begins to be mobilized when flow depth is slightly greater than 80% of bankfull depth (Parker 1979, ref. 97). Flushing flows recommended by Reiser *et al* (1989a) are of two types.

The first type is based on flow record and refined by field observations, and includes 200% average annual flow and the 5th < 17th percentile on flow duration curve. The second type involves sediment transport methods within particular reaches involving either direct field measurements of the threshold discharge for transport, e.g. using bed-load tracers, or modelling of sediment transport to predict the discharge which causes incipient motion of particles. An application of the latter is given by Reiser *et al* (1989b). Most commonly, flows are required to flush superficial accumulations of fines and to clear the surface gravel to a depth of approximately

0.5 < 1.0 times the average diameter of surface cobbles. This has been shown to be a realistic objective (Beschta & Jackson 1979).

The timing and duration of pulse releases is also important and must avoid harm to the biotic communities, such as by dislodgement and transport of eggs and fry. For example, flushing flows may have greatest benefit if they are provided prior to salmonid spawning, cleaning the gravels and enhancing egg and alevin survival. Clearly, knowledge of life histories for target species is important for determining the optimum timing of flows, although it is often assumed that the biota is adapted to the normal hydrograph, so that coincidence of flushing flows with normal peak-flow periods should prove beneficial. In any case, test flow releases should be made to enable field observations to assess the effectiveness of the recommended flows.

5.4 PROSPECT

Linking hydrology and ecology is a complex science because of the many ways in which discharge influences biota (by determining habitat suitability for each life stage) and biotic interactions (predation, competition, etc.). In the past, river management strategies have been directed most frequently to the protection of sport and commercial fisheries. Both implicitly and explicitly, it has been assumed that this strategy would also sustain adequate habitat for other organisms.

River management requires scientifically-sound operational tools to determine the allocation of water to meet instream, riparian and floodplain needs. The rapid natural recovery of fish of following severe drought (Bayley & Osbourne 1993), of invertebrates impacted by severe low flows following flow augmentation (Petts *et al* 1995), and of fish and invertebrates to flow restoration to remnant channels following channelization (Toth *et al* 1993) suggests that many natural systems can undergo self-restoration in response to rare extreme low-flow conditions. However, the assumption that enhanced minimum instream flow will result in the production of more or larger fish has not been demonstrated (Wolff *et al* 1989; Harris *et al* 1991).

This arises because other habitat factors, such as cover or temperature, may be limiting or because natural variations in abundance may mask any trends in short-term data sets.

The lack of evidence that the biota responds to changes in flow and the inability to predict population responses to flow alterations remain frustrations which will persist until intensive long-term research is initiated (Orth 1987). Development of deterministic ecosystem models may be an unrealistic objective because of the stochastic nature of the driving hydrological and geomorphological processes and the complexity of biological interactions. Nevertheless, concern for sustaining the biological integrity of ecosystems requires new approaches to ensure the maintenance of ecological processes, rather than maintenance of single target species (O'Keefe & Davies 1991).

Several authors have argued that benthic macroinvertebrate communities must be protected by prescribed flows to maintain biotic integrity and ecosystem functioning (Gore 1989). The macroinvertebrates have a key role in the energy dynamics of ecosystems and provide a primary energy link to the game and forage fishes. River margins – floodplains and riparian zones – also play an important role in maintaining the productivity of rivers, and lateral and vertical interactions and exchanges need to be incorporated into approaches to assessing flow needs. There is some information on habitat change and biological responses to suggest that at the regional scale, a hydrological approach, giving due regard to floodplain, riparian, channel and minimum-flow needs, can provide a practicable option for establishing an ecologically-acceptable flow regime. In the short term, the most cost-effective approach to achieving ecologically-sensitive water development may be to use integrated biological and habitat studies to evaluate hydrological methods for instream-flow assessment based upon a regional (river type) and longitudinal, within-river (river sector) channel classification.

REFERENCES

Alabaster JS. (1970) River flow and upstream movement and catch of migratory salmonids. *Journal of Fish*

Biology **2**: 1–13. [5.3]

Ambuhl H. (1959) Die Bedeutung der Stromung als okologischer Fakton. *Schweizerische Zeitschrift für Hydrologie* **21**: 133–264. [5.2]

Amoros C, Petts GE. (1993) *Les Hydrosystèmes Fluviaux*. Mason, Paris (to be published in Engish by Chapman & Hall, London). [5.1, 5.2]

Armitage PD. (1978) Downstream changes in the composition, numbers and biomass of bottom fauna in the Tees below Cow Green reservoir and in an unregulated tributary Maize Beck, in the first five years after impoundment. *Hydrobiologia* **58**: 145–56. [5.2]

Armitage PD, Ladle M. (1991) Habitat preferences of target species for application in PHABSIM testing. In: Bullock A, Gustard A, Grainger ES (eds) *Instream Flow Requirements of Aquatic Ecology in Two British Rivers*. Institute of Hydrology, Report 115, Wallingford, UK. [5.3]

Armitage PD, Petts GE. (1992) Biotic score and prediction to assess the effects of water abstraction on river macroinvertebrates for conservation purposes. *Aquatic Conservation* **2**: 1–18. [5.2]

Baxter G. (1961) River utilization and the preservation of migratory fish life. *Proceedings of the Institute of Civil Engineers* **18**: 225–44. [5.3]

Bayley PB. (1991) The flood-pulse advantage and the restoration of river-floodplain systems. *Regulated Rivers* **6**: 75–86. [5.2]

Bayley PB, Osbourne LL. (1993) Natural rehabilitation of stream fish populations in an Illinois catchment. *Freshwater Biology* **29**: 295–300. [5.4]

Beschta RL, Jackson WL. (1979) The intrusion of fine sediments into a stable gravel bed. *Journal of the Fisheries Research Board of Canada* **36**: 204–10. [5.3]

Bickerton M, Petts GE, Armitage P, Castella E. (1993) Assessing the ecological effects of groundwater abstraction on chalk streams: three examples from eastern England. *Regulated Rivers* **8**: 121–35. [5.2]

Binns NA, Eiserman FM. (1979) Quantification of fluvial trout habitat in Wyoming. *Transactions of the American Fisheries Society* **108**: 215–28. [5.3]

Bovee KD. (1982) *A Guide to Stream Habitat Analysis Using the Instream Flow Incremental Methodology*. Instream Flow Information Paper 12, FWS/OBS-82/26. Office of Biological Services, US Fish and Wildlife Service, Fort Collins, Colorado. [5.3]

Brooker MP. (1981) The impact of impoundments on the downstream fisheries and general ecology of rivers. *Advances in Applied Biology* **6**: 91–152. [5.2, 5.3]

Brookes A. (1988) *Channelized Rivers*. John Wiley, Chichester. [5.2, 5.3]

Brookes A. (1994) River channel change. In: Calow P, Petts GE (eds) *The Rivers Handbook*, Vol. 2, pp. 55–75. Blackwell Scientific Publications, Oxford. [5.2]

Bullock A, Gustard A. (1992) Application of the Instream flow incremental methodology to assess ecological flow requirement in a British lowland river. In: Carling PA, Petts GE (eds) *Lowland Floodplain Rivers: Geomorphological Perspectives*. John Wiley, Chichester. [5.2, 5.3]

Bullock A, Gustard A, Grainger ES. (1991) *Instream Flow Requirements of Aquatic Ecology in Two British Rivers*. Institute of Hydrology, Wallingford, Report 115. [5.3]

Chaveroche P, Sabaton C. (1989) An analysis of brown trout (*Salmo trutta fario* L.) habitat: the role of qualitative data from expert advice in formulating probability-of-use curves. *Regulated Rivers* **3**: 305–20. [5.2, 5.3]

Chorley RJ, Schumm SA, Sugden DE. (1984) *Geomorphology*. Methuen, London. [5.2]

Conder AL, Annear TC. (1987) Test of weighted usable area estimates derived from a PHABSIM model for instream flow studies on trout streams. *North American Journal of Fisheries Management* **7**: 339–50. [5.2]

Courot A. (1989) Determination of hydraulic parameters for instream flow assessments. *Regulated Rivers* **3**: 337–44. [5.3]

Creuze des Chatelliers MC, Reygrobellet JL. (1990) Interactions between geomorphological processes, benthic and hyporheic communities: First results on a by-passed canal of the French Upper Rhône River. *Regulated Rivers* **5**: 139–58. [5.2]

Crisp DT, Mann RHK, Cubby PR. (1983) Effects of regulation of the River Tees upon fish populations below Cow Green reservoir. *Journal of Applied Ecology* **20**: 371–86. [5.2]

Drake PJ, Sheriff JDF. (1987) A method for managing river abstractions and protecting the environment. *Journal of Water and Environmental Management* **1**: 27–38. [5.3]

Edwards RW, Garrod DJ. (1972) *Conservation and Productivity of Natural Waters*. The Zoological Society of London, Academic Press, London. [5.2]

Fraser JC. (1972) Regulated discharge and the stream environment. In: Oglesby RT, Carlson CA, McCann JA (eds) *River Ecology and Man*, pp. 263–86. Academic Press, New York. [5.2]

Gan K, McMahon T. (1990) Variability of results from the use of PHABSIM in estimating habitat area. *Regulated Rivers* **5**: 233–9. [5.3]

Gibert J, Dole-Olivier MJ, Marmonier P, Vervier P. (1990) Surface water/groundwater ecotones. In: Naiman RJ, Decamps H (eds) *Ecology and Management of Aquatic Terrestrial Ecotones*, pp. 199–225. Unesco, Paris; Parthenon Publishers, Carnforth. [5.2]

Gore JA. (1989) Models for predicting benthic macroinvertebrate habitat suitability under regulated flows.

In: Gore JA, Petts GE (eds) *Alternatives in Regulated River Management*, pp. 253–66. CRC Press, Boca Raton, Florida. [5.4]

Gore JA. (1994) Hydrological change. In: Calow P, Petts GE (eds) *The Rivers Handbook*, Vol. 2, pp. 33–54. Blackwell Scientific Publications, Oxford. [5.2]

Gore JA, Judy RD. (1981) Predictive models of benthic macroinvertebrate density for use in instream flow studies and regulated flow management. *Canadian Journal of Fisheries and Aquatic Sciences* **38**: 1363–70. [5.2]

Gore JA, Layzer JB, Russell IA. (1992) Non-traditional applications of instream flow techniques for conserving habitat for biota in the Sabie River of southern Africa. In: Boon P, Calow P, Petts GE (eds) *River Conservation and Management*, pp. 161–78. John Wiley, Chichester. [5.3]

Gustard A, Cole G, Marshall D, Bayliss A. (1987) *A Study of Compensation Flows in the UK*. Institute of Hydrology, Report 99. A summary is given in Gustard A. (1989) Compensation flows in the UK: a hydrological review. *Regulated Rivers* **3**: 49–60. [5.2]

Harris DD, Hubert WA, Wesche TA. (1991) Brown trout population and habitat response to enhanced minimum flow in Douglas Greek, Wyoming. *Rivers* **2**(4): 285–94. [5.4]

Hayes FR. (1953) Artificial freshets and other factors controlling the ascent and population of Atlantic salmon in the La Have River, Nova Scotia. *Bulletin of the Fisheries Research Board of Canada* **99**: 47 pp. [5.3]

Heggenes J. (1990) Habitat utilization and preferences in juvenile Atlantic Salmon (*Salmo salar*) in streams. *Regulated Rivers* **5**: 341–54. [5.2]

Heggenes J, Brabrand A, Saltveit SV. (1990) Comparison of three methods for studies of stream habitat use by young brown trout and atlantic salmon. *Transactions of the American Fisheries Society* **119**: 101–11. [5.3]

Hill MT, Platts S, Beschta RL. (1991) Ecological and geomorphological concepts for instream and out-of-channel flow requirements. *Rivers* **2**: 198–210, [5.1, 5.2, 5.3]

Howard A. (1992) Modeling channel migration and floodplain sedimentation in meandering streams. In: Carling P, Petts G (eds) *Lowland Floodplain Rivers* pp. 1–42. John Wiley, Chichester. [5.2]

Junk WJ, Bayley PB, Sparks RE. (1989) The flood-pulse concept in river-floodplain systems. *Special Publication of the Canadian Journal of Fisheries and Aquatic Sciences* **106**: 110–27. [5.2]

Kulik BH. (1990) A method to refine the New England Aquatic Base flow Policy. *Rivers* **1**: 8–22. [5.3]

Lambert TR, Hanson DF. (1989) Development of habitat suitability criteria for trout in small streams. *Regulated Rivers* **3**: 291–304. [5.2]

Maddock I. (1992) Instream habitat assessment. In: Petts GE (ed) *The River Glen: a Catchment Assessment*, Annex E. [5.3]

Marmonier P, Creuze des Chatelliers MC. (1991) Effects of spates on interstitial assemblages of the Rhône River. Importance of spatial heterogeneity. *Hydrobiologia* **210**: 243–51. [5.2]

Marmonier P, Dole-Olivier MJ, Creuze des Chatelliers MC. (1992) Spatial distribution of interstitial assemblages in the floodplain on the Rhône River. *Regulated Rivers* **7**: 75–82. [5.2]

Mathur D, Bason WH, Purdy EJ, Silver CA. (1985) A critique of the Instream Flow Incremental Methodology. *Canadian Journal of Fisheries and Aquatic Sciences* **42**: 825–31. [5.3]

Milner NJ, Scullion J, Carling PA, Crisp DT. (1981) The effects of discharge on sediment dynamics and consequent effects on invertebrates and salmonids in upland rivers. In: Coaker TD (ed) *Anvances in Applied Biology*, pp. 154–220. Academic Press, London. [5.2]

Milner NJ, Hemsworth RJ, Jones BE. (1985) Habitat evaluation as a fisheries management tool. *Journal of Fisheries Biology* **27**(Suppl. A): 85–108. [5.3]

Morin A, Harper PP, Peters RH. (1986) Micro-habitat preference curves of blackfly larvae (Diptera: Simuliidae): a comparison of three estimation methods. *Canadian Journal Fisheries and Aquatic Sciences* **43**: 1235. [5.2]

Naiman RJ, Lonzarich DG, Beechie TJ, Ralph SC. (1992) General principles of stream classification and the assessment of conservation potential in rivers. In: Boon PJ, Calow P, Petts GE (eds) *River Conservation and Management*. John Wiley, Chichester. [5.3]

Nestler JM, Milhous RT, Layzer JB. (1989) Instream habital modeling techniques. In: Gore JA, Petts GE (eds) *Alternatives in Regulated River Management*, pp. 295–315. CRC Press, Boca Raton, Florida. [5.3]

Newbury RW. (1984) Hydrologic determinants of aquatic insect habitats. In: Resh VH, Rosenberg DM (eds) *The Ecology of Aquatic Insects*, pp. 323–57. Praeger, New York. [5.2]

Nowell ARM, Jumars PA. (1984) Flow environments of aquatic benthos. *Annual Review of Ecology and Systematics* **15**: 303–28. [5.2]

Obrdlik P, Castella E, Foeckler F, Petts GE. (1992) Groundwater invertebrates of European alluvial rivers. *Regulated Rivers, Special Issue* **7**: 1. [5.2]

O'Brien JS. (1987) A case study of minimum streamflow for fishery habitat in the Yampa river. In: Thorne CR, Bathurst JC, Hey RD (eds) *Sediment Transport in Gravel-bed Rivers*, pp. 921–46. John Wiley, Chichester. [5.3]

Oglesby RT, Carlson CA, McCann JA. (1972) *River Ecology and Man*. Academic Press, New York. [5.2]

O'Keefe JH, Davies BR. (1991) Conservation and management of the rivers of Kruger National Park: suggested methods for calculating instream flow needs. *Aquatic Conservation* **1**: 55–71. [5.4]

Orth DJ. (1987) Ecological considerations in the development and application of instream flow-habitat models. *Regulated Rivers* **1**: 171–82. [5.4]

Orth DJ, Leonard PM. (1990) Comparison of discharge methods and habitat optimization for recommending instream flows to protect fish habitat. *Regulated Rivers* **5**: 129–38. [5.3]

Parker G. (1979) Hydraulic geometry of active gravel-bed rivers. *Journal of the Hydraulics Division ASCE* **105**: 1185. [5.3]

Petts GE. (1984) *Impounded Rivers*. John Wiley, Chichester. [5.2]

Petts GE. (1992) *The River Glen: a Catchment Assessment*. Report for the National Rivers Authority, Anglian Region, Peterborough. [5.2, 5.3]

Petts GE. (1993) *The River Babingley: Instream Flow Needs*. Draft Report for the National Rivers Authority, Anglian Region, Peterborough. [5.3]

Petts GE. (1994) Rivers: dynamic components of catchment ecosystems. In: Calow P, Petts GE (eds) *The Rivers Handbook*, Vol. 2, pp. 3–22. Blackwell Scientific Publications, Oxford. [5.2]

Petts GE, Wood R. (eds) (1988) River regulation in the United Kingdom. *Regulated Rivers, Special Issue* **2**: 3. [5.2]

Petts GE, Moller H, Roux AL. (eds) (1989) *Historical Changes of Large Alluvial Rivers: Western Europe*. John Wiley, Chichester. [5.2]

Petts GE, Maddock I, Bickerton M, Ferguson A. (1995) Linking hydrology and ecology. In: Ferguson A, Harper D (eds) *The Scientific Basis for River Management*. John Wiley, Chichester. 1–16 [5.3, 5.4]

Phillipson GN. (1954) The effect of water flow and oxygen concentration on six species of caddis fly (Trichoptera) larvae. *Proceedings of the Zoological Society of London* **124**: 547–64. [5.2]

Raleigh RF, Miller WJ, Nelson PC. (1986) *Habitat Suitability Index Models and Instream Flow Suitability Curves: Chinook Salmon*. Biological Report 82 (10.122), US Fish and Wildlife Service, Fort Collins, Colorado. [5.2]

Reiser DW, Ramey MP, Wreshe TA. (1989a) Flushing flows. In: Gore JA, Petts GE (eds) *Alternatives in Regulated River Management*, pp. 91–138. CRC Press, Boca Raton, Florida. [5.2, 5.3]

Reiser DW, Ramey MP, Beck S, Lambert TR, Geary RE. (1989b) Flushing flow recommendations for maintenance of salmonid spawning gravels in a steep, regulated stream. *Regulated Rivers* **3**: 267–76.

Resh VH. (1985) Periodical citations in aquatic entomology and freshwater benthic biology. *Freshwater Biology* **15**: 757–66. [5.2]

Salo JS. (1990) External processes influencing the origin and maintenance of inland water–land ecotones. In: Naiman RJ, Decamps H (eds) *The Ecology and Management of Aquatic–Terrestrial Ecotones*, pp. 37–64. Unesco-MAB, Parthenon, Carnforth, UK. [5.2]

Scarnecchia DL, Bergenson EP. (1987) Trout production and standing crop in Colorado's small streams, as related to environmental features. *North American Journal of Fisheries Management* **7**: 315–30. [5.3]

Scott D, Shirvell CS. (1988) A critique of the Instream Flow Incremental Methodology with observations on flow determination in New Zealand. In: Craig JF, Kemper JB (eds) *Regulated Streams: Advances in Ecology*. Plenum, New York. [5.3]

Sedell JR, Richey JE, Swanson FJ. (1989) The river continuum concept: a basis for the expected ecosystem behaviour of very large rivers? In: Dodge DP (ed) *Canadian Special Publication of Fisheries and Aquatic Sciences* **106**: 49–55. [5.2]

Shepherd BG, Hartman GF, Wilson WJ. (1986) Relationships between stream and intragravel temperatures on coastal drainages, and some implications for fisheries workers. *Canadian Journal of Fisheries and Aquatic Sciences* **43**: 1818–22. [5.2]

Shirvell CS. (1989) Ability of PHABSIM to predict Chinook salmon spawning habitat. *Regulated Rivers* **3**: 277–90. [5.3]

Smith SD, Wellington AB, Nachlinger JL, Fox CA. (1991) Functional responses of riparian vegetation to streamflow diversion in the eastern Sierra Nevada. *Ecological Applications* **1**: 89–97. [5.2]

Stanford JA, Ward JV. (1988) The hyporheic habitat of river systems. *Nature* **335**: 64–6. [5.2]

Statzner B, Gore JA, Resh VH. (1988) Hydraulic stream ecology: observed patterns and potential applications. *Journal of the North American Benthological Society* **7**(4): 307–60. [5.2]

Sterba O, Uvira V, Mathur P, Rulik M. (1992) Variations of the hyporheic zone through a riffle in the R. Morava, Czechoslovakia. *Regulated Rivers* **7**: 31–44. [5.2]

Stromberg JC. (1993) Instream flow models for mixed deciduous riparian vegetation within a semi-arid region. *Regulated Rivers* **8**: 225–36. [5.2]

Tennant DL. (1976) Instream flow requirements for fish, wildlife, recreation and related environmental resources. *Fisheries* **1**(4): 6–10. [5.3]

Toth LA, Obeysekera TB, Perkins WA, Loftin MK. (1993) Flow regulation and restoration of Florida's Kissimmee River. *Regulated Rivers* **8**: 155–66. [5.4]

Triska FJ, Duff JH, Avanzino RJ. (1993) Patterns of hydrological exchange and nutrient transformation in the hyporheic zone of a gravel-bottom stream: examining terrestrial–aquatic linkages. *Freshwater Biology* **29**: 259–74. [5.2]

Vannote RL, Minshall GW, Cummins KW, Sedell JR, Cushing CE. (1980) The river continuum concept. *Canadian Journal of Fisheries and Aquatic Sciences* **37**: 130–7. [5.2]

White DS. (1990) Biological relationships to convective flow patterns within stream beds. *Hydrobiologia* **196**: 149–58. [5.2]

Wickett WP. (1954) The oxygen supply to salmon eggs in spawning beds. *Journal of the Fisheries Research Board of Canada* **11**: 933–53. [5.2]

Wolff SW, Wesche TA, Hubert WA. (1989) Stream channel and habitat changes due to flow augmentation. *Regulated Rivers* **4**: 225–33. [5.4]

6: Environmentally Sensitive River Engineering

R. D. HEY

6.1 RIVER ENGINEERING

Traditional engineering practices

From time immemorial rivers have been harnessed, managed and engineered for the benefit of humans. Within the last century river engineering works have become more intrusive, in terms of the scale of modification, as mechanization has increased our ability to modify rivers and their local environment. Early engineering practices relied on trial-and-error procedures as schemes were implemented and subsequently managed to meet and maintain design objectives. Inevitably mistakes were made as design methods evolved.

Any engineering work that modifies the river system has the potential to cause instability and adversely affect the riverine environment. Attempts to impose an unnatural condition on a river can lead to major instability problems unless the river is heavily engineered. In turn, this can cause severe environmental degradation. The types of problem that can result may be illustrated by considering a range of river engineering works.

Flood control and land drainage works have traditionally involved different combinations of channel widening, dredging and straightening (see Brookes 1994). Not only does this destroy river and bankside flora and habitats, but it adversely affects the local sediment transport regime of the river and promotes channel instability (Hey 1987a). For example, long sections of the Lower Mississippi have been severely destabilized as a result of channel straightening. Headward erosion, both on the main river and its tributaries,

caused severe sedimentation problems in the modified reaches. Major spur-dyke fields have been constructed to prevent bank erosion while extensive dredging is required to maintain navigation depths (Winkley 1982). On rivers which do not transport significant amounts of bed material load, for example many of the lowland rivers in Eastern England, channel resectioning may not cause serious instability problems; any siltation that does occur is routinely dredged at approximately 10-yearly intervals. The environmental consequences are, however, still very damaging as instream habitats are destroyed and any rehabilitation that does occur is short lived.

River training works are often carried out to stabilize aggrading or degrading channels. For example, braided rivers can be stabilized by increasing their ability to transport the sediment supplied from upstream. Traditionally, this involves the construction of a straight channel, to maximize the gradient, with a relatively deep and narrow cross-section. This can only be maintained if the banks are artificially lined to prevent their failure. Inevitably this totally destroys the natural channel and creates a uniform, canalized river with little or no environmental value. The formerly braided Alpine Rhine in Switzerland was extensively trained in the 18th century in this manner. Land previously destroyed as the braided river shifted its position is now intensively farmed and flood risk is considerably reduced as sediment accretion is prevented from destroying the capacity of the channel (Visher 1986).

Major water resource development schemes, either surface water reservoirs or groundwater, can also destabilize a river system by reducing flood flows. The impact depends on the degree of regulation and the nature of the tributary channels. Immediately downstream from the reservoir or abstraction zone the impact will be considerable, but this will decline as unregulated tributaries join the main river.

Reservoirs, both direct supply and regulating, can cause bed degradation for a considerable distance downstream from a dam as well as promoting a coarsening or armouring of the bed as finer material is eroded but not replenished from upstream. Eventually a state is reached when relatively little bed material transport occurs. The bed then becomes imbricated as fines fill in the voids in the gravel framework and the bed is rendered relatively impermeable and unsuited for salmon and trout spawning. In addition the width of the river is reduced by vegetation encroachment as flood flows no longer occur (Raynov *et al* 1986).

Major groundwater development schemes, by drawing down the aquifer over large areas during dry periods, encourage increased recharge and reduced run-off during wet periods. Consequently the frequency of flood flows can, potentially, be reduced. If this occurs, then the river will adjust its bankfull morphology to the new imposed condition.

Basis for environmentally sensitive approaches

The stable morphology of natural alluvial channels, defined by the bankfull longitudinal slope, cross-section and plan shape of the river, is dependent on the flow and sediment transport regime, the nature of the bed and bank sediment, bankside vegetation and the slope of the valley. Any change in the flow regime or the dimensions of the channel through engineering works can destabilize the river and promote erosion and deposition not only within the engineered reach, but upstream and downstream from it (Hey 1986). For example, a section of the Homochitto River in southwest Mississippi was straightened between 1938 and 1946 and this caused degradation up to 40 km upstream by 1974.

An understanding of the physical processes controlling channel shape and dimensions (see Bettess 1994) is a prerequisite for developing and

implementing river engineering schemes that maintain channel stability and the natural range of habitat features which are vital for riverine flora, fisheries and fauna. Such schemes are also likely to be more cost-effective in the longer term.

6.2 FLOOD ALLEVIATION SCHEMES

Traditional and environmental options

A post-project appraisal has been carried out on 18 flood alleviation schemes in England and Wales to establish their engineering and environmental performance (Hey *et al* 1990). Schemes were chosen to be representative of urban and rural projects, as space and design standards often require different solutions, and upland and lowland schemes; the latter essentially enabled differentiation between those rivers which transport bed material load, and therefore are more susceptible to engineering change, and those which transport sand, silt and organic material and which are likely to be less affected.

In view of the criticism of the traditional methods of increasing flood capacity, on conservation grounds, more recently advocated environmental options were also evaluated.

Traditional methods

1 Resectioning. This involves dredging and/or widening the main channel to increase its inbank discharge capacity. In addition, bed slope may be steepened to increase flow velocities and further augment flood capacity. In urban areas rectangular flume-like channels are often constructed due to limited space. In order to maintain a stable bank, vertical sheet piling, concrete or masonry must be used to line the channel.

2 Realignment. Straightening the channel increases the gradient of the river and, thereby, flow velocity and flood capacity. This is often carried out in association with resectioning.

3 Adjacent flood banks. The construction of flood banks or levees is a common engineering solution to flood control. Conventionally these are constructed close to the river and, as a consequence, they need to be higher than distant flood banks to achieve the same level of protection.

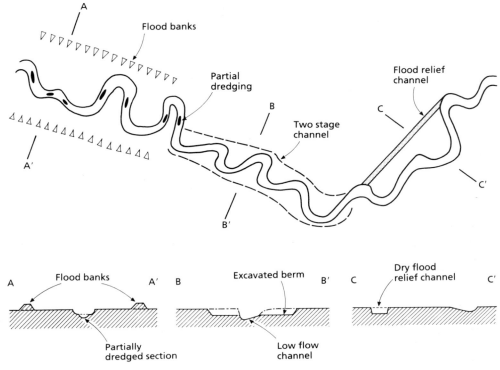

Fig. 6.1 Flood alleviation schemes: environmental options.

Environmental options

1 Relief channels. These are constructed to divert flow above a given stage away from the main channel. Such channels may be wet or dry during low flow periods. The natural channel is left intact (Fig. 6.1).

2 Partial dredging. A limited central section of the river is dredged to increase channel cross-sectional area, particularly at shallow riffle sections. The undisturbed bed acts as a biological store for recolonizing species (Fig. 6.1).

3 Distant flood banks. Where space is not limiting, the flood banks can be set back some distance from the river. Often the banks are located at the edge of the meander belt (Fig. 6.1).

4 Two-stage channels. These are created by excavating the upper section of the floodplain adjacent to the river. The natural low-flow channel is preserved while higher flows are contained within the newly created flood berm (Fig. 6.1).

Effect on channel stability

Traditional methods

Resectioning. On upland rivers this can cause severe instability in alluvial reaches as headcut erosion can promote significant deposition in the engineered reach, as the river attempts to re-establish its width, depth and slope, and erosion farther downstream (Hey 1987a). Harder engineering solutions are often employed, particularly in urban areas, to try to maintain the design channel. This often involves combinations of bank revetments and check weirs in the dredged section, and bed load traps farther upstream in order to control the transport regime of the river. Bed sills and bed load traps prevent headward erosion and limit the supply of sediment to the engineered reach, where it would be deposited, while the check weirs control local gradient at the entrance to the dredged section and prevent bed scour during floods. While this can protect the scheme, erosion can result farther downstream as sediment loads are substantially reduced.

In lowland areas instability problems are not as serious. Eventually the river would re-establish its original condition through reed encroachment from the bank and by bed aggradation. Dredging every 5–10 years can generally maintain the flood capacity of the river.

Realignment. On upland rivers, channel straightening can promote considerable instability with headcut erosion and the re-establishment of a meandering channel in the engineered reach (Hey 1987a). A bed sill at the head of the reach would prevent headcut erosion, while a series of check weirs along the straightened reach could maintain channel gradient and prevent bed scour. Bank revetments would be required to stabilize the banks.

On lowland rivers, straightening does not create the same problems unless increased gradients cause the bed to be scoured. Some form of bank protection may be required to prevent failure of the over-deepened banks.

Adjacent flood banks. The construction of flood banks adjacent to the river increases the in-bank flood capacity of the river and sediment transport capacity in comparison with neighbouring natural reaches. On upland rivers this can cause instability problems with erosion in the engineered reach and deposition farther downstream. In lowland rivers the increased velocities during flood events are unlikely to cause bed degradation and they will probably remain fairly stable.

Environmental options

Relief channels. Instability can occur at the intake into the relief channel in rivers transporting bed material load. The reduced transport capacity in the main river when the flow is divided precipitates deposition of coarse material. At the re-entry point, erosion can occur as the transport capacity of the river is significantly increased. This is especially the case if the angle of the

confluence is obtuse. Secondary flows generated by the flow from the relief channel can cause significant bed scour. In lowland rivers such problems are less likely as most sediment is transported in suspension. Care still needs to be exercised to ensure that return flows from the relief channel enter the river at an acute angle to prevent bed scour.

Partial dredging. On upland rivers the partially dredged section will rapidly become filled with coarse bed material. However, on lowland rivers it can be maintained by routine maintenance dredging every 5–10 years.

Distant flood banks. Flood banks set back from the river, which allow the river to meander freely within their bounds, enable the natural channel to remain intact. During overbank flows flooding is curtailed to a limited strip of floodplain. Provided space is available such schemes represent the best solution for flood alleviation. No instability problems are generated and provided the restricted flood plain is grazed or otherwise managed, the flood capacity of the scheme will be maintained.

Two-stage channels. The construction of a two-stage channel in upland rivers is unlikely to be successful. Local change in the bedload transport capacity of the river as it enters the two-stage channel would precipitate aggradation, rapid bank erosion and destruction of the newly created berm during flood flows. On lowland rivers they have proved to be more successful but even then they have to be carefully designed and managed. If the flood berm is excavated too close to the water table, then it cannot be grazed by cattle as it will not support their weight. A major maintenance cutting programme is then required to prevent reed encroachment as this would seriously impair flood channel capacity. In urban areas the flood berm could be maintained as a linear park.

Effect on instream and bankside flora

The environmental performance of the 18 flood alleviation schemes investigated were assessed to establish their impact on instream and bankside flora. For each type of scheme the following information was provided:

1 Species diversity: this gives the number of species found per 10 m length of river. For comparison purposes it should be noted that for natural reaches the mean diversity of instream species was 4.18 species per 10 m length of river and for bank species 4.22 per 10 m.

2 Diversity ranking: rank ordering of schemes on the basis of number of species per 10 m. Natural channels were ranked third for instream species and fifth for bank species on a scale 1–7.

3 Related species: species were identified which were associated with particular engineering works irrespective of geographical location.

Traditional methods

Resectioned and realigned. These schemes considerably limit habitat diversity, particularly if the banks are lined to prevent erosion. As a result they exhibit low species diversity (Table 6.1).

Adjacent flood banks. Bank height is artificially increased and thereby bank habitat diversity. Consequently bank species diversity is relatively high (Table 6.2).

Table 6.1 Environmental parameters for resectioned/realigned schemes

Parameter	Unlined	Lined
Species diversity	Instream 3.17; bank 4.04	Instream 2.73; bank 3.18
Diversity ranking	Instream 5th; bank 6th	Instream 6th; bank 7th
Related species	None	None

Table 6.2 Environmental parameters for schemes with adjacent flood banks

Parameter	Instream	Bank
Species diversity	3.33	5.67
Diversity ranking	4th	2nd
Related species	None	Fleabane

Table 6.3 Environmental parameters for moist relief channels

Parameter	Instream	Bank
Species diversity	2.17	6.67
Diversity ranking	7th	1st
Related species	None	Teasel

Environmental methods

Relief channels. Wet relief channels are those close to or below the water table. They are difficult to maintain and create a favourable environment for such undesirable species as algae and pondweed. Dry, higher channels only contain water during periods of high flow. For moist channels the results obtained are given in Table 6.3.

Distant flood banks. These showed slightly greater species diversity than natural channels, which probably reflects some partial dredging of point bars at the sites investigated (Table 6.4).

Two-stage channels. The low-flow channel is preserved while the bank habitat is changed considerably due to the proximity of the water table.

Table 6.4 Environmental parameters for distant flood banks

Parameter	Instream	Bank
Species diversity	5.48	5.38
Diversity ranking	2nd	3rd
Related species	Jointed rush; filamentous algae	Creeping yellow cress; creeping bent

Table 6.5 Environmental parameters for two-stage channels

Parameter	Instream	Bank
Species diversity	6.51	4.63
Diversity ranking	1st	4th
Related species	Marsh woodwort; unbranched burr reed	Yellow loosestrife; lesser-tufted sedge; yellow flag

For instream species it exhibits the highest species diversity, reflecting the provision of favourable marginal habitats, but a much lower diversity for bank species (Table 6.5).

Environmental design guidelines

Distant flood banks, where the banks are located along the edge of the meander belt, are the preferred solution as they have no impact on the natural stability of the river or on the riverine environment. Stability is maintained because the natural bankfull capacity of the river is unchanged. Should space limitations preclude their use, alternative procedures are required and these increase the 'inbank' capacity of the river. Any attempt to artificially increase the natural capacity of the river will cause instability and this will adversely affect its conservation value (Table 6.6).

In lowland urban areas, two-stage channels are a viable alternative as siltation will be minimal and they can actually increase environmental value. The flood berms can be maintained as an urban park. If insufficient space is available for this approach, adjacent flood banks are acceptable provided the natural alluvial bank is preserved.

Table 6.6 Engineering and environmental performance of flood alleviation schemes

Option	Engineering and environmental performance		
	Advantages	Disadvantages	Design limitations
Distant flood banks	Natural stability and flood capacity maintained. Instream and bankside habitats and flora unaffected		*Preferred solution.* Large space requirement which may be unavailable in urban areas. Possible need to change agricultural practice in flood storage zone in rural areas
Adjacent flood banks	On lowland rivers with negligible bed material load, no significant change on instream habitats and flora. Bank diversity may be enhanced	Scouring on upland rivers which transport bed material load unless bed is armoured. May be prevented by weirs. Restricts view of river across floodplain	*Not suited to upland-type rivers without additional engineering works*
Two-stage channel	On lowland-type rivers, instream low-flow habitats and flora unaffected. In short-term floral diversity increased on berm but unlikely to be maintained should reed bed become established without heavy maintenance	On upland-type rivers deposition of bed material load at entrance to two-stage section will promote instability. On lowland-type rivers need to ensure that flood berm is sufficiently high above the water table to allow grazing/mowing and prevent reed growth. If berm surface becomes overgrown, design flood capacity is lost	*Not suited to upland-type rivers.* Larger space requirement. In urban areas could be developed as a linear park
Relief channels	Instream and bankside flora and habitats unaffected	On upland-type rivers significant deposition likely to occur at entrance to relief channel and erosion at exit	*Not suited to upland-type rivers*

continued p. 86

Table 6.6 *Continued*

| Option | Engineering and environmental performance | | Design limitations |
	Advantages	Disadvantages	
Resectioning		On upland-type rivers severe erosion at head of dredged section, unless prevented by weir or bed sill, and deposition at downstream end. In lowland-type rivers siltation in dredged reach requiring regular maintenance dredging. Flood capacity impaired. Instream and bankside flora are totally destroyed	*Not recommended unless necessitated by lack of space.* Check sediment transport capacity for stability and ensure weirs and bank revetments have conservation/ architectural merit
Realignment		On upland-type rivers severe headward erosion, unless prevented by weir or bed sill, and deposition downstream of straightened section. Bank revetment probably required to maintain unnatural alignment and weirs to prevent bed erosion. Instream and bankside habitats and flora totally destroyed	*Not recommended unless no alternative.* Check sediment transport capacity for stability and ensure weirs and bank revetments have conservation/ architectural merit

Resectioning should only be contemplated as a last resort as it completely destroys the riverine environment and requires maintenance dredging.

At urban upland sites, adjacent flood banks are preferable to relief channels or resectioning since they have less impact on channel stability and the riverine flora. The latter can cause severe instability problems and should not be attempted. Two-stage channels are likely to cause similar instability problems.

In rural lowland regions two-stage channels can be successful provided the vegetation on the flood berm can be managed to preserve the design discharge capacity of the scheme. Instability need not be a problem, provided the flood channel is properly aligned, and the riverine environment is enhanced. Adjacent flood banks are preferable to relief channels and resectioning if space is limited. Resectioning should not be attempted, even if maintenance requirements are minimal, due to the very adverse environmental impact.

Adjacent flood banks are the only real alternative to distant flood banks in upland rural regions. Even these promote some instability depending on the degree of flood confinement. Instream flora is adversely affected although this is, in part, compensated by increased diversity of bankside species. All other procedures have been shown to cause expensive instability problems and a deterioration in riverine flora.

6.3 REGIONAL CHANNEL STABILIZATION

Nature of problem

Rivers become unstable when there is an imbalance between the sediment load supplies to the reach in question and the river's ability to transport it. Regional instability relates to large-scale and systematic degradation and aggradation, which can be natural or man-induced. It can progress downstream, due to change in sediment supply, or upstream as a result of local changes in transport capacity.

Incision along an alluvial reach of river can cause significant land loss as banks fail and the channel rapidly widens. In time the river would re-establish a regime-type condition with the river flowing within a new lower-level floodplain leaving the original floodplain as a terrace feature.

Severe aggradation, which results in the development of a braided channel form, can destroy the agricultural potential of floodplain areas due to rapid channel shift and increased flood frequencies. Eventually a new equilibrium would be achieved in which the river would either meander or form a multi-channel anastomosing system across a new, higher-level floodplain.

Erosion control options

Grade control

Incision along a reach of river is traditionally controlled by the construction of grade-control structures or check weirs at various points along its length. The requirement is to define the number, location and height of these structures to stabilize the river and prevent further headward erosion on the main river and its tributaries.

Three approaches are available: conventionally grade control is determined using tractive stress calculations or regime theory, but there is also a geomorphological alternative.

1 Tractive stress method. This determines the slope, velocity and depth of flow which will prevent the erosion of material from the bed or banks of the river (Lane 1937; Einstein 1950; Vanoni & Brooks 1957).

2 Modified regime approach. This allows sediment supplied to the reach, either upstream or from tributaries, to be transported through the system. Appropriate mobile-bed regime equations are used to predict slope, velocity and flow depth, depending on bed material size (sand, see Blench 1966; gravel, see Hey & Thorne 1986).

3 Geomorphological method. The method is based on an empirical geomorphological model of channel evolution, consequent upon the initiation of erosion, developed from field observations and measurements (Schumm *et al* 1984). Using a space for time substitution, the authors constructed a five-stage model of channel development from initial incision to final attainment of quasi-equilibrium (Fig. 6.2). For reaches that were in quasi-equilibrium, relations were obtained between channel top width, the 5-year discharge and the associated water surface slope. At unstable reaches the equation was used to calculate the allowable slope for existing top width and discharge, or the allowable width for existing top width and slope. The size, location and number of grade control structures or, alternatively, flow control reservoirs, can therefore be determined by calculating allowable slope or discharge criteria and by computing backwater profiles. Values for soil loss, from bed and banks, and the increase in top width can be ascertained which were relevant for the assessment of potential reservoir sedimentation rates if nothing was done to control the problem.

Lowered valley

For small alluvial channels (<20 m top width), where incision is of the order of the original bankfull depth of the river, it would be possible to stabilize the river by forming a new regime channel within a lowered valley in the incising section and by constructing a grade control structure to prevent continued headward erosion. Effectively this creates what nature would eventually produce in the incising section below the grade control structure without causing aggradation farther downstream.

The new valley floor would be formed at a level corresponding to the depth of incision and its width would need to accommodate the amplitude of the meanders of the new channel. Regime equations, as appropriate for the nature of the bed material, would be used to design the new channel given the bankfull discharge and sediment load for the natural reach upstream from the grade control structure. Regime equations only enable channel width, depth and slope to be

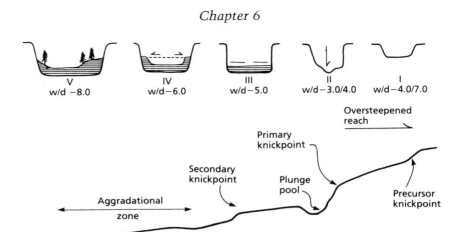

Fig. 6.2 Longitudinal and cross-sectional profiles of unstable river reach (5-stage evolution: channel width (*w*) to depth (*d*) ratios given; size of arrows indicates relative importance and direction of dominant processes) (from Schumm *et al* 1984).

determined but, as valley slope is prescribed, channel sinuosity – the ratio of channel length to valley length – can be determined from the ratio of valley slope to channel slope. This, together with meander arc length, the channel distance between inflexion points, which is given by 4–10 times channel width, uniquely prescribes the plan shape of the river (Hey 1976). Pools and riffles would need to be incorporated in the design and special attention given to the construction of meander bends to obtain a natural asymmetry and appropriate maximum flow depths.

Engineering and environmental performance

Grade control structures

The three methods outlined above were evaluated on an incising section of Oaklimiter Creek, Mississippi. Calculations showed that 15 grade control structures were required to stabilize the river according to the modified regime approach, 20 with the tractive stress method, and six with the geomorphological design procedure.

The traditional engineering solutions tend to produce an essentially constant low slope along the ponded reaches created by the weirs, while

the geomorphological procedure recognizes that a natural-equilibrium longitudinal stream profile is concave.

Although the six structures were not actually constructed to enable the method to be evaluated, this study suggested that significant costs savings could be made by adopting the geomorphological approach.

The design of the actual grade control structures is also crucially important for the success of the scheme. By creating fixed points on the bed of the river, bank erosion may be precipitated at the structure due to the development of strong vortices adjacent to the bank (Fig. 6.3). Knauss and Scheuerlein (1988) advocate the use of curved submerged sills, bowed upstream with gentle side contraction. This creates convergent overspill and associated slight scouring in mid channel, while the vortices adjacent to the bank are significantly reduced as the contraction at the bank is gradual (Fig. 6.3). Where high structures are constructed as, for example, on Long and Godwin Creeks in northern Mississippi, a baffle is required in the plunge pool to dissipate energy and prevent excessive scouring.

Even though grade control structures can successfully arrest bed degradation, the heightened over-steepened banks in the ponded reaches are potentially more prone to failure following

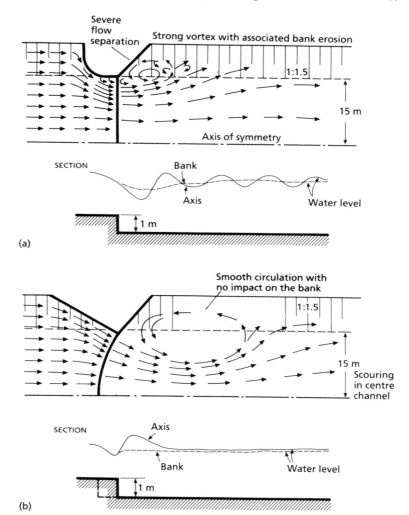

Fig. 6.3 Effect of sill geometry on bank erosion: (a) submerged sills, straight layout plan; (b) submerged sills, curved layout plan (after Knauss & Scheuerlein 1988).

incision. However, observations on Long Creek indicate that bank erosion is generally reduced since deposition in the ponded reach reduces bank heights and failed material is less readily removed (Biedenharn *et al* 1990). More recent evidence indicates that some failures are still occurring in meander bends where secondary flows are sufficiently strong to remove eroded debris and maintain local bank height.

No environmental assessments have been carried out to compare the performances of the three different approaches or to establish their absolute impact. The latter would be difficult to assess because the pre-condition is not in equilibrium and, by providing stability, there is scope for enhancement as flora, invertebrates and fisheries become established. However, as the geomorphological approach requires fewer structures and ponding behind the weirs is not total, it should create more habitat variety and have greater conservation potential.

Lowered valley

For smaller rivers where degradation would be less than natural channel depth, the lowered valley option probably represents a viable alternative to the construction of grade control structures.

A stable natural channel would be reinstated with its complementary range of instream and bankside habitat features, which would improve the conservation and fisheries value of the affected reach and enhance visual amenity.

Construction of the new channel and floodplain could constitute a problem unless the river was realigned. This would enable construction work to be carried out in relatively dry conditions and allow vegetation to become established before flood flows needed to be transmitted through the channel. Reconstructing the existing channel would involve working in difficult wet conditions and it would be prone to erosion and bank failure until vegetation became established.

Environmental design guidelines

Grade control structures represent the only sensible procedure for stabilizing large rivers and those where incision exceeds the original local bankfull flow depth. Deep excavations to create a new valley would be prohibitively expensive as large volumes of material would have to be removed (Table 6.7).

It would appear that the geomorphological approach for establishing the number of grade control structures to stabilize the river is better than alternative methods as it minimizes the number required. However, until schemes are implemented and evaluated in different river environments its potential is unconfirmed.

For smaller rivers where incision is limited, excavation of a lower-level valley would be a viable alternative, especially if it could be realigned to allow working in dry conditions (Table 6.7). Environmentally this would be the preferred solution as the reinstated river would provide a range of habitats for biological exploitation. Such an approach has been successfully employed when a stable, dredged, resectioned channel was diverted (Hey 1992) but it needs to be evaluated for stabilization schemes.

Aggradation control options

Resectioned and straightened channel

Where braiding results from sediment supplied from catchment source areas, a traditional engineering solution would be to straighten, narrow and deepen the channel in order to increase its capacity to transport sediment to match that supplied from upstream. This approach was adopted on the Alpine Rhine in Switzerland.

Natural channel

An alternative to resectioning and straightening would be to create an irregular sinuous channel. A rational design approach would be required involving appropriate flow resistance and sediment transport equations to determine bankfull depth, slope and velocity (Hey 1987b). Channel width would need to be selected, as no process-based equations are available to predict its value.

Table 6.7 Engineering and environmental performance of erosion control measures

| Option | Engineering and environmental performance | | |
	Advantages	Disadvantages	Design limitations
Grade control	Controls incision and reduces bank erosion	Artificially ponded. Adversely affects instream and bankside habitats	*Only option for incision greater than local stable channel depth*
Lowered valley	Controls incision and reduces bank erosion. Natural channel with range of habitat features recreated	Considerable excavation to create new lower valley	*Alternative option when incision less than local stable channel depth and for rivers less than approx. 20 m top width*

For gravel-bed rivers, equations developed by Hey and Thorne (1986) could be used on the assumption that the channel would effectively be tree-lined or incised; as the river would need to be revetted to maintain its width and planform, this would be a fair assumption. Once channel width is established and the required channel slope calculated, the plan shape of the channel can be determined given the overall valley slope (see p. 88).

Bank revetments would be crucial to preserve the integrity of the scheme and it is likely that hard engineering solutions involving blockstones or gabion baskets would be necessary, particularly on the outer bank in meander bends. However, it is possible that softer, bioengineering methods could be used on straighter sections and on the inside of meander bends (see Section 6.4).

Braiding that results from incision at adjacent upstream reaches, channel-derived sediment, would be treated by stabilizing the upstream eroding reach, as outlined previously, and constructing an appropriately designed sinuous channel to accommodate the reduced sediment load.

Engineering and environmental performance

Resectioning

This represents the cheapest solution, as the new channel has the shortest possible length, and it has been successfully used on the Alpine Rhine in Switzerland. Environmentally the river lacks instream and bankside flora, as the bed has few if any exposed bars, and the hard bank revetments preclude successful colonization. In addition the straightened river has little habitat variety and amenity value.

Natural channel

No information is currently available to quantify the engineering and environmental performance of these channels. Nevertheless it is apparent that it represents a 'softer' alternative to the control of aggradation. By creating a meandering channel with a variable bed geometry, a range of instream habitats are created which are beneficial for instream flora, invertebrates and fisheries.

The use of softer bank-protection measures, particularly those involving natural vegetation, provides a more sympathetic approach to bank stabilization that is aesthetically pleasing and provides cover for fish. Because of its longer length, it is more expensive to excavate than standard resectioning procedures, but savings could be made on bank protection costs and maintenance is likely to be cheaper.

Environmental design guidelines

In order to stabilize multi-channel braided systems some form of heavy engineering is required. The ecology of the riparian zone will be dramatically altered by such action but this might have to be accepted in order to satisfy economic and development interests.

The construction of a more natural sinuous channel would be preferable to resectioning as this would have greater morphological and hydraulic variability and, consequently, would have less environmental impact (Table 6.8)

6.4 LOCAL CHANNEL STABILIZATION

Nature of problem

Local instability problems are essentially concerned with bank protection and the maintenance of channel planform. Changes in bed elevation are reversible whereas width adjustments rarely are. Channels which are ostensibly in regime may also need training to prevent down-valley migration of meanders.

Bank protection options

Revetments

A range of measures are available to increase the erosional resistance of riverbanks, and it is not necessary to describe them all here. Recent publications have reviewed the available hard engineering methods and also considered more novel softer options (e.g. Hemphill & Bramley 1989).

Essentially the methods can be ranked from softer, natural vegetative treatments to harder,

Table 6.8 Engineering and environmental performance of aggradation control measures

Option	Engineering and environmental performance		Design limitations
	Advantages	Disadvantages	
Resectioning and straightening	Controls aggradation	Heavily engineered; lacks instream and bankside habitats	*Not recommended*
Natural channel	Controls aggradation. Sinuous channel created with variable bed topography	Bank revetment required	*Preferred option*

engineering methods with little potential for amelioration (Table 6.9).

Hydraulic controls

The aforementioned conventional and bioengineering approaches to bank protection provide stability by increasing the erosional resistance of the bank. Effectively this is treating the symp-

Table 6.9 Bank revetment procedures ranked according to erosional resistance (after Hey *et al* 1991)

Protection type	Flowchart symbol	Costs (£/m) (May 1991)
Grass	1	
Grass and jute	2	
Grass and geotextile	3	
Reeds	4	
Willow/osier	Soft 5	<50
Ash	6	
Gravel and geotextile	7	
Mastic and geotextile	8	
Woven wooden fence	9	
Riprap	A	<50
Riprap over geotextile	B	50–100
Gabion mattresses	C	100–150
Gabion riprap	D	100–150
Grouted riprap	E	50–100
Grouted gabion mats	F	
Grouted gabion baskets	G	
Jointed cellular blocks	Hard H	100–150
Interlocking blocks	I	
Cable-tied blocks	J	
Wooden boards	K	50–100
Sheet piling	L	
Masonry wall	M	>150
Concrete wall	N	

toms rather than the cause of the problem. An alternative is to modify the flow adjacent to the bank such that the erosional forces acting on the bank are reduced and bank failure prevented. In meander bends submerged vanes or hydrofoils have been developed which prevent bank failure by modifying the pattern of secondary flows in the meander bend (Odgaard & Mosconi 1987; Paice & Hey 1989). The structures are located (Fig. 6.4) to generate a secondary flow cell, which has opposite polarity to the main cell that results from flow curvature in the bend. Convergence of faster surface water then occurs in centre channel inside the line of the vanes and causes bed scouring. Material eroded from this zone is deposited in the original scour hole adjacent to the outer bank. As shear stresses against the outer bank and toe region and the bank height are reduced, bank retreat can be prevented and the natural bank preserved. Should deposition eventually cover the vanes the original secondary circulation pattern would re-establish itself. However, the resultant bed scour will re-expose them and further bank retreat will be prevented. The system is, therefore, self-regulatory.

Engineering and environmental performance

Revetments

A range of revetment types are available and it is necessary to establish which are appropriate in different circumstances bearing in mind the need for the adoption of bioengineering solutions wherever possible. The universal application of heavy engineering methods is no longer acceptable not only on environmental grounds but also

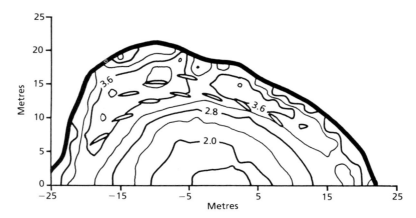

Fig. 6.4 Location of submerged vanes on River Roding, Loughton, Essex. Contours are depths below fixed zero datum (after Paice & Hey 1989).

on economic ones as many hard schemes are likely to be overdesigned.

Recent research has begun to address this issue (Hey *et al* 1991). Based on a post-project appraisal of the engineering performance of a range of schemes in different river environments in England and Wales, a series of flowcharts were developed which enable successful bank protection to be chosen for a particular site on the basis of local hydraulic, morphological, geotechnical, wave and tidal information. Effectively these enable the minimum level of protection to be specified to stabilize the bank against the factors causing failure. By entering information into the flowchart (Figs 6.5, 6.6 and 6.7; Table 6.9) a number of viable methods are identified and the softest one listed would be appropriate.

The post-project appraisal attempted to obtain precise information on the environmental impact, in terms of bankside flora, of the various revetment methods. Unfortunately pre- and post-scheme river corridor survey information was not available to allow this to be objectively carried out and recourse has had to be made to more subjective assessments (Table 6.9). Nevertheless it does enable the softest options to be chosen as appropriate for the local riverine environment.

On cost grounds the harder engineering options are often most expensive although they are generally relatively maintenance free. Table 6.9 lists the average costs of a range of protection methods, as of May 1991, but it should be recognized that considerable variation can occur around these average values due to problems of access, availability of plant, variations in bank height and economies of scale when protecting long lengths of bank.

Hydraulic controls

Submerged vanes or hydrofoils have been successfully used to reduce bank erosion on sand-and-gravel-bed rivers with widths ranging from 20 to 55 m (Odgaard & Mosconi 1987; Paice & Hey 1989). As they obviate the need to modify or cover the bank, the natural character is maintained. Over time sub-aerial weathering will cause bank angles to decline and they will eventually become vegetated. Being submerged even at the lowest flow they are not visually intrusive and actually enhance instream habitats.

As they are located towards the eroding bank and cause bed scouring in mid-channel, they can even be deployed on navigable rivers (Odgaard & Mosconi 1987).

Environmental design guidelines

Bank revetments have traditionally been used to prevent bank erosion. The requirement is to select the most environmentally acceptable type to stabilize a particular erosion problem; this can be achieved using the flowcharts (Figs 6.5–6.7). In high-energy environments, upland rivers or tidal areas, heavier protection measures may be required, whereas in lowland-type rivers

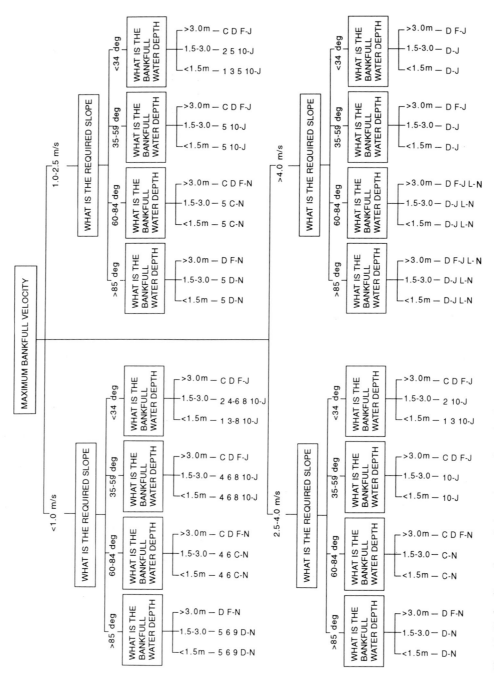

Fig. 6.5 Hydraulic and morphological controls on bank protection options (from Hey *et al* 1991).

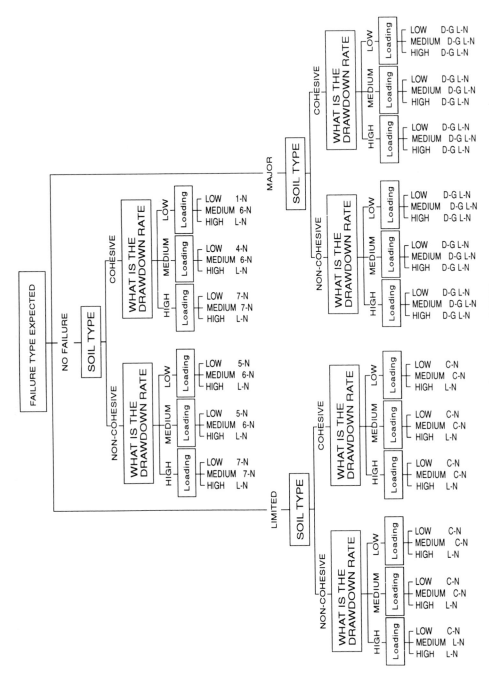

Fig. 6.6 Geotechnical controls on bank protection options (from Hey *et al* 1991).

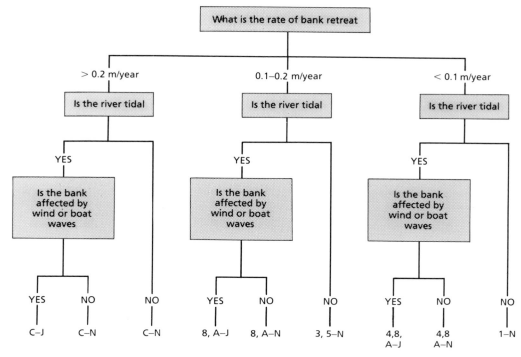

Fig. 6.7 Wave and tidal controls on bank protection options (from Hey *et al* 1991).

vegetative methods may be sufficiently robust. Where possible attempts should be made to soften harder treatments through selective planting (Table 6.10).

As the selection procedure assumes that protection works will be correctly implemented, failure may occur if this is not the case. Recommended installation practices have been identified for the various bank protection procedures, as determined from engineering experience and manufacturers' recommendations, together with methods for 'greening' harder structures (Hey *et al* 1991).

Harder bank revetment works are often an integral part of major schemes to control rivers for flood alleviation, particularly in urban schemes where space limitations preclude more natural solutions (Section 6.2), or for major stabilization works (Section 6.3). Protection is required to maintain an unnatural river condition. In such cases their impact should be ameliorated by planting or by maximizing their architectural merit.

Submerged vanes or hydrofoils are potentially cheaper than all harder revetment methods but do not have universal applications. To date they have been used to prevent bank erosion on meander bends on rivers which are ostensibly in regime, namely where the river migrates across its floodplain while maintaining a relatively stable meander pattern. They can also be used on rivers undergoing slight degradation, where the river is becoming more sinuous, provided some form of bed sill is installed to prevent further headward erosion. However, they are unlikely to be successful where major, systematic, regional erosion or deposition is occurring as they would be either undermined or submerged with sediment.

Environmentally, submerged vanes are preferable to revetment methods since the banks of the river are left undisturbed and natural recolonization is allowed to occur (Table 6.10).

Table 6.10 Engineering and environmental performance of bank protection works

Options	Engineering and environmental performance		Design limitations
	Advantages	Disadvantages	
Revetments			
Grass	Natural and unobtrusive		Lowest erosional resistance
Grass and jute			
Grass and geotextile			
Reeds			
Willows/osier			
Ash			
Gravel and geotextile	Natural but more obtrusive. Vegetation can become established		
Mastic and geotextile			
Woven wooden fence			
Riprap			Chosen option should be softest to prevent failure
Riprap over geotextile			
Gabion mattresses		Artificial but some vegetation can become established	
Gabion baskets			
Grouted riprap			
Grouted gabion baskets			
Jointed cellular blocks			
Cable-tied blocks			
Wooden boards		Artificial and cannot become vegetated	Highest erosional resistance
Sheet piling			
Masonry wall			
Concrete wall			
Hydraulic controls			
Submerged vanes	Natural bank retained. Vanes are submerged and unobtrusive. Instream habitats enhanced	Not appropriate where systematic bed degradation or aggradation	Suitable for bank erosion control in meander bends on rivers which are in regime

6.5 RIVER RESTORATION

Restoration requirements

River engineering works have, over the centuries, adversely affected hundreds of kilometres of rivers (Brookes 1988; Purseglove 1988). The ecological devastation that has been wrought by many of the traditional approaches to river engineering problems is well illustrated by the results of the environmental impact assessment of flood alleviation schemes (Hey *et al* 1990). Unsympathetic engineering treatments consistently reduced plant diversity, when compared with natural channels, while environmentally sensitive approaches actually increased diversity by creating a greater range of habitats. Limited information is currently available regarding the impact of different engineering treatments on fisheries. However, it has long been recognized that increased morphological diversity benefits the carrying capacity of a river and provides suitable habitats for the various stages in the life cycles of fishes, which is essential if the fishery is to be self-sustaining. It follows, therefore, that conventional engineering methods often have a deleterious effect on fisheries.

With the advantage of hindsight and experience it is possible to identify why problems have arisen. It is now a question of using our current level of understanding of river mechanics and its effect on channel form to restore degraded rivers to increase their environmental value in terms of flora, fisheries and amenity (Hey 1992). Essentially it is a question of removing the legacy of uniformity and recreating the diversity that is characteristic of natural channels.

Restoration options

As river shape and dimensions are essentially self-determined, then any habitat improvement or restoration scheme that imposes an unnatural condition on the river will inevitably lead to instability, loss of design performance and adverse environmental impact.

Upland rivers, because they transport considerable quantities of bed material load, are less forgiving than lowland rivers with regard to the implementation of restoration works. Badly designed schemes will quickly be destroyed as the river reacts to the imposed changes. An expensive maintenance programme would then be required to sustain the unnatural condition; this emphasizes the need for the development of sympathetic design procedures which are in harmony with local river conditions. With lowland rivers some flexibility is possible since they are less reactive to imposed change and a number of slightly different options may be feasible. Any adverse reaction by the river could subsequently be managed through a routine maintenance programme.

The basic requirement of any restoration works is to increase local morphological, hydraulic and sedimentological variability given the natural constraints of the river. Ideally any planned improvements need to be assessed with regard to their impact on channel stability, both bed and banks, and their influence on flow hydraulics (in terms of velocities, flow depths, etc.) and on the flood capacity of the channel. Only when these criteria are satisfied should the scheme be implemented. If several options are possible, then it is a question of establishing which produces the desired range of habitats. This presupposes that information is available regarding the habitat preferences of different species of fish during different stages in their life cycles. Ideally the created habitats should support every stage, from spawning to mature adult, in order that the improved reach will be self-sustaining and regular restocking will not be required. While there is considerable information available regarding habitat

preferences for salmonids, in terms of velocities, flow depths, substrate, etc. (Solomon 1983) there is little comparable information for coarse fish (Smith 1989). This remains a research priority as without such data informed decisions cannot be made when choices are available.

With regard to instream flora, some species preference charts have been developed, in terms of bankfull velocity, flow depth, cross-sectional area, bed substrate and bankslope, based on data from flood alleviation schemes and natural reaches (Hey *et al* 1990). These provide some guidance on likely species response to planned changes but here again more research is required to refine the method and improve its predictive capability.

There are two basic approaches to restoration and habitat improvement works: non-structural and structural.

Non-structural restoration

This method refers to the re-establishment of natural features within a reach that had previously been dredged and/or straightened. It could involve, *inter alia*, the restoration of meanders, pools, riffles, vertical banks and dead zones. Lowland rivers are particularly amenable to this type of treatment as they are less reactive to engineering change than upland ones. With the latter, riffles will rapidly re-form after dredging if bed material is actively being transported.

Irrespective of the scale of the planned restoration works a site survey is required to ascertain the nature of the existing bed topography and substrate characteristics. The geomorphological assessment should also map bankside features: eroding, vertical and slumped banks, tree-lined sections, submerged trees, areas of bank accretion, and the extent of any backwater from mills, weirs, etc. This identifies existing habitats that need to be preserved or enhanced and provides the baseline data for designing pool-riffle sequences. Appropriate regime equations, and/or data from local natural sections upstream and/or downstream from the affected reach, should be used to define required reach average widths, depths and slopes for the river. These enable the plan geometry of the channel to be defined over the reach if that also requires modification. The location of pools and riffles needs to correspond to the meander geometry of the river, with pools at the outside of the meander bends and dredged spoil used to form the point bar or shelf on the inner bank. Channel width in the bend needs to be less than that on the riffle to prevent siltation during high flows. The riffles should be located at the inflexion point between bends and constructed at a slight angle across the river in order that flow is directed towards the outer bank in the downstream bend. This skewing of the flow helps to generate secondary currents in the bend which, in turn, encourages scouring. The riffle crest should be high enough to create ponding upstream at low flow and needs to be formed of coarse enough material to maintain its stability. Large stones, 200–300 mm diameter, would make suitable foundation material and this would need to be covered by graded gravel slightly coarser than the local bed material size. The upstream face of the riffle would be steeper than the downstream one, the latter acting as an apron for the faster-flowing water overspilling the riffle at low flow. An example geomorphological map and resultant scheme design are given in Fig. 6.8 (Hey 1992).

If pools and riffles are being re-established in a straight channel, then the riffles would need to be spaced at 4–10 × channel width. In order that the pools are located adjacent to alternate banks, the riffles need to be slightly skewed. As riffle spacing is related to channel width, care should be exercised to ensure that widths used in the calculation are natural or predicted regime values, and not local values which may be artificially large due to dredging, if a natural width is going to be allowed to re-establish itself.

Attempts to recreate a pool-riffle sequence in a reach that is located in a backwater upstream from a weir or sluice is unlikely to be very successful. The riffle will be permanently drowned out and local velocity variations will, as a consequence, be minimal. The restored riffle needs to create a step in the water surface profile, by backing up water behind it, and this would necessitate the construction of an inordinately large riffle.

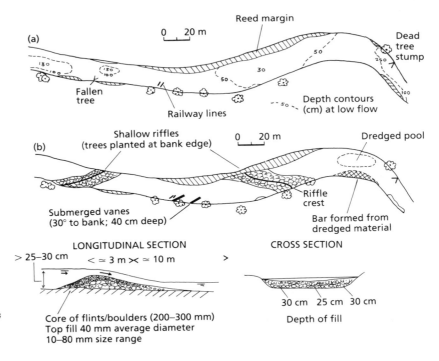

Fig. 6.8 Re-creation of pools and riffles at Lyng, River Wensum: (a) geomorphological map of original channel; (b) proposed pool-riffle sequence (from Hey 1992).

Structural restoration

These techniques refer to a range of artificial instream structures which can create ponded reaches and bar forms and prevent siltation to maintain substrate condition. Such structures are particularly useful where full restoration is not possible or, for example, where it is necessary to increase habitat diversity on urban flood alleviation schemes which have to be heavily engineered.

Weirs. A range of weirs and dams are available to create ponded reaches upstream and scouring in the overspill zone (Fig. 6.9). Full-width weirs can create different shaped plunge pools, depending on their crest form. Those V-ing downstream can precipitate bank failure as pools occur adjacent to the bank. Partial-width weirs accelerate flow through the gap and, thereby, cause scouring. All weirs require some form of bank protection to prevent bank erosion outflanking the structure. Sedimentation will occur in the ponded reach

upstream while material eroded below the structure will be deposited locally (Fig. 6.9).

Deflectors. Deflectors are structures which limit channel width and accelerate the flow through the constricted section. This causes local scouring and bar development. A variety of deflectors have been devised and these are illustrated in Fig. 6.9.

Wing deflectors can be triangular, with the leading edge angled at 45° to the flow, or straight but similarly angled, and extending up to three-quarters of the way across the channel in grossly overwidened and ponded reaches. In faster-flowing rivers a separation zone, or vortex, may develop downstream from the structure where flow expands. In extreme cases this may cause bank erosion. It can be avoided with triangular deflectors by reducing the angle of the trailing edge of the structure to allow gradual expansion to the flow. Both types have been successfully applied in a range of rivers (Hubbs *et al* 1932; White & Brynildson 1967).

At high discharges, when the structures are

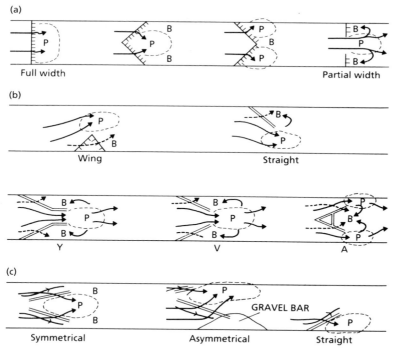

(a) Full width / Partial width
(b) Wing / Straight
(c) Y / V / A
Symmetrical / Asymmetrical / GRAVEL BAR / Straight

P, Pool; B, Bar; ⟶ Main/surface flow; →‑ Near bed flow; ‑‑‑▶ Over topping flow.

Fig. 6.9 River habitat improvement using structural measures: (a) weirs/dams; (b) deflectors; (c) vanes (from Hey 1992).

drowned out, flow is no longer fully constricted. Triangular deflectors cause overtopping flows to be directed back towards centre channel and encourage further scouring. Consequently it is not necessary for them to be constructed to bankfull level. In contrast, when the straight deflectors are overtopped, faster surface flow is directed towards the bank, which could cause bank failure if the banks are not protected. To avoid this problem, straight deflectors need to be constructed to bankfull level.

Instream deflectors take several forms: A, Y and V types, reflecting their shape. The apices of the Y and V structures lie upstream and flow accelerates through the central gap to create a scour hole. The A deflector points upstream with gaps adjacent to the bank. Pools generated adjacent to the bank may precipitate mass failure of the banks. When Y and V deflectors are overtopped, the secondary circulation that results will cause scouring at the base of the banks which may, ultimately, cause bank collapse. With the A deflector, overtopping will promote scouring in mid-channel. To avoid potential bank erosion problems with the Y and V structures, they would need to be constructed to bankfull levels. With the A deflector it is probably desirable for it to be overtopped at about half bankfull stage, otherwise bank erosion could be excessive.

Submerged vanes. Submerged vanes are instream structures which are designed to promote bed scouring by developing secondary circulation in the flow (Fig. 6.9) (Hey 1992). They are submerged even at low flow.

Pools can be created in two ways. The simplest is to install a vane, essentially a large wooden board, at 45° to the bank facing downstream and extending approximately a quarter to a third of the distance across the river. Faster surface flows overspill the vane and create a pool adjacent to the bank. Tree planting may be required to prevent bank failure and meander initiation. Alternatively two vanes can be installed facing upstream at approximately 30° to the flow. Gaps are left between the vanes and adjacent to both banks to allow for the passage of bed material load. Flow spilling over the vanes is directed towards mid-channel and this promotes bed scour.

If required twin-vane systems can be offset towards the banks, to create a series of alternate pools, or asymmetric vanes can be installed to initiate meander development.

Engineering and environmental performance

Non-structural restoration

More and more restoration schemes are being implemented but insufficient time has elapsed for any detailed assessments to be made of their engineering and environmental performance. However, provided appropriate design approaches are adopted (as outlined in Section 6.4), the restored reach should remain stable and maintain the discharge capacity of the river. By reinstating a natural range of habitat features the river will, in time, be recolonized by instream and bankside flora, invertebrates and fish. Experience indicates that this can be very rapid as freshwater crayfish, stone loaches and bullheads were observed to colonize restored riffles on the River Wensum at Lyng, Norfolk, during their construction.

Structural restoration

Weirs. Several authors (White & Brynildson 1967; Everhart *et al* 1975) argue that weirs/dams are really only beneficial in upland rivers which have steep gradients and where tranquil, ponded reaches are rare since lowland rivers are already ponded over considerable distances. However, if the original, undredged river exhibited pools and riffles, then the best restoration strategy is to let nature take its course and re-establish a natural bed topography through the reach.

On a heavily dredged reach of the River Neath at Maes Gwyn is South Wales, where riffles were removed over a 4-km reach of river, a number of blockstone weirs were installed to compensate for the loss of habitat diversity. Many of these were constructed between bends where riffles would naturally be located and, not surprisingly, they have since become submerged by gravel deposits. It should be emphasized that a natural pool-riffle sequence is unlikely to increase flow resistance during flood events, as no flow separation will occur, whereas the weirs may impair channel capacity.

The installation of weirs on rivers that are naturally relatively uniform, or devoid of pools, may be more successful provided they are appropriately located. Spacing of the weirs is critical and should be related to the width of the river as described previously. Provided they are properly spaced, there is the possibility that they will remain relatively sediment free. They are, however, likely to increase frictional resistance, even when they are drowned out at high flows, due to flow separation and, thereby, impair the discharge capacity of the river.

Many lowland rivers are ponded and it is a question of deciding whether fisheries benefits can be gained by installing more weirs. Velocities would be further reduced in the backwater zone, encouraging siltation, and scouring would be confined to the plunge pool below the weir. Anecdotal evidence suggests that the ponded section does improve coarse fish habitats and aeration is improved downstream from the dam. The structures are often constructed from wood, corrugated iron and chicken wire, and, regrettably, are often visually very intrusive. Consequently, consideration needs to be given to improvements in design techniques. The main problem with weirs on lowland rivers is their adverse effect on flood capacity, especially when they collect floating debris.

Deflectors. Wing or bankside deflectors aim to reduce the effective width of the river. As many rivers have been overwidened for land drainage purposes, this technique helps to restore a natural regime width and encourage bankside sedimentation and vegetative recolonization. Often deflectors are located on alternate sides of the river to recreate a natural pool sequence. Spacing the deflectors is crucial if this is to be successful. Where the river is grossly overwidened, there would be merit in constructing a number of deflectors, almost like a series of spur dykes, to restrict the width of the river. In ponded reaches, the channel would need to be constricted quite considerably to create any significant increase in velocity. Consequently it is anticipated that they would only maintain an existing pool in a silt-

free condition. On non-ponded reaches, deflectors may be constructed to scour a new pool as the constriction could cause local ponding and increased head.

There are potential problems with regard to the application of instream deflectors on upland-type rivers. High stream energy and associated bed material transport rates will ensure that the river will rapidly respond to the imposed structures and it is vital that they are located correctly. Essentially they are required to guide and amplify the natural flow pattern along the reach in question in order to increase morphological and hydraulic diversity. On lowland rivers the flow will need to be constricted quite considerably in order to produce the required velocities to cause scouring. This will be particularly the case on ponded reaches where it may only be possible to prevent siltation in an existing pool.

All deflectors adversely affect the discharge capacity of a river, particularly if they are blocked by debris. Before installing any deflectors, geomorphological surveys should be carried out to ensure that they are sited an appropriate distance apart and that they reinforce the natural tendency of the river. Their use in active gravel-bed rivers is probably limited in view of the high bed material transport rates. Due consideration also needs to be given to the height of the deflectors bearing in mind the problems that can arise when they are overtopped.

Environmental design guidelines

River restoration is best achieved using non-structural procedures as the natural character of the river can be recreated. This would involve the reconstruction of pools and riffles and, if necessary, the recreation of meandering channels.

Where lack of space, access or finance prevents re-creation of a meandering channel, or the requirement for heavier engineering works prevents the restoration of pools and riffles, then rehabilitation could be carried out using structural procedures (Table 6.11). On upland-type rivers weirs could be deployed to provide habitat variety in heavily engineered and dredged channels, provided they are fully drowned out during flood conditions. On lowland-type rivers they are

Table 6.11 Engineering and environmental performance of river restoration works

Options	Engineering and environmental performance		Design limitations
	Advantages	Disadvantages	
Non-structural	Natural solution which recreates range of habitats and improves visual amenity. Recreates pools and riffles in dredged section, narrows widened channels, and restores meanders in straightened rivers		*Preferred solution. For straightened channels needs sufficient space to restore meanders*
Structural Weirs	In heavily managed and dredged upland rivers where riffles removed, fish weirs may provide some local habitat variability. In heavily engineered urban upland reaches, weirs can provide some habitat variety and visual improvement	Can impair discharge capacity of river and trap sediment and floating debris	*Blockstone weirs beneficial on heavily engineered and managed upland rivers. On lowland rivers little benefit as long reaches already ponded*
Deflectors	Wing deflectors can create and sustain pools in overwide lowland channels. Can create sinuous course in straight reaches. Increases habitat diversity	A, Y and V deflectors very intrusive and unnatural. In ponded, backwater reaches significant constriction required. Likely to be destroyed on upland rivers. Can impair discharge capacity of channel	*Wing deflectors beneficial on non-ponded lowland rivers*
Submerged vanes	Unobtrusive. Create pools by guiding and amplifying natural scour processes. Increases habitat diversity.		*Simple wooden structures suitable for non-ponded lowland rivers. On upland-type rivers larger blockstone structures required*

unlikely to provide significant habitat improvement as ponded conditions are quite prevalent. Deflectors and submerged vanes are best suited to non-ponded lowland-type rivers as they create a local increase in the energy of the flow by narrowing the river (deflectors) or generate secondary flows (submerged vanes) to cause scouring of the bed.

6.6 FUTURE RESEARCH REQUIREMENTS

Research needs to be carried out to develop and define environmentally sensitive options for flood alleviation and river training. While preliminary results indicate that more natural approaches to river management are preferable to harder engineering solutions on conservation and economic grounds, few if any schemes have been implemented using such procedures to enable comparisons to be made with more traditional options and establish their range of application.

The basic requirement is for field trials to be carried out to evaluate the natural options across a range of river environments. For flood alleviation schemes and bank protection works this would supplement existing information (Hey *et al* 1990, 1991) but for channel stabilization the more natural methods have yet to be implemented and evaluated. Pre- and post-scheme surveys would be required to enable the engineering and environmental performance of each scheme to be assessed for comparison with traditionally designed schemes. In addition the cost-effectiveness of the various options needs to be determined based on both capital and maintenance costs.

Further research is also required to develop river restoration procedures and evaluate the impact and range of application of structural rehabilitation measures. Although more restoration and rehabilitation schemes are now being implemented many of these are based on visual and aesthetic approaches and lack any rigorous scientific base. In addition the lack of any baseline surveys precludes any objective evaluation of their merit.

A number of trials need to be carried out to evaluate natural restoration procedures in both upland and lowland rivers. As the former transport bed material load, their shape and dimensions are closely prescribed and design guidelines need to be strictly adhered to (Hey & Heritage 1993). With the latter there is more flexibility with design options.

Structural approaches to rehabilitate and soften heavily engineered reaches also merit further research, particularly the deployment of submerged vanes as their potential has not been fully evaluated. Attention should be focused on the design and size of each structure in order to create the required habitat, and how this may vary between different types of river, their location in order to be sustainable and their effect on the discharge capacity and stability of the river.

Finally, as all the recommended design procedures are based on knowledge of natural channel processes, it follows that further improvements are dependent on continued basic research.

REFERENCES

Bettess R. (1994) Sediment transport and channel stability In: Calow P, Petts GE (eds) *The Rivers Handbook*, Vol. 2, pp. 227–53. Blackwell Scientific Publications, Oxford. [6.1]

Biedenharn DS, Little CD, Thorne CR. (1990) Effects of low drop grade control structure on bed and bank stability. In: Chang HH, Hills JC (eds) *Hydraulic Engineering*. Proceedings of National Conference on Hydraulic Engineering, ASCE, San Diego, August 1990, pp. 826–31. [6.3]

Blench T. (1966) *Mobile Bed Fluviology*. University of Alberta Press, Edmonton. [6.3]

Brookes A. (1988) *Channelized Rivers*. John Wiley, Chichester. [6.5]

Brookes A. (1994) River channel change. In: Calow P, Petts GE (eds) *The Rivers Handbook*, Vol. 2, pp. 55–75. Blackwell Scientific Publications, Oxford. [6.1]

Einstein HA. (1950) *The Bedload Function for Sediment Transportation in Open-Channel Flow*. US Dept. of Agriculture, Technical Bulletin No. 1026. [6.3]

Everhart WH, Eipper AW, Youngs WD. (1975) *Principles of Fishery Science*. Cornell University Press, Ithaca. [6.5]

Hemphill RW, Bramley ME. (1989) *Protection of River and Canal Banks*. Butterworths, London. [6.4]

Hey RD. (1976) Geometry of river meanders. *Nature* **262**: 482–4. [6.3]

Hey RD. (1986) River mechanics. *Journal of the Institution of Water Engineers and Scientists* **40**(2): 139–58. [6.1, 6.3]

Hey RD. (1987a) River dynamics, flow regime and sediment transport. In: Thorne CR, Bathurst JC, Hey RD (eds) *Sediment Transport in Gravel-Bed Rivers*, pp. 17–37. John Wiley, Chichester. [6.1, 6.2]

Hey RD. (1987b) Regime stability. In: Brandon TW (ed) *River Engineering, Part 1, Design Principles*, pp. 139–47. The Institution of Water and Environmental Management, London. [6.3]

Hey RD. (1992) River mechanics and habitat creation. In: O'Grady KT, Butterworth AJB, Spillett RP, Domaniewski JCJ (eds) *Fisheries in the Year 2000*, pp. 271–85. Institute of Fisheries Management, Nottingham, UK. [6.3, 6.5]

Hey RD, Heritage GL. (1993) *River Engineering Works in Gravel-Bed Rivers*. R & D Project Record 387/1/W, 96, National Rivers Authority Bristol. [6.6]

Hey RD, Thorne CR. (1986) Stable channels with mobile gravel-beds. *American Society of Civil Engineers, Journal of Hydraulic Engineering* **109**(6): 842–51. [6.3]

Hey RD, Heritage GL, Patteson M. (1990) *Design of Flood Alleviation Schemes: Engineering and the Environment*. Ministry of Agriculture, Fisheries and

Food, London. [6.2, 6.5, 6.6]

Hey RD, Heritage GL, Tovey NK, Boar RR, Grant A, Turner RK. (1991) *Streambank Protection in England and Wales*, R & D Note 22, National Rivers Authority, London. [6.4, 6.6]

Hubbs HD, Greeley JR, Tarzwell CM. (1932) Methods for the improvement of Michigan trout streams. *Bulletin of the Institute for Fisheries Research* 1: 1–54. [6.5]

Knauss J, Scheuerlein H. (1988) Erosion control and environmental protection of low slope river ranges with flood plains. *Proceedings of the International Conference on Fluvial Hydraulics '88*, pp. 185–90. Research Centre for Water Resource Development, Budapest. [6.3]

Lane EW. (1937) Stable channels in erodible material. *Transactions of the American Society of Civil Engineers* **102**: 123–94. [6.3]

Odgaard AJ, Mosconi CE. (1987) Streambank protection by submerged vanes. *American Society of Civil Engineers, Journal of Hydraulic Engineering* **113**(3): 520–36. [6.4]

Paice C, Hey RD. (1989) Hydraulic control of secondary circulation in meander bends to reduce outer bank erosion. In: Albertson ML, Kia RA (eds) *Design of Hydraulic Structures 89*, pp. 249–54. A.A. Balkema, Rotterdam. [6.4]

Purseglove J. (1988) *Taming the Flood*. Oxford University Press, Oxford. [6.5]

Raynov S, Pechinov D, Kopaliany Z, Hey RD. (1986) *River Response to Hydraulic Structures*. UNESCO, Paris. [6.1]

Schumm SA, Harvey MD, Watson CC. (1984) *Incised Rivers*. Water Resources Publications, Colorado. [6.3]

Smith RP. (1989) Habitat requirements and distribution of Chub in some rivers in Eastern England. Unpublished PhD thesis, University of East Anglia. [6.5]

Solomon DJ. (1983) *Salmonid Enhancement in North America*. The Atlantic Salmon Trust, Pitlochry, Scotland. [6.5]

Vanoni VA, Brooks NH. (1957) *Laboratory Studies of the Roughness and Suspended Load of Alluvial Streams*. US Army Corps of Engineers, Missouri River Division, Sediment Series No. 11. [6.3]

Visher D. (1986) *Swiss River Training in the 18th and 19th Centuries*. Publication No. 14 of the Hydrology Centre, Christchurch, New Zealand. [6.1]

White RJ, Brynildson OM. (1967) *Guidelines for Management of Trout Stream Habitat in Wisconsin*. Technical Bulletin 39, Department of Natural Resources, Division of Conservation, Wisconsin. [6.5]

Winkley BR. (1982) Response of the Lower Mississippi to river training and realignment. In: Hey RD, Thorne CR, Bathurst JC (eds) *Gravel-Bed Rivers*, pp. 659–81. John Wiley, Chichester. [6.1]

7: Rehabilitation of River Margins

A. R. G. LARGE AND G. E. PETTS

7.1 INTRODUCTION

Since Welcomme's (1979) influential work on the importance of annually-inundated floodplains for sustaining fish production, attention has increasingly focused on the role of river margins in sustaining the biological integrity of both riverine and terrestrial systems (Naiman & Décamps 1990; Lachavanne 1993). Rivers, together with their marginal, ecotonal, systems, provide corridors through the landscape; their margins provide buffers between the watercourse and the variety of land uses within the catchment. However, throughout Europe and North America, this intimate relationship between land and water has been interrupted, degraded, and in extreme cases destroyed, by human activity (e.g. Bravard et al 1986; Petts et al 1989; Dister et al 1990; Petts 1990a). Swift (1984) has catalogued the nationwide loss of riparian habitat in the USA, estimating that of 75–100 million ha only 25–35 million ha remain. Rehabilitation of river margins has two important roles in river management: (i) to enhance values of nature conservation, and (ii) to improve water quality. This section assesses the benefits for river management of preserving, rehabilitating and restoring river margin ecosystems.

The spatial context

A river corridor comprises active and abandoned channels, the aquatic margins of these channels, the riparian zones along the channel banks and any floodplains. Although complicated by the legacy of climatic change over the Quaternary, and longer time-scales in some cases, and by the effects of neotectonic activity and human interference, a river may be viewed as a longitudinal continuum changing in a more or less predictable way from source to mouth (Vannote et al 1980). Along this continuum, the corridor can be seen to comprise a changing set of soil/vegetation patches – patches of different type and of different age that reflect the underlying geomorphological structure (Salo 1990; Petts 1990a; Cummins 1992).

For simplicity, the river continuum may be divided into three primary zones. First, headwater channels – first- to third-order streams – may be viewed as the production zone: the major source area tapping water, solute and sediment supplies from the hillslopes. Secondly, the middle river, or transfer zone, is characterized by high environmental heterogeneity and high species richness. Thirdly, the lowland floodplain river represents the depositional or storage zone. Rivers of fourth order and above are usually isolated from adjacent hillslopes by the river margin systems, which become especially important along reaches with major floodplains, although throughout the temperate zone, and increasingly elsewhere, these are the reaches that have been most severely impacted by human activity. The potential for managing river margins will differ in each of these three main zones of the river network.

7.2 THE CASE FOR RIVER MARGINS IN RIVER MANAGEMENT

The protection, rehabilitation and restoration of river margins should have a high priority in catchment-based river management. River margins have a range of important characteristics

Table 7.1 The role of riparian vegetation in natural river ecosystem dynamics (after Large & Petts 1992)

Primary roles	Functions addressed
Provision of important habitats for flora and fauna	High biological diversity High biological productivity Source for species dispersal
Regulation of ecosystem dynamics	Influence movement and migration of fauna Control surface runoff Regulate sub-surface flows Provide organic matter to the river Store water
Enhancement of visual quality and amenity value	
Enhancement of ecological patch diversity of floodplain rivers	Incorporate a range of habitat patches, especially small woods, cut-off channels and wetlands of different successional stages

(Table 7.1) typical of ecotonal systems (Naiman & Décamps 1990). The case for including river margins in river management is based on the four key functions: (i) water-quality control; (ii) nature conservation; (iii) instream habitat enhancement; and (iv) recreation and amenity. Functions (i) and (iii) are most effective within Zone 1 whereas functions (ii) and (iv) offer opportunities for environmental enhancement throughout river networks.

River margins for water-quality control

In temperate situations, it has been clearly demonstrated that riparian buffer zones, particularly those with organic-rich riparian soils, can significantly reduce the concentration of nutrients in surface water and groundwater entering streams (Howard-Williams et al 1986; Cooke & Cooper 1988; Pinay & Décamps 1988; Fustec et al 1991), and more specifically influence the quality of water passing from agricultural systems into the aquatic system (Haycock & Burt 1990, 1991).

Grassed buffer zones can reduce sediment-bound phosphorus and nitrogen inputs to streams by 80–87% and groundwater nitrate inputs by more than 90% (Smith et al 1989; Cooper 1990). Alluvial forests are known to play a particularly important role in reducing diffuse-source pollution (Labroue & Pinay 1986; Welsch 1991). Rhodes et al (1985) found nitrate removal from Zone 1 streams in the Sierra Nevadas to be 99% through uptake by riparian forests and wetlands. In one case study of the effectiveness of forested wetlands, along the Rhode River, Maryland, USA, Peterjohn and Correll (1984) found annual removal of nitrate-N was of the order of $45 \, kg \, ha^{-1} \, yr^{-1}$ in subsurface runoff and 11 kg particulate organic-N in surface runoff. Thus, Peterjohn and Correll concluded that coupling natural systems and managed habitats within river basins may effectively reduce diffuse-source pollutions.

Three primary processes are active in controlling water quality in areas of semi-natural vegetation along river margins.

1 Retention through interception of sediment-bound nutrients, pesticides and other contaminants transported by surface runoff, which is particularly important in the case of phosphorus.

2 Uptake by vegetation or microbes of soluble nutrients – the primary process for nitrate removal.

3 Absorption by organic and inorganic soil particles.

However, the key parameter is the flow path (Hill 1990; Haycock 1991). Groundwater flow is rarely perpendicular to the channel flow, and the effect of variable permeability of floodplain sediments influencing oblique pathways means that actual retention times of groundwater are often greater than expected. Furthermore, channelled surface runoff may pass rapidly through buffer zones during storm runoff and care needs to be taken to ensure that buffers are not by-passed by pollutant transport pathways (Osborne & Wiley 1988; Risser 1990).

River margins for wildlife conservation

River margins provide both important habitat and linear connecting corridors through the landscape. The importance of the interaction between geomorphology and vegetation in floodplain environments for maintaining biotic diversity has been displayed (Bravard *et al* 1986; Salo *et al* 1986; Amoros *et al* 1987b; Pautou & Décamps 1989; Castella *et al* 1991; Greenwood *et al* 1991; Petts *et al* 1992). Furthermore, recent research has clearly demonstrated the need to consider river corridors as three-dimensional systems, especially where deep valley fill deposits create major alluvial aquifers (see *Regulated Rivers* Special Issues 6.4 and 7.1). In such systems, Stanford and Ward (1988), for example, have pointed to the importance of the hyporheic zone (the interstitial habitat influenced by surface water–groundwater interactions) of floodplains for maintenance of invertebrate diversity.

Animals

River margins are especially important for mammals, reptiles and amphibians (e.g. Brinson *et al* 1981; Cross 1985; Dickson & Huntley 1985) and river margins support some of the richest terrestrial vertebrate faunas (Risser 1990). With respect to large mammals, particular attention has been given in North America to the beaver (Naiman *et al* 1988) and in Europe to the otter (MacDonald & Mason 1983).

Birds. Much attention has focused on breeding-bird densities (Anderson & Ohmart 1977; Johnson *et al* 1977; Knopf 1985; Knopf *et al* 1988; Triquet *et al* 1990) because the loss of river margin systems can severely impact bird populations. Thus, Hehnke and Stone (1978) have described how the removal of riparian vegetation along the Sacramento River resulted in 95% fewer birds and 32% fewer species.

Fish. Many authors describe the value of hydraulically-diverse river margins for fish (e.g. Copp 1989). Along large Zone 3 rivers, especially those in the tropics with a predictable flood season, fish productivity is highly correlated with flood magnitude and the area inundated (e.g. Welcomme 1979; Copp & Penaz 1988). Thus, Bayley (1991) defined the 'flood-pulse advantage' as the amount by which annual multi-species fish yield exceeds that from a system lacking annual flood-plain inundation.

Riparian zones to protect instream habitats

Riparian vegetation is especially important in determining instream habitats in Zone 1 streams, providing shade, cover and organic debris. The input of particulate organic matter (mainly twigs and leaves) has been established as being particularly important for aquatic ecosystems, especially invertebrate populations (e.g. Bilby & Likens 1980; Gregory 1992), since organic carbon is the most important fuel for running-water food webs (see Hildrew 1994). The provision of shade, regulating instream temperatures and limiting growth of macrophytes and algae, is also an important function of riparian vegetation (e.g. Burton & Likens 1973; Karr & Schlosser 1977). Thus, in the UK, the Salmon Advisory Committee (1991) have described the introduction of riparian buffer zones as an attainable benefit of an integrated approach to catchment management. They conclude that the benefits of such an approach would include (i) allowing bankside vegetation to develop to provide cover; (ii) provision of food in the form of invertebrates; (iii) reduction of fine solid material; (iv) reduction of the risk of chemical pollution; and (v) reduction of the input of fertilizers.

Recreation and amenity

In river corridors two features particularly influence landscape quality: the existence of the land–water interface and its degree of naturalness (see Petts 1990b; Cosgrove & Petts 1990). Diversity (i.e. 'patchiness') and nature conservation interest are also important.

Researchers in both the UK and the USA (Sweep *et al* 1985; Simcox & Zube 1989; Cook 1991; Green & Tunstall 1992) highlight positive public attitudes towards preservation of multiple-use river corridor amenities including wildlife habitat, riparian vegetation and open space. Thus, multi-purpose management functions have been advocated for riparian areas in lowland, urban and upland situations (Budd *et al* 1987; Cohen *et al* 1987; Rinne 1990), stressing the aesthetic and recreational potential of such areas, as well as their role in water quality and erosion control.

7.3 PROCESSES INFLUENCING NATURAL RIVER MARGINS

The degree of heterogeneity is an important feature of the riparian ecotone. In the natural situation, such heterogeneity is determined mainly by flow variability, topography (i.e. elevation in relation to river level), sediment permeability, and the frequency of destructive events (floodplain erosion and channel cut-off). It is the geomorphological structure of the river margin that provides the template for the operation of other physical, chemical and biological processes.

Geomorphological processes

Natural river margins consist of a complex mosaic of patches of different type, size and age (Plate 7.1, facing p. 112 and Table 7.2) that reflect

Table 7.2 Vegetation types mapped using remote sensing and large-scale mapping of the alluvial plain of the lower River Ain (from Roux 1986)

Patch number	Dominant vegetation type present
A Patches at the aquatic–terrestrial interface	
26	*Phalaris arundinacea*
9	*Phragmites australis, Urtica dioica, Calystegia sepium*
12	*Phragmites australis, Scirpus lacustris*
17	*Urtica dioica*
24	*Melilotus alba*
26	*Phalaris arundinacea*
B Patches with shallow ground water-tables, inundated for lengthy periods	
13	*Salix viminalis, S. triandra*
14	*Alnus incana, A. glutinosa, Ulmus minor*
16	*Salix alba, Carex acutiformis*
20	*Salix alba, Salix triandra*
21	*Salix alba, Impatiens glandulifera*
28	*Salix alba, Phalaris arundinacea*
36	Diverse *Salix* spp.
45	*Salix elanganos*
55	*Bromus erectus*
69	*Salix alba, Alnus glutinosa*
C Patches with deeper water-table and less persistent inundation than group B	
7	*Quercus robur, Populus alba, Carex pendula*
21	*Salix alba, Impatiens glandulifera*
29	*Ulmus minor*
31	*Fraxinus excelsior*
32	*Populus nigra*
43	*Bromus erectus*
48	*Fumana procumbens*
57	*Crataegus monogyna*
62	*Poa trivialis, Dactylis glomerata* (pasture)

the geomorphological setting. The development of riparian systems through time is part of a directional sequence known as the reversible process concept (Amoros *et al* 1987a,b) within which the directional sequences are rejuvenated by erosion, deposition and flood disturbance. Of sediment reaching streams, 29–93% is stored in alluvial wetlands (Phillips 1989a). Although progressive sedimentation leads to terrestrialization and a loss of wetland habitat, new 'wet' habitat is created by channel cut-off and lateral migration elsewhere along the river sector so that, over time, optimal areas for particular fauna shift to different parts of the hydrosystem. Periodic replacement of older soil-vegetation complexes by pioneer patches (e.g. gravel or sand deposits) leads to an increase in both the biodiversity and the primary biological productivity of these systems.

Hydrological processes

Flooding is important in providing seasonal connectivity both between the different components of the drainage network and locally between patches, and in stimulating biological responses. Morphological and physiological adaptations directly related to flooding and waterlogging occur in riverine plants and collectively these adaptations determine a species' success in different moisture conditions (Ernst 1990). These adaptations are mainly concerned with the change of several of the nutrients present from an oxygenated to a reduced state. Life cycles of many fish species are also highly adapted to changes of flow: in temperate rivers salmonids require freshets to stimulate upstream migration (Fraser 1972) and many tropical fish are highly adapted to the predictable annual flood (Welcomme 1979; Bayley 1991).

Biogeochemical processes

Plant growth in waterlogged soils may be greatly affected by reduced minerals such as ammonium, manganous and ferrous ions, and sulphide (Ernst 1990; Laanbroek 1990). The length of the waterlogged period will influence the necessary physiological adaptations to these chemically reduced states. The principal effect of flooding is to reduce primary production in terrestrial species in the riparian and floodplain zone as these can only use CO_2 as a carbon source (whereas aquatic plants can utilize HCO_3^-). A feature of actively growing aquatic plants is that they release generally between 1 and 10% of their photosynthetically-fixed carbon to the water in the form of dissolved organic compounds (Carpenter & Lodge 1986).

In terms of nutrient dynamics, riparian wetlands can be described as valves (Kibby 1978), taking in nutrients in spring and early summer and releasing them in late summer and autumn. With regard to phosphorus for example, the rate of uptake correlates with measures of metabolic activity (see Newbold 1994), with the phosphorus content of leaf detritus then increasing during decomposition. The significant removal of nitrate in wetland soils is long evident in the literature (Lee *et al* 1975; Patrick & Reddy 1976; Richardson *et al* 1978). Flooding provides an input of organic carbon into the system, fuelling denitrification processes within anoxic floodplain soils (Cooper *et al* 1987). The ability of semiaquatic communities characterized by high transpiration to absorb large quantities of water, assisting in absorption of nutrients, is also important here (Pautou & Décamps 1989), with accumulation of nitrogen in nitrate form during winter in soils with less waterlogging (Pinay *et al* 1989). Vegetation uptake will retain nitrate in the summer period, as denitrification is often lowest at this time of year (Ambus & Lowrance 1991) due to aeration of the soil.

7.4 RIVER MARGINS AS BUFFER ZONES FOR RIVER MANAGEMENT

It is the ecotonal qualities of natural river margins that have particular value for river and landscape management (Petts 1990b). Protection, rehabilitation and restoration of river margins can be partially achieved by using 'structural' measures but will be fully realized only if the appropriate flow variability and geomorphological instability are sustained.

Table 7.3 Some recommended widths for naturally-vegetated zones to enable ecosystem functions to be carried out in river margins

Function	Study	Relevant details	Recommended width (m)
Wildlife protection	Brown *et al* (1990)	Provision of food, water, cover	99–169
	Rabeni (1991)	Fish, amphibians, birds	7–60
	Newbold *et al* (1980)	Invertebrate populations	>30
	Brinson *et al* (1981)	Mammals, reptiles, amphibians	200
	Stauffer & Best (1980)	Breeding bird communities	11–200
	Budd *et al* (1987)	Organic debris provision	15
	Cross (1985)	Small mammals	9–20
Fisheries protection	Williamson *et al* (1990)		10 < 20
	Karr & Schlosser (1977)		
Streambank stability	Erman *et al* (1977)	Low order streams	30
	Rabeni (1991)		<5
Water-quality control	Ahola (1989, 1990)	General improvement	50
	Hoek (1987)	As above	150
	Rabeni (1991)	As above	Various
	Pinay & Décamps (1988)	As above	1–2
	Keskitalo (1990)	As above	30
	Pinay & Décamps (1988)	As above	Narrow
	Peterjohn & Correll (1984)	Nitrate control	20–30
	Correll & Weller (1989)	As above	30
	Rhodes *et al* (1985)	As above	1–2
	Peterjohn & Correll (1984)	Phosphorus control	
	Smith *et al* (1989)	As above	
Sediment control	Rabeni (1991)	US State Legislation	23–183.5
	Brown *et al* (1990)	As above	213
	Peterjohn & Correll (1984)	Nutrient control	19
	Erman *et al* (1977)	Control stream turbidity	30
	Budd *et al* (1987)		15

Structural characteristics of river margins

Minimal area and shape of wildlife habitat are important determinants of species productivity, and this is especially true in relation to the narrow, linear habitat of stream corridors (Diamond 1975; Simberloff 1976). In the urban situation, management strategies need to protect food resources and include a corridor concept connecting fragmented habitat to larger rural populations (Greer 1982). Décamps *et al* (1987) found that avian species richness increased following fragmentation of the riparian corridor, but studies reviewed by Brinson *et al* (1981) suggest that 5–6-ha riparian habitat 'islands' are needed to support near maximum bird diversity, with larger areas required to support raptors. However, in terms

of cost, restoration of a large contiguous river-floodplain area may be more cost-effective than restoring a similar area comprising smaller, disjointed areas along the river (Bayley 1991). Recommended dimensions of buffer zones are given in Table 7.3.

Continuity of the buffer zone is an important variable, not least if optimum management of riparian and instream biota is to be achieved. In one example, Dawson (1978) has outlined a plan where trees are planted along the south side of a stream to provide shade, but gaps of approximately 20 m are left at 70-m intervals to permit instream primary production, especially macrophyte growth, which provides shelter for invertebrates and fish and is an important source of autochthonous detritus. Certainly along floodplain rivers, the buffer zone should be a mosaic of patches rather than a continuous strip, thus maximizing heterogeneity.

Buffer width for water-quality control

In some studies, the recommended buffer width to protect wildlife habitat has depended on the extent of groundwater draw-down and the slope of the groundwater table. Where groundwater pollution is a major problem, wider buffer zones are required. Work in the Netherlands (van der Hoek 1987) has discussed the disappearance of vulnerable and rare plant species due to eutrophication of groundwater, recommending a buffer zone of 150 m to improve groundwater flow, and to increase floristic diversity in the riparian fringe.

With reference to specific width recommendations to achieve the function of water-quality control, a fairly narrow riparian strip can be highly effective (Table 7.3). In a study in France, a 30-m width of alluvial forest was shown to be sufficient to remove all nitrate with denitrification of up to 50 mg of $N_2 m^{-2}$ day^{-1} being observed (Pinay & Décamps 1988). However, not all studies point to definite trends towards an increase in water quality. Studies in the eastern USA have concluded that the 23-m buffer zone width provided for in State legislation is inadequate for non-point pollution removal and recommend instead an 80-m width, particularly in estuarine situations (Phillips 1989b).

US Department of Agriculture recommendations for minimum widths to minimize sedimentation problems in streams range from 23 m for coarse sand to 138.5 m for silt, concluding that control over clay sedimentation cannot be met by buffers alone but requires wider-scale land management strategies. Buffers have been shown to fail in specific cases due to channelization influences (Dillaha *et al* 1986), and some sediment will almost certainly be remobilized during high flows and flood events; most, however, may be retained for a prolonged period of time (Lowrance *et al* 1986).

Overall there is wide variability in the effectiveness of buffer zones, with a range of 15–80 m being appropriate for various land/soil/vegetation complexes in riparian situations (Phillips 1989c). The pollutant-holding characteristics of emergent aquatic and wetland vegetation has been exploited in another way through the construction of artificial wetlands, and these may be particularly useful as barriers to protect streams from well-defined sources, such as drains and ditches, or any first/second-order stream (e.g. Hammer 1989).

Wildlife criteria

The size, arrangement and connectivity of patches depend on the geographical setting and should give due regard both to the nature of the natural riparian zone and to the existing features of the proposed buffer. The relationship between patches is especially important as a particular target species could be sustainable in a relatively small area if it is found in association with, or connected to, certain other patches. The factors which need, therefore, to be addressed in any scheme for ecological enhancement or river restoration include both the minimum area and configuration necessary to retain both plant and wildlife values in different riparian habitats, as well as the maximum distances which can separate islands of given habitat type before adverse effects to, and even loss of wildlife species or populations occur (Johnson *et al* 1977; Knopf *et al* 1988). In addition, the optimal as well as minimal requirements for enhancing wildlife values for a given habitat type (e.g. plant species type and cover) need to be determined in addition to information relating to their resilience under unfavourable conditions. Quite small seminatural and natural patches on the floodplain have the potential to act as refugia (Sedell *et al* 1990; Large *et al* 1994). These patches can be defined as conveying spatial or temporal resistance or resilience to biotic communities impacted by biophysical disturbances.

Rabeni (1991), in a review primarily focusing on water quality protection, but also including habitat values for wildlife, quotes examples of mandatory buffer widths in the USA. Widths were shown to vary from 1.5 m (for forested streams in Idaho) to 92 m (in Wisconsin). Between these bounds there is a wide variation in buffer

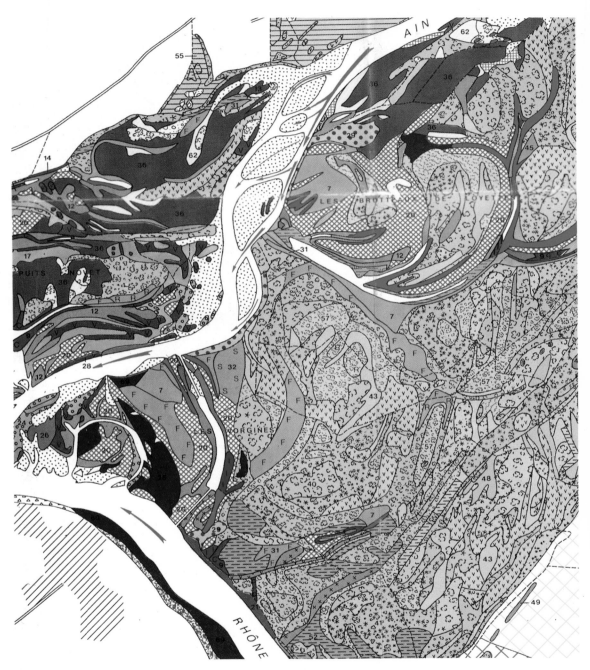

Plate 7.1 Vegetation patch mosaic within the corridor of the River Ain at the Rhone confluence, France. Vegetation patches (defined in Table 7.2) reflect the underlying geomorphological structure. Patches are of different type and age. Provided by J. Girel, University of Grenoble, and C. Amoros, University of Claude Bernard, Lyon.

[*facing page 112*]

width, even in those recommended for similar land uses in different States. In Iowa, bird species diversity has been found to increase with increasing width of wooded riparian habitats (Stauffer & Best 1980) but Brinson *et al* (1981) showed most mammal, reptile and amphibian species to concentrate within 60 m of the edge of the stream. In the USA, the Washington Department of Ecology (1981) found wildlife habitat to extend beyond the stream bank a minimum of 27.4 m into the upland areas of the river corridor. Relatively wide buffers are required to provide sufficient habitat for riparian wildlife and plants and to function as wildlife corridors linking larger areas of riparian habitat (Rabeni 1991), a feature also seen in discussions of buffer zones for wildlife protection in east central Florida (Brown *et al* 1990).

River margins and fluvial processes

Vegetation has been shown to exert significant control over fluvial processes in five main ways: flow resistance, flow interruption by log jams, interception and storage of sediment, bank strengthening, and concave bank bench deposition (Hicken 1984; Gregory & Gurnell 1988). Vegetation exerts a particularly important control on bank erosion rates (Hemphill & Bramley 1989) but in general there is little information available to show how wide buffers need to be specifically for bank protection. Whipple *et al* (1981) found a correlation between buffer width and bank stability, while for low-order north California streams, Erman *et al* (1977) found 30-m vegetated buffers adequate for controlling bank erosion.

Corridor restoration

In order to effectively implement restoration, attention needs to be paid to the already-existing 'natural' and semi-natural communities present along river margins. In Germany, Arnold *et al* (1989) have argued for at least the creation of 'pocket-sized' wet biotopes and for the broadening of floodplain to at least five times the width of the main channel for any ecological improvement to be possible through re-creation of meanders, riparian forests and meadows. In the UK this aspect relating to riverine plant communities has become more topical with the introduction in the 1980s of detailed river corridor surveys (Gardiner 1991), which have complemented other works discussing distribution of herbaceous and woody riparian vegetation along a series of studied reaches in both upland and lowland situations (Mason *et al* 1984; Curry & Slater 1986; Mason & MacDonald 1990).

Individual conflicts arise. In discussing the benefits of riparian trees for ecological management of watercourses in the UK, Mason *et al* (1984) urge replanting or encouraging natural regeneration of *Quercus* species, *Acer pseudoplatanus* and *Fraxinus excelsior*. The mature root systems of these species provide secure holts for otter, but these trees are rejected as unsuitable by the engineer, as their horizontal root systems permit undercutting of the channel bank. A balance has therefore to be struck by planting a strategic mix of both vertical and horizontal rooting species. Elsewhere some workers advocate setting aside strips of land uncultivated (Newbold & Rush 1989; Nature Conservancy Council 1991), while others, for example Risser and Harris (1989) in the USA, discuss use of specific riparian species to restrict recreation access to sensitive areas as well as improving degraded wildlife habits and improving bank stability.

7.5 PRACTICAL IMPLEMENTATION OF RESTORATION

River margins have considerable ecological importance throughout the drainage network providing (i) buffer zones between the terrestrial and aquatic systems, and (ii) corridors through the landscape. However, research on river margins highlights four key points. First, river margins have an important vertical dimension extending from the subsurface groundwater zone, to the above-ground vegetation structure. Thus, Anderson *et al* (1978) discuss the importance of re-vegetating riparian floodplain areas for wildlife, with vertical foliage density being positively correlated with the number of species in an area. Secondly, the replacement of naturally-occurring riparian woody species with commercial crop alternatives can lead to loss of both species abundance and diversity in riparian areas (Geier &

Table 7.4 Design options for integrated catchment management incorporating river margins

Zone	Ecological significance
1 Production zone	Buffer *zones* significant in maintaining the quantity and quality of the river flows downstream, and for conserving running-water habitats, as well as providing conservation areas in their own right. Bank stability is also improved by increasing vegetation cover. Buffers act as barriers to eutrophication of small streams
2 Transfer zone	*Strips* provide important linear habitats, not only within the riparian fringe but also along the channel margin, including shading and cover for fish. Floodplains can occur here and will be geomorphologically active. Buffers can aid channel stability in these cases
3 Storage zone	Riparian *strip* has important ecological value but considerable opportunities exist for environmental enhancement in former floodplain areas by managing *patches* for nature conservation

Best 1980). Thirdly, a significant feature of river margin systems is their inherently dynamic nature (Naiman & Décamps 1990), a property that has direct implications for river restoration and management. Fourthly, the primary reasons for river margin restoration differ in relation to location within the drainage network: water-quality control is the primary role in headwater systems and nature conservation becomes most important along larger rivers. Table 7.4 summarizes design options for integrated catchment management using restored river margins.

Headwater streams

All vegetated river margins act as buffers between land and water ecosystems and have benefits for water-pollution control, but several water-quality problems, such as pollution by nutrients such as nitrates, phosphates or pesticides, relate to diffuse sources and require management within the headwater production zone.

Land management practices on hillslopes can affect river water-quality in four ways: via over-land flow, shallow subsurface flow, pipe flow and deep subsurface flow. Buffer zones can be very effective where problems are caused by diffuse overland flow or shallow subsurface flow. However, they may be by-passed by channelized surface runoff, pipe flow or deep subsurface flow. In many lowland areas the vegetated buffer could be by-passed by flow in under-drains. New drain designs and the incorporation of reconstructed wetlands and catch-water systems to intercept

pipe flow, are being investigated to overcome this problem.

To maximize their effectiveness, all streams and ditches within the production zone need to be bounded by buffer zones; this represents a considerable length of channel. One alternative option is to combine buffer zones along second- and third-order streams with the creation of wetlands and/or storage ponds to intercept flow from first-order streams and ditches. Constructed wetlands and reed beds have been advocated as land-treatment alternatives in sewage systems for removal of biochemical oxygen demand (BOD) and solids leading to downstream improvement of water quality (e.g. Gersberg *et al* 1984a,b; Burka & Lawrence 1990; Upton & Griffin 1990). Although some studies show the potential of these schemes for nitrogen removal is uncertain (Bayes *et al* 1989), others (Boyt *et al* 1977; Tilton & Kadlec 1979; McIntyre & Riha 1991) demonstrate that constructed vegetated riparian areas have distinct potential for water-quality control. In relation to seasonal factors, leakage, especially of phosphorus, may occur (Richardson 1985; Mann 1990; Vanek 1991) following senescence and decomposition of the plant material. However, this can be controlled by maintenance through harvesting of biomass and, in extreme cases, removal of saturated sediment.

Middle and lower river

In the mid-channel situation, vegetated buffers will have value for water quality but their main

Fig. 7.1 Components of a rehabilitated river margin (after Petts 1990b): (1) channel with restored pattern and bedform; (2) restored riparian zone (see Chapter 9); (3) flood berm excavated and planted to create new wetlands; (4) flood embankments set well back from the river's edge; (5) additional embankment set away from river to create (6) emergency flood control channel and/or floodplain lake with link to main channel controlled by sluices, weirs or gated ducts.

role would be for environmental enhancement. Even narrow riparian strips along riverbanks having little management are important for many species, and would markedly improve the conservation value along river reaches that are currently cultivated up to the channel banks. The value of buffer zones for environmental enhancement increases directly with habitat diversity. Along the channel margin of the floodplain river, primary habitats of gravel bars, sandbanks, eroding banks in alluvium, cut-off channels and backwaters linked to the main channel are of particular value. While these habitats have been severely affected by recent and historic river management, studies of remnant patches have demonstrated their considerable importance for nature conservation (e.g. Petts *et al* 1992). Wetland and woodland patches also have particularly high conservation value.

Management requires three distinct levels of

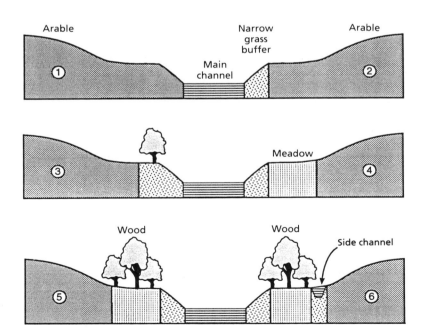

Fig. 7.2 Scenarios for river margin rehabilitation. The functions provided by each scenario are summarized in Table 7.5 (after Large & Petts 1992).

involvement. First, options should be considered to sustain the hydrological and geomorphological processes that determine the ecology of the river margin, riparian zone and floodplain. Secondly, management should seek to maintain the diversity of patches within the buffer zone. Finally, it is necessary to develop an ecologically sustainable maintenance programme to maximize the structural and sustainable functional characteristics. The structural components of ecologically sensitive, artificial river margins are illustrated in Fig. 7.1.

The landscape scale

Buffer zones fulfil a number of functions in the riparian landscape. These include increasing biotic diversity and enhancing the nature conservation value of the riparian zone and reducing water-quality problems both above ground in surface flows and groundwater quality. The benefits to bank stability and increase in water storage capability increase as the complexity of the buffer design increases. Attendant improvements in recreation potential and aesthetic quality can also be achieved.

Figure 7.2 illustrates different types of rehabilitated river margin which are suitable for use in a range of situations. Table 7.5 shows the functions achieved by the different buffer types. These range from the situation where no buffer is present and the adjacent land uses impact directly on the aquatic system (Scenario 1), to the situation where an ecologically diverse buffer incorporating a range of habitat types and including wetland patches has been established in the river corridor (Scenario 6).

A situation where no buffer is present (Scenario 1) scores zero for the seven functions outlined. Many floodplains have old channels cutting across them, often at the base of the hillslope. Such channels act as natural interceptors for surface and subsurface runoff from cultivated hillslopes and should be exploited, perhaps by dredging to create wetland areas for diffuse-source pollution control and conservation. With full restoration of floodplain function, including use of old channel courses, a range of vegetation patches to enhance biotic diversity and to aid control of both surface and subsurface runoff, scores for each of the functions can be maximized (Scenario 6).

Minimizing the flood problem

The major perceived disadvantage of river margin restoration is reduction in flood control. In several instances, the increasing hydraulic roughness of the channel margin and adjacent floodlands has been raised as an argument for *not* enhancing the ecological quality of river corridors. Any ecological advantages provided by a

Table 7.5 Functions carried out by vegetated buffer strips and patches in the riparian landscape. Scenarios range from no buffer present (1) to ecologically-complex protection mechanism (6). Maximum scores allocated in each scenarios represent the optimum management attainable using a structure of that type. This will not necessarily correspond to 100% efficiency in practice

Function	Maximum score	Scenario: increasing buffer complexity (score)					
		1	2	3	4	5	6
Biotic diversity/environmental enhancement	3	0	0/1	1/2	1/2	2	3
Overland flow control	3	0	1	1	2	3	3
Subsurface flow control	3	0	0	0/1	0	1 < 3	3
Bank stability	3	0	1	2	1	3	3
Water storage capability	3	0	0	1	1/2	3	3
Recreation provision	3	0	1	2	2	3	3
Aesthetic value	3	0	1	2	2	3	3

continuous belt of riparian forest could be outweighed by enhanced flood problems. However, the feasibility of using land adjacent to a river for flood storage and the use of the patch concept for environmental enhancement could minimize these problems. The ecological benefits of a series of small patches, connected by ditches, floodways, wetlands or grassland, designed to minimize hydraulic resistance at the landscape scale, would be considerable. In such situations the buffer zone may be visualized as a series of patches that should be connected but may appear as a 'string of beads' (Large & Petts 1992) in a landscape sense.

Longer-term maintenance

In any plan for managing river margins, commitment to habitat maintenance is obviously important and this is especially so if the natural hydrological and geomorphological dynamics that determine the natural disturbance regime cannot be fully restored. Without maintenance the conservation value may actually become quite depressed through internal competition reducing floristic diversity. Planning is required to ensure that any such maintenance is minimal, but this planning needs to be set in a long-term context. In reality, the maintenance of river margins may simply involve the redistribution of costs from current maintenance programmes.

Particular attention needs to be paid to the potential problem of invasion by undesirable species (Brock *et al* 1993). For example, *Impatiens glandulifera*, *Reynoutria japonica* and *Heracleum mantegazzianum* are examples of vascular species which have proved to be a problem along the waterways of England and Wales. Leaving areas fallow along the margins of waterways will provide potential sites for invasion, and thus a programme of continued management to prevent colonization will need to be implemented in areas where spread of such species is a potential threat.

Year-round management of water regime and the vegetation structure therefore is essential to maintain the effectiveness of any buffer for water quality. Decomposition processes and nutrient release in freshwater and wetland systems have a strong seasonality (e.g. Brinson 1977; Polunin 1982, 1984). Furthermore, in unmanaged riparian buffer zones, nutrient release may occur due to senescence and decomposition of the vegetation *in situ*.

With regard to the spiralling of phosphorus, for example, wetland systems tend to be quite leaky with a significant release from the dead plant community throughout the year (Magette *et al* 1989; Dillaha & Hayes 1991). There is also evidence to suggest that some floodplain wetlands used as a sink for phosphorus in time will become ineffective, releasing phosphorus back into circulation in the system. Examples of other problems are: (i) that some vegetated zones may not be efficient enough through nitrate uptake to reduce significantly the nitrate load during the growing season; (ii) that soil waterlogging may not be long enough to provide the anaerobic conditions for denitrification of sufficient duration to reduce loads; and (iii) that organic carbon provided by flood events and through litter fall may not be sufficient to sustain microbial respiration necessary for denitrification. Long-term effects of near-stream vegetation in reducing stream nutrients may be enhanced if buffers are used in conjunction with other practices, such as timing nutrient applications on a wider catchment basis to maximize uptake by crops and minimize loss to the aquatic system.

7.6 PROSPECT

To be effective, restoration of river margins requires legislation at governmental level to encourage landowners to set land aside for enhancement of the conservation value of the riparian zone and the river corridor in general. It has been shown that putting arable land over to grass as part of a set-aside programme is of value for nature conservation. Along larger rivers, such a policy might require arable land to be converted to grassland on all floodplain and former floodplain areas within a statutory distance of the channel bank. This distance could be fixed, a function of channel width or stream order, or based on historic flooding or channel migration (as determined from old maps and field observation).

In Europe, Dister *et al* (1990) have described the reduction of habitat on the Rhine floodplain by transformation of floodplain forests into monoculture plantations, and call for 'renaturalization' quoting the changing nature of EEC policy as a spur for implementation. Management perspectives based on isolated components of the catchment are ecologically incomplete. Phillips (1989d) recommends management in the context of the catchment rather than discrete units, and Lowrance *et al* (1985) conclude that management must occur on a catchment-by-catchment basis Nilsson *et al* (1988) highlight the fact that each river has largely unique features. However, thus far in the area of resource management, more emphasis has been placed on gathering information than on effective and efficient use of available information for decision-making and problem-solving. This is especially true with respect to whole-catchment management.

Whilst attempting to maintain the integrity of land–water interactions in otherwise altered catchments (Karr & Schlosser 1978), management must remain within the constraints posed by multiple-use objectives for the catchment (Ward & Stanford 1989). River margins have important benefits for society and progress in catchment management could be achieved by developing a programme of river margin rehabilitation. The starting point is to conceptualize river margins as the primary ecotone between the aquatic and terrestrial systems. Along many rivers of the temperate zone only a thin strip of natural vegetation remains due to a long history of fluvial landscape management. Nevertheless, these fringing zones along with small, presently isolated, wetland and woodland patches can act as refugia for flora and fauna already at the limits of their ecological tolerance limits. In many cases these refugia will provide logical starting points for rehabilitation programmes.

REFERENCES

Ahola H. (1989) Vegetated buffer zone project of the Vantaa River river basin. *Geografisk Tidsskrift* **89**: 22–5. [7.4]

Ahola H. (1990) Vegetated buffer zone examinations of the Vantaa river basin. *Aqua Fennica* **20**: 65–9. [7.4]

Ambus P, Lowrance R. (1991) Comparison of denitrification in two riparian soils. *Soil Science Society of America Journal* **55**: 994–7. [7.3]

Amoros C, Rostan J-C, Pautou G, Bravard J-P. (1987a) The Reversible Process Concept applied to the environmental management of large river systems. *Environmental Management* **11**: 607–17. [7.2, 7.3]

Amoros C, Roux AL, Reygrobellet JL, Bravard J-P, Pautou G. (1987b) A method for applied ecological studies of fluvial hydrosystems. *Regulated Rivers: Research and Management* **1**: 17–36. [7.2, 7.3]

Anderson BW, Ohmart RD. (1977) Vegetation structure and bird use in the Lower Colorado River Valley. In: Johnson RR, Jones Jr DA (eds) *Importance, Preservation and Management of Riparian Habitat: a Symposium*, pp. 23–4. USDA Forest Service General Technical Report RM-43. [7.2]

Anderson BW, Ohmart RD, Disano J. (1978) Revegetating the riparian floodplain for wildlife. In: Johnson RR, McCormick JF (eds) *Strategies for Protection and Management of Floodplain Wetlands and Other Riparian Ecosystems*, pp. 318–31. USDA Forest Service, General Technical Report WO-12. [7.5]

Arnold U, Höttges J, Rouvé G. (1989) Removing the strait-jackets from rivers and streams. *German Research* **1**: 22–4. [7.4]

Bayes CD, Bache DH, Dickson RA. (1989) Land-treatment systems: design and performance with special reference to reed-beds. *Journal of the Institution of Water and Environmental Management* **3**: 588–97. [7.5]

Bayley PB. (1991) The flood-pulse advantage and the restoration of river-floodplain systems. *Regulated Rivers: Research and Management* **6**: 75–86. [7.2, 7.3, 7.4]

Bilby RE, Likens GE. (1980) Importance of organic debris dams in the structure and function of stream ecosystems. *Ecology* **61**: 1107–13. [7.2]

Boyt FL, Bayley SE, Zoltek J. (1977) Removal of nutrients from treated municipal wastewater by wetland vegetation. *Journal of the Water Pollution Control Federation* **49**: 789–99. [7.5]

Bravard J-P, Amoros C, Pautou G. (1986) Impact of civil engineering works on the successions of communities in a fluvial system: a methodological and predictive approach applied to a section of the Upper Rhône River. *Oikos* **27**: 92–111. [7.1, 7.2]

Brinson MM. (1977) Decomposition and nutrient exchange of litter in an alluvial swamp forest. *Ecology* **58**: 601–9. [7.5]

Brinson MM, Swift BL, Plantico RC, Barclay JS. (1981) *Riparian Ecosystems: Their Ecology and Status.* US Fish & Wildlife Service FWS/OBS 82/17. [7.2, 7.4]

Brock JH, Childs LE, de Waal LC, Wade PM. (eds)

(1993) *Ecology and Management of Invasive Aquatic Plants*. John Wiley & Sons, Chichester. [7.5]

Brown MT, Schaefer J, Brandt K. (1990) *Buffer Zones for Water, Wetlands and Wildlife in East Central Florida*. Center for Wetlands Publication 89-07, University of Florida, Gainsville. [7.4]

Budd WW, Cohen PL, Saunders PR, Steiner FR. (1987) Stream corridor management in the Pacific Northwest, I. Determination of stream corridor widths. *Environmental Management* **11**: 587–97. [7.2, 7.4]

Burka U, Lawrence PC. (1990) A new community approach to waste treatment with higher water plants. In: Cooper PF, Findlater C (eds) *Constructed Wetlands in Water Pollution Control*, pp. 359–71. Pergamon Press, Oxford. [7.5]

Burton TM, Likens GE. (1973) The effect of strip-cutting on stream temperatures in the Hubbard Brook experimental forest, New Hampshire. *BioScience* **23**: 433–5. [7.2]

Carpenter SR, Lodge DM. (1986) Effects of submersed macrophytes on ecosystem processes. *Aquatic Botany* **26**: 341–70. [7.3]

Castella E, Richardot-Coulet M, Roux C, Richoux P. (1991) Aquatic macroinvertebrate assemblage of two contrasting floodplains: The Rhône and Ain Rivers. *Regulated Rivers: Research and Management* **6**: 289–300. [7.2]

Cohen PL, Saunders PR, Budd WW, Steiner FR. (1987) Stream corridor management in the Pacific Northwest. II. Management strategies. *Environmental Management* **11**: 599–605. [7.2]

Cook EA. (1991) Ecosystem modeling as a method for designing synthetic fluvial landscapes: a case study of the Salt River in Arizona. *Landscape and Urban Planning* **20**: 291–308. [7.2]

Cooke JG, Cooper AB. (1988) Sources and sinks of nutrients in a New Zealand hill pasture catchment. III. Nitrogen. *Hydrological Processes* **2**: 135–49. [7.2]

Cooper AB. (1990) Nitrate depletion in the riparian zone and stream channel of a small headwater catchment. *Hydrobiologia* **202**: 13–26. [7.2]

Cooper JR, Gilliam JW, Daniels RB, Robarge WP. (1987) Riparian areas as filters for agricultural sediment. *Soil Science Society of America Journal* **51**: 416–20. [7.3]

Copp GH. (1989) The habitat diversity and fish reproductive function of floodplain ecosystems. *Environmental Biology of Fishes* **26**: 1–27. [7.2]

Copp GH, Penaz M. (1988) Ecology of fish spawning and nursery zones on the flood plain, using new sampling approach. *Hydrobiologia* **169**: 209–24. [7.2]

Correll DL, Weller DE. (1989) Factors limiting processes in freshwater wetlands: an agricultural primary stream riparian forest. In: Sharitz RR, Gibbons JW (eds) *Freshwater Wetlands and Wildlife*, pp. 9–23. USDoE Symposium Series 61. [7.4]

Cosgrove D, Petts GE (eds). (1990) *Water Engineering and Landscape*. Belhaven. London. [7.2]

Cross SP. (1985) Responses of small mammals to forest riparian perturbations. In: Johnson CD et al (eds) *Riparian Ecosystems and Their Management: Reconciling Conflicting Land Uses*. USDA Forest Service General Technical Report RM-120, Fort Collins, Colorado. [7.2, 7.4]

Cummins K. (1992) Catchment characteristics and river ecosystems. In: Boon PJ, Calow P, Petts GE (eds) *River Conservation and Management*, pp. 125–36. John Wiley & Sons, Chichester. [7.1]

Curry P, Slater FM. (1986) A classification of river corridor vegetation from four catchments in Wales. *Journal of Biogeography* **13**: 119–32. [7.4]

Dawson FH. (1978) Aquatic plant management in semi-natural streams: the role of marginal vegetation. *Journal of Environmental Management* **6**: 213–21. [7.4]

Décamps H, Joachim J, Lauga J. (1987) The importance for birds of the riparian woodlands within the alluvial corridor of the River Garonne, SW France. *Regulated Rivers: Research and Management* **1**: 301–16. [7.4]

Diamond JM. (1975) The island dilemma: lessons of modern biogeographic studies for design of natural reserves. *Biological Conservation* **7**: 129–46. [7.4]

Dickson JG, Huntley JC. (1985) Streamside management zones and wildlife in the South Coastal Plain. In: Johnson CD et al (eds) *Riparian Ecosystems and Their Management: Reconciling Conflicting Uses*. USDA Forest Service General Technical Report RM-120, Fort Collins, Colorado. [7.2]

Dillaha TA, Hayes PE. (1991) *A Procedure for the Design of Vegetative Filter Strips*. US Soil Conservation Service. [7.5]

Dillaha TA, Sherrard JH, Lee D. (1986) *Long-Term Effectiveness and Maintenance of Vegetative Filter Strips*. Virginia Water Resources Research Centre Bulletin No. 153. Blaksburg, Virginia. [7.4]

Dister E, Gomer D, Obrdlik P, Petermann P, Schneider E. (1990) Water management and ecological perspectives of the Upper Rhine's floodplains. *Regulated Rivers: Research and Management* **5**: 1–15. [7.1, 7.6]

Erman DC, Newbold JC, Roby KB. (1977) *Evaluation of Streamside Buffer Strips for Protecting Aquatic Organisms*. California Water Resources Center, University of California, Davis, California. [7.4]

Ernst WHO. (1990) Ecophysiology of plants in water-logged and flooded environments. *Aquatic Botany* **38**: 73–90. [7.3]

Fraser JC. (1972) Regulated discharge and the stream environment. In: Oglesby RT, Carlson CA, McCann JA (eds) *River Ecology and Man*, pp. 263–86. Academic Press, New York. [7.3]

Fustec E, Mariott A, Grillo X, Sajus J. (1991) Nitrate

removal by denitrification in alluvial groundwater: role of a former channel. *Journal of Hydrology* **123**: 337–54. [7.2]

Gardiner JL. (1991) *River Projects and Conservation: A Manual for Holistic Appraisal.* John Wiley & Sons, Chichester. [7.4]

Geier AR, Best LB. (1980) Habitat selection by small mammals of riparian communities: evaluating effects of habitat alterations. *Journal of Wildlife Management* **44**: 1–16. [7.5]

Gersberg RM, Elkins BV, Goldman CR. (1984a) Wastewater treatment by artificial wetlands. *Environmental Science and Technology* **17**: 443–50. [7.5]

Gersberg RM, Elkins BV, Goldman CR. (1984b) Use of artificial wetlands to remove nitrogen from wastewater. *Journal of the Water Pollution Control Federation* **56**: 152–6. [7.5]

Green CH, Tunstall SM. (1992) The amenity and environmental value of river corridors in Britain. In: Boon PJ, Calow P, Petts GE (eds) *River Conservation and Management*, pp. 425–42. John Wiley & Sons, Chichester. [7.2]

Greenwood MT, Bickerton MA, Castella E, Large ARG, Petts GE. (1991) The use of Coleoptera (Arthropoda: Insecta) for patch characterisation on the floodplain of the River Trent, UK. *Regulated Rivers: Research and Management.* **6**: 321–32. [7.2]

Greer DM. (1982) Urban waterfowl population: ecological evaluation on management and planning. *Environmental Management* **6**: 217–29. [7.4]

Gregory KJ. (1992) Vegetation and river channel process interactions. In: Boon P, Calow P, Petts GE (eds) *River Conservation and Management*, pp. 225–70. John Wiley & Sons, Chichester. [7.2]

Gregory KJ, Gurnell AM. (1988) Vegetation and river channel form and process. In: Viles HA (ed) *Biogeomorphology*, pp. 11–42. Blackwell Scientific Publications, Oxford. [7.4]

Hammer DA (ed). (1989) *Constructed Wastelands for Wastewater Treatment.* Lewis, Chelsea, Michigan. [7.4]

Haycock NE. (1991) Riparian land as buffer zones in agricultural catchments. Unpublished DPhil Thesis, University of Oxford. [7.2]

Haycock NE, Burt TP. (1990) Handling excess nitrates. *Nature* **348**: 29. [7.2]

Haycock NE, Burt TP. (1991) The sensitivity of rivers to nitrate leaching; the effectiveness of near-stream land as a nutrient retention zone. In: Allison RJ, Thomas DSG (eds) *Landscape Sensitivity*, pp. 261–72. John Wiley & Sons, Chichester. [7.2]

Hehnke M, Stone CP. (1978) Value of riparian vegetation to avian populations along the Sacremento River system. In: Johnson RR, McCormick JF (eds) *Strategies for protection and Management of Floodplain Wetlands and Other Riparian Ecosystems*, pp.

228–35. USDA Forest Service, General Technical Report WO-12, Fort Collins, Colorado. [7.2]

Hemphill RW, Bramley ME. (1989) *Protection of River and Canal Banks.* CIRIA and Butterworths, London. [7.4]

Hicken EJ. (1984) Vegetation and river channel dynamics. *Canadian Geographer* **28**: 111–26. [7.4]

Hildrew AG. (1994) Food webs and species interactions. In: Calow P, Petts GE (eds) *The Rivers Handbook*, Vol. 1, pp. 309–30. Blackwell Scientific Publications, Oxford. [7.2]

Hill AR. (1990) Groundwater cation concentrations in the riparian zone of a forested headwater stream. *Hydrological Processes* **4**: 121–30. [7.2]

Hoek D van der. (1987) The input of nutrients from arable lands on nutrient poor grassland and their impact on the hydrological aspects of nature management. *Ekologia* **6**: 313–23. [7.4]

Howard-Williams C, Pickmere S, Davies J. (1986) Nutrient retention and processing in New Zealand streams: the influence of riparian vegetation. *New Zealand Agricultural Science* **20**: 110–14. [7.2]

Johnson RR, Haight LT, Simpson JM. (1977) Endangered species vs. endangered habitats: a concept. In: Johnson RR, Jones Jr DA (eds) *Importance, Preservation and Management of Riparian Habitat: a Symposium*, pp. 68–79. USDA Forest Service General Technical Report RM-43, Fort Collins, Colorado. [7.2, 7.4]

Karr JR, Schlosser IJ. (1977) *Impacts of Nearstream Vegetation and Stream Morphology on Water Quality and Stream Biota.* EPA-600/3-77-097. Environmental Research Laboratory, Environmental Protection Agency, Athens, Georgia. [7.2, 7.4]

Karr JR, Schlosser IJ. (1978) Water resources and the land–water interface. *Science* **201**: 229–34. [7.4, 7.6]

Keskitalo J. (1990) Occurrence of vegetated buffer zones along brooks in the catchment area of Lake Tuuslanjärvi, South Finland. *Aqua Fennica* **20**: 55–64. [7.4]

Kibby HV. (1978) Effects of wetlands on water quality. In: Johnson RR, McCormick JF (eds) *Strategies for Protection and Management of Floodplain Wetlands and Other Riparian Ecosystems*, pp. 289–98. USDA Forest Service General Technical Report WO-12, Fort Collins, Colorado. [7.3]

Knopf FL. (1985) Significance of riparian vegetation to breeding birds across an altitudinal cline. In: Johnson RR *et al* (eds) *Riparian Ecosystems and Their Management: Reconciling Conflicting Uses*, pp. 105–11. USDA Forest Service General Technical Report RM-120, Fort Collins, Colorado. [7.2]

Knopf FL, Johnson RR, Rich T, Samson FB, Szaro RC. (1988) Conservation of riparian ecosystems in the United States. *The Wilson Bulletin* **100**: 272–84. [7.2, 7.4]

Laanbroek HJ. (1990) Bacterial cycling of minerals that affect plant growth in waterlogged soils: a review. *Aquatic Botany* **38**: 109–25. [7.3]

Labroue L, Pinay G. (1986) Epuration naturelle des nitrates des eaux souterraines: possibilités d'application au réménagement. *Annales Limnologie* **22**: 83–8. [7.2]

Lachavanne J-B (ed). (1993) *Biodiversity in Land/Inland Water Ecotones*. UNESCO-MAB, Paris. [7.1]

Large ARG, Petts GE. (1992) *Buffer Zones for Conservation of Rivers and Bankside Habitat*. R&I Project Record 340/5/Y, National Rivers Authority, Loughborough. [7.2, 7.5]

Large ARG, Prach K, Bickerton MA, Wade PM. (1994) Alteration of patch structure and boundary types on the floodplain of the River Trent, England. *Regulated Rivers: Research and Management* **9**(1). [7.4]

Lee GF, Bentley E, Amundson R. (1975) Effects of marshes on water quality. In: Hasler AD (ed) *Coupling of Land and Water Systems*, pp. 105–27. Springer-Verlag, New York. [7.3]

Lowrance RR, Leonard R, Sheridan J. (1985) Managing riparian ecosystems to control non-point pollution. *Journal of Soil and Water Conservation* **40**: 87–91. [7.6]

Lowrance RR, Sharpe JK, Sheridan JM. (1986) Long-term sediment deposition in the riparian zone of a coastal plain watershed. *Journal of Soil and Water Conservation* **41**: 266–71. [7.4]

MacDonald SM, Mason CF. (1983) Some factors affecting the distribution of otters (*Lutra lutra*). *Mammal Review* **13**: 1–10. [7.2]

McIntyre BD, Riha SJ. (1991) Hydraulic conductivity and nitrogen removal in an artificial wetland system. *Journal of Environmental Quality* **20**: 259–63. [7.5]

Magette WL, Brinsfield RB, Palmer RE, Wood JD. (1989) Nutrient and sediment removal by vegetated filter strips. *Transactions of the American Society of Agricultural Engineering* **32**: 663–7. [7.5]

Mann RA. (1990) Phosphorus removal by constructed wetlands: substratum adsorption. In: Cooper PF, Findlater C (eds) *Constructed Wetlands in Water Pollution Control*, pp. 97–105. Pergamon Press, Oxford. [7.5]

Mason CF, MacDonald SM. (1990) The riparian woody plant community of regulated rivers in eastern England. *Regulated Rivers: Research and Management* **5**: 159–66. [7.4]

Mason CF, MacDonald SM, Hussey A. (1984) Structure, management and conservation value of the riparian woody plant community. *Biological Conservation* **29**: 201–16. [7.4]

Naiman RJ, Décamps H. (eds) (1990) *The Ecology and Management of Aquatic–Terrestrial Ecotones*. Parthenon Publishing, Carnforth. [7.1, 7.2, 7.5]

Naiman RJ, Johnston CA, Kelley JC. (1988) Alteration of North American streams by beaver. *Bioscience* **38**: 753–62. [7.2]

Nature Conservancy Council. (1991) *Nature Conservation and Pollution From Farm Wastes*. Nature Conservancy Council, Peterborough. [7.4]

Newbold C, Rush A. (1989) Set aside and extensification of agricultural production: implications and opportunities for nature conservation and the river engineer. In: *Proceedings of Institute of Water and Environmental Management Annual Symposium, York 1989*. IWEM, London. [7.4]

Newbold JD. (1994) Cycles and spirals of nutrients. In: Calow P, Petts GE (eds) *The Rivers Handbook*, Vol. 1, pp. 379–410. Blackwell Scientific Publications, Oxford. [7.3]

Newbold JD, Erman DC, Roby KB. (1980) Effects of logging on macroinvertebrates in streams with and without buffer strips. *Canadian Journal of Fisheries and Aquatic Sciences* **37**: 1076-85. [7.4]

Nilsson C, Grelsson G, Johnansson M, Sperens U. (1988) Can rarity and diversity be predicted in vegetation along riverbanks? *Biological Conservation* **44**: 201–12. [7.6]

Osborne LL, Wiley MJ. (1988) Empirical relationship between land use/cover and stream water quality in an agricultural watershed. *Journal of Environmental Management* **26**: 9–27. [7.2]

Patrick WH, Reddy KR. (1976) Nitrification–denitrification reactions in flooded soils and water bottoms: dependence on oxygen supply and ammonium diffusion. *Journal of Environmental Quality* **5**: 469–72. [7.3]

Pautou G, Décamps H. (1989) Ecological interactions between the alluvial forests and hydrology of the Upper Rhône. *Archiv für Hydrobiologie* **104**: 13–37. [7.2, 7.3]

Peterjohn WT, Correll DL. (1984) Nutrient dynamics in an agricultural watershed: observations on the role of a riparian forest. *Ecology* **65**: 1466–75. [7.2, 7.4]

Petts GE. (1990a) Forested river corridors – a lost resource? In: Cosgrove D, Petts GE (eds) *Water Engineering and Landscape*, pp. 12–34. Belhaven, London. [7.1]

Petts GE. (1990b) The role of ecotones in aquatic landscape management. In: Naiman RJ, Décamps H (eds) *The Ecology and Management of Aquatic–Terrestrial Ecotones*, pp. 227–62. Parthenon Publishing, Carnforth. [7.2, 7.4, 7.5]

Petts GE, Moller H, Roux AL. (eds) (1989) *Historical Changes of Large Alluvial Rivers: Western Europe*. John Wiley & Sons, Chichester. [7.1]

Petts GE, Large ARG, Greenwood MT, Bickerton MA. (1992) Floodplain assessment for restoration and conservation: linking hydrogeomorphology and ecology. In: Carling P, Petts GE (eds) *Lowland Floodplain Rivers: Geomorphological Perspectives*, pp. 217–34.

John Wiley & Sons, Chichester. [7.2, 7.5]

Phillips J. (1989a) Evaluation of North Carolina's estuarine shoreline area of environmental concern from a water quality perspective. *Coastal Management* **17**: 103–17. [7.3]

Phillips J. (1989b) Nonpoint source pollution risk assessment in a watershed context. *Environmental Management* **13**: 493–502. [7.4]

Phillips J. (1989c) Non-point source pollution control effectiveness of riparian forest along a coastal plain river. *Journal of Hydrology* **110**: 221–37. [7.4]

Phillips J. (1989d) Fluvial sediment storage in a wetland. *Water Resources Bulletin* **25**: 867–73. [7.6]

Pinay G, Décamps H. (1988) The role of riparian woods in regulating nitrogen fluxes between the alluvial aquifer and surface water: a conceptual model. *Regulated Rivers: Research and Management* **2**: 507–16. [7.2, 7.4]

Pinay G, Décamps H, Arles C, Lacassin-Seres M. (1989) Topographic influence on carbon and nitrogen dynamics in riverine woods. *Archiv für Hydrobiologie* **114**: 401–14. [7.3]

Polunin N. (1982) Processes contributing to the decay of reed (*Phragmites australis*) litter in fresh water. *Archiv für Hydrobiologie* **94**: 182–209. [7.5]

Polunin N. (1984) The decomposition of emergent macrophytes in fresh water. *Advances in Ecological Research* **14**: 115–66. [7.5]

Rabeni CF. (1991) *Buffer Zones for Riparian Zone Management: A Literature Review.* Department of the Army, New England Division, Corps of Engineers, Waltham MA. [7.4]

Rhodes J, Skau CM, Greenlee D, Brown D. (1985) Quantification of nitrate uptake by riparian forests and wetlands in an undisturbed headwaters watershed. In: Johnson RR *et al* (eds) *Riparian Ecosystems and Their Management: Reconciling Conflicting Uses*, pp. 175–9. USDA Forest Service General Technical Report RM-120. [7.2, 7.4]

Richardson CJ. (1985) Mechanisms controlling phosphorus retention capacity in freshwater wetlands. *Science* **228**: 1424–7. [7.5]

Richardson CJ, Tilton DL, Kuclee JA, Chamie JDM, Wentz AW. (1978) Nutrient dynamics of northern wetland ecosystems. In: Good RE, Whigham DF, Simpson RL (eds) *Freshwater Wetlands: Ecological Processes and Management Potential*, pp. 217–42. Academic Press, New York. [7.3]

Rinne JN. (1990) The utility of stream habitat and biota for identifying potential conflicting forest land uses: Montane riparian areas. *Forest Ecology and Management* **33**: 363–83. [7.2]

Risser PG. (1990) The importance of land/land-water ecotones. In: Naiman RJ, Décamps H (eds) *The Ecology and Management of Aquatic–Terrestrial Ecotones*, pp. 7–22. Parthenon Publishing, Carnforth. [7.2]

Risser RJ, Harris RR. (1989) Mitigation for impacts to riparian vegetation on western montane streams. In: Gore J, Petts GE (eds) *Alternatives in Regulated River Management*, pp. 235–65. Boca Raton Press. [7.4]

Roux AL. (1986) *Recherches Interdisciplinaires sur les Ecosystemes de la Basse-plaine de l'Ain, France. Potentialities Evolutives et Gestion.* Laboratoire de Biologie Végétale, Saint-Martin d'Hères. [7.3]

Salmon Advisory Committee. (1991) *Factors Affecting Natural Smolt Production.* Ministry of Agriculture, Fisheries & Food, Lowestoft. [7.2]

Salo J. (1990) External processes influencing origin and maintenance of inland water–land ecotone. In: Naiman RJ, Décamps H (eds) *The Ecology and Management of Aquatic–Terrestrial Ecotones*, pp. 37–64. Parthenon Publishing, Carnforth. [7.1]

Salo J, Kalliola R, Häkkinen I, Mäkinen Y, Niemelä P, Puhakka M, Coley PD. (1986) River dynamics and the diversity of Amazonian lowland forest. *Nature* **322**: 254–8. [7.2]

Sedell JR, Reeves GH, Hauer FR, Stanford JA, Hawkins CP. (1990) Role of refugia in recovery from disturbances: modern fragmented and disconnected river systems. *Environmental Management* **14**: 711–24 [7.4]

Simberloff DS. (1976) Island biogeography theory and conservation practice. *Science* **191**: 285–6. [7.4]

Simcox DE, Zube EH. (1989) Public value orientations toward urban riparian landscapes. *Society and Natural Resources* **2**: 229–39. [7.2]

Smith CM, Williamson RB, Cooper AB. (1989) Riparian retirement: the effects on streambank stability and water quality. In: *Changing Times. Proceedings of the New Zealand Soil and Water Conservation Annual Conference*, pp. 27–35. Nelson, New Zealand. [7.2, 7.4]

Stanford JA, Ward JV. (1988) The hyporheic habitat of river ecosystems. *Nature* **335**: 64–6. [7.2]

Stauffer DF, Best LB. (1980) Habitat selection by birds of riparian communities: evaluating effects of habitat alterations. *Journal of Wildlife Management* **44**: 1. [7.4]

Sweep D, Zilincar JM, Smith B, Hardy R. (1985) Integration of riparian management strategies within the context of multiple land management programs in southwestern Wyoming. In: Johnson RR *et al* (eds) *Riparian Ecosystems and Their Management: Reconciling Conflicting Uses*, pp. 371–3. USDA Forest Service General Technical Report RM-120, Fort Collins, Colorado. [7.2]

Swift BL. (1984) Status of riparian ecosystems in the United States. *Water Resources Bulletin* **20**: 223–8. [7.1]

Tilton DL, Kadlec RH. (1979) The utilization of a freshwater wetland for nutrient removal from secondarily treated wastewater effluent. *Journal of Environmental Quality* **8**: 328–33. [7.5]

Triquet AM, McPeek GA, McComb WC. (1990) Song-bird diversity in clearcuts with and without a riparian buffer strip. *Journal of Soil and Water Conservation* **45**: 500–3. [7.2]

Upton J, Griffin P. (1990) Reed bed treatment for sewer dykes. In: Cooper PF, Findlater C (eds) *Constructed Wetlands in Water Pollution Control*, pp. 391–8. Pergamon Press, Oxford. [7.5]

Vanek V. (1991) Riparian zone as a source of phosphorus for a groundwater-dominated lake. *Water Research* **25**: 409–18. [7.5]

Vannote RL, Minshall GW, Cummins GW, Sedell JR, Cushing CE. (1980) The river continuum concept. *Canadian Journal of Fisheries and Aquatic Science* **37**: 130–7. [7.1]

Ward JV, Stanford JA. (1989) Riverine ecosystems: the influence of man on catchment dynamics and fish ecology. *Canadian Special Publication of Fisheries and Aquatic Sciences* **106**: 55–64. [7.6]

Washington Department of Ecology. (1981) Western Washington urban stream assessment. Washington Department of Ecology, Office of Water Programs. Water Quality Planning. Olympia, WA. [7.4]

Welcomme RL. (1979) *Fisheries Ecology of Floodplain Rivers*. Longmans, New York. [7.1, 7.2, 7.3]

Welsch DJ. (1991) *Riparian Forest Buffers: Function and Design for Protection and Enhancement of Water Resources*. USDA Forest Service. Northeast Area. Report NA-PR-07-91, Radnor, Pennsylvania. [7.2]

Whipple W, DiLouie JM, Pytalr T. (1981) Erosion potential of streams in urbanizing areas. *Water Resources Bulletin* **17**: 36–45. [7.4]

Williamson RB, Smith RK, Quinn JM. (1990) *The Effects of Riparian Protection on Channel Form and Stability of 6 Grazed Streams, Southland, New Zealand*. Water Quality Centre Publication 19, DSIR, Hamilton, New Zealand. [7.4]

8: Restoration of River Corridors: German Experiences

P. LARSEN

8.1 INTRODUCTION

Until the end of the 1970s river training in Germany was based on technical criteria, sometimes supplemented with aesthetic considerations. Emerging public concern for the environment, awakened by works such as Rachel Carson's book *Silent Spring*, first published in 1962, gradually had its impact on the profession and on the water authorities. Around 1980 the first guidelines, instructions and laws regarding 'nature-related river training' and 'maintenance' were issued. The emphasis on 'renaturalization' has now (1992) been strengthened by laws in most of the German states.

The earliest attempts to restore stretches of smaller watercourses were undertaken by enthusiasts, who were looked upon with benevolent amusement by the authorities and by hydraulic engineers. Such projects date back to the 1960s and 70s. Today, ecological criteria are considered on an equal footing with technical criteria.

Much of the information in this chapter is based on experience of river restoration in the southwestern part of Germany. The approach has been developed over the last decade and has proved to be effective in ways that may well make it relevant to other parts of the temperate zone. Restoration of a river corridor requires both the knowledge and the co-operation of specialists representing several disciplines. The approach is necessarily comprehensive because in highly developed and densely populated countries, such as Germany, very little can be left to chance. Its application to other countries would require some modification because of the inevitable variety of regulations, authorities involved, type of watercourse, aim of restoration, economic constraints, etc.

The term 'renaturalization' should be properly interpreted. Even if a 'natural' condition could be defined, the goal of 'back to nature' is usually impossible to reach. People are now and have been for centuries modifying their ecosystem. Not many stretches of the world's rivers could be called natural in their present states. Much effort has already been spent in acquiring knowledge on various aspects of river corridor restoration, but the state of the art is still in its infancy. In Germany, hundreds of kilometres of river channel have been engineered to states that are far from natural. The experience gained so far with their restoration – the reversal of this process – may be useful to planners elsewhere. Planners in countries in which river systems may be in a more natural state should also take note: an ounce of prevention is worth a pound of cure, i.e. protection against degradation will always prove to be more cost-effective and ecologically effective than restoration.

8.2 BACKGROUND TO RIVER RESTORATION IN GERMANY

History of degradation

In many areas, particularly in the industrialized part of the world, rivers and watercourses have undergone progressive changes away from their natural state. Mankind has been attracted to natural waterways to enjoy their scenic value and to use them for fishing, power, transport, waste disposal, etc. Settlements began near rivers. As they grew, many areas that previously had been flooded during high water became more and more densely populated. The resultant protection of these areas reduced the river valley's natural retention of floodwater. Flood peaks downstream were thereby increased, and still further protection was needed for people living in other flood-prone areas. A second major activity, hydropower utilization, often created dams with large storage areas upstream and sections of the river downstream were deprived of normal water flows. Also the discharge of wastes produced different but seriously detrimental effects. Rivers flowing through farmland have been altered to improve drainage and to improve the layout of fields used for crops. Competition in food production led to increases in the usage of fertilizers and of pesticides, causing diffuse loads of pollutants added to those of community wastes. Such activities as these have had far reaching ecological consequences. Figure 8.1 shows, as an example, endangered plant species contained in the German Red Data Book and the causes for their reduction.

The foregoing changes were originally perceived as improvements, but the decisions that led to them were based solely on technical and economic concepts; their planning, some years ago, failed to include proper attention to possible ecological consequences. The result, in many areas, has been serious ecological deterioration, such as reductions in the variety of plant and animal life, and even the extinction of many species. Also, aesthetically pleasing features have been lost: straight channel alignment and geometric homogeneity of cross-section have replaced the winding river with its charming — and ecologically important — contrasts. Rows or groves of trees, which once marked the river path, are gone; natural habitats for birds and animals have been destroyed.

As these consequences became more and more serious, public awareness led to requests, and later to demands, for a more comprehensive consideration of ecological aspects. Public pressures in this direction were probably stronger in West Germany than in any other country; the main reasons were the extensiveness of the rectification

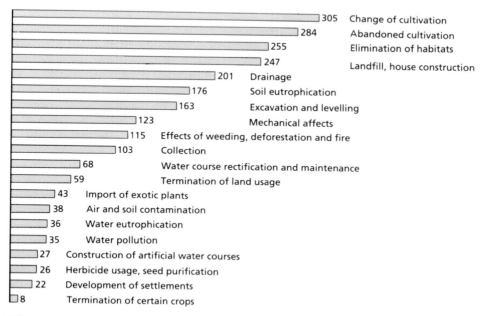

Fig. 8.1 The causes that endanger 711 species (from the *Red Data Book*, Germany) arranged in descending order of the endangering cause. The sum of the figures shown exceeds the number of species because some are endangered by more than one cause. (Source: Bundesforschungsanstalt für Naturschutz und Landschaftsökologie, 1989.)

of running waters and of the reclamation of wetlands that had occurred, the high population density and the generally high standard of living.

History of restoration

In the state of Baden-Württemberg, river restoration projects, primarily those on the Murr river near Stuttgart (Bürkle *et al* 1985), were begun in the 1970s. Guidelines and regulations were issued by the German Association for Water Resources and Land Improvement (DVWK) and by water authorities in several states. In the course of time, the emphasis on naturalization was strengthened by the enactment of legal regulations.

The proposed (1991) modification of the water law of Baden-Württemberg requires that a nature-like condition of the watercourses must be strived for; the conservation and restoration of the ecological function of a watercourse has to be given priority. The natural retention of floodwater must be preserved or increased, and increased discharge capacity is allowed only if important reasons, like the protection of settlements from flooding, can be documented. Those responsible for the maintenance of rivers shall, provided no overriding reasons in terms of such public disadvantages stand against it, convert rectified watercourses into nature-like ones within a reasonable period of time. Their efforts are to be monitored by those water authorities that have the responsibility to enforce compliance.

In the mid-1980s, the Ministry of Environment (then the Ministry of Nourishment, Agriculture, Environment and Forestry) of Baden-Württemberg inaugurated a research project proposed by the Institute of Hydraulic Structures and Agricultural Engineering at the University of Karlsruhe. Its purpose was to obtain information and experience with the renaturalization of the watercourses within the State. Fifteen sections of streams distributed throughout the State were selected as pilot projects, and these are to be executed and monitored during a 10-year period. A few of these projects have reached the monitoring stage, i.e. ecological and morphological consequences of the alterations are being surveyed.

A 2-km section of the River Enz was restored in 1990 after a period of comprehensive planning

and detailed hydraulic model studies. Figure 8.2 shows a part of this section as it looked before, in 1989, and after modification in the summer of 1991. The difference will be even more marked once the vegetation becomes fully developed.

The Danube within Baden-Württemberg, a 160-km stretch of the river between its source and the point where it crosses the boundary with Bavaria, is in various stages of investigation and pre-planning; restoration is the ultimate goal. A 2-km subsection was selected as a pilot project, and detailed planning, including hydraulic model studies, has been carried out. Land adjacent to the river has been purchased and implementation began in 1991.

Also for the biggest river, the Rhine, that flows along the southern and western border of the State, restoration programmes have been established. Thus an Integrated Rhine River Programme covering a reach of about 220 km between Basle and Mannheim and an international programme Salmon 2000, covering the entire river downstream of Lake Constance have been formulated.

In present-day planning of coventional hydraulic projects ecological requirements play a role comparable to those of techniques and costs. Permission for project implementation requires, by law, thorough studies of the environment and the expected impact of the project on it. Regulations often call for proposals of alternative measures to compensate for ecological features that may be lost. These are detailed in the environmental impact assessment law. Binder (1984) presents some examples of projects on the River Lech in Bavaria, in which environmental considerations have played an essential role.

Other German states have undertaken developments similar to those in Baden-Württemberg. Bavaria has been a forerunner in the renaturalization and care of rivers. As part of the Baden-Württemberg research project, a survey of projects in progress or being executed, the state of the art in some of the German states and existing regulations was conducted (Kern & Nadolny 1986). The information thus gained was used in defining goals and methods, and in selecting the 15 pilot sections mentioned above.

All available experience with river restoration

(a)

(b)

Fig. 8.2 A section of the River Enz, Baden-Württemberg, before (a) and after (b) renaturalization.

gained from projects in Baden-Württemberg has been documented, and from the information thus compiled, a guide to river restoration, contained in the same volume, has been prepared (Ministerium für Umwelt 1992).

Components of river restoration planning

The classification of running waters has proved to be an important prerequisite to the process of corridor restoration. The state of Baden-Württemberg contains a large variety of landscapes and types of watercourses. A research project is in progress on two natural units that were selected because they have landscapes of distinctly different characteristics. These are being comprehensively surveyed with the aim of establishing a methodology for stream classification adapted to the requirements of restoration planning. One goal is to typify about 20 varieties of streams in the State, and to do so in such a way that the process does not require undue effort. The results of the research project are compiled in Forschungsgruppe Fliessgewässer 1993 (Bostelmann *et al.* 1993). Following a review of stream classification methodologies the main issues are interdisciplinary characterization of stream types and leitbild development.

An important part of river restoration is to provide for the migration of both fish and invertebrates. Numerous river-training projects have effected longitudinal slope corrections in a stepwise manner by the construction of a series of drop structures, and these often obstruct fish migration. They must be replaced by structures that are passable by fish – gently sloping ramps that are covered with rip-rap made of varying stone size plus a finer substrate. At weirs and dams, by-pass structures with the same function and effectiveness must be provided. A comprehensive research project on this topic has been completed (Gebler 1991). Figure 8.3 shows an appropriate drop structure constructed to replace a vertical, impassable structure in the River Elz. This was one of several full-scale structures designed and tested in that study.

Channelization has caused a reduction in the variety of habitats and the loss of a number of species of both flora and fauna. Figure 8.4 shows the threat to fishes in German waters. Uniform channels that have been constructed cause the substrates to become impoverished and uniform. Deposition of fine material clogs the substrate surface and seals off the paths to deeper layers. Straight channels that eliminate meanders increase the hydraulic gradient and thereby aug-

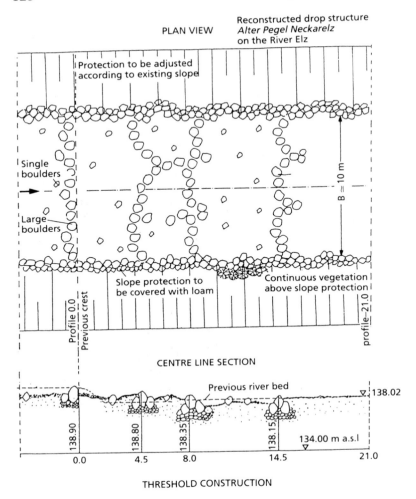

PLAN VIEW   Reconstructed drop structure
                 Alter Pegel Neckarelz
                 on the River Elz

Protection to be adjusted
according to existing slope

Single
boulders

Large
boulders

B ≈ 10 m

Slope protection to
be covered with loam

Continuous vegetation
above slope protection

Profile 0.0
Previous crest

profile 21.0

CENTRE LINE SECTION

Previous river bed

▽ 138.02

138.90   138.80   138.35   138.15   134.00 m a.s.l
                                         ▽

0.0   4.5   8.0   14.5   21.0

THRESHOLD CONSTRUCTION

Selected, large
flatlings

Boulders, largest side
length 0.9–1.2 m

Sub-structure of existing
slope protection stones
d = 25–35 cm
layer thickness > 2d

Existing material
d_{85} = 70 mm

Fig. 8.3 Drop structure
designed to allow passage of the
aquatic fauna.

ment the transport of sediment. Lower bed levels and the accompanying lower water levels cause the groundwater table to be lower also. The capacity of aquifers is diminished and the floodplain wetlands, which contribute to ecological quality with their special habitats, are lost. The intermittent flooding of the floodplains adjacent to a natural river is extremely important to its ecosystem. The lateral exchanges between river and floodplain of inorganic and organic matter, living and dead, are key features of ecosystem dynamics. Dister *et al* (1990) give a number of reasons why

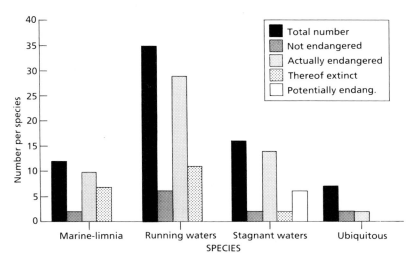

Fig. 8.4 Threat to fishes according to environment (Germany). (Source: Bundesforschungsanstalt für Naturschutz und Landschaftsökologie, 1988–89.)

the inundation of floodplains is so vitally important for balancing out anthropogenic effects.

Where the connection between the main channel and abandoned channels has been closed off spawning possibilities for fish are reduced and exchanges of aquatic life are eliminated. A variety of wetland plants depend for their continued existence on annual inundations, thus an altered succession takes place on previously flooded areas, marked by dying off of existing natural species. Many fishes, not only the salmonids, depend for their existence on migration and movement to refugia. Re-establishment of aquatic life after accidental losses, for example caused by chemical spill, is dependent on the existence of refugia such as marginal backwaters and flood-plain channels.

River regulation that prevents the flooding of the areas outside the main channel precludes this exchange. The two-stage channel, which is favoured by some specialists (e.g. Hey *et al* 1991), has limited value in river corridor restoration. This conclusion is supported by experience with such channels in Germany. They have been constructed in large numbers for decades, and now considerable effort is required to alter them. The limited discharge capacity, accurately determined during engineering hydraulic design, severely constrains the possibilities of renaturalization.

8.3 RESTORATION GOALS

The primary goal of river restoration is to re-establish the variety of habitats required for the natural diversity of biota in and along the river.

Knowledge of the consequences of river construction projects on the environment suggests some important goals for restoration: the primary one is the conservation of nature; the others are water resources management and landscape planning.

Conservation of nature

The re-establishment and preservation of the natural environment is the dominant objective of restoration. However, it is important to define the target end-point (see Chapter 12). A claim that maximum possible species variety should be a central goal must be stated in relative terms: each river is special and the ecology along a given river in its natural state varies with location. Therefore, it is not the species variety *per se*, but the site-specific flora and fauna that should be supported.

The features of dynamic river morphology must be re-established. Artificial bank protection should be eliminated so that streams, where possible, are free to develop their natural courses. The land required for natural channel changes to occur may need to be purchased from the present owners. Exchanges with intermittently inundated floodplains should also occur naturally. Hence, some dikes will have to be removed and, where water levels or grades require adjustment, ecologically compatible structures should be used. In addition the channel capacity has to be reduced to natural conditions to secure frequent flooding of the adjacent wetlands. The natural development of site-specific flora and fauna is based on free migration in and along the river channel. Migration paths, suitable for both fish and invertebrates, must be continuous. The complex ecosystem of a natural river depends not only on the properties of the river channel and its floodplains but also on exchanges with its tributaries. Thus restoration planning requires consideration of some ecological features of the whole river valley.

Water resources management

The primary purpose of flow management is usually the reduction of flooding. Normally a discharge of a certain probability of occurrence, depending on the values of the areas to be protected, determines a maximum discharge up to which flood protection should be guaranteed. Reduction of this design discharge, often a politically determined quantity, can be achieved by increased retention of water, i.e. physically reducing the discharge of a certain probability of occurrence. Also, the broadening of the basis for the balance between costs of flood damage and costs of prevention affects the magnitude of the design discharge. For example, the use of lower values for farmland, a common tendency, works in favour of more retention storage. Also, where the cost of flooding of farmland is the determining factor, a lower design discharge may be selected since reimbursement for flooded crops and other damages will be less.

Determination of the discharge capacity (the flow rate for a given water level) of a renaturalized watercourse to ensure that the design discharge can pass, presents the hydraulic engineer with a difficult problem. Its technical aspects are discussed further in Section 8.5, below. If the groundwater table has been lowered by the degra-

dation of the river bed, it may require corrective actions to raise it again. Any structures installed to raise the water level need also to satisfy the requirement that the aquatic fauna can migrate along the river.

Water quality is, of course, a paramount factor in restoration planning. Although self-purification is enhanced by naturalization, it is not a primary goal of renaturalization. If the water quality is poor because of discharges of wastes from human activities, renaturalization is doomed to fail and any money to be spent on it would be better invested in waste-water treatment.

Improved quality of landscape

Restoration targets can extend from local improvements in appearance near settlements to the renaturalization of a whole stream. Whatever the goal or its extent, the changes made will affect the landscape. Renaturalization should include the creation of areas suitable for human recreation of various kinds. In this task, the conflict between the ecological requirement of undisturbed habitats and that of free human activity must be considered and a suitable compromise be found.

Model image

Even though 'back to nature' is not a realistic objective, a survey of a river's historical development is an important part of planning, as will be explained below. Such studies must include a summary of the recent geological history, natural morphological changes with time, man-made alterations, previous land use and historical changes of vegetation. Information of this kind forms the basis on which to establish a 'model image', i.e. a description of the river as it would have appeared, had it not been subjected to human activities. [The German word *Leitbild* (Kern *et al* 1986), analogous to the word *Leitmotif*, used also in English, describes this concept well.]

The model image serves as a benchmark. It is a description of an idealistic goal that helps to guide the planner. It will normally not be achievable because of a number of constraints caused by irreversible changes of abiotic and biotic factors, and by consequences of cultural ecology. Examples of the former are changes of the runoff regime and the sediment load, and rigid boundaries like bridge crossings and roads, that prohibit lateral movement of the stream bed and thus limit the dynamics of natural morphology. An example of the latter is the extinction of species due to effects of modern agricultural techniques.

8.4 A PROGRAMME FOR RESTORATION PLANNING

The planning of corridor restoration is distinct from engineering river training in that it cannot be limited to the space between the river banks; it must include the entire floodplain. Technical data, such as significant discharges, river stages and sediment properties, make up only part of the information on which such panning should be based. The necessarily more diversified approach requires additional information about geology, morphology, biology, pedology and landscape. The hydraulic engineer, who would traditionally be in charge of such projects, now finds himself to be only one member of a team that includes botanists, limnologists, geologists, geographers and landscape architects.

The planning and execution of a river corridor restoration project includes the following steps:
1 establishment of model image;
2 preliminary assessment;
3 survey and evaluation;
4 pre-design with possible options;
5 final design and acquisition of permits;
6 planning of project execution;
7 construction and supervision.
Obviously, the extent of the various activities will vary in accordance with the actual conditions. The boundaries between the steps are not rigid: some activities may run in parallel. Discussions of each of these steps follow.

Historical maps

A succession of historical maps may help to establish the model image. They may provide not only the present planform of the river, but also its past forms and thus illustrate the mobility of the river bed. Another important source of information is aerial photography, including infrared images; these may reveal previous oxbows and other features that could not be detected by direct observation.

In some cases, where a section of river, either of the same river or of a neighbouring one that flows through a similar natural region, has been left in its natural state or nearly so, its study may provide some of the information required to establish the model image.

Preliminary assessment

In a preliminary assessment, the general situation is assessed to obtain a first indication as to the feasibility of a restoration project. Items to be studied include water quality, availability of land for purchase, boundary constraints like roads and bridges, buried conduits, power cables and land borders. The results of the preliminary assessment should be discussed among representatives of the various authorities and professional disciplines that will be involved, owner associations and, of course, the project sponsor. Based on the assessed need for the restoration and expectation of success the essential goals of the project should be stated and the areas to be included in the project should be agreed upon.

Survey and evaluation

The goals and extent of the project will determine the type and comprehensiveness of field investigations. As distinct from traditional engineering projects, the major tasks are the collection of ecological data and a comprehensive pre-design, comprising various alternatives. An extensive investigation and evaluation of the present environmental conditions is a necessary prerequisite in any restoration of a river corridor. Subdivision of this task into collection of data on the catchment, on the riverine area and on the river, is convenient.

Catchment

The purpose of a catchment inventory is to collect information on *all* factors that influence the ecology and the flow regime in the river corridor to be restored.

Relevant data describe the size of the catchment; the extent of its lakes, climate, geology and relief; and existing natural units, and land utilization (forest, crop fields and pastures, villages and housing developments, sports fields, etc.). Natural and artificial drainage systems with possible waste-water influx should be noted as well as water utilization and hydraulic structures. Also important are existing wetlands, nature reserves, occasionally inundated areas and habitats of special concern.

A substantial part of this information can be obtained from maps – topographical, geological, pedological, and vegetation maps – and from aerial photographs. Inventories made by the water authorities may provide information on water quality, existing water rights, water utilization and water management structures. Field visits and interviews with local residents may help to round off the inventory.

Riverine area

The riverine area is the central object of the restoration; it includes the land that in its natural state was occasionally or regularly flooded, and the stretch of river within it. The purpose of its inventory is to assess the possibility of establishing habitats and their potential for development. Information on natural biotic communities and their development is essential to this process.

The inventory should comprise information on the natural situation: valley morphology, geology, soil types and textures, groundwater table, existing natural vegetation and the potential for other desirable vegetation. It should also include the historical development of the cultivated landscape down to its present state. The latter would include former land use, infrastructure development, dumps and landfills, including those that have been abandoned and possibly covered. Present land use and official plans for future developments are important as regards their possible incorporation into the restoration activities. Accordingly, land ownership, private and public, must be ascertained.

Landscape elements worthy of protection, such as small lakes, ponds, oxbows and wetlands with their specific vegetation, are important components of the inventory. A faunistic survey comprising typical insects, birds and mammals, and of course those species belonging in the *Red Data Book*, is normally part of the survey.

Data should also be included on drainage systems, natural and artificial, on the groundwater table, including its annual variations, and on water protection areas.

The sources of information are much the same as those mentioned above for 'Catchment'. Land ownership can be obtained from land registers and data on groundwater from well observations.

River

Information on the river is needed to perceive its past development, to determine the need for restoration, and to examine limiting conditions that may form constraints on proposals for conservation measures.

The category to which the river belongs needs to be determined in accordance with a standard classification system. Information is collected on previous rectification works, structures for regulation purposes, weirs and dams for water utilization, etc. If possible, morphological changes before human actions changed the state of the river should be documented.

Details of present utilization obviously belong to this inventory. These include waterpower, abstractions, sources of waste water, fishing and other recreational activities. Also necessary is information on hydraulic structures, such as flood control structures, plans for future developments, and ownership of water and fishing rights.

Regarding hydraulic data, discharge values and corresponding water levels at selected sites for significant probabilities of occurrence must be obtained. Water-quality observations include degree of pollution, usually in terms of saprobic level, and types of pollutants and their origins.

The morphological condition of the river channel is characterized in terms of sediment load, aggradation or degradation, boundary stability, substrate types and their structures. The extent of erosion protection and the materials used must be recorded; likewise the tendencies

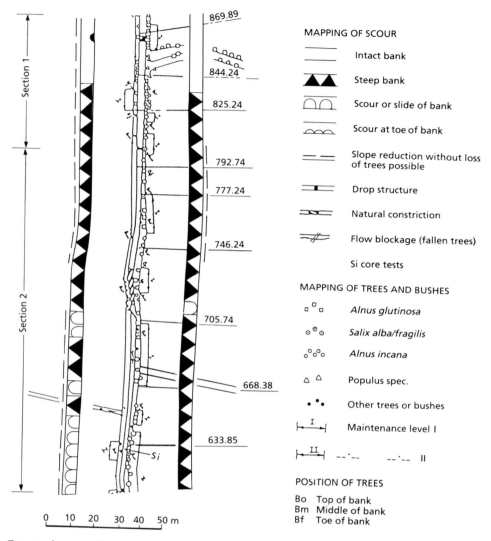

MAPPING OF SCOUR

—————— Intact bank

▲▲ Steep bank

⌒⌒ Scour or slide of bank

⌒⌒ Scour at toe of bank

— — Slope reduction without loss of trees possible

■ Drop structure

⊃⊂ Natural constriction

⫽ Flow blockage (fallen trees)

Si core tests

MAPPING OF TREES AND BUSHES

□ □ □ *Alnus glutinosa*

○ ○ ○ *Salix alba/fragilis*

○○○○ *Alnus incana*

△ △ *Populus spec.*

• • Other trees or bushes

⊢ I ⊣ Maintenance level I

⊢ II ⊣ —·— —·— II

POSITION OF TREES

Bo Top of bank
Bm Middle of bank
Bf Toe of bank

0 10 20 30 40 50 m

Fig. 8.5 Cutout of a map of scour and vegetation along a brook.

for channel alignment to change on unprotected stretches of the riverbanks should be noted.

The report should describe the system for the maintenance of the river, detailing the nature of the works and costs of upkeep; it should also include information on who is responsible for maintenance.

A biological report concludes the survey. It should contain information on fish and inver-

tebrates and on plant communities — in the river, on its banks and on adjacent flood-prone areas.

The huge amount of data collected in the various surveys requires suitable reduction and thorough editing to produce a clear account of the important facts. The explanatory text should be accompanied by a variety of maps. Figure 8.5 shows one such specialized map.

Pre-design with possible options

The facts derived from the evaluation of the survey form the basis for the elaboration of measures that will lead to more nature-like conditions. These are presented in a preliminary design, possibly including alternatives, that is the basis for presentations and discussions of the project with those responsible for it. This should lead to a decision on whether and – if it is a positive decision – how to carry out the project.

The pre-design shall explain the achievable goals and the means of reaching them under the constraints imposed by water management, ecology, engineering and economy. The goals have various time perspectives: immediate, intermediate and long term. The immediate goals are achieved by the engineering and planting operations to be carried out, while the further goals will be achieved through suitable maintenance. Long-term goals, to be reached through immediate operations, and maintenance works, are conceived in terms of the model image described in Section 8.3, above.

An important need is for open discussions of the plans. All parties involved or affected by the restoration measures should be given the opportunity to participate in the deliberations. The reasons for selecting the project layout, its goals and any restrictions, should be clearly presented. Such openness may help to defuse opposition and save considerable time later, particularly in the course of obtaining the implementation permit.

Final design and acquisition of permits

The project option that is chosen in the pre-design phase is further elaborated and described in the text and supplemented by detailed drawings. Since these documents form the basis for the project initiator's final decision and for that of the various authorities regarding the execution permit, they need to be both complete and final. In the case of governmental subsidy, usually the case in Germany, they also constitute the basis for such allocations. If land is to be purchased the information needed for legal procedures comes partly from these documents.

The final design is determined while maintaining close communication among the various specialists and the project initiator. The final design documents comprise: (i) a written report; (ii) a set of drawings; (iii) hydraulic computations; (iv) design and stability analysis of hydraulic structures; (v) cost analysis; and (vi) reports and comments from experts.

Written report. This explains the reasons for, and recounts the deliberations that have led to, the selection of the actual project layout and includes a full description of the project. It also includes lists of measures to be executed, their location on a survey, cross-sections, scour protection measures, planting schemes, expected developments of morphology and vegetation as well as directions regarding future maintenance.

Drawings. The drawings that are included comprise an overall plan view and maps showing design, land requirements, ground acquisition, stock and vegetation, areas under protection, and locations of adjacent agricultural areas on which farming measures are to be modified.

Hydraulic computations. These substantiate the required flood discharge capacity (to be maintained after the vegetation has reached maturity!), expected sediment transport and any measures to resist scour.

Design and stability analyses. These are required for structures used to regulate flow or water levels, such as gently sloping drop structures, fish paths, etc.

Cost analysis. A detailed cost analysis must comprise costs of acquiring land, legal permits, planning, execution (including supervision), materials, plants and expected costs of maintenance.

Expert reports. Reports and comments on the various fields represented by the multidisciplinary team members engaged in the project evolution should be appended to the final design report.

Based on this comprehensive set of information, tender documents can be prepared. These include a time schedule for the various activities, specification of materials to be used and the quality the finished work is to achieve.

Construction

Experience shows that the construction phase also differs from that for conventional engineering projects. The success of restoration depends greatly on the supervisory participation of experts during the execution. For example, excavator operators are accustomed to be guided by straight lines and constant slopes or levels, which are often not suitable for this type of project. If such guidance is not provided, and often it is not, greater understanding and flexibility on the part of the operator is required. He has to work in close co-operation with the designer, who in turn needs to comprehend field practices in some detail. Planting operations must also be supervised by people with horticultural or silvicultural skills, and these people must also know how to work effectively with the contractor. Multidisciplinary co-operation thus prevails throughout all phases of the river corridor restoration project.

Contrary to normal river construction projects, execution of, the restoration proceeds from upstream to downstream. In this way completed areas are essentially spared sedimentation of silt and sludge, brought into suspension during the various operations.

The time schedule of the execution must take account of planting seasons, of expected periods of low discharges and of the possibility of utilizing the winter period.

8.5 HYDRAULIC COMPUTATIONS AND MODEL TESTS

The conveyance capacity of the watercourse is normally required to comply with the stated design discharge, for example Q_{50} or Q_{100}, including a certain allowance for a freeboard. The hydraulic computations are straightforward as far as regular, engineered channels are concerned: experience with such computations is usually available in the form of Manning coefficients for both single-stage and two-stage channels. Backwater computations render reliable relations between stage and discharge for a range of flows.

With natural or renaturalized watercourses the situation is different: little is known about flow resistance caused by vegetation in its varied forms and stages of growth. Considerable effort was invested in laboratory studies in the early and mid-1980s, financed by the German Research Foundation. However, the results have only limited practical value because the tests were performed using simulated bushes or tree trunks in rows, and in channels that were sufficiently long to produce uniform flow. The results are valuable in so far as semi-theoretical models could be developed and checked against them. These rather complicated models have been used to produce computer programs capable of predicting flow resistance under these particular conditions (Pasche 1984; Arnold *et al* 1987). However, their utility is quite limited in studies of actual rivers with groups of trees, irregularly located bushes (Fig. 8.6), patches of rushes, etc. in a channel that is anything but straight and uniform.

The importance of effects due to these types of 'roughness' is illustrated by results of model tests performed in connection with the reconditioning of the Enz, mentioned in Section 8.2 and shown in Figs 8.2 and 8.7. The two-stage channel with a width of about 90 m had a conveyance capacity of $800 \, \text{m}^3 \, \text{s}^{-1}$, far in excess of the design discharge of $450 \, \text{m}^3 \, \text{s}^{-1}$. The freeboard with this discharge was about 1 m in excess of that normally required. Hence, a large increase in flow resistance could be tolerated, even though the reconditioning was to take place only between the flood levees. However, just the process of reshaping the low-stage channel to create 'meanders' and a few islands raised the floodwater level by 0.4 m at the upstream end of the 1.3-km river section. Another 0.6 m of depth was shown to be required to allow for flow resistance caused by short rows of willows, essential for erosion protection, to be planted on alternate sides of the channel. The limited extent of mature willows to be tolerated was determined in the model tests, shown in Fig. 8.7.

The simulation of natural vegetation in model tests is difficult. It requires that a sufficient num-

Fig. 8.6 Group of willows resisting flow (the River Enz, 230 m³ s⁻¹).

ber of field measurements be made to provide calibrations at various discharges. The process could take decades. At present, bushes are simulated by models that essentially block the flow. This is a condition that occurs in nature if debris, brought by the flood flow, catches on the bushes. The advantage of physical model tests is that the model reproduces the combined effects of channel curvature, branching channels, patches of vegetation, etc. At the present state of mathematical modelling, such complexity cannot be accounted for.

The present approach to computing water levels is like that used in model testing: it is assumed that groups of trees or bushes block the flow, and the corresponding cross-sectional areas are subtracted from the flow section. This rather coarse and somewhat subjective method tends to render results that are 'on the safe side', i.e. they overestimate the height of the water level.

An extensive series of model tests with two-stage channels is in progress at the Theodor Rehbock Laboratory, University of Karlsruhe. Their aim is to improve the ability to account for natural flow resistance by providing data on which a Manning roughness coefficient can be estimated by the superposition of the various effects that contribute to the overall resistance. A similar approach is contained in Chow's book (1959) on open channel flow; however, the data on flow resistance due to vegetation are rather limited.

With two-stage channels, where the flood levees cannot be removed, or even displaced, as was the case for the Enz, restoration is essentially limited to measures between the levees. Normally these measures are severely constrained because the carrying capacity was accurately determined in the original design to meet the prescribed flood discharge. In this respect, the Enz, with its excess capacity, was an exception. If the flood levees are not raised, a measure that conflicts with renaturalization, the only way to achieve additional carrying capacity is to lower the floodplains. Increased cross-sectional area, and thus decreased average water velocities, can provide for reshaping the low-stage channel and for limited planting of vegetation whilst still maintaining the necessary capacity to carry the design discharge.

Restoration and renaturalization, for areas not restricted by flood levees, must provide ample areas to carry the flow. The discharge computations, required to show that the watercourse can convey the design flood, must take account of a

Fig. 8.7 Model (scale 1 : 40) of a
section of the River Enz.

Fig. 8.8 Map of Baden-
Württemberg.

future state with fully grown vegetation. Subsequently, maintenance may require thinning of the growth to maintain carrying capacity.

8.6 CASE-STUDY: PLANNING THE RESTORATION OF THE DANUBE IN BADEN-WÜRTTEMBERG

The Baden-Württemberg section of the Danube is an illuminating example of the planning of a river corridor restoration. The Danube originates in the Black Forest (Fig. 8.8). Two tributaries, the Brig and the Bregach, join at the town of Donaueschingen; their junction is the beginning of the Danube. It flows through the Swabian Alb in a deep and narrow valley, geologically a karst region. In this section seepage causes a substantial loss of discharge, a flow that returns to the surface within the catchment of the River Rhine. The Danube then flows along the edge of the Swabian Alb and passes the Bavarian border at the city of Ulm. The distance along the river between Donaueschingen and Ulm is 160 km.

The geomorphology is rather complicated because successive glacial periods have left their marks on the landscape: ancient fluvial systems have eroded the higher ground and transported the sediments down to the valleys. The catchment of the Danube was once much larger and had a much higher sediment yield.

After leaving the Jurassic formation of the Swabian Alb, the river enters rather soft layers of molasses, a fossiliferous sediment found in and near Switzerland. At the edge of the Swabian Alb it again hits resistant Jurassic formations. These almost entirely prevent erosion and lead to gradients of about 0.001. In this section the morphology of the river is similar to that of lowland river; also similar are the widths of the valley and extent of the floodplains.

Figure 8.9 is a map of a section of the Danube, 7 km long, near the town of Blochingen. The path of the river in 1840 and the channel of today are shown, as are numerous traces of oxbows in the floodplain area. Regulation works began in the middle of the 19th century, and they included the cutting off of all meanders along the edge of the Swabian Alb. These changes shortened the river channel by about 20% and increased the gradient accordingly. As a result of the higher gradient, erosion has lowered the bed by as much as 2.5 m in some places during the past 90 years. The water levels dropped by the same amount, and this in turn lowered the groundwater table. The few wetland habitats that had escaped cultivation were thereby further endangered.

Confronted with this undesirable outcome, in 1988 the water authorities embarked on a restoration programme that has gradually been extended to include the entire stretch of the Danube within Baden-Württemberg. The programme is in various stages of completion and includes the implementation of a pilot section. Planning was initiated by selecting a 40-km

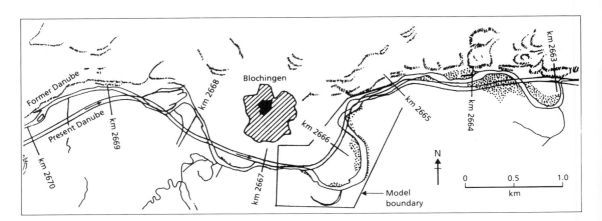

Fig. 8.9 Old map of a stretch of the Danube near the town of Blochingen.

Table 8.1 Project planning schedule for the restoration project of a 40-km section of the Danube (after Kern & Schramm 1988)

Investigation phase					Planning phase	Implementation phase
		Survey and evaluation	(s-e)	*Model image* (m-i)		
Investigations, surveys for planning basis	p-i 1	River morphology	s-e 1	'Old Danube'		
pre-investigation (p-i)	p-i 2	Landscape ecology	s-e 2	m-i 1		
	p-i 3	Water resources management	s-e 3	Deficiencies and restrictions		
	p-i 4	Limnology	s-e 4	m-i 2		
	p-i 5	special investigations	s-e 5			
Planning		pilot project		Concretization of planning goals	*Master planning* m-p	*Planning of specific measures*
		p-p 1		m-i 3	m-p 1	
		p-p 2				
		p-p 3				
		p-p 4				
Implementation	Purchase of land, preferably at the river, former river beds, oxbows, wetlands. Steps toward extensive agriculture, particularly in flood-prone areas					
	Pilot project p-p 5					*Implementation of specific measures, supervision*
Monitoring of development	*Pilot project monitoring of development* p-p 6					*Monitoring of development.* Observation of changes in river morphology, flow regime, groundwater levels, flora and fauna. Survey and data collection of initial conditions after implementation. Possible maintenance measures

Explanations to abbreviations included in Tables 8.2 to 8.6.

section between the towns of Sigmaringen and Zwiefaltendorf and assignments were given to various bureaus and institutes. The Institute of Hydraulic Structures and Agricultural Engineering, University of Karlsruhe, was commissioned to collect the available data and propose a detailed planning procedure for the restoration of the Danube corridor. This proposal resulted in specialist studies listed below. The survey and its partial evaluation are included in a report of 130 pages, of which 50 pages are a record of source material used and information on where it is available. The report essentially follows the outline presented in Section 8.4. The proposed planning schedule included may serve as a con-

Table 8.2 Pre-investigation (p-i)

p-i 1
Compilation of data on water resources management and landscape ecology

p-i 2
Pre-evaluation focusing on river morphology

p-i 3
Task identification; statement of planning goals

p-i 4
Consideration of possible solutions for proper river morphology

p-i 5
Structuring of planning activities

Table 8.3 Pilot project (p-p)

p-p 1
Water resources management and ecological surveys

p-p 2
Project planning; consideration of pilot-project goals

p-p 3
Hydraulic model tests to verify and optimize the design

p-p 4
Presentation of the pilot project to the public, including visit to the hydraulic model

p-p 5
Statutory permits and execution

p-p 6
Development monitoring

Table 8.4 Survey and evaluation (s-e)

s-e 1: River morphology
Survey of the river bed: size distribution of sediment, strata, erodibility, natural armouring
Investigation of sediment budget: sediment transport, sediment balance
Morphological development; information from old maps, etc.
Adoption of sediment transport model: calibration, range of applicability

s-e 2: Landscape ecology
Mapping of present and previous usage of the corridor
Mapping and evaluation of biotopes: wetlands, drylands, other biotopes
Mapping and evaluation of tributaries: morphological features, sediment delivery, water discharge
Mapping of stand characteristics: soil properties, humidity, climate, potential for natural vegetation
Changes in stand properties due to human activities: water management, artificial fertility, reversibility

s-e 3: Water resources management
Investigation of groundwater management; limits on water level
Investigations of flooding and flood protection
Establishment of a register of sewage and waste-water discharges

s-e 4: Limnology
Survey of the Danube, its tributaries and still waters
Chemical and physical parameters
Fish fauna, invertebrates, macrophytes

s-e 5: Special investigations
Potential for re-establishing plant societies
Biotope requirements of (especially) endangered species: grassland birds, fishes, amphibians

densed summary of the report. It lists the various project phases and the activities to be executed in chronological order (Tables 8.1 to 8.6).

The following investigations were included in the survey and evaluation phase concerning the 40-km section:
- analysis of the historical river morphology;
- mapping of riparian vegetation and of ecology of riverbanks;
- physical and chemical parameters;
- insect larvae and fish species;
- weirs and drop structures in respect of migration;
- geohydrological survey;

Table 8.5 Model image: 'old Danube' (m-i)

m-i 1: Description of the old Danube landscape as it appeared at the beginning of the 19th century: river morphology and ecological aspects of landscape
    Watercourse system
    Uses of land and water
    Biotope conditions
    Riverine dynamics
    Assumed species diversity
    Landscape structure

m-i 2: Deficiencies and restrictions
    Deficiencies in comparison with present conditions
    Restrictions due to present usage
    Changes that cannot be reversed

m-i 3: Confirmation of planning goals
    Landscape ecological and landscape planning goals
    Goals for water resources management and river
      morphology

Table 8.6 Master planning (m-p)

m-p 1: Short, intermediate and long-term measures
    Restoration of river morphology along the entire
      Danube section (specification of measures to be
      carried out)
    Restoration of former river courses
    Regeneration of riverine woodlands, typical of the old
      Danube
    Biotope development and interconnection for
      biotopic continuity
    Landscape improvements

- vegetation and land use of the former floodplain;
- selected groups of insects and birds;
- hydrological and hydraulic studies for flood protection.

The last point was added after a devastating flood ravaged the upper Danube in February 1990.

A pilot project, to be implemented in advance, is incorporated in the schedule, and is described in more detail in the following section.

Tables 8.1 to 8.6 constitute a list of activities and measures to be taken throughout the project development, and they are ordered chronologically. This compilation may well serve as a checklist for any river corridor restoration project, with omissions and additions as appropriate in specific cases, of course.

The pilot project

The Institute was asked to prepare a design proposal for a 1.4-km subsection of the Danube and to validate its hydraulic performance through model tests in the Theodor Rehbock Laboratory. The planning of this project, situated downstream of the town of Blochingen (Fig. 8.9), is presented in more detail. Figure 8.9 shows that the short-cutting of a large bend in 1874 shortened the Danube substantially. An aerial view of that section revealed remains of the old channel, partly lined by a row of trees. Only extreme floods, like the one in 1990, show the depressions in the floodplain that mark the former channels. The land between the old channel and the present one has been cultivated, but with little success because of the poor soil – coarse, very permeable fluvial sediments. The high permeability and the low level of the groundwater, lowered as the river eroded, rendered this land quite dry.

What would the 'model image' of this section look like? Morphologically, the soil would pose little resistance to bank erosion; thus the channel could readily shift laterally. Old maps substantiated this trend: once, the channel had moved 100 m in only 30 years. Extreme floods caused short-cuts to occur, leaving oxbows behind, and these eventually were filled in either by siltation or by human activity. In the model, therefore, the river bed would be rather broad with gravel bars and possibly split by islands. The channel would probably carry little more than the annual flood. The water surface and the groundwater level would vary within a limited range just below the level of the floodplain. Nevertheless, the habitats adjacent to the river would be rather dry, except in former oxbows, because of very permeable sediments. The floodplain and the riverbanks would be forested.

What irreversible damage has the river system suffered? What restrictions must be considered in developing a restoration scheme for this section of the Danube? Not much is known about sediment transport in the 'old Danube'. The banks and many of the tributaries have been protected against erosion, and weirs for water-power plants located upstream retain sediments artificially. Consequently, it is reasonable to assume that

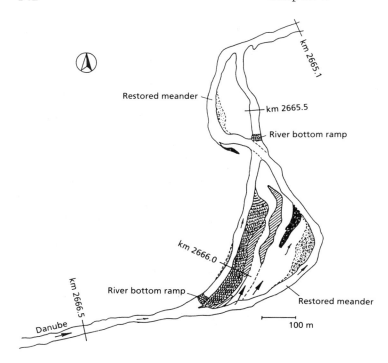

Fig. 8.10 Pilot project layout, adopted solution.

sediment transport has been substantially reduced.

Some formerly endemic fish species are now extinct; other species have been introduced. Water quality is satisfactory, classified as 'less polluted'. Flood protection for the nearby village of Blochingen has to be considered: present flood levels must not be raised.

The solution that was adopted is a river diversion that reactivates the old channel (Fig. 8.10). This included two migratable drop structures in the existing river channel, one at each diversion. The two islands thus formed and the adjacent floodplains will be landscaped with ridges and depressions. No bank protection is to be provided along the new channel and part of that along the existing channel will be removed and used for constructing the gently sloping drop structures.

The hydraulics of this concept were optimized in a model study performed at a scale ratio of 1 to 40 in the Theodor Rehbock Laboratory. The modification raised the water level at mean flow $(24\,\mathrm{m^3\,s^{-1}})$ by almost 1 m. The bed had been lowered through erosion by between 1.1 and 1.3 m in this section of the river and by up to 2.5 m farther downstream. Although the water levels were raised up to a flow of $160\,\mathrm{m^3\,s^{-1}}$, the design permits high flows to pass with lower levels than before. The stage for the 100-year flood $(400\,\mathrm{m^3\,s^{-1}})$ will be 0.3–0.4 m lower at the village of Blochingen. The improved flood conditions helped convince the public to view the project favourably.

The existing (artificial) channel will be used mainly for flood relief; about 75% of the 100-year flood will flow in it. In contrast, the mean flow will pass almost entirely through the restored meanders.

What will be achieved?

• Restoration of the former average water level and unrestricted morphological dynamics in the new channel.

• Raising of water levels for flows of up to $160\,\mathrm{m^3\,s^{-1}}$, which corresponds to the average annual flood.

• Relief for floods higher than the annual flood.

• Channel banks will be able to erode freely; a

strip of land 100 m wide along the outer bank of the meander has been purchased to allow for later movement.

- Control of bed erosion (as deduced from velocities derived from the model study).
- Raising of groundwater levels in riparian areas.
- Improvement of floodplain habitats.
- Improvement of aquatic habitats.

What concessions must be made?

- Drop structures are not typical for the Danube in this section.
- The habitat of the present channel will correspond neither to that in the still water at the oxbows nor to that of free flow of a channel.
- Recolonization of vegetation and fauna will necessarily take place under present-day conditions, rather than under the original ones.
- Costs for restoration are high: the estimated cost for this 1.3-km section is 1.3 million DM.

The project, implemented in 1991, will also be used as a full-scale test model. It includes intensive surveys of the morphological and ecological developments. The experience from this project will serve as a guide to further restoration projects, on the Danube and elsewhere. The government has allocated a budget of 100 million DM for the entire 160 km of the Danube within Baden-Württemberg, and the planning of restoration measures is now in progress.

REFERENCES

Arnold U, Gabrbrecht G, Pasche E *et al.* (1987) *Hydraulische Probleme beim naturnahen Gewässerausbau.* Forschungsbericht DFG, VCH Verlagsgesellschaft mbH, Weinheim Germany. [8.5]

Binder W. (1984) Der Lech zwischen Landsberg und Augsburg – Umgestaltung einer süddeutchen Flusslandschaft in den letzten 100 Jahren. In: *Fluss und Lebensraum.* Verlag Paul Parey. [8.2]

Bostelmann R, Braukmann U, Briem E, Humborg G, Nadolny I, Steib K, Weibel U. (1993) *Forschungsgruppe Fliessgewässer 1993. Fliessgewässertypologie – interdisziplinäre Studien an naturnahen Gewässern und*

Auen in Baden-Württemberg mit Schwerpunkt Buntsandstein-Odenwald und Oberrheinehene. Reihe Umweltforschung Baden-Württemberg, Ecomed Verlag, Landsberg am Lech, Germany, p. 226. [8.2]

Bürkle F, Arnold O, Buck H *et al.* (1985) *Ökologische Untersuchungen an der unteren Murr, Landkreis Ludwigsburg 1977–1982.* Landesanstalt für Umweltsschutz Baden-Württemberg, Karlsruhe. [8.2]

Chow VT. (1959) *Open-Channel Hydraulics.* McGraw-Hill, New York. [8.5]

Dister E, Gomer D, Obrdlik P, Petermann P, Schneider E. (1990) Water management and ecological perspectives of the Upper Rhine's floodplains. *Regulated Rivers, Research and Management* 5(1): 1–15. [8.2]

Gebler R. (1991) *Naturnahe Bauweisen zur Vernetzung von Fliessgewässern.* Mitteilungen Heft 181, Institut für Wasserbau und Kulturtechnik, University of Karlsruhe. [8.2]

Hey RD, Heritage GL, Patteson M. (1991) *Design of Flood Alleviation Schemes: Engineering and The Environment.* Ministry of Agriculture, Fisheries and Food, London. [8.2]

Kern K, Nadolny I. (1986) *Naturnahe Umgestaltung ausgebauter Fliessgewässer – Projectstudie.* Mitteilungen Heft 175, Institut für Wasserbau und Kulturtechnik, University of Karlsruhe. [8.2]

Kern K, Schramm M. (1988) Sanierung der Donau zwischen Sigmaringen und Zwiefaltendorf. Institut für Wasserbau und Kulturtechnik, University of Karlsruhe (unpublished report to the Ministy of Environment, Stuttgart). [8.6]

Kern K, Anselm R, Bürkle F *et al.* (1986) *Naturnahe Umgestaltung ausgebauter Fliessgewässer – Beiträge zum wasserbaulichen Kolloquium am 14. Febr., 1986, Karlsruhe.* Mitteilungen Heft 174, Institut für Wasserbau und Kulturtechnik, University of Karlsruhe. [8.3]

Ministerium für Umwelt. (1992) *Handbuch Wasserbau, Naturnahe Umgestaltung von Fliessgewässern.* Heft 2: Teil I: Leitfaden, Teil II: Dokumentation ausgeführter Projekte. Ministerium für Umwelt, Baden-Württemberg. [8.2]

Pasche E. (1984) *Turbulenzmechanismen in naturnahen Fliessgewässern und die Möglichkeit ihrer mathematischen Erfassung.* Mitteilungen Nr. 52, Institut für Wasserbau und Wasserwirtschaft, TH Aachen. [8.5]

9: Management of Macrophytic Vegetation

P. M. WADE

9.1 INTRODUCTION

Consensus as to the acceptable level of vegetation occurring within and along a river channel is rarely achieved. At one extreme the flood defence engineer and navigation manager wish to minimize plant growth, at the other the nature conservationist argues for minimum interference. First and foremost, the vegetation is a key component of the riverine environment, being the primary producer and a significant factor in maintaining channel stability. Vegetation fixes solar radiation, making this energy available for a wide range of herbivores including invertebrates, fish, birds and mammals. The aquatic vegetation can be important in aerating the water, providing shelter and a spawning or egg-laying medium for fish and freshwater invertebrates. Emergent and marginal plants provide shelter and nesting habitat for a variety of fauna including birds and invertebrates. The vegetation is also important in the consolidation of the river bed and banks.

A number of negative effects brought about by the vegetation of the river channel and its margins can be identified. Direct effects include the impedance of the flow of drainage and irrigation water; the hindrance of navigation; an increase in sedimentation by the trapping of silt particles; a decrease in human food production, especially fish; harbouring host organisms for various diseases; interference with recreation such as water skiing and angling; restriction of access to the river including a decrease in the possibilities for washing and bathing; and deoxygenation resulting from the decomposition of large amounts of vegetation within the water.

In the temperate zone, flow resistance brought about by vegetation is regarded as the main problem associated with riverine vegetation; this is reviewed by Pitlo and Dawson (1990). The presence of such vegetation may affect flow in a channel by:

1 reducing water velocities and consequently raising water levels in the channel and in the water table in adjacent land causing it to become waterlogged;
2 increasing the incidence of flooding;
3 encouraging the deposition of suspended sediment;
4 changing the magnitude and direction of currents thus causing local erosion or reducing bank erosion.

Interference with the movement of boats is mainly a problem of tropical areas but can also be serious in temperate navigable waterways used for seasonal recreation (Murphy & Eaton 1983). Floating mats of weeds in particular may cause serious problems as they can cut off remote settlements from the outside world.

This chapter recognizes the different uses to which a stretch of river is put and outlines the various forms of vegetation management which can be employed to maintain a particular use, paying attention to the effects of such management on the ecology of the river. Plants and plant communities growing in a river can be inimical to human activity, but in other situations they might need to be fostered and encouraged. The chapter does not seek to prescribe an ideal balance between these various demands; such a decision should be based on the integrated knowledge of any given river and its catchment.

Aquatic plant management or weed control?

Vegetation management for rivers is often referred to as weed control (e.g. Seagrave 1988; Pieterse & Murphy 1990) with an emphasis on weed cutting and the use of herbicides. In many instances, however, the need to manage the vegetation arises from inappropriate uses or management of the river as a system. Eutrophication by effluents from sewage treatment works, river regulation and the siting of human settlements in river floodplains, all result in changes to the river system which can induce the need to manage vegetation either because biomass has increased to a nuisance level or because hydrological criteria for the river have changed. The management of river systems increasingly acknowledges the desirability to manage the river as nature intended, for example the introduction of tertiary treatment at sewage reclamation works associated with ecological water quality objectives for a particular river or section of river. The benefits of such an approach are not expected to be immediate due to such factors as the accumulation of nutrients in the substrate of the river; nevertheless over time a more sustainable approach to the river resource can be achieved.

The avoidance of the need for weed control through these means is not yet possible for many rivers and given certain hydrological criteria related to, say, flood defence in a heavily engineered stretch, direct manipulation of the vegetation is and will remain necessary for rivers.

The first two stages in this management process are the identification of the species and community or communities of plants which need management, and an assessment of the extent and distribution of the beds of macrophytes.

Plant recognition

Successful vegetation management needs to be based on the correct taxonomic identification of the plant species. This information enables the selection of appropriate management strategies such as a control agent for use against an unwanted stand of a particular species (e.g. MAFF 1986; Westerdahl & Gestinger 1988). Details of the species occurring within a system will give an indication of the habitat conditions (Melzer 1976; Standing Committee of Analysis 1987) and consequently the likely pattern of recolonization. Cook *et al* (1974) and Cook (1990) provide comprehensive catalogues of the genera of the aquatic macrophytes of the world, though none of the continents enjoys a full description of aquatic plant species within the confines of a single publication. Hotchkiss (1972) comes close to this for the USA and Canada, as does Aston (1973) for Australia, and Casper and Krausch (1980, 1981) for Europe. Wade (1987) reviewed the provision made for the identification of aquatic and wetland plants around the world and listed over 100 manuals and other publications to aid the recognition of aquatic flora.

Vegetation assessment

The assessment of marginal and emergent vegetation is relatively straightforward, being achieved through methods similar to those used for terrestrial vegetation. Submerged and floating vegetation is more difficult to assess as it is often inaccessible and in the case of the former out of sight. A basic methodology is provided in such texts as Wood (1975), Haslam (1978), Hellawell (1978) and Murphy (1990). More recently river corridor surveys have been pioneered by the National Rivers Authority (1992), a survey technique which includes a description of the riverine vegetation. Haslam and Wolseley (1981) describe a methodology for British rivers, and techniques for working in chalk streams have been developed through such studies as Wright *et al* (1982). Larger, deeper rivers pose more of a challenge especially as substantial beds of macrophytes can be present but unseen by the assessor, for example the submerged forms of *Nuphar lutea* and *Sagittaria sagittifolia*, both commonly overlooked in turbid eutrophic rivers.

Increasing use is being made of aerial photography for extensive surveys of marginal, emergent and floating vegetation (e.g. Haslam 1979) including the use of aerial video film of the river corridor (V. Holt, personal communication). Remote sensing by aerial photography and satellite survey methods using colour, false-colour and infrared photography offer the possibility of rapid, large-scale monitoring anywhere in the world over whatever time-scale is required (Murphy 1990). An important aspect of these assessment techniques is that they enable an accurate record to be established of the vegetation at a given point in time by which to measure the success of vegetation management techniques.

9.2 MAINTENANCE OF SUSTAINABILITY

The aim of the river manager should be the development of a strategy for given sections of river corridor or river catchment with agreed levels of usage including drainage function, potential for water abstraction and reception of discharges, and recognition of such resources as nature conservation and fisheries. Such approaches to sustainable resource utilization are being adopted throughout Europe, Australia and North America and are rapidly becoming part of river and vegetation management practice. Although an acknowledged improvement in management strategy, such practices struggle to recognize the fundamental factors controlling plant growth, namely nutrient loading and hydrological characteristics. Both the standing crop and the species composition of aquatic plant communities are controlled by these factors and regulation of nutrient inputs and flow manipulation could be used to manage the nature of the aquatic plant element of any given river. Likewise strategies are being developed for riparian and floodplain vegetation to further the sustainable approach to river management.

Nutrient availability

The first stage in developing a vegetation management strategy is to agree upon the target nutrient loading and flow characteristics for a given river in relation to the desired plant communities. Data already collected for rivers can provide basic water quality characteristics and a crude indication of past plant species composition. Only very rarely, however, do data exist

for the size of standing crops and other such quantitative estimates. Nutrient concentration data are, of themselves, of limited value in that they need to be converted into mass flow and give no indication as to nutrient availability in sediments. This is of potential significance as roots have been identified as an important site of nutrient uptake for certain aquatic macrophyte species (Chambers *et al* 1989), a fact also established for rooted aquatic plants growing in lakes (Barko & Smart 1981; Smith & Adams 1986). Studies on European streams and rivers have shown that aquatic macrophyte biomass and tissue nutrient concentration are not correlated with open-water nutrient concentrations (Owens & Edwards 1961; Ladle & Casey 1971), again pointing to the importance of sediment nutrients for plant growth in flowing waters. However, Kern-Hansen and Dawson (1981) observed that aquatic plant biomass and tissue concentration in 19 Danish streams were not correlated with either openwater or sediment concentrations, suggesting that some other factor or factors limited growth. If root uptake is important for riverine macrophyte nutrition, the impact of decreased nutrient loading on growth will depend upon nutrient availability and particle size of the river-bed sediments.

In one attempt to implement aquatic plant control through nutrient limitation, results were unclear (Charlton & Bayne 1986). Water quality and nuisance aquatic plant growth were monitored in the Bow River, Canada, after the installation in 1982–83 of phosphorus removal at Calgary's two sewage treatment works. Charlton and Bayne (1986), in an analysis of the results of the first 2 years, 1984–85, did not show a consistent reduction in plant biomass in spite of an 80% reduction in total phosphorus loading. An evaluation of nutrients and plant growth in the river from 1986 to 1988, however, revealed that a significant decrease in macrophyte biomass had occurred since 1983 at six of the 22 regularly sampled sites, with biomass also appearing to decline at some other sites (Sosiak 1990). Most of the sites with a significant decline in biomass were in the mixing zone for Calgary's sewage treatment effluent.

Aquatic vegetation and flow characteristics

As early as the 1920s, Butcher (1933) recognized that changes in water flow or velocity can alter the biomass and species composition of the submerged plant community, though it is only recently that this relationship has been explored in any detail. Physiological studies have shown that photosynthetic rates are positively correlated with current speeds over the range likely to occur in weed beds (i.e. $0-0.2\,m\,s^{-1}$) (Westlake 1967; Madsen & Sondergaard 1983). Ecological studies, on the other hand, have failed to show any consistent relationship between water movement and the distribution and abundance of submerged plant communities. In the River Lambourn, UK, the 1971–80 expansion and recession of *Ranunculus* beds was positively correlated with discharge rate (Ham *et al* 1981), whereas in the River Wye, Wales, macrophyte cover and peak biomass were negatively correlated with flow (Brooker *et al* 1978). Similarly, in a Swedish stream, Nilsson (1987) observed that macrophyte cover increased at low current velocities ($<0.3\,m\,s^{-1}$), yet decreased at higher speeds. Biomass and shoot density in the Bow River, Alberta, Canada, decreased with increasing current velocity within a weed bed over the range $0.001-1\,m\,s^{-1}$, and at current speeds in excess of $1\,m\,s^{-1}$ aquatic macrophytes were rare (Chambers *et al* 1991). Although the impact of flow characteristics on plant growth in rivers is not sufficiently well understood to use manipulation of such factors for the control of plant growth in all rivers, the potential does exist. The effect of the current can be direct-acting upon plant metabolism, but current velocity may also exert an indirect effect on aquatic macrophyte growth by altering the composition of the river bed and hence nutrient availability (Chambers *et al* 1991). Spillet (1981) used wooden groynes to direct water flow to influence downstream weed beds and silting to improve the fishery in the River Thames.

Identifying appropriate plant communities

Deriving targets for the species content, extent and biomass for beds of vegetation will be a particular challenge. Earlier descriptions of the flora of the river will be valuable in reconstructing past community composition and extent. An investigation to determine the previous flora of the Rivers Test and Itchen, UK, involved consulting previous reports on the river vegetation, the records of botanists, the use of local floras and plant records acquired from herbaria (E. Cranston, personal communication). However, information on the biomass for any given sections of the river were almost non-existent. Where management necessitates influencing community composition, reintroductions may be necessary and it will be important to refer to those agencies regulating or co-ordinating introductions. Recognition is needed of the dynamic nature of riverine plant communities and the need for management to either direct successional processes or to slow them down in line with the strategy for that particular river or catchment.

Bank protection

Although relatively little attempt has been made to regulate plant growth through nutrient control, the need to maintain ecological stability has been identified for certain components of the river habitat, especially the riverbank.

The use of vegetation for bank stabilization and protection is described in detail by Hemphill and Bramley (1989). Four zones of vegetation are identified in relation to water level, the dominant factor affecting plant growth along the river margin. The four zones are based on the vegetation horizons along a river bank (Seibert 1968) (Fig. 9.1).

1 Aquatic plant zone in which the plants can provide protection near the water surface, an effect which decreases with increasing depth.

2 Marginal and emergent zone, comprising plants which either grow up out of the water with emergent leaves and stems or grow along water margins with roots extending below the water table. Emergent plants grow in depths up to $2\,m$, but most species are confined to depths less than $0.5\,m$.

3 Damp, seasonally flooded zone, the principal zone for natural bank protection, supporting grass and fast-growing shrub and tree species.

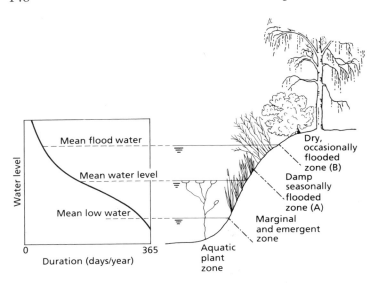

Fig. 9.1 Vegetation horizons along a riverbank (after Seibert 1968).

4 Dry, occasionally flooded zone in which plant life is relatively unaffected by the water level regime.

This chapter, being concerned with aquatic and marginal plant management, focuses on zones 1, 2 and 3.

The aquatic plant zone is rarely encouraged as a deliberate river stabilization policy even though it has a protective influence on the emergent vegetation, for example through the damping effect of species such as *Sagittaria sagittifolia* and water-lilies such as *Nuphar lutea*. Such plants also contribute positively to the visual impact of the river. The disinterest in these plants is mainly because they have a significant potential to reduce channel capacity. Elimination of in-channel vegetation, especially in small unshaded channels, using a weed-cutting boat or herbicides can, however, put the bank at greater risk, placing emphasis on the need for active management of the marginal and emergent zone and the damp, seasonally flooded zone. On the other hand, a fringe of submerged and floating aquatic plants is often maintained in a large waterway such as the River Thames to prevent bank erosion due to boat wash.

Emergent riparian aquatic plants can be important in protecting riverbanks and the floodplain from damage due to high flows and, in navigable rivers, boat traffic (Siebert 1968; Keown *et al*

1977). Murphy *et al* (1980) assessed the protective potential of reedswamp species on the lower slopes and stoloniferous grasses on upper slopes of canal banks in Britain: *Glyceria maxima* and *Sparganium erectum* grow in this marginal zone effecting good protection. *Agrostis stolonifera* is useful on the bankward part of this zone due to its binding root system and pliable upper parts.

Studies on the River Thames, UK, have investigated the dissipation of energy waves produced by boats for various species. Sixty per cent of boat-wave energy is dissipated by a 2-m band of *Phragmites australis*, 70% by a 2–5-m band of *Scirpus lacustris*, 75% by a 2–4-m band of *Acorus calamus* and 60% by a 2–3-m band of *Typha angustifolia*. Such vegetation also encourages siltation by absorbing current-flow energy, and thus reducing the sediment-carrying capacity of the flow (Hemphill & Bramley 1989). Figure 9.2 illustrates a range of different planting situations for the marginal and emergent zone.

The damp, seasonally flooded zone is traditionally regarded as the principal zone for natural bank protection, supporting grass and fast-growing shrub and tree species. The favoured vegetation type is that of grass-based communities which can be mown to encourage rooting and to minimize potential resistance to flow in periods of high precipitation. More recently it has become acceptable on certain lowland rivers to alternate

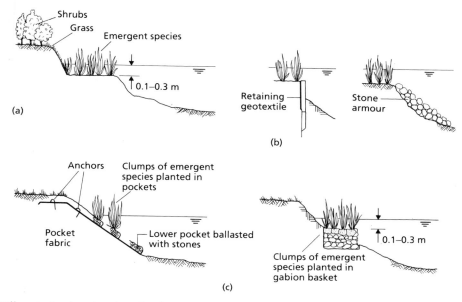

Fig. 9.2 Different planting situations for the marginal and emergent zone (after Hemphill & Bramley 1989).

bank cutting on a year-to-year basis, i.e. leaving one bank uncut for a given year. The stimuli for this change in management have been economics, nature conservation objectives and possibly lower flows in the channel. For some rivers it is acceptable to plant trees along the bankward edge of this zone. These can be useful in shading the river and reducing plant growth as well as stabilizing the bank, creating wildlife habitat and areas of river out of the sun which are preferred by certain species of fish.

Planting can be achieved manually or by using machinery such as a dredger. The dredged plant material can be used either to return to sections of the river being managed, or for transplantation to another stretch of the same or other river. Some species colonize more aggressively than others, and care must be taken in choosing the most appropriate species to prevent problems arising through excessive growth and channel obstruction. It is best to use fresh, native, and preferably abundant plants, taken where possible from the same river or one of its tributaries. This approach is both practical and conforms to good practice from the nature conservation viewpoint. Some countries have legislation restricting the

removal of plants. In the UK, for example, Section 13 of the Wildlife and Countryside Acts 1981 prohibits the uprooting of any plants without the permission of the landowner or occupier. The first prosecution under this Act was for the removal of *Stratiotes aloides* from a watercourse by a landscape gardener.

The planting of mixtures of species rather than single stands leads more rapidly to a more balanced community with a reduction in the likelihood of excessive growths of one species. Planting in early spring as the shoots first appear above ground level is recommended (Lewis & Williams 1984), and it is preferable to transfer sediment with the plant material to aid establishment and protect the plants from any late frosts. Cuttings or clumps of plant material should be placed in a hole in shallow water and firmed with the heel of a boot (Lewis & Williams 1984). Hemphill and Bramley (1989) and Kite (1980) provide specific advice on the water depth, soil type, water quality, flow velocity, planting method and growth for a range of emergent species commonly used in bank protection (Table 9.1). Most aquatic plants are easy to propagate from cuttings, whole plants or rhizome fragments

Table 9.1 Range of species used for planting in the reed-bank zone, with their habitat requirements and planting method (data from Hemphill & Bramley 1989; Kite 1980)

Species	Water depth	Soil type	Water quality	Flow velocity	Remarks	Planting method	Growth
Common or Norfolk reed (*Phragmites australis*)	Very shallow, 0.1 m max.	Sand	Clean	Very low	Least useful emergent. Does not like water motion	Rhizome and shoot clumps / Shoot cuttings	Poor* / Poor
Common club-rush (*Schoenoplectus lacustris*)	Deep to medium 1.0 m max.	Clay silt	Clean to moderate	Low to fast	Very useful emergent. Good resistance to flowing water	Rhizome and shoot clumps	Moderate*
Reed mace or bulrush (*Typha latifolia*)	Shallow 0.5 m max.	Clay silt	Clean	Low	Good bank protector	Rhizome and shoot clumps	Excellent
Greater pond-sedge (*Carex riparia*)	Medium 0.5 m max.	Clay silt / Peat	Clean to poor	Low to moderate	Can be invasive. Useful bank protector	Rhizome and shoot clumps / Shoot cuttings	Excellent / Excellent
Lesser pond-sedge (*Carex acutiformis*)	Medium 0.5 m max.	Clay silt	Clean to poor	Low to moderate	Can be invasive. Useful bank protector in moderate flows	Rhizome and shoot clumps / Shoot cuttings	Very good / Very good
Slender tufted-sedge (*Carex acuta*)	Medium 0.5 m max.	Clay silt	Clean	Low to moderate	Needs constantly high water level	Rhizome and shoot clumps / Shoot cuttings	Good / Poor†
Reed sweet-grass (*Glyceria maxima*)	Deep to medium 1.0 m max.	Clay silt	Clean to poor	Low to moderate	Good bank protector	Rhizome and shoot clumps	Excellent*
Yellow iris or yellow flag (*Iris pseudacorus*)	Medium 0.5 m max.	Clay silt	Clean	Low to moderate	Good bank protector	Rhizome and shoot clumps	Good*
Galingale (*Cyperus longus*)	Shallow 0.2 m max.	Clay silt	Clean	Low	Typically a species of southern England and Wales	Shoot cuttings	Very good*
Sweet-flag (*Acorus calamus*)	Shallow 0.5 m max.	Clay silt	Clean to poor	Low	Useful in slower flowing stretches	Rhizome and shoot clumps	Good
Hard rush (*Juncus inflexus*)	Very shallow–dry, 0.1 m max.	Clay silt	Clean to poor	Low to moderate	Good for protecting the drier margins	2-year-old plants	Moderate
Branched bur-reed (*Sparganium erectum*)	Shallow to medium, 0.6 m max.	Clay silt	Clean to poor	Low	Can be invasive in shallow waters. Good bank protector	Rhizome and shoot clumps.	Moderate

* Grazed by birds or water voles but not killed. † Smothered by overhanging vegetation.

(Lewis & Williams 1984). *Phragmites australis* is an exception, being noted for its unreliability as a species for planting. Propagation can be achieved from planting clumps, cuttings, by layering and using seed (Lewis & Williams 1984). Planting clumps and cuttings was found to be usually successful. It was important to plant clumps above the mean water level (rhizomes planted below water level will usually rot), to avoid damage by trampling to the shoots in the donor stand and in the planted material, and in the case of cuttings, to plant at water level and set them so that at least three leaf nodes are buried. Advice on the best time of year for planting varies: March to May (Hemphill & Bramley 1989) or October to March (Lewis & Williams 1984). Lewis and Williams (1984) prescribe the conditions necessary for germinating *P. australis* seeds.

Protection of the planted material is often necessary to ensure establishment of the emergent vegetation. Fencing might be necessary to prevent grazing or excessive trampling, and might aid against vandalism. Protection from wave action can be achieved in different ways, the nature of the protection depending upon the severity of scour (Hemphill & Bramley 1989). Care should also be taken to avoid the invasion of the planting by alien species such as *Fallopia japonica* (*Reynoutria japonica*), *Impatiens glandulifera* and other such alien species which readily establish in such conditions (Child *et al* 1992).

Nature conservation, wildfowl and fisheries resources

Given the damage and changes to which rivers have been subject, there is a growing need in certain circumstances to repair the river habitat, whilst in others it requires protection from what some users would regard as damaging activities. Managing for nature conservation can involve a number of objectives: the maintenance of plant and animal communities as a nature conservation resource; the encouragement of certain plant species to act as a food source or for nesting or spawning; and establishing roosting or refuge for wildfowl and fish. These objectives are not always compatible. Rehabilitation and conservation range from the management of short stretches of river, including the designation of restrictive practices, to the reclamation of significant lengths of river. Most such management has focused on certain sections or components of rivers, the marginal zone being one of the more common foci (Lewis & Williams 1984; Hemphill & Bramley 1989). The submerged and floating communities have received relatively little attention and rarely feature in practical guidance. Very few examples of the restoration of plant communities have been reported in the literature. Communities have been manipulated in order to try to improve water quality and to achieve bank consolidation (Oksiyuk *et al* 1978).

Landscape

Vegetation is a key component of the river landscape, good examples being the floating, emergent and marginal zones of lowland rivers incorporating such species as *Nuphar lutea*, *Phalaris arundinacea* and *Lythrum salicaria*. These species contribute both form and colour to the landscape, elements recognized by workers such as Burkle (1978) and Kijlstra (1978).

9.3 CONTROL OF VEGETATION

River management is typically based on a traditional approach related to the main function of a river, e.g. navigable sections of river and canals for transportation. The drainage function of rivers has been dominant for many years, supporting agricultural development and serving to limit flooding of property, a consequence of which is that all aquatic and riparian plants have been seen as weeds in need of control. In recent decades rivers have increasingly been recognized as multiuse resources and not simply transportation or drainage structures. The National Rivers Authority in the UK, for example, manages certain rivers for drainage, angling, nature conservation, leisure boating and informal countryside recreation leading to management strategies based on an understanding of the landscape ecology of the resource.

Many rivers have developed plant communities which require direct control of marginal and/or in-channel vegetation. Different river conditions will dictate the type of vegetation control to be applied, and a number of organizations have drawn up guidelines and strategies for those rivers and waterways under their management (e.g. National Rivers Authority, undated; British Waterways Board 1981).

Mechanical control

Mechanical control of unwanted plants in rivers dates back to when people first used their hands and sticks to clear away weeds blocking the passage of boats or denying access to fishing. Manual methods provide a highly selective approach to weed control and can be applied to the management of fisheries, e.g. in chalk streams (e.g. Ham *et al* 1981), wildfowl and stretches of river with high nature conservation value (e.g. Lewis & Williams 1984). Seagrave (1988) provides a useful description of such techniques as cutting and hoeing, raking, pulling and the use of booms. The increasing cost of labour in many countries has made this method expensive compared with other techniques. In other countries with cheap labour, especially those in the developing world, manual control remains the most economic method (Wade 1990).

The mechanization of aquatic plant control is achieved by adapting agricultural machinery for the cutting and harvesting of bankside and aquatic vegetation. With the application of hydraulics, considerable control and sophistication can be achieved from both boat- and bank-based machinery.

Specialized weed-cutting boats are available for purchase or hire from specialist engineers and contractors (Fig. 9.3a). Such boats are craft with shallow draft driven by a paddle-wheel or screw. Most models have reciprocating cutting blades on a U- or ⊥-shaped beam. Using hydraulics this beam can be adjustd to cut at any depth down to a maximum of approximately 2 m. The boat should be light and easily handled by one person, being transportable by trailer between rivers or from one part of a river to another. The swath widths of the cutter bar on these boats range from 1–2 m to 4–5 m, the larger sizes being fitted on to barges to improve their capacity for cutting weed. Wade

(1990) reviews a range of these machines, considering their advantages and disadvantages.

A bewildering range of cutting mechanisms has been developed which can be operated from the riverbank (Fig. 9.3b,c). The variety of machinery is associated specifically with the cutting and harvesting of the vegetation. The technique of dredging, which removes both vegetation and sediment, is typically of a similar design and nature.

The reach of such cutting and harvesting machinery varies: that of a tractor-mounted flail mower is approximately 7 m; a weed-cutting bucket mounted on a hydraulic excavator, 11 m; and a weed-cutting bucket on a dragline, 18 m (Cave 1981). The most widely used device is the weed-cutting bucket attached to the hydraulic jib of a tractor or excavator. The lower edge of the bucket has a cutter bar, which may range from 2 to 4 m in length, and it is lowered to the substrate surface and pulled towards the excavator cutting the weeds in its path. The bucket is able to cut weeds on the banks and the bed of the river and, given a wide enough reach, both banks can be managed in one sweep. The cut weeds can be dumped on the bank or in a truck.

Rotary, reciprocating and flail cutters provide an important range of machinery for cutting emergent and bankside vegetation (Robson 1975) (Fig. 9.3d,e). Small self-propelled pedestrian and ride-on cutters can be used on slopes with a gradient less than 2:1, although under certain conditions Allen motor scythes can work on steeper slopes (Price 1981). A review of bank-based machinery undertaken by Murfitt and Haslam (1981) indicated that reciprocating drum and disc mowers could be used in any section of the channel. The rotary devices, although needing higher power, were very much more robust than the reciprocating cutters. Flail cutters and mowers were limited in use to the area above the water.

The criteria for an ideal machine able to deal with both bank and channel are that it should be robust and reliable, be able to control rooted and non-rooted weeds at one pass without affecting the stability of the banks, have variable geometry to cater for a channel bed of 0.6–1.2 m and bank slopes of 30–45 degrees, and remove weeds to a

(a)

(b)

(c)

(d)

Fig. 9.3 A range of machines for managing aquatic vegetation. (a) A weed-cutting boat. (b) Weed basket with cutter bar (InteDrain (England) UK); (c) channel clearance (Bicycle tractor, InteDrain (England) UK); (d) flail mower Bradshaw H-6710 tracked mower with three different types of flail cutters; (e) bank clearance (AEBI TT90 InteDrain (England) UK).

(e)

stable position above 1.2 m up the bank (Wade 1990). Price (1981) presented data on the characteristics of eight weed-control machines related to these criteria giving advantages and disadvantages. The two best machines had an estimated output of approximately 2.4 km day^{-1} and 4.2 km day^{-1} allowing for normal down-time and obstructions.

A significant disadvantage of cutting and harvesting vegetation, particularly submerged and floating species, is that the underground material remains. More thorough control is achieved by dredging, which removes both plant material and accumulated sediments. Draglines have the advantage of a considerable reach whereas hydraulic excavators have greater control over the form of the bank created. The intervals between dredging are much longer than intervals between weed cutting or herbicide treatment. Where the depth of water is increased through the removal of sediment, the amount of light reaching the bottom may be reduced. Disadvantages associated with dredging are the cost and time involved and the problem of disposing of the spoil.

A number of shortfalls can be identified in the efficiency of currently available mechanical techniques. These include the following:

1 Timing. The optimal time for managing vegetation, especially the submerged and floating plants, is poorly understood; indeed, certain cutting regimes actually promote plant growth. A good example is the management of *Ranunculus* beds in chalk streams in the UK (Westlake & Dawson 1982, 1986).

2 Removal of cut material. Machinery can be ineffective in harvesting the cut plants. This is particularly so with boat-based techniques, though recent developments have overcome some of the inherent difficulties in handling large amounts of wet material (H. Miller, personal communication) (Fig. 9.3a).

3 Training. The efficient use of machines can be improved through training. This should include recognition of plant species, understanding of the role of vegetation and recovery processes, reduction of down-time, and recognition of different management objectives including nature conservation (Newbold *et al* 1989).

4 Development of new machines. Current machinery is based on the design of agricultural equipment and is seen as a means of eliminating plant species. A more sound approach would be to consider such techniques as a part of environmental management, for example shifting a river from one developmental stage with associated plant community to another with a more acceptable community structure given the use of the river. This method requires a different approach to the machinery and is the basis for emerging new designs (Wade 1990).

The ecological effects of mechanical control

Evidence of the ability of macrophytes to recover from aquatic plant management is limited, with most studies of river management being of the impact of dredging. Such fundamental management alters the habitat, and recovery of the aquatic plant community can take a long time. The recolonization of the Boro River, Botswana, after dredging was still only in its early stages 8 years after dredging, with the re-establishment of small colonies of *Rotala myriophylloides*, *Ottelia kunenensis*, *Najas pectinatus*, *Potamogeton thunbergii*, *P. trichoides* and *Nymphaea caerulea* (Lubke *et al* 1981, 1984). The dredging had resulted in the creation of a deep channel in the centre with steep sides, which, coupled with turbidity of the water, limited regrowth. The removal of natural meanders increased water flow considerably, further exacerbating recovery (see also Brookes 1988). At the other end of the spectrum, the recovery from dredging of a millstream in southern England dominated by *Elodea canadensis* with some *Nuphar lutea* and *Potamogeton pectinatus* was a faster process (Crisp & Gledhill 1970). The predredging community was succeeded by sparse growth of *E. canadensis* in the spring following management, extending through the summer to cover most of the bed despite a minor incident of pollution. The *E. canadensis* was removed by spate flow and immigrant *Ranunculus penicillatus* var. *calcareus* developed extensive growth in the second year after dredging, being replaced by *E. canadensis* and floating mats of *Apium* during the summer of that year.

Research into the recovery of chalk streams subjected to annual cutting regimes found that previously managed streams which were left unmanaged had a wider, more extreme range of both dissolved oxygen and water temperature than regularly managed streams (Dawson *et al* 1981; Dawson & Henville 1985). The morphological changes associated with the management of streams tended to create stress within the system because the system is modified to cope with winter flooding rather than allowing the channel to become naturally adjusted by flood erosion. The biomass levels at which management occurred coincided with the maximum biomasses found in unmanaged streams. Thus lack of management did not cause flooding and the fauna did not suffer the destabilizing effects of plant removal (Dawson 1989).

Concern has been expressed that cutting, harvesting and dredging remove most of the invertebrates attached to the vegetation and living in or on the mud of a watercourse; the evidence here is more extensive. The impact of dredging in certain cases can be long lasting, in others recovery is rapid. The macroinvertebrate community usually recovers rapidly after weed cutting. Free-swimming species, such as Coleoptera and Hemiptera, are left behind although in reduced numbers, though recolonization by flying and swimming species does not usually take place until suitable habitat conditions have developed in the channel. For example, oviposition by Odonata will not occur unless the required type of vegetation is available (Corbet *et al* 1960). Recolonization by species with limited powers of movement, e.g. Gastropoda and Lamellibranchia, is an even slower process, and if dredging is carried out on an extensive scale, the status of such animals will decline and, in intensively managed areas, become eradicated altogether (George 1976). Toner *et al* (1965), investigating a tributary of the River Moy, Ireland, observed that the recovery of the invertebrates after dredging was slow although large numbers of Chironomidae and Ephemeroptera were found 2 years after management. Trichoptera larvae were more seriously affected than other taxa.

In other situations macroinvertebrate re-establishment has been rapid and recovery has occurred within 12 months despite the severity of the management. Crisp and Gledhill (1970) considered that the recovery of the macrofauna of a millstream in southern England was complete about 1 year after draining and dredging. Chironomidae, Oligochaeta and Mollusca together formed 85% of the benthos and all three groups were present from the autumn of the year of management, but whereas the Chironomidae were numerically important from the outset, the Oligochaeta and Mollusca took almost a year to build up their numbers. In a similar investigation on a canalized section of the River Hull, UK, no dramatic changes in community composition were shown. Most species were recovering their numbers 6 months after dredging and both variety and numbers were expected to have returned to normal by 8–9 months after dredging (Pearson & Jones 1975). As well as removal by the dredger, it was suggested that a large number of animals were lost in downstream drift.

The effects of weed cutting on the macroinvertebrate fauna of the River Hull (Pearson & Jones 1978) were similar to those made in the earlier dredging study (Pearson & Jones 1975). As the substrate was not disturbed the recovery was more rapid although large numbers of invertebrates were removed in the cut weed. The timing of weed cutting proved to be important. In this case, Chironomidae and *Caenis horaria* had emerged prior to weed cutting with no impact on the breeding population. The effect of weed cutting on invertebrate drift was investigated by Kern-Hansen (1978) in four small Danish lowland streams. Total macrophyte clearance increased the drift of *Gammarus pulex* while partial cutting programmes resulted in only small increases in drift density. Similar increases in invertebrate drift density have been recorded in a small stream in Germany (Statzner & Stechmann 1977). In both cases the biomass of invertebrates removed from the river was significant.

Fish are not able to respond as rapidly to changes resulting from weed control as are invertebrates and macrophytes. Hence fishermen often regard mechanical weed control as deleterious to their fishery. On the Hampshire Avon, UK, anglers felt that the timing, extent and severity of weed cutting had caused destruction of cyprinid spawn, removal of habitat for fry development, a decrease of invertebrate diet and loss of cover for adult fish (Frake 1979). This view can certainly be substantiated for rivers. Swales (1982) has shown how potentially serious mechanical weed control is, through disruption of feeding, reproduction and other behaviours. Cutting, harvesting and dredging can result in the removal of large numbers of invertebrates with the weed, and increases in the level of invertebrate drift (Kern-Hansen 1978; Pearson & Jones 1975, 1978; Statzner & Stechmann 1977). A 30% decrease was observed in the fry of salmonid fish after dredging, though part of this was due to natural mortality, and within 2 years population estimates compared favourably with pre-dredging estimates (Toner *et al* 1965). A cut of *Callitriche*, *Berula* and *Ranunculus* in a tributary of the River Itchen, UK, to improve fishing did not encourage increased use of the stretch for the spawning of *Salmo trutta*, although it increased the area of exposed gravel. A count of redds, however, showed no increase over the previous years (Soulsby 1974).

Some fish, such as *Leuciscus leuciscus* and *Tilapia* spp., utilize aquatic macrophytes as a direct food source (Swales 1982; Lubke *et al* 1981). Removal of large amounts of vegetation can, therefore, have serious effects on fish feeding and growth. Macrophytes are also an important spawning substrate for phytophilous fish (Mills 1981) and weed cutting and dredging may remove potential spawning areas and incubating eggs, and eliminate the slack water needed for fry development. Mortensen (1977) found that weed cutting and the clearing out of stream weed beds increased mortality of *Salmo trutta*. Reductions in water level through weed cutting may adversely affect spawning by stranding incubating eggs (Mills 1981).

A crucial factor determining the impact of weed cutting on fisheries and spawning in particular is the timing of the weed control (Pearson & Jones 1978). Swales (1982) attributed low population levels of *Rutilus rutilus* in the River Perry, UK, to the effects of annual weed cutting on the reproductive success of the species. He also showed fish distribution in uncut and partially cut sections of river to be strongly associated with weed

cover, particularly cover provided by overhanging bankside vegetation. Increased fish movements were caused by the operation of the weed-cutting launch and manual cutting was suggested as a preferable form of control because it is more selective. Indeed, selective weed cutting can be used to improve species diversity and fishing. This is difficult to achieve and is not normally attempted in the UK except in some of the more valuable trout fisheries (Barrett 1978). Frake (1979) described a reduction of the weed cut on the Hampshire Avon, UK, based on a flexible programme fitted to the pattern of weed growth and land drainage requirement with marginal strips of weed left on one or both banks where possible and in some cases a strip down the centre.

Chemical control

The use of herbicides in or near the aquatic environment has always been a sensitive issue, never more so than today when a number of agencies in Europe and North America are severely restricting herbicide application in or adjacent to waters, if not banning such use altogether. Different herbicides have been cleared for use in or near water in different countries (e.g. MAFF 1986); their most intensive use is in lowland alluvial plains where their application is compatible with the use of the water and where the plants can create a serious flood hazard (Haslam 1987). Murphy and Barrett (1990) conclude a review of the chemical control of aquatic weeds: '[herbicides] are not a panacea solution to all problems, nor are they to be rejected out of hand because of their potential ecological side-effects. As with any weed control measure, aquatic herbicides have their limitations and dangers but the record of their use to date in terms of both efficacy and environmental safety, is generally good'.

The treatment of vegetation in or near water is well described in such texts as Seagrave (1988) and Riemer (1984). The control of submerged vegetation with a herbicide in rivers limits the applicability of most herbicides, effective treatment being achieved with special formulations such as alginate and granules. It is emphasized that there is considerable legislation dictating which herbicides can be used in or near water, requirements prior to application, and the method of application itself. This legislation varies from one country to another, or from one administrative area of a country to another, as in the various USA states.

Bankside and emergent vegetation is treated using standard techniques although the range of herbicides for use near water is typically limited. In the UK herbicides such as dalapon, glyphosate and 2,4-D amine can be used for emergent and bankside vegetation. Maleic hydrazide can be used for the suppression of grass growth, fosamine ammonium for control of deciduous trees and shrubs, and asulam for bracken and dock control. These chemicals and their application are considered in detail by Seagrave (1988).

Both the bipyridinium herbicides, diquat and paraquat, are readily absorbed by submerged aquatic plants but despite this they are not generally effective in water flowing at more than about $100 \, m \, h^{-1}$, probably because the availance is insufficient (Murphy & Barrett 1990). This problem has been overcome by adding sodium alginate to the formulation, converting it into a sticky viscous solution (Barrett 1978). The formulation is applied from a strengthened or special applicator as a pencil jet on to the water surface where it breaks up to form discrete strings and droplets in the water. The jet can be projected up to 10 m. The strings and droplets are dense and sink rapidly into the weedbeds where they stick to the plants and release the active ingredient. Diquat-alginate effectively controls weeds in fast-flowing rivers (Barrett & Murphy 1982; Fox *et al* 1986). Diquat is strongly adsorbed and inactivated by clays and other organic particles (Narine & Guy 1982) and adsorption on to suspended material is very rapid. Hence the performance of diquat is greatly reduced in turbid waters or where plants are covered by deposits of silt and salts. High water hardness also reduces the uptake of this herbicide (Parker 1966).

Acrolein acts as a contact herbicide and has the ability to give useful weed control in fast-flowing waters because it needs only a very short contact time (Bowmer & Sainty 1977; Gaddis & Kissel 1982). Acrolein can be injected at a high concen-

tration such that a pulse of herbicide with a peak concentration of about $15 \, mg \, a.i. \, l^{-1}$ moves downstream killing all aquatic plant growth as it passes (Bowmer & Smith 1984). The disadvantage of acrolein is that it is toxic to both plants and animals and the above management practice would also kill much of the animal life in the treated section of the river (Murphy & Barrett 1990). It is also hazardous to work with, being a lacrimatory agent and causing skin and lung damage; it is also explosive. Concentrations of less than $15 \, mg \, a.i. \, l^{-1}$ in irrigation water are generally safe for crops (USDA 1963) and it is rapidly lost from water by degradation to non-toxic residues and by volatilization (Bowmer & Higgins 1976). It is banned in many countries but is still used in certain situations in Australia, Canada, Egypt, Argentina and the USA.

Terbutryne, one of the methylthio-triazines, has a primary mode of action through photosynthetic inhibition with little translocation or activity away from the leaves (Murphy 1982). The principal target weeds are submerged and free-floating species. Terbutryne is also a potent algicide (Robson *et al* 1976). The herbicide is applied in a granular form spread evenly from the bank or a boat in order to achieve an availance of $0.05-1.0 \, mg \, a.i. \, l^{-1}$ for $7-16$ days. It can be used in situations with flowing water so long as this concentration can be maintained. The efficacy of terbutryne can be reduced by its adsorption to clays, uptake by phytoplankton and chemical and microbial decomposition. It is also possible that the chemical is photodegraded. These processes tend to reduce its persistence considerably in the field (Murphy & Barrett 1990).

Dichlobenil is preferentially taken up by plant roots and subsequently transported around the plant. The formulation recommended for aquatic use is a clay-based granule containing 20% active ingredient. The granules have a slow-release property enabling them to carry the chemical down into the root region and release it slowly into the hydrosoil/water interface region (Tooby & Spencer-Jones 1978; Murphy & Barrett 1990). The properties associated with this particular formulation are such that it can be useful in slowly flowing rivers. Treatment is most effective early in the growing season when the chemical is translocated rapidly to growing points. Dichlobenil must not be used in potable water supplies nor in water to be used for irrigation nor for livestock watering. Fish from treated waters should not be used for human consumption or for animal feed for a period of 90 days following application (Riemer 1984).

Murphy and Barrett (1990) identify a number of areas of current research into herbicides for use in or near water. Those which are applicable to the management of rivers include the following:

1 Improvement of application methodology such as advances in controlled-release technology with the aims of maximizing impacts on target weeds and minimizing effects on non-target organisms.

2 Development of more rigorous assessment procedures to determine the environmental safety of aquatic herbicides.

3 Finding and developing new selective compounds to control major nuisance species or groups, one outstanding need being an algicide.

4 Determining the compatibility of herbicides with other aquatic weed control methods for use in integrated management programmes.

Effects of the use of herbicides

The impacts of herbicides upon aquatic ecosystems have been considered in detail by Brooker and Edwards (1975), Newbold (1976) and Robson and Barrett (1977). The effects are either direct toxicity to both target and non-target species, or indirect effects brought about by either the death/damage or removal of the target species.

Herbicide treatments can affect non-target species in two ways. First the herbicide might have an impact on non-target plant species, including algae, occurring in the section of river treated. The susceptibilities of the more common and abundant macrophyte species are given in manuals and guides for the use of herbicides (e.g. MAFF 1986). Likewise the toxic effects of most aquatic herbicides on non-target phytoplankton or other algal populations are well documented (e.g. Robson *et al* 1976). It is the less common and rare macrophyte species for which little information is available. Secondly, herbicide moving outside the treated area by drift or movement in water currents can have ecological significance, and there has been concern over long-term im-

plications for non-target plant communities of the accumulation of inactivated residues of the bipyridinium herbicides where regular treatment has occurred (Corwin & Farmer 1984).

The direct toxic effects on herbicides on microorganisms, invertebrates, fish and other vertebrates are comprehensively reviewed by Murphy and Barrett (1990).

The short-term indirect effects of herbicidal control are concerned with the following factors:

1 Alterations in dissolved gas and pH brought about by decaying vegetation (see Brooker & Edwards 1975; Marshall 1981; Murphy *et al* 1981).

2 Toxin and nutrient release from decaying vegetation (see Ahmed *et al* 1981, 1982).

3 Habitat loss or alteration for non-target organisms (see Brooker & Edwards 1973a,b; Hanbury *et al* 1981; Clare & Edwards 1983).

4 Increases in detritus (see Carter & Hestand 1977; Newbold 1975; Strange 1976).

5 Development of replacement growth of opportunist plant species (see Carter & Hestand 1977; Hestand & Carter 1977).

Other forms of control

Outside of the more traditional physical and chemical control methods, there are other techniques which can be used to limit vegetation growth in rivers. These are shading, hydrological manipulation and biological control.

Shading

Shading is an effective control measure which, in some rivers, has been used for many years to limit weed growth and to draw current to the weedless areas, e.g. the chalk streams of southern England (National Rivers Authority, undated). Krause (1977) and Lohmeyer and Krause (1974, 1975) advocated full shade to remove vegetation, rather than partial shade, with the retention of some vegetation for a better ecological balance. On the sandy unstable banks of streams in the Luneberger Heide, Germany, planting was achieved with *Alnus glutinosa*, a species chosen because of its tolerance to damp conditions and its deep-rooting stabilizing roots. A 10–15-year rotation of tree cutting prevents farmland being shaded excessively. The costs were less than half those of weed cutting and dredging (excluding the loss of a small amount of agricultrual land), though even with shading some macrophytes occurred beneath occasional breaks in the canopy. The autumn leaf fall was not found to hinder flow and added organic matter to the stream compensating for the loss of that from river plants.

Dawson and Kern-Hansen (1979a,b) developed these initial ideas, leading to a recommendation of light reduction of approximately 50%. This achieved a satisfactory ecological balance with planting on the north and south sides of stream sections of various widths flowing in an east–west direction. The light available at the water surface is related to the effective tree and bank height, and the orientation of the bank and its vegetation in relation to the width of the river, emphasizing the importance of channel morphology. Narrow streams with high banks can be deeply shaded by the bank and low vegetation, e.g. the sunken streams of Norwegian farmland (Haslam 1987). On lowland streams approximately 2 m in width with banks 1–2 m wide,

little other control is needed where there is no grazing and tall herbs can grow. Streams 3–8 m wide will need bushes or small trees for effective shading, and those 15+ m wide may require mature trees (Dawson 1978). With full shading from the south, aquatic growth can be considerable in east–west streams because of the light availability from the north. In a chalk stream with macrophytes present in winter and an annual average of 15% of light reaching the water, the amount of light in summer was as low as 6%, and in winter it reached 30–40%'' Westlake & Dawson 1976).

A summary of the influence of channel orientation on effectiveness of weed control is given in Fig. 9.4a. Dawson (1976, 1980) shows that leaf fall provides adequate organic matter to compensate for the loss of that from macrophytes within the stream and better conditions for breakdown of organic matter.

The provision of gaps in a shade belt to allow patches of aquatic plants to grow maintains a better balanced habitat in which leaf litter from the trees decomposes more easily; otherwise it

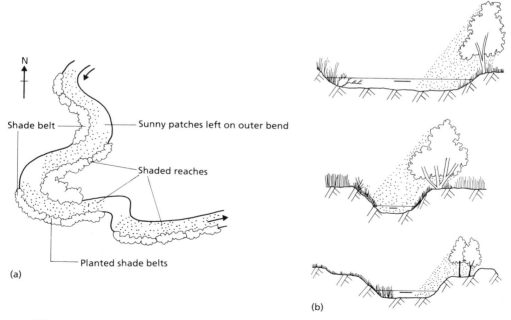

(a)

(b)

Fig. 9.4 (a) The influence of channel orientation on the effectiveness of weed control. (b) Optimal planting of trees to shade river channel.

tends to form a dense, slimy deoxygenated mass on the channel bed (Fig. 9.4b) (Lewis & Williams 1984). A survey of the River Tone, England, in which tree-shaded and open sections of river were alternated at 40–50-m intervals, demonstrated that a greater variety of habitats for nature conservation is created compared with continuously shaded sections and that this approach maintains an attractive landscape for people (Lewis 1981).

Floating vegetation, e.g. water-lilies, can also provide shading to suppress submerged plant growth (Pitlo 1982). This approach is unlikely to be useful in rivers in general as floating species are not adapted to growing in flowing water. However, there is the possibility of using floating leaved plants in slow-flowing lowland rivers.

Investigation has also been undertaken of the application of artificial covering to shade out weeds (Dawson 1981; Dethioux 1982; Dawson & Hallows 1983). Dawson and Hallows (1983) describe the use of lengths of gas-permeable opaque material to control vegetation in narrow watercourses. The material is moved from one section of channel to another on a rotational basis, remaining in one place for 4–12 weeks, the duration varying with species (e.g. *Ranunculus* species are killed sooner than *Elodea canadensis*) and whether or not temporary die-back or elimination is required.

Dawson and Haslam (1983) comment that although some data are available to guide the choice of vegetation and the amount of shade provided by such vegetation (e.g. Krause 1977), detailed information dealing with all aspects of half-shade conditions is not currently available. Lewis and Williams (1984) provide a useful consideration of a number of tree species including *Alnus glutinosa*, *Salix* tree and shrub species, *Populus nigra*, *Acer pseudoplatanus* and *Fraxinus excelsior*.

Shading can present problems to river managers, especially with respect to other forms of river maintenance, exacerbating the risk of flooding and complicating landscape management. As they age, dead and diseased limbs may fall off into the river; with time the channel may be undercut or erode behind a mature tree until it falls into the channel. Likewise trees below flood level will catch trash and this may contribute to their falling in severe storms. Such dead and fallen wood is nevertheless an important natural component of rivers. Along lowland rivers in particular, access is required for bankbased machinery such as dredgers for the maintenance of sediments and banks. Trees and shrubs can prevent such access and can contribute to the hydraulic roughness of the channel or its floodplain, increasing the likelihood of flooding. Close liaison between those managing the aquatic plants and the engineer is essential to achieve a positive approach to shading as a form of plant control.

Hoogerkamp and Rozenboon (1978) drew attention to the inappropriate nature of trees in certain landscapes, in this case the flat Dutch landscape. Dawson and Haslam (1983) illustrate the alternative view that in other situations such planting can enhance the landscape. Hoogerkamp and Rozenboon (1978) also expressed concern that trees might interfere with crops through shading and reduction of drying period, increase insect nuisance to cattle, and increase the incidence of lightning damage. Hermans (1975) and Pitlo (1978), on the other hand, advocated control by shading in the Netherlands, the former finding that the cost is less than half that of other methods of weed control.

The basic principles of shading control can be summarized as follows:

1 Half shade by deciduous vegetation is the optimum for aquatic plant control in streams and rivers.

2 Vegetation, if on the south bank, should at maximum be as high as the distance to the north bank; otherwise more vegetation is required and this should aim to intercept up to two-thirds of the light near the centre of the channel around mid-summer; it is more efficient to intercept the sun path near midday.

3 The vegetation should be in regularly intermittent stands occupying two-thirds of one bank.

4 Vegetation should be considered as part of a planned cycle of planting and cropping; replanting of trees should begin in and around the gaps in those stands halfway to maturity; alternative weed control is particularly important during the first few years following establishment.

Channel deepening

The deepening of the river channel by dredging or raising water levels can effectively put plant growth out of reach of incident light, an effect observed to occur naturally in deeper rivers. This effect has been observed in a number of situations (e.g. Lubke *et al* 1981; Pitlo 1982), occasionally being enhanced by an increase in turbidity due to alterations in flow characteristics. In order to compensate for loss of the submerged plant communities as a result of channel deepening, it is preferable to introduce a shallow-water berm in which replacement plant communities can develop (Lewis & Williams 1984). This can be important for nature conservation, wildfowl and fisheries uses.

Biological control

The most widely used biological control agent for aquatic vegetation in Europe and North America is the grass carp (*Ctenopharyngodon idella* Val.), a fish which under the right conditions can effect good control of water weeds (Seagrave 1988). Limiting the movement of fish stocked in a given piece of water is essential for two reasons. First, the fish need to concentrate at an appropriate stocking density to effectively control the weeds. If the fish stock is dissipated over a too wide an area it will not achieve the level of control required. Despite the unlikely event of this fish species reproducing – it requires very specific conditions – there is concern that the grass carp, if unrestricted in its movement, could cause damage to sensitive plant communities, and at worst, despite predictions to the contrary, could establish a breeding population. It is primarily for these reasons that grass carp are most unlikely to be used to any extent in river systems. There is some potential for their use in smaller lowland rivers, canals and drains. Successful use has been demonstrated in small drains in the Netherlands and England.

Integrated management

There is an increasing recognition of the value of integrated control in river management. In its simplest form this can be a combination of two management techniques, for example weed mowing for the banks and emergent vegetation and the application of diquat alginate to control submerged vegetation. Integrated management should recognize the uses agreed for a river and the ecological processes occurring within and associated with the river, and can range from control of the nutrient budget to agreeing acceptable levels of aquatic plant biomass within the channel. The achievement of an acceptable river vegetation could take a number of years, and the management techniques would need to change over this period; for example, the growth of trees and shrubs would alter the intensity of management needed for aquatic vegetation. This period of time should also be used to understand better the dynamics of the vegetation in relation to management. This has been well illustrated in the case of chalk stream vegetation typically dominated by *Ranunculus* spp. and the advantages and disadvantages of cutting at different times of the year (Dawson 1989).

9.4 PROSPECT

The management of the aquatic and riparian vegetation of rivers has been regarded as simply weed control for too long, and there is a pressing need to put this management into a broader context in which the vegetation is seen as a key component of the river, and one which should be incorporated into an agreed strategy for that river or even the catchment as whole. River management is undertaken by a number of different agencies, ranging from the national agencies such as the National Rivers Authority in England and Wales, through to those responsible for drainage districts such as the Internal Drainage Boards and the individual landowners managing streams and smaller watercourses. Dawson (1989) reports an estimate of the total cost of aquatic plant control in flowing waters in England and Wales, made by the Water Research Centre; this is between 45 and 75 million pounds per annum and could be as high as £100 million. Main rivers were costing £8 million and streams managed by groups or individuals also £8 million. Given the relatively large resources spent on this aspect of river management by independent and often uncoordinated agencies, significant environmental and economic benefits could be derived through the development of integrated and ecologically-based river vegetation management.

REFERENCES

Ahmed SA, Ito M, Ueki K. (1981) Water quality as affected by water hyacinth decomposition after 2,4-D and ametryne application. *Weed Research* **25**: 386–93. [9.3]

Ahmed SA, Ito M, Ueki K. (1982) Water quality as affected by water hyacinth decomposition after cutting or 2,4-D application. *Weed Research* **27**: 34–9. [9.3]

Aston HI. (1973) *Aquatic plants of Australia.* Melbourne University Press, p. 368. [9.1]

Barko JW, Smart RM. (1981) Sediment based nutrition of submersed macrophytes. *Aquatic Botany* **10**: 339–52. [9.2]

Barrett PRF. (1978) Aquatic weed control: necessity and methods. *Fisheries Management* **9**: 93–101. [9.3]

Barrett PRF, Murphy KJ. (1982) The use of diquat-alginate for weed control in flowing waters. In: *Proceedings EWRS 6th Symposium on Aquatic Weeds 1982*, pp. 200–8. Novi Sad. [9.3]

Bowmer KH, Higgins ML. (1976) Some aspects of persistence and fate of acrolein herbicide in water. *Archives of Environmental Contamination and Toxicology* **5**: 87–96. [9.3]

Bowmer KH, Sainty GH. (1977) Management of aquatic plants with acrolein. *Journal of Aquatic Plant Management* **15**: 40–6. [9.3]

Bowmer KH, Smith GH. (1984) Herbicides for injection into flowing water: acrolein and endothal-amine. *Weed Research* **24**: 201–11. [9.3]

British Waterways Board. (1981) *Vegetation Control and Management.* British Waterways Board, London. [9.3]

Brooker MP, Edwards RW. (1973a) Effects of the herbicide paraquat on the ecology of a reservoir I. Botanical and chemical aspects. *Freshwater Biology* **3**: 157–76. [9.3]

Brooker MP, Edwards RW. (1973b) Effects of the herbicide paraquat on the ecology of a reservoir. II. Community metabolism. *Freshwater Biology* **3**: 383–92. [9.3]

Brooker MP, Edwards RW. (1975) Review paper: aquatic herbicides and the control of water weeds. *Water Research* **9**: 1–15. [9.4]

Brooker MP, Morris DL, Wilson CJ. (1978) Plant flow relationships in the R. Wye catchment. In: *Proceedings EWRS 5th Symposium on Aquatic Weeds*, pp. 63–70. Amsterdam. [9.2]

Brookes A. (1988) *Channelized Rivers. Perspectives for Environmental Management.* Wiley, Chichester. [9.3]

Burkle F. (1978) Natural construction on watercourses. *Garten und Landschaft* **1**: 18–24. [9.2]

Butcher RW. (1933) Studies on the ecology of rivers. I. On the distribution of macrophyte vegetation in the rivers of Britain. *Journal of Ecology* **21**: 58–91. [9.2]

Carter CC, Hestand RS. (1977) Relationship of regrowth of aquatic macrophytes after treatment with herbicides to water quality and phytoplankton populations. *Journal of Aquatic Plant Management* **15**: 65–9. [9.3]

Casper SJ, Krausch H-D. (1980, 1981) *Susswasserflora von Mitteleuropa.* 23, 1 (Lycopodiaceae bis Orchidaceae), pp. 1–403 (1980); 23, 2 (Saururaceae bis Asteraceae), pp. 404–943 (1981). Fischer-Verlag, Jena. [9.1]

Cave TG. (1981) Current weed control problems in land drainage channels. In: *Proceedings of the Conference on Aquatic Weeds and their Control, 1981*, pp. 5–14. Association of Applied Biologists, Wellesbourne, UK. [9.3]

Chambers PA, Prepas EE, Bothwell ML, Hamilton HR. (1989) Roots versus shoots in nutrient uptake by aquatic macrophytes in flowing waters. *Canadian Journal of Fisheries and Aquatic Sciences* **46**: 435–9. [9.2]

Chambers PA, Prepas EE, Hamilton HR, Bothwell ML. (1991) Current velocity and its effect on aquatic macrophytes in flowing waters. *Ecological Application* **1**: 249–57. [9.2]

Charlton SED, Bayne D. (1986) *Phosphorus Removal: the Impact Upon Water Quality in the Bow River Downstream of Calgary, Alberta. Bow River Data Base 1980–1985.* Pollution Control Division, Alberta Environment, Edmonton. [9.2]

Child L, de Waal LC, Wade PM. (1992) Control and management of *Reynoutria* species (knotweed). *Aspects of Applied Biology* **29**: 295–307. [9.2]

Clare P, Edwards RW. (1983) The macro-invertebrate fauna of the drainage channels of the Gwent Levels, S. Wales. *Freshwater Biology* **13**: 205–27. [9.3]

Cook CDK. (1990) *Aquatic Plant Book.* p. 228. SPB Publishing, The Hague. [9.1]

Cook CDK, Gut BJ, Rix EM, Schneller J, Seitz M. (1974) *Water Plants of the World: a Manual for the Identification of the Genera Freshwater Macrophytes*, p. 561. Junk, The Hague. [9.1]

Corbet PS, Longfield C, Moore NW. (1960) *Dragonflies.* Collins, London. [9.3]

Corwin DL, Farmer WJ. (1984) Nonsingle-valued adsorption-desorption of bromacil and diquat by freshwater sediments. *Environmental Science and Technology* **18**: 507–14. [9.3]

Crisp DT, Gledhill T. (1970) A quantitative description

of the recovery of the bottom fauna in a muddy reach of a mill stream in Southern England after draining and dredging. *Archiv für Hydrobiologie* **64**: 502–41. [9.3]

Dawson FH. (1976) Organic contribution of stream edge forest litter fall to the chalk stream ecosystem. *Oikos* **27**: 13–18. [9.3]

Dawson FH. (1978) Aquatic plant management in semi-natural streams: the role of marginal vegetation. *Journal of Environmental Management* **6**: 213–21. [9.3]

Dawson FH. (1980) The origin and composition of downstream transport of plant material in a small chalk stream. *Freshwater Biology* **10**: 419–35. [9.3]

Dawson FH. (1981) The reduction of light as a technique for the control of aquatic plants – an assessment. In: *Proceedings of the Conference on Aquatic Weeds and their Control, 1981*, pp. 157–64. Association of Applied Biologists, Wellsbourne, UK. [9.3]

Dawson FH. (1989) Ecology and management of water plants in lowland streams. *Annual Report Freshwater Biological Association* **57**: 43–60. [9.3, 9.4]

Dawson FH, Hallows JB. (1983) Practical applications of a shading material for macrophyte control in watercourses. *Aquatic Botany* **17**: 301–8. [9.3]

Dawson FH, Haslam SM. (1983) The management of river vegetation with particular reference to shading effects of marginal vegetation. *Landscape Planning* **10**: 147–69. [9.3]

Dawson FH, Henville P. (1985) Characteristics, calibration and output optimisation of Mackereth-type dissolved oxygen sensor. *Journal of Physics E: Scientific Instruments* **18**: 526–31. [9.3]

Dawson FH, Kern-Hansen U. (1979a) The effect of natural and artificial shade on the macrophytes of lowland streams and the use of shade as a management technique. *Internationale Revue gesamten Hydrobiologie und Hydrographie* **69**: 437–55. [9.3]

Dawson FH, Kern-Hansen U. (1979b) The effect of natural and artificial shade on the macrophytes of lowland streams. In: Symoens JJ, Hooper SS, Compère P (eds) *Studies on Aquatic Plants*, pp. 214–21. Royal Botanic Society of Belgium, Brussels. [9.3]

Dawson FH, Kern-Hansen, Westlake DF. (1981) Water plants under temperature and oxygen regimes of lowland streams. In: Symoens JJ, Hooper SS, Compère P. (eds) *Studies on Aquatic Vascular Plants. Proceedings of International Colloquium on Aquatic Vascular Plants*, Brussels, 214–221. [9.3]

Dethioux M. (1982) Les saules dans nos payages. *Parca Nationaux* **37**: 111–18. (*Notes techniques du centre d'écologie forêtière et rurale (ISRA), 43.*) [9.3]

Fox AM, Murphy KJ, Westlake DF. (1986) Effects of diquat alginate and cutting on the submerged macrophyte community of a *Ranunculus* stream in Northern England. In: *Proceedings EWRS/AAB 7th Symposium on Aquatic Weeds, 1986*. pp. 105–12. Loughborough. [9.3]

Frake A. (1979) The Hampshire Avon Survey. In: *Proceedings of the 1st British Freshwater Fisheries Conference, 1979*, pp. 100–5. University of Liverpool, Liverpool. [9.3]

Gaddis CW, Kissel CL. (1982) Acrolein in irrigation waterways. In: *Proceedings EWRS 6th Symposium on Aquatic Weeds, 1982*, pp. 164–70. Novi Sad. [9.3]

George M. (1976) Mechanical methods of weed control in watercourses – an ecologist's view. In: *Proceedings of Symposium on Aquatic Herbicides*. Monograph 16, pp. 91–9. British Crop Protection Council, Oxford. [9.3]

Ham SF, Wright JF, Berrie AD. (1981) Growth and recession of aquatic macrophytes on an unshaded section of the River Lambourn, England, from 1971 to 1976. *Freshwater Biology* **11**: 381–90. [9.2]

Hanbury RG, Murphy KJ, Eaton JW. (1981). The ecological effects of 2-methylthio triazine herbicides used for aquatic weed control in navigable canals. II. Effects on macro-invertebrate fauna, and general discussion. *Archiv für Hydrobiologie* **91**: 408–26. [9.3]

Haslam SM. (1978) *River Plants*. Cambridge University Press, Cambridge. [9.1]

Haslam SM. (1979) Infra-red colour photography and *Phragmites communis* Trin. *Polskie Archiwum Hydrobiologie* **26**: 65–72. [9.1]

Haslam SM. (1987) *River Plants of Western Europe*. Cambridge University Press, Cambridge. [9.3]

Haslam SM, Wolseley PA. (1981) *River Vegetation: its Identification Assessment and Management*. Cambridge University Press, Cambridge. [9.1]

Hellawell JM. (1978) *Biological Surveillance of Rivers*. Natural Environment Research Council/Water Research Centre, Stevenage. [9.1]

Hemphill RW, Bramley ME. (1989) *Protection of River and Canal Banks: A Guide to Selection and Design*. Butterworths, London. [9.2]

Hermans LCM. (1975) Levendgroen, II. Groene beken in Limburg. *Tijdschrift der Nederlandschè Leidemaatschappij* **86**: 476–81. [9.3]

Hestand RS, Carter CC. (1977). Succession of various aquatic plants after treatment with four herbicides. *Journal of Aquatic Plant Management* **15**: 60–4. [9.3]

Hoogerkamp M, Rozenboon G. (1978) The management of vegetation on the slopes of waterways in the Netherlands. In: *Proceedings EWRS 5th Symposium on Aquatic Weeds, 1978*, pp. 203–11. Amsterdam. [9.3]

Hotchkiss N. (1972) *Common Marsh, Underwater and Floating-leaved Plants of the United States and Canada*, p. 124. Dover Publications, New York. [9.1]

Keown MP, Oswald NR, Perry EB, Dordeau JDA. (1977)

Literature Survey and Preliminary Evaluation of Stream-bank Protection Methods. Technical Report H-77-9, May 1977. [9.2]

Kern-Hansen U. (1978) Drift of *Gammarus pulex* L. in relation to macrophyte cutting in four small Danish lowland streams. *Verhandlungen der Internationalen Vereinigung für theoretische und angewandte Limnologie* **20**: 1440–5. [9.3]

Kern-Hansen U, Dawson FH. (1981) The standing crop of aquatic plants of lowland streams in Denmark and the inter-relationships of nutrients in plant, sediments and water. In: *Proceedings EWRS 5th Symposium on Aquatic Weeds, 1978*, pp. 143–50. Amsterdam. [9.2]

Kijlstra BC. (1978) Nature conservation and aspects of landscape planning. In: *Proceedings 5th Symposium on Aquatic Weeds, 1981*. Amsterdam. [9.2]

Kite D. (1980) Getting to the root of river ecology. *Surveyor* 10 July: 24–25. [9.2]

Krause A. (1977) On the effect of marginal tree rows with respect to the management of small lowland streams. *Aquatic Botany* **3**: 185–92. [9.3]

Ladle M, Casey H. (1971) Growth and nutrient relationships of *Ranunculus penicillatus* var. *calcareous* in a small chalk stream. In: *Proceedings EWRC 3rd Symposium on Aquatic Weeds, 1971*, pp. 53–64. Oxford. [9.2]

Lewis G. (1981) *Somerset Rivers Survey: A Survey of the Rivers Tone, Yeo, Cary and Northmoor Main Drain, to Map and Describe their Flora and Fauna.* Somerset Trust for Nature Conservation/Wessex Water Authority (unpublished report). [9.3]

Lewis G, Williams G. (1984) *Rivers and Wildlife Handbook: A Guide to Practices Which Further the Conservation of Wildlife on Rivers.* Royal Society for the Protection of Birds/Royal Society for Nature Conservation, Bedford. [9.2, 9.3]

Lohmeyer W, Krause A. (1974) Uber den Geholzbewuchs und Kleinen Fleissgewassern Nordwestdeutschlands und seine Bedeutung für den Uperschutz. *Naturschutz und Landschaftsplanung* **49**: 323–30. [9.3]

Lohmeyer W, Krause A. (1975) Uber die Auswirkungen des Geholzbewuchses an kleinen Wassertaufen des Munsterlandesauf die Vegetation im Wasser und anden Boschungen in Hinblick auf die Unterhaltung der Gewasser. *Schriftenreike fuer Vegetationskunde* **9**: 1–105. [9.3]

Lubke RA, Raynham PE, Reavell PE. (1981) Reassessment of plant succession on spoil heaps along the Boro River, Okavango Delta, Botswana. *South African Journal of Science* **77**: 21–3. [9.3]

Lubke RA, Reavell PE, Dye PJ. (1984) The effects of dredging on the macrophytic vegetation of the Boro River, Okavango Delta, Botswana. *Biological Conservation* **33**: 211–36. [9.3]

Madsen TV, Sondergaard M. (1983) The effects of current velocity on the photosynthesis of *Callitriche stagnalis* Scop. *Aquatic Botany* **15**: 187–93. [9.2]

MAFF (Ministry of Agriculture, Fisheries & Food). (1986) *Guidelines for the Use of Herbicides on Weeds in or Near Water Courses and Lakes.* MAFF Booklet 2078. [9.1, 9.3]

Marshall EJP. (1981) The ecology of a land drainage channel. 1. Oxygen balance. *Water Research* **15**: 1075–85. [9.3]

Melzer A. (1976) Makrophytische Wasserpflanzen als Indikatoren des Dewasserzustandes oberbayerischer Seen. *Dissertationes Botanicae* **34**: 1–195, Cramer, Vaduz. [9.1]

Mills CA. (1981) The spawning of roach, *Rutilus rutilus* L. in a chalk stream. *Fisheries Management* **12**: 49–54. [9.3]

Mortensen E. (1977) Density-dependent mortality of trout fry (*Salmo trutta* L.) and its relationship to the management of small streams. *Journal of Fish Biology* **11**: 613–17. [9.3]

Murfitt RFA, Haslam SM. (1981) Some unanswered questions relating to the mechanical control of weeds in water channels. In: *Proceedings of the Conference on Aquatic Weeds and their Control, 1981*, pp. 87–91. Association of Applied Biologists, Wellesbourne, UK. [9.3]

Murphy KJ. (1982) The use of methylthio-triazine herbicides in freshwater systems: a review. In: *Proceedings EWRS 6th Symposium on Aquatic Weeds, 1982*, pp. 263–77. Novi Sad. [9.3]

Murphy KJ. (1990) Survey and monitoring of aquatic weed problems and control operations. In: Pieterse A, Murphy KJ. (eds) *Aquatic Weeds – the Ecology and Management of Nuisance Aquatic Vegetation*, pp. 228–37. [9.1]

Murphy KJ, Barrett PRF. (1990) Chemical control of aquatic weeds. In: Pieterse AH, Murphy KJ (eds) *Aquatic Weeds.* Oxford University Press, Oxford. [9.3]

Murphy KJ, Eaton J. (1983) Effects of pleasure-boat traffic on macrophyte growth in canals. *Journal of Applied Ecology* **20**: 713–29. [9.1]

Murphy KJ, Bradshaw AD, Eaton JW. (1980) *Plants for the Protection of Canal Banks.* Report, Department of Botany, University of Liverpool. [9.2]

Murphy KJ, Hanbury RG, Eaton JW. (1981) The ecological effects of 2-methylthio triazine herbicides used for aquatic weed control in navigable canals. I. Effects on aquatic flora and water chemistry. *Archiv für Hydrobiologie* **91**: 294–331. [9.3]

Narine DR, Guy RD. (1982) Binding of diquat and paraquat to humic acid in aquatic environments. *Soil Science* **33**: 356–63. [9.3]

National Rivers Authority. *Managing Aquatic Plants.* Information Sheet. Education Series 14. National

Rivers Authority (Southern Region). [9.3]

National Rivers Authority. (1992) *River Corridor Surveys. Methods and Procedures.* Conservation Technical Handbook No. 1. NRA, Bristol. [9.1]

Newbold C. (1975) Herbicides in aquatic systems. *Biological Conservation* 7: 97–118. [9.3]

Newbold C. (1976) Environmental effects of aquatic herbicides. In: *Proceedings of Symposium on Aquatic Herbicides*, pp. 78–90. Monograph 16, British Crop Protection Council, Oxford. [9.3]

Newbold C, Honnor J, Buckley K. (1989) *Nature Conservation and the Management of Drainage Channels.* Nature Conservancy Council and Association of Drainage Authorities, Peterborough. [9.3]

Nilsson C. (1987) Distribution of stream-edge vegetation along a gradient of current velocity. *Journal of Ecology* 75: 513–22. [9.2]

Oksiyuk OP, Merezhko AA, Volkova TF. (1978) Use of higher aquatic plants in canal bank consolidation. *Water Resources* 5: 556–62. [9.2]

Owens M, Edwards RW. (1961) The effects of plants on river conditions II. Further crop studies and estimates of net productivity of macrophytes in a chalk stream. *Journal of Ecology* 49: 119–26. [9.2]

Parker C. (1966) Water hardness and phytotoxicity of paraquat. *Nature (London)* 212: 1465. [9.3]

Pearson RG, Jones NV. (1975) The effects of dredging operations on the benthic community of a chalk stream. *Biological Conservation* 8: 273–8. [9.3]

Pearson RG, Jones NV. (1978) Effects of weedcutting on the macro-invertebrate fauna of a canalised section of the River Hull, a North England chalk stream. *Journal of Environmental Management* 7: 91–9. [9.3]

Pieterse AH, Murphy KJ (eds). (1990) *Aquatic Weeds.* Oxford University Press, Oxford. [9.1]

Pitlo RH. (1978) Regulation of aquatic vegetation by interception of daylight. In: *Proceedings EWRS 5th Symposium on Aquatic Weeds, 1978*, pp. 91–9. Amsterdam. [9.3]

Pitlo RH. (1982) Flow resistance of aquatic vegetation. In: *Proceedings EWRS 6th Symposium on Aquatic Weeds, 1982*, pp. 225–34. Novi Sad. [9.3]

Pitlo RH, Dawson FH. (1990) Flow resistance of aquatic weeds. In: Pieterse AH, Murphy KJ (eds) *Aquatic Weeds*, pp. 74–84. Oxford University Press, Oxford. [9.1]

Price H. (1981) A review of current mechanical methods. In: *Proceedings of the Conference on Aquatic Weeds and their Control, 1981*, pp. 77–86. Association of Applied Biologists, Wellesbourne, UK. [9.3]

Riemer DN. (1984) *Introduction to Freshwater Vegetation.* AVI Publishing, Westport, USA. [9.3]

Robson TO. (1975) *A Survey of Aquatic Weed Control Methods used in Internal Drainage Boards, 1973.* Technical Report No. 35, Agricultural Research Council Weed Research Organisation, Oxford. [9.3]

Robson TO, Barrett PRF. (1977) Review of effects of aquatic herbicides. In: Perring PM, Mellanby K (eds), *Ecological Effects of Pesticides*, pp. 111–18. Academic Press, London. [9.4]

Robson TO, Fowler MC, Barrett PRF. (1976) Effect of some herbicides on freshwater algae. *Pesticide Science* 7: 391–402. [9.3]

Seagrave C. (1988) *Aquatic Weed Control.* Fishing News Books, Farnham. [9.1, 9.3]

Siebert P. (1968) *Importance of Natural Vegetation for the Protection of the Banks of Streams, Rivers and Canals. Freshwater.* Council of Europe Nature and Environment Series No. 2, pp. 33–67. [9.2]

Smith CS, Adams MS. (1986) Phosphorus transfer from sediments by *Myriophyllum spicatum. Limnology and Oceanography* 31: 1312–21. [9.2]

Sosiak AJ. (1990) *An Evaluation of Nutrients and Biological Conditions in the Bow River, 1986 to 1988.* Internal report of Environmental Quality Monitoring Branch, Environmental Assessment Division, Alberta Environment, Edmonton. [9.2]

Soulsby PG. (1974) The effect of a heavy cut on the subsequent growth of aquatic plants in a Hampshire chalk stream. *Journal of the Institute of Fisheries Management* 5: 49–53. [9.3]

Spillet PB. (1981) The use of groynes and deflectors in river management. In: *Proceedings of the Conference on Aquatic Weeds and their Control, 1981*, pp. 189–98. Association of Applied Biologists, Wellesbourne, UK. [9.2]

Standing Committee of Analysts (1987) Methods for the examination of waters and associated materials. In: *Methods for the Use of Aquatic Macrophytes for Assessing Water Quality 1985–6*, p. 176. HMSO, London. [9.1]

Statzner B, Stechmann DH. (1977) Der Einfluss einer mechanischen Entkrautenseebach. *Faunistisch-Okologische Mittelungen* 5: 93–109. [9.3]

Strange RJ. (1976) Nutrient release and community metabolism following the application of herbicide to macrophytes in microcosms. *Journal of Applied Ecology* 13: 889–97. [9.3]

Swales S. (1982) Impacts of weed cutting on fisheries: an experimental study in a small lowland river. *Fisheries Management* 13: 125–38. [9.3]

Toner ED, O'Riordan A, Twomey E. (1965) The effects of arterial drainage works on the salmon stock of a tributary of the River Moy. *Irish Fisheries Investigations Series A (Freshwater)* 1: 36–55. [9.3]

Tooby TE, Spencer-Jones DH. (1978) The fate of the aquatic herbicide dichlobenil in hydrosoil, water and roach (*Rutilus rutilus* L.) following treatment of areas of a lake. In: *Proceedings EWRS 5th Symposium on Aquatic Weeds, 1978*, pp. 323–31. Amsterdam. [9.3]

USDA. (1963) *Chemical Control of Submerged Water-*

weeds in Western Irrigation and Drainage Canals.
US Department of Agriculture Agricultural Research
Service and US Department of the Interior: Recla-
mation Joint Report ARS 34–57. [9.3]

Wade PM. (1987) A review of the provision made for
the identification of wetland macrophytes. *Archive
fur Hydrobiologie Ergebnisse Limnologie* **27**: 105–
113. [9.1]

Wade PM. (1990) Physical control of aquatic weeds. In:
Pieterse AH, Murphy KJ (eds) *Aquatic Weeds*, pp.
93–135. Oxford University Press, Oxford. [9.3]

Westerdahl HE, Gestinger KD. (1988) *Aquatic Plant
Identification and Herbicide Use Guide. 2. Aquatic
Plants and Susceptibility to Herbicides.* Technical
Report A-88-9, US Army Engineer Waterways Experi-
ment Station, Vicksburg, Mississippi. [9.1]

Westlake DF. (1967) Some effects of low-velocity currents on the metabolism of aquatic macrophytes.
Journal of Experimental Botany **18**: 187–205. [9.2]

Westlake DF, Dawson FH. (1976) The construction and

long term field use of inexpensive aerial and aquatic
integrating photometers. In: Evans GG, Bainbridge R,
Rackham O (eds) *Light as an Ecological Factor II*, pp.
27–42. British Ecological Society Symposium, 16.
Blackwell Scientific Publications, Oxford. [9.3]

Westlake DF, Dawson FH. (1982) Thirty years of weed
cutting on a chalk stream. In: *Proceedings EWRS 6th
Symposium on Aquatic Weeds 1982*, pp. 132–40.
Novi Sad. [9.3]

Westlake DF, Dawson FH. (1986). The management of
Ranunculus calcareus by pre-emptive cutting in
Southern England. *Proceedings EWRS/AAB 7th
Symposium on Aquatic Weeds 1986*, pp. 395–400.
Loughborough. [9.3]

Wood RD. (1975) *Hydrobotanical Methods.* University
Park Press, Baltimore. [9.1]

Wright JF, Cameron AC, Hiley PD, Berrie AD. (1982)
Seasonal changes in biomass of macrophytes on
shaded and unshaded sections of the River Lambourn,
England. *Freshwater Biology* **12**: 271–83. [9.1]

10: Direct Control of Fauna: Role of Hatcheries, Fish Stocking and Fishing Regulations

D. P. DODGE AND C. C. MACK

10.1 INTRODUCTION

This chapter describes the benefits and deficiencies inherent in directly controlling biological populations, as opposed to habitat manipulation, as part of a scheme to manage riverine resources. Here, the use of hatchery-reared fish is discussed. The key to successful management of fish in any catchment is cut from three principles that support all animal culturing whether intensive feedlot operations for domestic stock or open-water harvest of pelagic fishes.

First, a manager must have extensive understanding of the habitat and general environmental conditions into which it is intended to introduce a reared species. Will the existing habitats limit the success of a stocking programme? Are the limiting factors irreversible, or can selected undertakings alter conditions to increase the probability of success? Might extremes in environmental conditions occur that could prevent success even when average conditions appear suitable? Can these extremes be mitigated? Is there sufficient knowledge about the habitat requirements of the selected species in order to match them with location and quantity of riverine habitat?

Secondly, the manager needs knowledge about the species to be cultured. How adaptable is the chosen species to episodes of stress resulting from extreme environmental fluctuations? Are there developed and tested gene pools or stocks of the species that are adapted to the kinds and quantities of habitat available in the river system? Does the manager want self-sustaining stocks or will the programme depend on reared stocks or on some combination of the two? Is the selected species compatible with native species in the

system, or should one expect such success that diversity of native species will decline? Will the reared individuals interbreed with wild individuals of the same species or with similar species to produce hybrids? Can any of these negative effects be mitigated?

Finally, the public must be consulted and the manager must ensure that the public understands the risks and benefits of stocking.

This chapter will propose answers to some of these questions. As will also become apparent, there may not be any answers to some of the questions, until assessments produce data about stocking activities sufficient to make adequate analyses of these kind of projects.

Scope and context

One cannot overestimate the value of planning, not only as a means of putting ideas on paper, but also as a way of testing those ideas. To realize the potential for fish production in any river system, managers should prepare plans for catchments which also have regard for creating and protecting stable and diverse fish assemblages as part of the bigger picture of water and land management. Also, a manager needs to appreciate that the productivity of a river depends on nutrients dissolved in the terrestrial systems of its catchment, and how these nutrients reach the aquatic environment depends on the interface between land and water (Zalewski et al 1991). Total reliance on fish culture for recruitment is fraught with as many pitfalls and subsequent disasters as for any other artificially sustained system. Wherever possible managers should select goals that advocate managing fish on the basis of self-sustaining, naturally reproducing native fish populations. Hatchery fish are a means to achieve this kind of goal, but are not by themselves the *raison d'être* for fish management. Obviously we are advocating re-habilitation over mitigation as the first choice for managers of riverine fisheries. However, there will be many situations where mitigation using hatchery fish is the only means available for river management, e.g. where spawning habitat is permanently lost or water quality changes prevent self-sustained populations. The demand for high-quality, inexpensive and readily available protein may eliminate most if not all options except the use of hatchery fish for a put-grow-and-take fisheries management system. In the Orient, and in many European and African river systems, fish communities necessary for human survival would fail without the support of stocking.

Our examples focus on multi-agency experiences derived from nearly 150 years of managing fish communities and their fisheries in the Laurentian Great Lakes Region and other parts of North America. On the one hand, this chapter may not serve managers from Europe and Asia who are working with rivers with longer management experiences and already altered fish communities. However, we feel the North American experience is relevant for river managers in developing countries facing major demands for increased fish extraction from severely-stressed native fish communities, and who are trying to develop a place and purpose for fish culture to maintain some form of sustainability. North Americans made horrendous decisions in the mid-1800s that continue to this day to thwart sustainability of fish communities in the Great lakes (e.g. introduction of the smelt, *Osmerus mordax*). These lessons, and the 1990's approach to managing the Great Lakes ecosystem with hatcheries as a major component, can help river managers throughout the world.

For the purposes of this chapter, we have con-fined our discussion to the intentional release of chosen species. There is no doubt that similar and often more disastrous effects can be traced to introductions of new species that have escaped confinement or that were accidentally introduced by an unsuspected vector. One hundred years of rainbow trout (*Oncorynchus mykiss*) culture and stocking worldwide have created naturalized, often self-sustaining, populations which have already caused most of their potential effects. However, rainbow trout escapes from intensive pond culture (e.g. in southern England) threaten native brown trout (*Salmo trutta*). Similarly, the introduction of ruffe (*Gymnocephalus cernus*) into Lake Superior from ballast water taken at a European port carries the potential for an eco-logical disaster for native Great Lakes percid communities (e.g. *Stizostedian vitreum*, *Perca flavescens*).

All this points up the importance of planning, of understanding the needs of the fish being cul-tured (or being considered for culture and intro-duction) and of assessing the potential effects on endemic fish communities from the stocked fish before one puts great reliance on a fish culture system to sustain a fishery.

This chapter is divided into sections that ex-amine first the basic principles of fish culture and the product desired; secondly, the factors that influence the survival and growth of the fish; and finally the role of regulations.

10.2 HATCHERIES AND FISH STOCKING

History of stocking

The art and science of fish culture are ancient pursuits. The Chinese cultured carp (*Cyprinus carpio*) and goldfish (*C. crassus*) for food and ornamentation as early as 4000 B.P. (MacCrimmon 1968; Balon 1974). Although little evidence is available showing that these and other species were purposely introduced into 'wild' environ-ments, there is no doubt that ponds and raceways failed as frequently then as they have in modern times so that cultured fish were released to new environments to start new populations.

Despite a common misconception, trout and salmon culture is a relatively young industry. In the mid-1700s, Stephen Jacobi successfully stripped and fertilized trout eggs and noted the effects of light and temperature on the developing embryos. Although his successes in Germany were well publicized, a Frenchman, Joseph Remy, is credited with the establishment of the first trout farm. Remy, a professional fisherman, noticed declining fish stocks and in 1840 decided to try to breed trout artificially. Assisted by friends and interested parties with influence, the success of his operation induced the French government to fund the construction of a large fish farm.

Following the success and publicity of Remy's operations, trout farming started developing in Britain, Europe and Russia. Researchers began detailing operations, describing facilities and recognizing the need for proper management of wild stocks, so intensive fish culture grew and flourished worldwide.

Hatching success was low (10–20%) in the early operations, until in 1850 a Russian (Wrasski) discovered the technique of dry spawning. This method has been used ever since in salmonid culture with good results.

Except for a greater understanding of that physiological entity called a 'fish', modern fish culture continues to work with the same basic factors of growth, survival and feed conversion as did the earliest culturists.

Fish stocking of natural waters to provide better commercial fishing or angling became an important tool for fisheries in the mid-1800s with the development of fish hatchery systems in Europe and North America. Of special significance was the evolution of cold-water culture techniques that allowed the raising of very large numbers of salmon and trout which survived long distances and time from hatchery to planting sites. Seth Green and Samuel Wilmot led these advances in North America. Tremendous increases in ranges through successful introductions of salmon and trout (MacCrimmon & Marshall 1968; MacCrimmon 1971) resulted from the application of their techniques.

Stocking objectives

Stocking is a method used in the management of fish stocks as integral parts of aquatic ecosystems. Stocking programmes must share the objectives of effective aquatic ecosystem management in order to provide benefits on a sustainable basis.

Protecting and rehabilitating fish stocks

Protection of aquatic ecosystems should be a fundamental management objective of any fisheries programme. Fish culture can play an important role in protecting endangered stocks by acting as a reservoir of genetic material. The establishment of broodstocks of selected species and strains is an effective way of protecting endangered fish stocks. Although there is always a risk that artificial systems like hatcheries may select towards a lower level of fitness, broodstock husbandry ensures that some of the original genetic material is always available. For example, the Aurora trout, a unique strain of brook trout (*Salvelinus fontinalis*), was approaching extinction due to acidification of the Northern Ontario lakes it inhabited. Hatcheries played a major role in preserving this strain until rehabilitation of its habitat allowed successful natural reproduction.

Rehabilitation is an important objective in managing aquatic ecosystems where they have been degraded. Stocking can play an important role in rehabilitating existing native fish stocks, providing it is used in conjunction with efforts to restore habitat and control exploitation. Examples include re-establishing fish stocks after major pollution events or when destroyed spawning habitat has been restored.

Rehabilitating fisheries with introductions

In many areas, degradation of aquatic ecosystems has been so severe that the restoration of native fish stocks has been deemed unfeasible. Fisheries managers faced with this situation have often chosen to 'rehabilitate a fishery' by using species other than those originally present. An example of this management technique was the introduction of chinook and coho salmon (*Oncorhynchus tshawytscha* and *O. kisutch*) to the Great Lakes and its tributaries in North America. Unfortunately, the introduction of these exotic species has drastically altered the fish community structure of these water bodies, and may be a major impediment to restoring native fish stocks when human commitment and technological advances enable the rehabilitation of these ecosystems.

In Africa, the primary purpose of introductions

of fish species was to maintain or increase yields and harvests. Some introductions met this purpose but others may have compromised long-term sustainable harvests, in part by altering the aquatic environment and competing with native species. The short-term benefits have increased the fish protein supply in these countries but more research and assessment are necessary to understand how introductions serve the reaching of long-term objectives (Ogutu-Ohwayo & Hecky 1991). Holcik (1991) identified at least 134 fish species that had been introduced or relocated within 29 European countries, especially Central and Eastern Europe. He noted that poor success was recorded for most cases, as well as measurable ill-effects on native fish and their habitat.

For further reading, especially for analyses about the implications to fish genetics and aquaculture from introductions, the publication by Billington and Hebert (1991) is an excellent reference.

It is imperative that fisheries managers use some disciplined decision-making when considering introductions as a means to re-establish a fishery. One approach applied by the Province of Ontario (Canada) as a procedure to evaluate proposals to stock species beyond their current range in Ontario waters is a sequential decision model adapted from Kohler and Stanley (1984). Using this model, the decision process continues until the first 'REJECT' decision is reached. Successful completion of the decision model would lead to a decision to approve the stocking (see also Fig. 10.1).

1 (a) Are reasons for introduction valid (including demonstrated need which cannot be met by other management actions)? [No – REJECT]
  (b) Would adequate precautions be taken to safeguard against introduction of disease and parasites? [No – REJECT]
2 (a) Would the species be able to survive in the range of habitats that would be available? [No – REJECT]
3 (a) Would the species have adverse ecological impacts? [Yes – REJECT]
  (b) Would the species potentially be hazardous to humans? [Yes – REJECT]
  (c) Is the species endangered, threatened or rare in its native range? [Yes – REJECT]

Unless:
  (i) purpose is to create a refuge, to prevent species extinction, and/or
  (ii) source of fish is a hatchery stock or naturalized population(s) which is (are) not threatened in any fashion.
4 (a) Was database adequate to develop a complete species synopsis? [No – FURTHER RESEARCH]
5 Based on all available information, do the benefits of the fish introduction outweigh the risks? [No – REJECT; Yes – APPROVE; Unclear – FURTHER RESEARCH]

Hatchery-dependent fisheries

Stocking is also used to provide a fishery in water bodies where natural reproduction cannot occur. These hatchery-dependent fisheries often provide important social and economic benefits, and the lack of natural reproduction may actually be beneficial since it may limit the damage caused by bad stocking decisions.

However, hatchery-dependent fisheries have often been used without adequate consideration of biological, social or economic implications. For example, the adaptability of introduced species to reproduce naturally in water bodies where they 'couldn't' has tested the credibility of many respected fisheries biologists. An example of casual approaches to a potential disaster is the treatment of the spread of the wide-ranging cyprinid, the rudd (*Scardinius erythrophthalmus*), throughout North America. Although the species arrived in the USA in 1916 (Cahn 1927), Courtenay *et al* (1986) considered the species as part of a group of non-native fish whose populations were in decline, as if there were unlikely now to be any effects. However, the rudd was being cultured in ponds in central USA and distributed extensively to anglers, who preferred it as bait to catch bass. Now Burkhead and Williams (1991) report that the rudd has interbred with the native cyprinid golden shiner (*Notemigonus crysoleucas*) to produce the first non-salmonid intergenic hybrid in North America. The potential effects on any fish community where golden shiner is the major forage species may be horrific; the loss of the genetic pool called golden shiner is immoral.

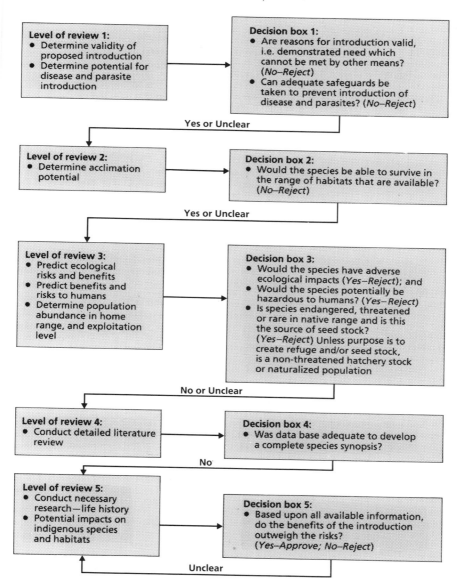

Fig. 10.1 Sequential decision model for evaluating fish species introductions (after Kohler & Stanley 1984).

Supplemental stocking over native populations

Perhaps the most damaging stocking practice still in common use is supplemental stocking over existing self-sustaining native populations. This practice often occurs in water bodies where demand for fishing exceeds supply, particularly when exploitation cannot be effectively regulated. Environmental and genetic effects on fish reared in hatcheries often result in a loss of fitness compared to their wild counterparts. Stocking hatchery fish over native populations could ultimately result in degradation of the health of the

Table 10.1 Impacts of hatchery-reared sportfish on wild fish populations (from Marnell 1986)

Introduction of pathogens and parasites
Hybridization, introgression, intergradation
Trophic alterations:
   Predation, cannibalism
   Food competition
Spatial alterations
   Territorial shifts, altered dominance hierarchies
   Stress and aggression
   Altered movements, temporal changes in activities
Altered growth and survival characteristics
   Altered growth rates
   Changes in natural mortality
   Changes in vulnerability to angling
Displacement, replacement, extinction

native stock by adversely affecting the genetic diversity of the native gene pools. The potential disadvantages of this practice range from minor interruptions in resident fish communities to drastic changes in the aquatic systems including major genetic shifts and even extinction (Table 10.1).

The debate about this issue is causing concern amongst fisheries professionals in the USA. Some scientists see the debate as counterproductive and consuming so much energy that political and economic decisions are being made without adequate biological input, because scientists are spending so much time debating hatcheries and their effects on wild stocks (Martin *et al* 1992).

Again, the manager must balance many aspects of fish production and riverine management before deciding if supplemental stocking is worth the risk. In some cases environmental changes have precluded natural reproduction of the native fish so that the remnant population must be sustained by plantings of hatchery fish. Moreover, in an economic and social climate where fish are essential for human survival, planting hatchery fish over native stocks must happen when no viable alternatives exist to provide the needed protein.

Another risk, potentially lethal, is also associated with intensive aquaculture especially in subtropical climates. Scholtissek (1992) has postulated that the mixing of birds, swine and fish farming sets in motion a process whereby swine act as mixing vessels in which lethal new forms of human Type A influenza viruses are produced.

In summary, stocking can be an effective tool in protecting and rehabilitating existing native fish communities, and can provide increased social and economic benefits. However, stocking fish species which are more adaptable to surviving in degraded aquatic ecosystems, without parallel programmes to restore the degraded systems, and supplemental stocking that degrades existing native populations are two practices which are incompatible with the objective of providing sustainable benefits from healthy aquatic ecosystems.

Stocking strategies

Several strategies are available to fisheries managers using stocking as a management tool. These include selection of species, strains and life stages which are best suited to meet management objectives. An ecosystem approach to fisheries management requires that fish stocking only be used as a tool to achieve balanced fish communities. Fish community objectives should, therefore, form the basis for identifying stocking requirements.

Fisheries managers considering a stocking programme should first evaluate the possibility of using other management options. Increased enforcement, habitat rehabilitation, and harvest control techniques are just three examples of other management tools which are often cheaper, less damaging to native stocks, and more effective than stocking.

Species selection

Fish culture has played a major role in the introduction or range extension of fish species into waters in which the species did not occur naturally. While some of these introductions have created naturally reproducing populations which are generally deemed as beneficial to society, others have resulted in irreversible damage to native fish communities. For example, rainbow trout (*Oncorynchus mykiss*), introduced to tributaries to the Great Lakes, have provided very large, self-sustaining fisheries, but in the process have significantly reduced the range and numbers of the native charr (*Salvelinus fontinalis*). Similar effects are predicted to happen to brown trout (*Salmo trutta*) in the UK as rainbow trout become more established.

In several jurisdictions, a more conservative approach is being used to select species for fisheries management programmes. Many governments have enacted legislation and policies which restrict the movement of fish within their jurisdictions. In cases where waters are shared between nations, such as the Great Lakes in North America, co-operative policies and protocols have been developed to ensure that introductions or range extensions of species are not made without adequate consultation with stakeholders, and that proper assessment of the environmental risks involved is undertaken. Another example of multinational protocols is the Code of Practice adopted by the European Inland Fishery Advisory Committee (EIFAC) in 1987 for the regulation and control of fish introductions.

For most stocking applications, only native fish species should be considered. Native species will provide the most predictable results, with the least risk of environmental consequences. However, most species of fish are not homogeneous in terms of their characteristics; fish stocking programmes which use the wrong genetic strain for a specific purpose can be just as damaging to local, native fish communities as if a non-native species were introduced.

Genetic strain

A fish species may consist of many unique genetic strains which have evolved as a result of distinct geographical, behaviourial or temporal factors. Ignorance of the importance of protecting fish stocks has led to the loss of genetic diversity in many fish populations, causing loss of population fitness. Recent developments in fish culture, such as rotational line crossing of broodstock lines to reduce inbreeding, and the use of large numbers of randomly selected wild brood fish to maximize genetic diversity, can reduce the loss of genetic diversity in fish populations. Selection cannot be eliminated entirely. Nature does not always act randomly, and fish collection techniques are often selective. Even if we were able to

maintain genetic diversity, environmental factors occur in fish culture which are fundamentally different to those in a wild environment.

Broodstock management

The management of broodstocks in a fish culture programme should be aimed not only to ensure an adequate and consistent supply of eggs for rearing and eventual stocking, but also to establish careful breeding programmes, and to maintain the genetic diversity of those stocks over several generations. Genetic variability is important for maintaining maximum hatchery production levels, for disease resistance, and for the ability of progeny to adapt to new environments after stocking.

Artificial propagation and rearing procedures used in contemporary fish culture tend to reduce the genetic diversity of captive broodstocks, resulting ultimately in inbreeding and associated loss of vigour. The protection afforded by the hatchery environment enables less fit individuals to survive, and because fewer parents produce relatively higher numbers of offspring than in natural conditions, the potential for siblings to be crossed one with another is greater.

To avoid the potential inbreeding effects of fish culture practices a number of principles should be considered in establishing and propagating broodstocks held in fish culture stations.

In collections of eggs from the wild to establish a new broodstock, and in propagating captive broodstocks in hatchery:
1 parents should be a random sample from the spawning population with no selection on the basis of size, appearance or other characteristics;
2 select from the entire spawning season or run, preferably with 25% of parents spawned when 15% of females are ripe, 50% spawned when 40% are ripe, and the remaining 25% when 70–80% of females are ripe;
3 a minimum of 50 spawning pairs should be used;
4 matings should be on a single pair basis, i.e. single males should be used to fertilize the eggs of single females with no pooling of eggs or milt;
5 individual families should be kept separate from fertilization through to incubation;

6 at eye-up, or preferably swim-up, equal numbers of eggs/fry from each family should be randomly taken to create the broodstock pool of individuals so that no family is represented more than any other — the number of eggs or animals to be taken per family will depend upon the number of families and the target number for a broodstock lot.

Thus, in a single year, a culturing station can establish one line of breeding for a broodstock. A minimum of two lines are required (three to five are preferred) in order to minimize losses of genetic variability.

The sources of establishment of these other lines of breeding are many.

1 In succeeding years follow the same process as described above so that in 3 years you will have established three lines; and/or:

2 Fish culture facilities exchange eyed-eggs at that time in the year when lines-of-breeding are being established. Disease control and certification systems are necessary to make this exchange safe for recipient fish culture facilities. It is advisable, also, to have some isolation facilities for rearing exchanged lines. It would be possible by this method to establish the minimum lines-of-breeding to maintain broodstocks in 1 year; or:

3 Use a co-operative, centralized facility to maintain lines-of-breeding.

Rotational line crossing

Once a captive broodstock is established in a fish culture station, in addition to the above procedures for the establishment of a stock, a breeding scheme is required which will prevent the mating of siblings or half-sibs. Thus inbreeding is minimized through successive generations. The technique is known as rotational line crossing (Kincaid 1977).

At the time a broodstock is established, three distinct lines are created from a single year class, or three lines are created in succession with three separate year classes. The three lines, which may be called A, B and C, must be held in separate units or marked by fin clips, branding or some other means by which they can be distinguished one from another.

All three lines may be used for producing eggs for production purposes in any given year, but when the time comes to produce the next generation of broodstock, a specific breeding scheme must be followed. For example, the females of line A are crossed with males from line B; the females of B are fertilized with males from C; and the females of C are fertilized with line A males. This creates three new lines, AB, BC and CA. The next generation is then produced from those three lines, again by crossing females and males from different lines. The creation of three

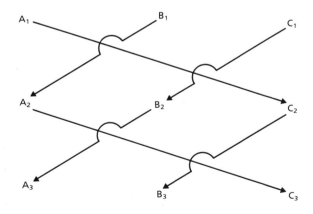

A_1 male is bred with C_2 female	*then*	A_2 male is bred with C_3 female
B_1 male is bred with A_2 female		B_2 male is bred with A_3 female
C_1 male is bred with B_2 female		C_2 male is bred with B_3 female

Fig. 10.2 Rotational line crossing (after Kincaid 1977).

lines for each generation may be carried out in a single year, or as is preferred for longer-living species, in three successive years (Fig. 10.2).

Evaluation

Evaluation of success of programmes that rehabilitate or introduce species using hatchery fish is fraught with many problems in river management. Sampling is very difficult, especially for small fish, and population estimates are usually very unreliable except by direct count methods of migratory fish at fishways (McMenemy & Kynard 1988; Beamesderfer & Rieman 1988). Sampling people who catch or eat fish may provide useful information about riverine fish, especially with artisanal fisheries (Bayley & Petrere 1989) but the quantitative methods to estimate fish production, survival and yield are poorly developed relative to approaches for the same parameters for lakes, small streams and reservoirs. Casselmann *et al* (1990) surveyed 73 scientists from 12 countries for their experience in sampling large river systems. This survey reviewed and evaluated many types of sampling gear but concluded that none was suitable for sampling large river systems in all types of habitat and situations.

10.3 FACTORS INFLUENCING SUCCESS

As stated earlier in this chapter, there must be a commitment by river catchment managers to include fisheries management as a component of their plans. Therefore, the catchment planning process becomes the most important factor that could influence the success of any fish stocking scheme. From the very beginning of this process, it should be evident from the catchment plan as to what quality and quantity of fish habitat will be delivered by the plan. Further, the plan must indicate where the various fish habitats will be in the catchment, what variability can be expected and when, in any one year, those changing conditions are likely to occur. Nelson *et al* (1992) used a hierarchical system to classify locations and sites in northeastern Nevada, USA. The system is based on the integration of geology, geomorphology and local habitat features. The authors were able to develop preliminary criteria

for assessing a fishery on a large scale (km^2) to save time and money, by analysing detailed habitat attributes on those sites most likely to be important for the chosen fish community.

The application of the ideas and concerns outlined in the remainder of this section is predicated singularly on the forewarning any catchment plan should provide. It is at this level of preparation that the public and their legislative representatives become involved. Consultation over and acceptance of catchment plans and their fish management components provide greater assurance that fiscal resources and commitment to sustainability will be forthcoming.

The concept of sustainability is an important part of planning for fisheries in a river catchment. Gardiner (1991) argues for ecological sustainability that includes social, political and legal components where economic and environmental sustainability are very much interrelated. His paper is an excellent treatise on the value of planning at the catchment level to achieve holistic management of riverine systems.

Water quality and quantity

Water-quality management for fish production and survival of hatchery fish includes the optimizing of not only discharges for current and volume, but also of the water levels and wetted margins of streams. The complicated interrelationships between instream flow and fish production have caused many problems in fish and river management. Often fisheries managers have had neither expertise nor data readily available to help plan for the effects of changes in hydrological regimes. However, Gustard (1992) reported significant advances in the understanding of river regimes, including international databases that could help in the understanding of global influences on floods and their frequency.

Water abstraction schemes, e.g. cooling, drinking-water supplies, especially those that withdraw large volumes (>500 m^3 min^{-1}), present major hazards to fish, and could 'harvest' major portions of planted species intended to rehabilitate a river system. Various fish protection devices have been designed for water extraction systems, but few, if any, prevent entrapment and impingement of all species of fish (Fletcher 1985).

Even with the most efficient and effective fish culture programme, the success of planted fish depends equally on the water quality of the river system into which they are introduced. Many factors interact with the fish as they strive to establish themselves within the existing fish communities and their environment.

Nutrient concentrations and the resulting primary productivity of a river limits the growth and development of the hatchery fish. Correlations between fish production and nutrients in streams have been well documented (Welcomme 1985).

Many water quality and physical characteristics affect the survival and growth of fish introduced into river systems. In fact, the concentrations of certain parameters will dictate whether or not a hatchery-supported fisheries can ever be successful. For example, the penetration of light and its association with primary and secondary production is a key component to the survival of salmonids (Lloyd 1987). Besides affecting the quality and quantity of light penetration, suspended particles in the water column influence the proficiency with which fish see and catch prey. Also, particles, especially colloidal clay materials, can accumulate on gill filaments and other body parts to such an extent that fish die or are easy prey for larger predators. Readers should refer to Walling and Webb (1992) and Webb and Walling (1992) for more detailed descriptions of water quality parameters and their ranges expected in riverine systems.

Habitat suitability

Essential to this matching of fish with habitat is the need to understand the effects on fish production of physical processes in rivers (Heede & Rinne 1990). Similarly, the generation, transport and deposition of organic and inorganic particles, so much related to hydrological processes, can affect the success of fish stocking into rivers (Newcombe & MacDonald 1991).

River and basin management schemes also influence the quantity and size of sediment that travels suspended and/or settles in the river bed. These factors also have great influence on the survival, growth and reproductive potential of hatchery-reared and wild fish (Reiser & White 1988). Large rivers move large particles, and es-

pecially during flood events, can redefine very large portions of river bottoms. These major alterations frequently remove and destroy essential spawning, nursery and staging areas for riverine fish. Losses of gravel, for example, preferred for spawning salmonids, could mean the demise of any annual recruitment based on natural reproduction. Deforestation of headwaters of tributaries to Lake Ontario in North America created severe erosion that eventually covered spawning habitat for landlocked Atlantic salmon with several metres of sand, silt and clay. Similar changes to the quality and quantity of essential habitat are well-documented worldwide (e.g. Ward & Stanford 1989).

The essence of successful fisheries management in rivers is the matching of fish stock with suitable habitat. In many cases, however, habitat requirements for many fish species, especially needs for early-life survival and growth, are not usually understood. The interrelationships of riverine fishes with their environments, and the spatial and temporal scales one must use to understand these relationships and how fish species have adapted, are reviewed in detail by Bayley and Li (1992).

Allocation/overharvest

Management of riverine fish stocks involves more than just planting hatchery-reared fish and harvesting these stocks for food, recreation and revenue. Certain basic decisions are necessary before committing resources to hatcheries and fish production. First, are artificially-reared hatchery fish the best means to optimize fish production or should managers be rehabilitating habitat and changing fishing scenarios to allow existing stocks to stabilize and thus optimize the potential for riverine production based on those existing stocks? Inherent in this decision is the question of how much of the annual production of fish should be allocated to the long-term maintenance of the resource. Of the remainder of fish production, what quantity of fish would be ecologically and economically sound to allot to fishing, and when and how could this resource extraction take place that would maintain these two principal allocations?

Welch and Noakes (1991) designed an optimal

economic and resource protection policy for harvesting Adams River sockeye salmon (*Oncorhynchus nerka*). The policy proposed that a subdominant run be fished at 50% harvest rate in the first year and a moratorium be imposed on fishing off-year runs for a period of 8–12 years. This proposal would put all the gains from a reduced rate of harvest into increasing the size of the spawning population. When an optimal escapement level was achieved, harvesting would be reinitiated. Unfortunately, senior management appeared to be more sensitive to the reduction in fishing times and local employment, so the policy was considered impractical even though the proposal could contribute up to $600 million (Can) to the net value of the fish stock.

Major river diversions on the scale of those in Siberia and northern Quebec (Kierans 1988; Berkes 1989) present different hazards to fish management dependent on fish stocking. As well as significant shifts in habitat, in local climates and in stage discharge patterns, diversions eventually change the character of the native fish assemblages such that new or existing species increased by fortuitous habitat shifts may prevent the successful management of the intended fish species. Reliance on cultured fish to offset these changes is inevitably misplaced.

However, once major ecologically profound changes have been accomplished within a river catchment, fisheries managers have to get on with the job of managing this altered environment to maximize fish production on a sustainable basis. In many cases, fish are an essential food item so that restoration of fish production as soon as possible is often close to an emergency. At the same time, it would be a risky investment to take just any approach. Planning will lead one through a logical sequence asking questions and seeking answers until the best solution can be identified for the management of the fish community in the new environment.

Conflicting land/water use

The best fish culture strategies and practices in the world rarely offset the detrimental results of major land and water management practices which destroy certain components of a river system essential to the production and maintenance

of fish stocks. For example, Raymond (1988) showed that major alterations in dam and impoundment management combined with large releases of smolt from hatcheries offset the decline of steelhead (*Oncorhynchus mykiss*) in the Columbia River, but failed to compensate for major losses of returning chinook (*O. tschawytscha*). Also, most returning adults were of hatchery origin, suggesting native gene pools had also been lost. Here may be a case for arguing for the establishment of hatchery stocks from broodstocks of local origin.

Management of established reservoirs can influence the survival and growth of hatchery-reared fish. Fisheries previously dependent in the main on hatchery productions can be boosted and even made self-sufficient by changes and innovations in reservoir management. In mid-western America, populations of centrachids (Centrachidae) dominate impoundment fisheries and are enhanced by increased time of storage of flood waters (Mitzner 1981). At the same time, cool and cold-water fish populations usually decline so that any maintenance of these species becomes almost exclusively hatchery dependent. Even coldwater tailrace fisheries are usually based on stocking.

Genetic integrity of wild and hatchery stocks

The overall fitness of any species and of any of its many stocks should be a major concern of a manager using hatchery fish to rehabilitate and maintain a riverine fish community. Undoubtedly, there are major differences among various species and stocks in their predilection to adapt to rigorous environmental conditions in any river over any annual cycle. Testing of stocks for these abilities would be an ideal screening mechanism to increase probability of returns of planted fish and also to reduce costs for fish culture programmes. Challenge-testing of stocks and their responses to success-limiting stresses showed stocks of coho salmon (*O. kisutch*) had different capabilities (McGeer *et al* 1991). Such differences should influence which stock is chosen to culture.

The danger to native populations from large-scale escapes of farmed fish reflects the same hazard that comes with intentional use of hatchery fish from inappropriate gene pools. In

Norwegian rivers, farmed Atlantic salmon (*Salmo salar*) are threatening native fish through cross-breeding of wild with farmed fish, with the subsequent risk of losing genetic material essential for the survival of local populations (Gausen & Moen 1991). The river catchment manager must always be aware of this kind of threat.

The dangers inherent in introductions are further enhanced by the blind faith put in recent genetic 'breakthroughs' where managers were made to believe large populations of desexed fish established by stocking would never produce off-spring. An excellent example of this fallacious assumption was the release of (reportedly sterile) grass carp (*Ctenopharyngodon idella*) into the Mississippi River and the subsequent colonization of the system as naturally-reproduced populations established rapidly (Brown & Coon 1991), all of this despite caution advised by scientists well-placed to predict ecological disasters.

Effect of environmental contaminants

Residues of persistent, toxic substances that bio-accumulate have been linked to the reproductive failures of wildlife (e.g. bald eagle *Haliaeetus leucocephalus*) and fish (e.g. lake trout *Salvelinus naymaycush*). Obviously the body burden carried by any hatchery fish and the potential to accumulate more in the environment into which it has been introduced must be considered as factors affecting the overall success of fish survival and growth. It is possible that mega fish stocking programmes will fail to re-establish self-sustaining fish populations in rivers because of uncontrolled toxic effluents and high concentrations of contaminated sediment (Gilbertson 1992).

One pertinent criterion often ignored by managers is whether or not the species chosen for a river fish culture programme has the propensity to accumulate persistent toxic substances that may threaten human health. Notwithstanding any effects that biomagnified toxic body burdens may have on the general health of the carriers and on the specific reproductability of mature fish, there is the fundamental issue of effects from toxic substances in fish on humans, especially women and children. Swain (1988) identified significantly damaging effects on maternal health

and showed the risks associated with trans-placental transmission to infants *in utero* and for nursing infants.

10.4 ROLE OF REGULATIONS

Regulations are an important mechanism for controlling risks to native fish communities which may result from stocking-related activities. Regulations can be used directly to control the choice of species or strains used for stocking, including the use of exotics, or to prevent the introduction or spread of serious fish disease agents.

Indirectly, regulations play a major role in contributing to the success of a stocking programme. Fishing seasons and access can be controlled to protect stocked fish when they are most vulnerable, such as at the stocking site, or in the case where anadromous species are stocked in a river as pre-smolts, prior to their movement downstream to a lacustrine environment. More fundamental regulations controlling exploitation can be used to eliminate the need for starting a stocking programme.

Regulations are needed to provide protection at continental, regional or local levels. Man-made boundaries (i.e. national, territorial or local government) are the main mechanism used to develop, implement and enforce regulations. The fact that fish do not recognize man-made boundaries poses a major challenge to the effectiveness of regulations. For this reason, international commissions such as the North Atlantic Salmon Conservation Organization, EIFAC and the Great Lakes Fishery Commission play an important role in developing international agreements and co-ordinated strategies which assist in managing large watersheds.

National or territorial controls provide the major framework for implementing legislation, regulations and policy. These controls are often easier to enforce, because they are based on clearly defined boundaries. Territorial legislation can be used as the basis for regulations which control at the local level, such as specifying the location of fish sanctuaries.

Fish disease regulations

The risk of transferring serious fish disease agents with live or dead fish has been recognized as a serious problem by many agencies. Until recently, fish diseases have largely been regarded as a hatchery-related problem. Recognition of the importance of fish diseases in the wild environment is a recent phenomenon which resulted from the occurrence of large epizootics such as ulcerative dermal necrosis (UDN) in the UK, and the huge mortalities of chinook salmon in Lake Michigan which were, in part, attributable to bacterial kidney disease. These and other events have shown that fish diseases can have serious economic and environmental consequences.

Harvest control/allocation

Fishing regulations that restrict the harvest of both hatchery and wild fish are developed to protect fish stocks from depletion. Most regulations use controls on fishing methods, seasons and bag limits as the major means of controlling harvest. In many cases, these regulations never achieve their intended purposes because total harvest (annual) is never controlled. Recent changes in regulations in North America, especially those related to catch-and-release (Anderson & Nehring 1984), suggest fishing quality and angler satisfaction can be maintained along with maintenance of appropriate fish stocks.

10.5 CONCLUSIONS

For a chapter dedicated to fish stocking, we are likely to be accused of being very much anti-stocking. But we have seen many native stocks lost to stocking and have witnessed many wasted efforts on ill-planned and poorly monitored schemes for fish stocking. We wish managers to view fish stocking as only one of many tools available for fish management and not the only and best tool.

When managers are required to use stocking to sustain use of riverine fish populations, they must ensure that they match the appropriate scheme with the management plan for the river catchment. Then, managers need to match the selected fish species and strain with the habitat quality and quantity available in the river. Here, we emphasize that money and resources should always go as a priority to promote the restoration and conservation of native fish species before putting any reliance on the culture and introductions of non-native species.

ACKNOWLEDGEMENTS

M. Succi typed many drafts and made order and legibility from scribbles and notes. We also acknowledge the comments by an anonymous reviewer of an earlier draft. Any bias we project in this chapter results from our collective experiences being centred in the Laurentian Great Lakes of North America.

REFERENCES

Anderson RM, Nehring RB. (1984) Effects of a catch-and-release regulation on a wild trout population in Colorado and its acceptance by anglers. *North American Journal of Fisheries Management* **4**: 257–65. [10.4]

Balon EK. (1974) *Domestication of the Carp* Cyprinus carpio L. Life Science Miscellaneous Publication, Royal Ontario Museum, Toronto. [10.2]

Bayley PB, Li HW. (1992) Riverine fishes. In: Calow P, Petts GE (eds) *The Rivers Handbook, Vol. 1*, pp. 251–81. Blackwell Scientific Publications, Oxford. [10.3]

Bayley PB, Petrere M Jr. (1989) Amazon fisheries: assessment methods: current status and management options. In: Dodge DP (ed) *Proceedings of the Large River Symposium*, pp. 385–98. Canadian Special Publication Fisheries and Aquatic Sciences 106, Ottawa. [10.2]

Beamesderfer RC, Rieman BE. (1988) Size selectivity and bias in estimates of population statistics of smallmouth bass, walleye and northern squawfish in a Columbia River reservoir. *North American Journal of Fisheries Management* **8**: 505–10. [10.2]

Berkes F. (1989) Editorial: impacts of James Bay development. *Journal of Great Lakes Research* **15**: 375. [10.3]

Billington N, Hebert PDN (eds). (1991) International symposium on the ecological and genetic implications of fish introductions (FIN). *Canadian Journal of Fisheries and Aquatic Sciences* **48** (Suppl. 1): 181. [10.2]

Brown DJ, Coon TG. (1991) Grass carp larvae in the lower Missouri River and its tributaries. *North American Journal of Fisheries Management* **11**: 62–6. [10.3]

Burkhead NM, Williams JD. (1991) An intergenic hybrid of a native minnow, the golden shiner, and an exotic minnow, the rudd. *Transactions of the American Fisheries Society* **120**: 781–95. [10.2]

Cahn AR. (1927) The European rudd (*Scardinius*) in Wisconsin. *Copeia* **162**: 5. [10.2]

Casselmann JM, Penczak T, Carl L, Mann HK, Holcik J, Woitowich WA. (1990) An evaluation of fish sampling methodologies for large river systems. *Polskie Archiwum Hydrobiologii* **37**(4): 521–51. [10.2]

Courtenay WR Jr, Hensley DA, Taylor JN, McCann JA. (1986) Distribution of exotic fishes in North America. In: Hocutt CH, Wiley EO (eds) *The Zoogeography of North American Freshwater Fishes*, pp. 675–98. John Wiley, New York. [10.2]

Fletcher RI. (1985) Risk analysis of fish diversity experiments: pumped intake systems. *Transactions of the American Fisheries Society* **114**: 652–94. [10.3]

Gardiner JL. (1991) Towards sustainable development in river basins: new professional perspectives? Paper presented to the International Symposium on Effects of Watercourse Improvements: Assessment, Methodology, Management Assistance, September 1991, Namur, Belgium. [10.3]

Gausen D, Moen V. (1991) Large-scale escapes of farmed Atlantic salmon (*Salmo salar*) into Norwegian rivers threaten natural populations. *Canadian Journal of Fisheries and Aquatic Sciences* **48**: 426–8. [10.3]

Gilbertson M. (1992) PCB and dioxin research and implications for fisheries research and resource management. *Canadian Journal of Fisheries and Aquatic Sciences* **49**: 1078–9. [10.3]

Gustard A. (1992) Analysis of river regimes. In: Calow P, Petts GE (eds) *The Rivers Handbook, Vol. 1*, pp. 29–47. Blackwell Scientific Publications, Oxford. [10.3]

Heede BH, Rinne JN. (1990) Hydrodynamic and fluvial morphologic processes; implications for fisheries management and research. *North American Journal of Fisheries Management* **10**: 249–68. [10.3]

Holcik J. (1991) Fish introductions in Europe with particular reference to its central and eastern part. *Canadian Journal of Fisheries and Aquatic Sciences* **48** (Suppl. 1): 13–23. [10.2]

Kierans T. (1988) Recycled run-off from the North. *Journal of Great Lakes Research* **14**: 255–6. [10.3]

Kincaid HL. (1977) Rotational line crossing: an approach to the reduction of inbreeding accumulation in trout brood stocks. *Progressive Fish Culturist* **39**: 179–81. [10.2]

Kohler CC, Stanley JG. (1984) A suggested protocol for evaluating proposed exotic fish introductions in the United States. In: Courtney WR Jr, Stauffer JR Jr (eds) *Distribution, Biology and Management of Exotic Fishes*. Johns Hopkins University Press, Baltimore. [10.2]

Lloyd DS. (1987) Turbidity as a water quality standard for salmonid habitats in Alaska. *North American Journal of Fisheries Management* **7**: 34–45. [10.3]

MacCrimmon HR. (1968) *Carp in Canada*. Bulletin 168, Fisheries Research Board of Canada, Ottawa. [10.2]

MacCrimmon HR. (1971) World distribution of rainbow trout (*Salmo gairdneri*). *Journal of the Fisheries Research Board of Canada* **28**: 663–704. [10.2]

MacCrimmon HR, Marshall TL. (1968) World distribution of brown trout, *Salmo trutta*. *Journal of the Fisheries Research Board of Canada* **25**: 2527–48. [10.2]

McGeer JC, Baranyi L, Iwama GK. (1991) Physiological responses to challenge tests in six stocks of coho salmon (*Oncorhynchus kisutch*). *Canadian Journal of Fisheries and Aquatic Sciences* **48**: 1761–71. [10.3]

McMenemy JR, Kynard B. (1988) Use of inclined-plan traps to study movement and survival of Atlantic salmon smolts in the Connecticut River. *North American Journal of Fisheries Management* **8**: 481–8. [10.2]

Marnell LF. (1986) Impact of hatchery stocks on wild fish populations. In: Stroud RH (ed) *Fish Culture in Fisheries Management*, pp. 339–47. American Fisheries Society, Bethesda, Maryland. [10.2]

Martin J, Webster J, Edwards G. (1992) Hatcheries and wild stocks: are they compatible. *Fisheries* **17**: 4. [10.2]

Mitzner L. (1981) Influence of floodwater storage on abundance of juvenile crappie and subsequent harvest at Lake Rathbun, Iowa. *North American Journal of Fisheries Management* **1**: 46–50. [10.3]

Nelson RL, Platts WS, Larsen DP, Jensen SE. (1992) Trout distribution and habitat in relation to geology and geomorphology in the North Fork Humboldt River drainage. *Transactions of the American Fisheries Society* **121**: 405–26. [10.3]

Newcombe CP, MacDonald DD. (1991) Effects of suspended sediments on aquatic ecosystems. *North American Journal of Fisheries Management* **11**: 72–82. [10.3]

Ogutu-Ohwayo R, Hecky RE. (1991) Fish introductions in Africa and some of their implications. *Canadian Journal of Fisheries and Aquatic Sciences* **48** (Suppl. 1): 8–12. [10.2]

Raymond HL. (1988) Effects of hydroelectric development and fisheries enhancement on spring and summer chinook salmon and steelhead in the Columbia River Basin. *North American Journal of Fisheries Management* **8**: 1–12. [10.3]

Reiser D.W., White R.G. (1988) Effects of two sediment size-classes on survival of steelhead and chinook salmon eggs. *North American Journal of Fisheries Management* **8**: 432–7. [10.3]

Scholtissek C. (1992) Cultivating a killer virus. *Natural*

History January 1992; pp. 2–6. [10.2]

Swain WR. (1988) Human health consequences of consumption of fish contaminated with organochlorine compounds. *Aquatic Toxicology* **11**: 357–77. [10.3]

Walling DE, Webb BW. (1992) Water quality I. Physical characteristics. In: Calow P, Petts GE (eds) *The Rivers Handbook, Vol. 1*, pp. 48–72. Blackwell Scientific Publications, Oxford. [10.3]

Ward JV, Stanford JA. (1989) Riverine ecosystems: The influence of man on catchment dynamics and fish ecology. In: Dodge DP (ed) *1989 Proceedings of the International Large River Symposium (LARS)*, pp. 56–64, Canadian Special Publication Fisheries and Aquatic Sciences 106, Ottawa. [10.3]

Webb BW, Walling DE. (1992) Water quality II. Chemical characteristics. In: Calow P, Petts GE (eds) *The Rivers Handbook, Vol. 1*, pp. 73–100. Blackwell Scientific Publications, Oxford. [10.3]

Welch DW, Noakes DJ. (1991) Optimal harvest rate policies for rebuilding the Adamo River sockeye salmon (*Oncorhynchus nerka*). *Canadian Journal of Fisheries and Aquatic Sciences* **48**: 526–35. [10.3]

Welcomme RL. (1985) *River Fisheries*. FAO Fisheries Technical Paper 262, Rome. [10.3]

Zalewski M, Thorpe JE, Gaudin P. (eds) (1991) *Fish and Land/inland-water Ecotones*. UNESCO MAB, tódź, Poland. [10.1]

11: Spatial and Temporal Problems with Monitoring

A. J. UNDERWOOD

11.1 INTRODUCTION

Despite the enormous and widespread need to be able to identify and, where possible, predict the effects of human disturbances in natural ecosystems, there is still insufficient attention paid to the basic requirements of design of sampling and analysis of quantitative data from field surveys. This is increasingly discussed in the context of experimental ecology (e.g. Underwood 1981, 1986; Hurlbert 1984). It does not yet seem to have been the focus of sufficient attention in the areas of environmental monitoring and assessment of anthropogenic impact, even though there have been some excellent accounts of general procedures (notably Green 1979; Clarke & Green 1988).

Monitoring, as an ongoing exercise in many habitats, is in particular need of justification of procedures and rationales (see Underwood 1989 for examples). The purpose of this review will be to consider some of the problems associated with sampling and testing hypotheses about spatial and temporal patterns in rivers, as they relate to such issues as environmental impacts. Some of the inadequacies of routine monitoring programmes, where there are no clearly articulated logical hypotheses (e.g. Connor & Simberloff 1986; Underwood 1990) will also be discussed. The context of this discussion is devoid of any particular understanding of the nuances of sampling procedures in freshwater systems. There are two justifications for this, given the author's background in marine habitats (which might be excusable if they were thought of as very salty, very wide rivers?). First, these topics are discussed elsewhere in this volume (see Chapter 3) as

are the potential disturbances and impacts (see Chapter 12). Second, and perhaps more importantly, the issue are general and transcend particularities of habitat, although obviously the organisms to be examined and their associations in assemblages will be very different from one habitat to another. A discussion of the sampling problem in rivers is presented by Norris *et al* (1994).

The general approach used will be to examine deficiencies in certain sorts of sampling and monitoring programmes with a view to increasing the relationships between the data that can be gathered in routine sampling, testable hypotheses and interpretations in relation to causation. The particular emphasis will be to increase the usefulness of sampling to establish causality between an observed disturbance and a measurable biological response (see also Clarke & Green 1988; Underwood & Peterson 1988). For this reason, the focus will be on measurements of abundances of populations of single species, although any other appropriate variable could be examined in the designs discussed (e.g. species diversity, rate of growth of individuals, production per unit area, scope for growth, etc.). Sophisticated multivariate procedures exist for many types of environmental monitoring involving numerous species in an assemblage (e.g. Clarke 1993; Warwick 1993), but these do not extend to the complex scenarios and designs that are often needed to detect impacts in very patchy and variable habitats (Clarke 1993).

Types of disturbance

Broadly, there are three types of human disturbances to natural habitats. These are sometimes classed as 'press' and 'pulse' disturbances (Bender *et al* 1984) and 'catastrophes'. Although there are some problems with this type of trichotomy (see below), it is useful to think about the nature, time-course and possible responses of populations to the various types of anthropogenic influences. *Pulse disturbances* are acute, short-term episodes of disturbance, for example an accidental discharge of chemicals through an outfall would, if it caused any biological effect, create a temporary pulse of change in a population. The disturbance is removed quickly and the response of the system is short-term, although a short-term change may itself cause long-term consequences. In contrast, a *press disturbance* is a sustained or chronic interference with a natural population. For example, building a weir and altering the rate of flow of water is a long-term environmental change that may have an impact on downstream populations because of changed physical features of the habitat. In this case, there would be long-term and usually non-recoverable changes in the populations. Finally, *catastrophes* are major, often planned, destructions of habitat. In these cases, there is no possibility that the organisms could recover – their habitat is removed. This is an easily predicted outcome.

There are some difficulties because, for example, a pulse disturbance may actually cause long-term effects. For example, there may be a pulse that removes predators temporarily from an area. Their prey then have a temporary escape from predation and remain in large numbers through a critical period of growth so that when the pulse disturbance is gone and the predators can recolonize from elsewhere, they cannot consume the prey that escaped them during or immediately after the disturbance. As a result, there can be long-term changes in dominance in the assemblage in such a habitat (Dayton 1971; Connell 1975).

As another problem, there are many cases where environmental disturbances will involve both types of perturbation. Thus, building a weir will cause a pulse disturbance due to disruption of sediments and, often, the introduction of chemicals during the construction phase. After it is built, there is a permanent press on the flow of water. Both may cause effects on populations and the interpretation of subsequent changes in the abundances of organisms may only be interpretable in the light of knowledge of the interaction between short-term and long-term disturbances.

A further difficulty lies in the definition of time-scales for the organisms concerned. For example, the presence of a mine may affect local rivers during its operation (Underwood 1991). If the mine is active for, say, 40 years, that will represent a press for many populations with shorter turnover times. For any longer-lived species, the closure of the mine after 40 years means that it was short-term and therefore a pulse. Obviously, the time-course of either type of disturbance is intimately related to the life cycle and longevity of the potentially affected organisms (Frank 1981; Connell & Sousa 1983). This makes the dichotomy between the two types of disturbance less useful than if there were no ambiguities.

Nevertheless, it is instructive to think in terms of the different types of disturbance. Where there is a pulse, environmental management requires that the time-course and rate of change of the population be considered (Bender *et al* 1984). The effect on abundance will depend on the inertia and resilience of the populations being affected (Underwood 1989; see later). The crucial issues for conservation of species will be their capacity to tolerate short-term disruptions to their habitat and their capacity to recolonize once the disturbance has ended.

Where press disturbances are happening, the major issue will be the changed abundances in the longer term, i.e. the new long-run averages of the population after the disturbance starts. Management must then focus on long-term sustenance of the population, for example to ensure that it retains the minimal numbers necessary to continue to breed.

Where there are planned or unfortunate catastrophes and habitat is permanently lost, the issues for management are the capacity of populations elsewhere to continue to persist once the populations are lost from some parts of their range. Of course, for very spatially localized species, no loss is tolerable and prediction of a catastrophe becomes very important.

In the latter case, there is no point in monitoring to detect an impact – the impact can be very well predicted from the nature of the planned disturbance. In the case of press and pulse disturbances, however, there is every need to decide in advance (where the disturbance is planned) exactly what sort of disturbance it will be and what sorts of effects it may have so that the sampling can be designed with appropriate time-scales to detect the effects. If a pulse disturbance is anticipated, it is essential to have sampling on sufficiently small time-scales to detect its effects, to ensure that the changes to abundances of relevant populations are not going outside the predicted ranges, or that populations are not actually heading to extinction. Otherwise, no remedial or alleviatory action could be taken and the populations will not be able to recover once the pulse has finished.

Where a press is concerned, there will be a need to sample at appropriate longer time intervals to determine the new long-run mean abundance (or the new pattern of temporal change – see below; Underwood 1991). Thus, for management of environmental impacts, a categorization of disturbances is helpful to planning, even if the disturbances do not neatly fall into the categories.

Disturbances affecting mean abundance

By and large, the literature on environmental changes that affect abundances of populations is obsessed with changed patterns of mean abundance (Fig. 11.1). For example, Green's (1979) excellent book does not consider any other types of

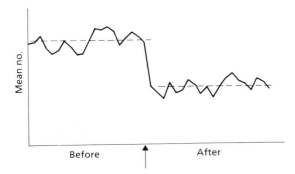

Fig. 11.1 Environmental impact (at the time indicated by the arrow) resulting in a long-term (press) decrease in mean abundance of a population.

impacts. The common notion is that a human disturbance to an environment will cause a change in average abundance. Usually, the argument becomes more irrational and the change is considered an impact only if it reduces the abundance. Increased abundances of some organisms are considered to be 'beneficial' (Underwood 1991), ignoring the obvious interactive relationships among species. For example, environmental changes that increase local habitat to favour the survival of some predatory fish (something often applauded by anglers!) must have some effect on the abundances of species of prey. These, of course, do not have political lobby-groups supporting them and therefore can be seriously depleted because of interactions with those species for which an increase in abundance is deemed desirable.

Sampling programmes to detect long-run alterations of mean abundance are widely discussed in the literature, as will be considered below. They are not the only possible environmental impacts and should not be treated as such.

Disturbances affecting temporal variances

Some potential environmental disturbances have no effect on the average numbers in a population (at least at some temporal scales) but are nevertheless extremely important for the long-term persistence or conservation of a species (Underwood 1991). Consider an impact that affects the rates of reproduction and the rates of mortality in a population. For example, construction of a sewerage outfall in a river may cause some pattern of increased flow of nutrients to an area downstream. This may well result in increased reproduction of organisms that use the nutrients, resulting in increased abundance. Every now and then, however, the discharge may be toxic (for example, there may be toxic chemicals discharged with the sewage, or the quantities of sewage may be excessive). Then the populations will crash. Thus, the impact may result in a pattern of increased and decreased abundance on a very sudden time-scale (Fig. 11.2). The average after the disturbance starts is actually the same as that prevailing before. Yet, the possibility that the population will go locally extinct is now much greater, because any new stress imposed during periods of

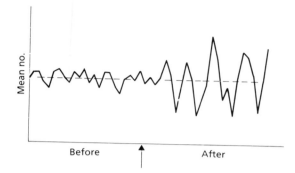

Fig. 11.2 Environmental impact (at the time indicated by the arrow) resulting in no change in mean abundance of a population, but having a long-term effect on temporal fluctuations in abundance. This would not be detected by routine environmental monitoring, unless the timing of samples happened to be appropriate.

crash will potentially reduce the already depressed abundance to zero.

Traditional methods of sampling to test hypotheses about changed mean abundance will not detect such environmental impacts, even though they may require very intense intrusive management to alleviate their effects (Underwood 1991). Instead, sampling is required that will detect changed temporal variances in numbers in the population (see later). Posing hypotheses about altered variability in time requires that the life cycle and time-courses of the populations are well-understood and that it has been realized that changed time-courses may be the effect of a disturbance.

Disturbances affecting spatial variances

Another class of disturbances does not affect overall mean abundance but instead, alter the spatial dispersion of the organisms. Again, traditional, random sampling in an area will fail to detect such impacts. Consider an organism that is scattered in clumps across the substratum, for example in those sites that provide shelter during periodic flooding of a river (Fig. 11.3). Animals do not survive outside shelters when the river floods. Some of the patches of organisms are lost because of accidents befalling some of the sheltered sites (for example, they may become scoured

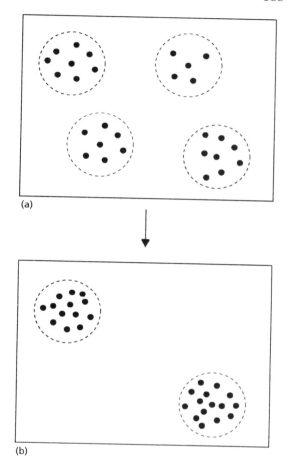

(a)

(b)

Fig. 11.3 Environmental impact (at the time indicated by the arrow) resulting in no change in mean abundance of a population, but having a long-term effect on spatial dispersion of the individuals. After the impact (b), there are less suitable patches of habitat for the organisms than was the case before (a).

by vegetation being washed down with the flood). The long-term persistence of a species is guaranteed by the existence of sufficient sheltered sites to 'spread the risk' (den Boer 1979, 1981).

Now, a human disturbance causes some alteration of some of the shelters, making them uninhabitable. For example, building flood-gates may cause sediments to fill some hollows. The animals are not actually killed or otherwise directly damaged by the disturbance – they simply redistribute themselves by moving out of the shelters and into others. This creates a greater density in the remaining shelters, but no overall change in the abundance of the population. Technically, the intensity of the pattern is altered by the disturbance (Pielou 1969). Of course, next time there is a flood, there will be greater loss of animals from the few patches that are accidentally, but naturally, demolished. If the decrease in available shelters due to the extra human disturbance is sufficient, the population may disappear at the first natural disturbance because there is no longer sufficient patchiness in its distribution. An example of this type of disturbance was investigated experimentally by Clifford (1982), who repeatedly disturbed the bed of an area of a stream. The substratum became more homogeneous (although in this case the mean abundances of many taxa also declined).

Sampling for such environmental effects requires more than simple random sampling to determine average abundance – the spatial variance of the population is the parameter affected by the disturbance.

What should be monitored?

So, the above considerations lead to the notion that environmental monitoring should only be done in response to clear advance understanding of the nature, time-courses and likely effects of some planned, or a range of possible, accidental disturbances. At this stage, the requirement is that there be much greater thought about the sorts of biological effects humans might have on the natural populations. This will then enable clear and unambiguous hypotheses to be proposed about the various possibilities (e.g. Underwood 1990). Only then can a proper plan of sampling be considered (Green 1979).

If better thought is given to the problems to which monitoring is to be addressed, there is actually little need to monitor at all, in the routine sense. Instead, the sampling is designed around specific anticipated (hypothesized) processes and results. It then fits much better into the mainstream framework of experimental ecology and can be designed much more appropriately to answer the questions.

It is interesting that to complete a piece of

'academic' experimental ecology by publishing it requires considerable demonstration (for example, by the journals) that the problems addressed and the methods used are clear and well related. Only then are interpretations accepted (although there are obviously problems with this sort of idealized approach; Hurlbert 1984; Underwood 1986). The irony is that monitoring and environmental sampling for eventual management and conservation of habitats and species can apparently often operate with a much looser framework of logic and design. This, at the very least, seems back-to-front – because, presumably, the latter type of science is potentially more important in the short term than the former!

The designs of sampling programmes discussed below are a sequence from early programmes to more recent ones, including those that are the preliminary answers to problems of environmental disturbances that do not affect long-run averages, but alter spatial or temporal variances. The solution of what to monitor is now translated to a better understanding of what sorts of effects are anticipated.

11.2 DESIGN OF SAMPLING

Unreplicated, uncontrolled before/after sampling

Some environmental assessment is based on the (incorrect) premise that populations show no natural temporal variability. A measured differ-

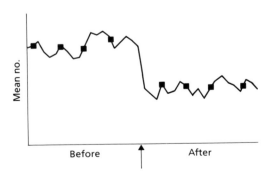

Fig. 11.4 Temporally replicated sampling to detect an impact (at the time indicated by the arrow) causing a long-term change in mean abundance of a single population.

ence in mean abundance from before to after a disturbance is then interpreted as being due to the disturbance. The situation is somewhat improved by taking replicate samples at each of several replicate times before and after the putative impact (Fig. 11.4). Then, a consistent change of mean associated with the onset of the disturbance will often be interpreted as being caused by the disturbance. This is illogical — the sampling is uncontrolled. Any environmental change that is coincidental with the start of the perturbation might have caused the sampled shift in abundance.

Unreplicated, but controlled BACI designs

To control for such natural temporal changes, Green (1979) proposed a so-called BACI design, in which there are replicate samples Before and After the planned disturbance, in each of an undisturbed control and the putatively impacted locations (Fig. 11.5). An impact due to the disturbance will cause the difference in mean abundance from before to after in the impacted location to differ from any natural change in the control. This would be detected as a statistical interaction (Table 11.1).

There are several problems with this interpretation. First, a sample taken at a single time before and again after the disturbance may not be representative of the abundance of the population. If there is much natural temporal variation, the

Table 11.1 Analysis of BACI design of sampling to detect environmental impact. n replicate samples are taken in each of two locations (the putatively impacted and a single control) once before and once again after the disturbance occurs (as in Fig. 11.5). Environmental impact would be detected as a significant interaction $(B \times L)$

Source of variation	Degrees of freedom	F-ratio versus	Degrees of freedom
Before versus after = B	1		
Control versus impact = L	1		
B × L	1	Residual	$1, 4(n-1)$
Residual	$4(n-1)$		
Total	$4n - 1$		

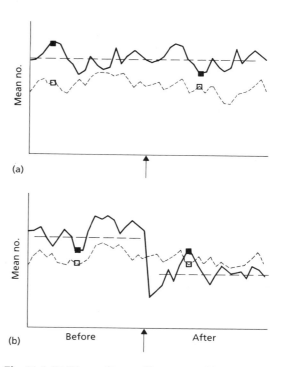

(a)

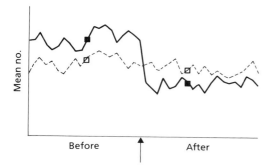

(b) Before   After

Fig. 11.6 BACI sampling to illustrate problems caused by lack of temporal replication. In (a) there is no impact and long-term mean abundance before and after a disturbance is the same. Because of temporal fluctuations, a single sample (at the time of the squares) would detect a difference in abundance in the impact (solid line), but not the control (dashed line) location. In (b) the disturbance in the impact location (solid line) causes a long-term decline in mean abundance, but this is not detected because of natural temporal fluctuations and lack of replication.

Fig. 11.5 Before–after/control–impact (BACI) sampling at a single time before and after an impact (indicated by the arrow) that affects the long-term mean abundance of a population in the impacted (solid line), but not the control (dashed line) location.

apparent or sampled difference from before to after in either location may be due to chance fluctuations (Fig. 11.6a). Alternatively, a real difference associated with the disturbance may be cancelled out by chance fluctuations (Fig. 11.6b). In either case, the wrong conclusions is reached because of lack of replication (see also Hurlbert 1984; Stewart-Oaten *et al* 1986; Underwood 1991).

A solution of the problem of lack of temporal replication was proposed by Bernstein and Zalinski (1983) and Stewart-Oaten *et al* (1986), following Green's (1979) suggestion that replicated sampling through time could be done. This involved taking samples (of several replicates each) at several times before and several times after the disturbance (Fig. 11.7). Stewart-Oaten *et al* (1986) proposed that the difference between the mean of each sample in the putatively impacted location and that in the control location be used as a variable. The average of these differences before the disturbance will be different from that after the disturbance, if it causes some impact on the population.

In the scheme of Bernstein and Zalinski (1983) and Stewart-Oaten *et al* (1986), these differences are examined by a *t*-test. Alternatively, the data can be examined by analysis of variance (Table 11.2). This analysis is identical to the *t*-test, but has the property that it can be modified for situations where it is impossible to sample both

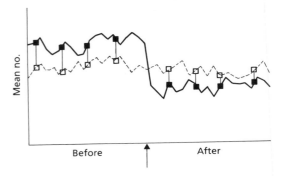

Fig. 11.7 BACI sampling with replicated temporal sampling in the impacted (solid line) and a single control (dashed line) location. Data from each time of sampling are paired (as indicated by the vertical lines) and the difference between the two locations is analysed (Stewart-Oaten *et al* 1986).

locations at the same time (Table 11.3; see Underwood 1991 for details).

This type of sampling still suffers from *confounding*, more recently termed pseudoreplication (Hurlbert 1984). The problem is that any two places may show a difference in time that has nothing to do with the human disturbance to one location. For example, Green (1979) discussed the possibility, where an outfall pipe enters a river, of using an area upstream of the pipe as the Control for the downstream, potentially Impacted location. There are difficulties with this because of

Table 11.2 Analysis of temporally replicated BACI design of sampling to detect environmental impact. *n* replicate samples are taken in each of two locations (the putatively impacted and a single control) at *t* replicated times before and again after the disturbance occurs (as in Fig. 11.7). The two locations must be sampled at the same times. Environmental impact would be detected as a significant interaction L × T(B) (or, if there were no differences between the two locations in the time-courses of abundances before and after the disturbance, as a significant interaction B × L)

Source of variation		Degrees of freedom	*F*-ratio versus	Degrees of freedom
Before versus after	= B	1		
Control versus impact	= L	1		
B × L		1*	L × T(B)	1, 2(t − 1)
Times (B)	= T(B)	2(t − 1)		
L × T(B)		2(t − 1)*	Residual	2(t − 1), 4t(n − 1)
Residual		4t(n − 1)		
Total		4tn − 1		

* This is an identical test to the paired *t*-test recommended by Stewart-Oaten *et al* (1986).

Table 11.3 Analysis of temporally replicated BACI design of sampling to detect environmental impact when sampling cannot be done at the same times in each location. *n* replicate samples are taken in each of two locations (the putatively impacted and a single control) at *t* replicated times before and again after the disturbance occurs (as in Fig. 11.7). Th two locations are not sampled at the same times. Environmental impact would be detected as a significant interaction B × L

Source of variation		Degrees of freedom	*F*-ratio versus	Degrees of freedom
Before versus after	= B	1		
Control versus impact	= L	1		
B × L		1	T(B × L)	$1, 4(t-1)$
Times (B × L)	= T(B × L)	$4(t-1)$		
Residual		$4t(n-1)$		
Total		$4tn - 1$		

possible non-independence (see later). Nevertheless, it will illustrate the point. Suppose that the organisms being sampled are insects, with an intrinsically patchy distribution of egg-laying. At about the time the outfall pipe is built, adults happen to arrive and lay eggs in the upstream Control location, but not, by chance, in the downstream area. As a result, the subsequent sampling (after the disturbance starts and the outfall begins its discharge) will reveal an apparent impact due to the pipe. The same conclusion would be reached if adults happened to visit the downstream, but not the upstream location. The sampling is clearly confounded and any effect of the disturbance cannot be distinguished from natural variation between locations. If there is an environmental impact, it is *necessary* for it to cause a change in the differences in abundance between two locations. Such change is not, however, *sufficient* evidence that an impact has occurred — see Hurlbert's (1984) review.

One final difficulty besets this type of sampling. If there is an interaction in the differences between mean abundances in the two locations *before* the human disturbance, the data cannot be analysed for environmental impact. This is discussed in full by Stewart-Oaten *et al* (1986). Where the temporal trend of mean abundance already differs between two locations before the impact, there must be an interaction in the data. This is a major problem because many populations, particularly of short-lived or widely-dispersing species, have different temporal patterns of abundance in different patches of habitat. Thus, the

Bernstein and Zalinski (1983) and Stewart-Oaten *et al* (1986) protocol will not be useful for many populations.

Beyond BACI: impact versus several controls

The solution to the spatial confounding identified above is to replicate the sampling. Obviously, it is usually impossible (and would always be undesirable!) to replicate potentially impacting disturbances solely to create a more valid statistical property of the data. There is, however, no reason that replicate control locations should not be used (Underwood 1989, 1991, 1992). What is needed is a set of locations, chosen to represent a particular habitat (i.e. with similar water-flow, depth, bottom, acidity of water, etc.). The only constraint on this set is that one of the locations must be the one in which a development or disturbance is planned (Fig. 11.8). Note that the locations are not supposed to be identical; this was not a requirement of the single control location. They must, however, come from a population of locations of which, for any variable of interest, the potentially impacted location is also a member. There will, of course, be difficulties with finding such locations, but it is not an impossible task for many habitats.

Now, the analysis is an asymmetrical one (Winer 1971; Underwood 1978, 1984, 1986, 1991, 1992) involving a contrast between the putatively impacted location and the set of controls. Of greatest importance is the analysis of interaction. An environmental impact must cause a greater

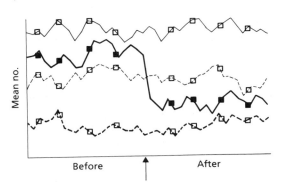

Mean no.

Before   ↑   After

Fig. 11.8 Beyond BACI: sampling to detect effects of an environmental disturbance in the impacted (solid line) and several replicated control (dashed lines) locations. Samples are taken several times before and after the disturbance.

difference from before to after in the impacted than in the control locations. This is analysed in Table 11.4 and described in full in Underwood (1992).

Such asymmetrical analyses can also be used to solve the problem of temporal interactions occurring before the possible impact (Stewart-Oaten *et al* 1986). The details are not presented here, but an environmental impact affecting a population in one (the impacted) location will cause a different magnitude of temporal interaction after, compared with before, for that location than occurs in the control locations. These interactions can be compared in statistical tests based on the asymmetrical analysis of all the data (Underwood 1992). Thus, analyses of environmental impact can be on a more secure logical foundation than where there is only a single control. They can also use more types of data than is the case in the more usual BACI designs (Bernstein & Zalinski 1983; Stewart-Oaten *et al* 1986).

Where it is not possible to sample several locations at the same time, because of logistic constraints, these procedures can be modified to provide some partial tests for the presence of impacts (Underwood 1991).

Confusion of space and time

A major problem besetting any biological sampling is that temporal and spatial patterns are not simple to separate (e.g. Pielou 1969). For some investigations, this may not be important.

Table 11.4 Analysis of temporally and spatially replicated 'Beyond BACI' design of sampling to detect environmental impact. *n* replicate samples are taken in each of several locations (*l*) (the putatively impacted and a set of controls) at *t* replicated times before and again after the disturbance occurs (as in Fig. 11.8). The locations must be sampled at the same times. Environmental impact would be detected as a significant interaction B × I, indicating a different temporal pattern in the difference between the impacted and control locations after the disturbance than occurred before. If there are significant differences among the locations in the time-courses of abundances before and after the disturbance, the interaction T(B) × I can be analysed further (Underwood 1992)

Source of variation		Degrees of freedom		
Before versus after	= B	1		
Among locations	= L	$(l-1)$		
Impact versus controls	= I		1	
Among controls	= C		$(l-2)$	
B × L		$(l-1)$		
B × I			1	
B × C			$(l-2)$	
Times (B)	= T(B)	$2(t-1)$		
T(B) × L		$2(t-1)(l-1)$		
T(B) × I			$2(t-1)$	
T(B) × C			$2(t-1)(l-2)$	
Residual		$2lt(n-1)$		
Total		$2ltn-1$		

Understanding the natural temporal changes in populations is, however, essential for any interpretation of their ecology and, particularly, for any programme of management and conservation. It is impossible to make realistic predictions about future abundances if temporal changes are not understood.

There are two circumstances where spatial variations in abundance will become very confused with apparent temporal changes in numbers in a population. First, in a heterogeneous, patchy habitat, if only a small number of replicate samples are taken at each of several occasions, they may sample different patches. Consider the bed of a river where there are patches of habitat which support large densities of an organism and other areas where the organisms are sparse. If only a few replicated samples are used to estimate abundances, they may, by ill chance, land predominantly in one type of habitat on one occasion and in the other at some subsequent time (Fig. 11.9). The different mean abundance in the two samples will be interpreted as a change in abundance.

Where the patterns of distribution are readily visible, a 'map' can be made and sampling done in a repeated fashion by stratifying the area to be sampled and then taking the same number of replicates in each 'stratum' or type of patch during

each time of sampling. Thus, if 20% of the area consists of patches of gravel (and gravel may have a different density of a sampled species than is found in other substrata), it would be prudent to put a similar number of quadrats in areas of gravel every time samples are taken. There have been many reviews of procedures for stratifying sampling (Cochran & Cox 1957; Cox 1958; Elliott 1977; Andrew & Mapstone 1987). There are different procedures when different types of information are available about the spatial variations in abundance.

As a second situation, apparent changes of mean abundance will be seen from time to time if the organisms sampled show behavioural changes in dispersion. This is well known, but not often considered in detail. Thus, if animals are very clumped at some times of the year or at some stages of the life cycle (or under some physical conditions, such as during and immediately after floods), but are more spread out at other times (or under other weather conditions), unless very large numbers of samples are taken on each occasion, mean abundances will appear to have changed. When the organisms are clumped (unless there are very many or very large clumps), many replicate sample units will be in the sparser areas between clumps. For example, if the clumps occupy 10% of the total area being sampled, and sample units are smaller than clumps, the probability of not hitting a clump in a sample of 10 units is 0.35; more than one-third of such samples do not measure densities reliably. The mean abundance will be small (although the variance among sample units will, on average, be relatively large). When the organisms are more scattered, there will be more in most of the sample units and mean abundance will be larger (with, usually, smaller variance among sample units). The change in density is, however, not real, but simply reflective of the behavioural change in dispersion.

One method for determining whether sampling is reliably estimating abundances at appropriate spatial scales, so that temporal patterns are clearly separable from spatial differences, is pilot sampling at short time-intervals. Sampling is done at some pre-determined spatial scales of placement of sample units. Sampling is then repeated after a

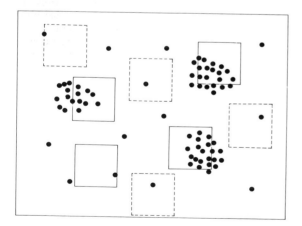

Fig. 11.9 Sampling a very heterogeneous (spatially dispersed) population with few replicates. At one time of sampling (solid squares) density is estimated to be larger than at the next time (dashed squares).

short time, short enough that no alteration of abundance (through recruitment, migration or mortality) could be expected. Then, if there *is* a difference between the two samples, it would identify an inadequacy of the spatial arrangement of sample units, or short-term changes in dispersion of the organisms (which could be examined by investigating the spatial variances), because it could not reflect a temporal change. This has rarely been done, but an example was described by Kennelly and Underwood (1985).

Unconfounding spatial scales

A different confusion of space and time occurs when a habitat is not sampled at appropriate spatial scales. Suppose, for example, that there is a general gradient of density across a river, such that more animals are found per unit area in its centre than at the edges. Unless some effort is made to ensure that sampling is equally representative on all occasions, there will, again, be apparent differences in abundance from time to time because of different patterns of spatial sampling. As an example in the ecology of rivers, Arthur *et al* (1982) compared the fauna in experimental channels, one at elevated temperature of the water. There was, however, only one channel

at each temperature and no estimation was made of the magnitude of differences between the abundances of fauna in the two channels due to their different siting, history and any events during the study that were not identical in the two places.

This was a major problem identified by Hurlbert (1984) in his review of ecological confounding. Where geographical (or temporal) differences from plot to plot cause differences in abundance (size, growth or any other variable) from plot to plot (or time to time), comparisons between two plots, one representing one treatment (or time) and the other a different treatment (or time), cannot be used to conclude that the treatment (or passage of time) caused the observed differences. The solution, not discussed by Hurlbert (1984), is to attempt hierarchical or nested sampling (Snedecor & Cochran 1967; Green & Hobson 1970; Underwood 1981; Andrew & Mapstone 1987).

Instead of placing sampling units (quadrats, grabs, nets, trays) at random throughout the area, they are placed in sets according to a number of spatial scales (Fig. 11.10). Arbitrarily defined plots (at some spatial scale say 30 m on a side) are imposed on the area to be sampled. Some of these are picked at random to be sampled. Then, these plots are further subdivided (e.g. into sub-plots of

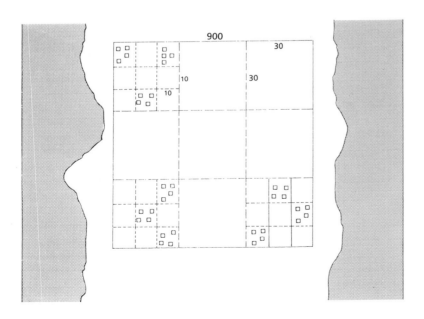

Fig. 11.10 Hierarchical (nested) sampling at several spatial scales. The area to be sampled (in a river) is divided into 30 × 30-m plots, of which three are chosen at random to sample. Each plot is divided into 10 × 10-m sub-plots, three of which are chosen at random to sample. Each sub-plot is sampled with four random, replicate sample-units. See text for further details.

side 10 m). Again, some of these are picked at random to be sampled. These could be further subdivided into areas (say, squares 5 × 5 m). In randomly-chosen areas, several replicate sampling units (nets, grabs, etc.) are used. The choice of scales is not necessarily arbitrary, but may be dictated by known biological features of the populations being sampled. For example, if the animals routinely travel 10 or 20 m up or downstream in search of food, it would be appropriate to have some sampled scale within this and one somewhat larger scale to detect any resulting spatial variances in abundance that might be related to such behaviour.

Data from such hierarchically organized sampling are amenable to nested analysis of variance (e.g. Green & Hobson 1970; Winer 1971; Sokal & Rohlf 1981; Underwood 1981). This will detect those spatial scales at which there are variations in abundance. These scales will then need to be sampled on each occasion to ensure that spatial variations do not become confused in assessment of temporal change. One great advantage of nested sampling of a hierarchy of spatial scales is that the data are readily amenable to cost-benefit procedures to determine how best to allocate effort (i.e. number of replicate samples) of each spatial scale (e.g. Snedecor & Cochran 1967; Green 1979; Underwood 1981; see Kennelly & Underwood 1984, 1985 for particular examples).

Where data are available from several hierarchical spatial scales, they can be analysed to determine whether some environmental disturbance has altered the spatial variance at some scale, regardless of whether the mean abundance has been changed (a problem raised earlier; see Fig. 11.3). The procedures are not discussed here, because of lack of space, but a similar approach was used by Green and Hobson (1970) to compare patchiness in abundance of a bivalve in different places on a beach.

Unconfounding temporal scales

To determine temporal patterns of abundance, hierarchical (nested) time-scales are necessary. This has rarely been the case in published studies. Usually, if sampling is done, say, every 3 months, to examine seasonal trends in abundance of a

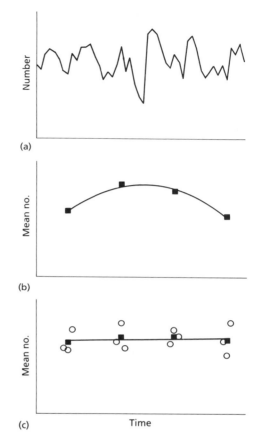

Fig. 11.11 Seasonal sampling with inadequate temporal replication. (a) True, but unknown pattern of abundance of a population; there is no seasonal pattern. (b) Apparent seasonal pattern in four widely separated samples. (c) Nested sampling (three different times in each season) gives seasonal averages that show, correctly, no pattern.

population, several (spatially scattered) replicates are taken at each time of sampling. If significant differences are found among the times of sampling, these are assumed to represent seasonal differences. This conclusion is, however, not necessarily correct because the data are, in fact, confounded or pseudo-replicated (Hurlbert 1984). There is only one sample per season. The differences may not represent seasonal differences, but simply unpatterned temporal fluctuations. This is illustrated in Figs. 11.11 and 11.12.

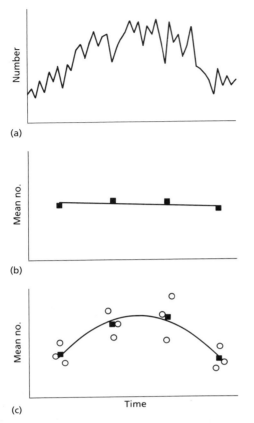

(a)

(b)

(c)

Time

Fig. 11.12 Seasonal sampling with inadequate temporal replication. (a) True, but unknown pattern of abundance of a population; there is a marked seasonal pattern. (b) Apparent lack of seasonal pattern in four widely separated samples. (c) Nested sampling (three different times in each season) gives seasonal averages that show, correctly, the seasonal pattern.

arranged, will estimate spatial variance at one time. Thus, if there is little spatial variance in abundance, there will be small within-sample variances and considerable statistical power to detect differences among seasonal samples.

What is required to be sure that there are, in fact, seasonal differences in abundance is temporal replication (see also Underwood 1991). To demonstrate seasonal variation requires that there are larger differences among mean abundances from season to season than occur at much shorter time-scales. This is illustrated in Figs. 11.11 and 11.12, where samples are taken several times in each season. At each time, there are replicate (spatial) samples. The data are hierarchically arranged with two time-scales – 'Seasons' and 'Times within each season'. Only if there is significant variation among the means for each season, over and above the variation within seasons, is it possible to demonstrate that there really are seasonal differences. A nested analysis of variance is needed for these data (Table 11.5) and the previous comments about cost-benefit procedures and the efficient allocation of sampling units (how many times to sample in each season and how many replicates to take at each time) can also be applied to this problem. These nested arrangements of sampling are also necessary to detect impacts that affect temporal variation (Fig. 11.13; see Underwood 1992).

The previous discussion does not imply that sizes of samples (i.e. replication, numbers of times sampled, number of locations) need to be huge. Although considerable thought must be given to the best way to allocate time, effort and money to sampling, the power of such analyses to detect impacts is quite large, even with relatively modest sizes of replication (Underwood 1993). Insufficient examples exist to determine appropriate guidelines for designing asymmetrical 'Beyond BACI' programmes. Nevertheless, it is probable that a re-allocation of numbers of replicates from one control location to several would not dramatically increase costs. In general, it is probably better to reduce the intensity of arbitrarily-chosen temporal patterns of sampling (routine monitoring) and re-allocate effort to several spatial controls. Simulations of environmental impacts (A.J. Underwood, unpublished data)

In the first case (Fig. 11.11a), there is no temporal pattern of abundance, but the mean abundance at the four times of sampling appears to show a seasonal cycle (Fig. 11.11b). In contrast, if there is sufficient short-term temporal variation (or 'noise'), the samples may show no trend (Fig. 11.12b), even though there is a clear seasonal cycle (Fig. 11.12a). The chances of detecting statistical differences among the means of the seasonal samples is entirely dependent on the design and intensity of sampling at each time. But the replicated sampling, however the sample units are

Table 11.5 Analysis of temporally (but not spatially) replicated 'Beyond BACI' design of sampling to detect environmental impact that affects temporal fluctuations but not long-run means. Replicate samples are taken in each of two locations (the putatively impacted and a control) at two temporal scales. Samples are taken in p replicate periods before and again after the disturbance occurs (as in Fig. 11.13, where $p = 2$ for the impacted location). In each period, there are t replicate times of sampling ($t = 3$ in Fig. 11.13). n replicate samples are taken at each time. The locations must be sampled at the same times. Environmental impact would be detected as a significant interaction L × P(B) or L × T(P(B)), depending on the time-scale at which the impact altered the temporal pattern of abundance in the impacted versus the control location (see Underwood 1991 for full details)

Source of variation		Degrees of freedom	*F*-ratio versus	Degrees of freedom
Before versus after	= B	1		
Control versus impact	= L	1		
B × L		1		
Periods in before or after	= P(B)	$2(p - 1)$		
L × P(B)		$2(p - 1)$	L × T(P(B))	$2(p - 1)$, $2p(t - 1)$
Times within periods	= T(P(B))	$2p(t - 1)$		
L × T(P(B))		$2p(t - 1)$	Residual	$2p(t - 1)$, $2lt(n - 1)$
Residual		$2lt(n - 1)$		
Total		$2ltn - 1$		

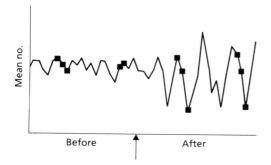

Fig. 11.13 Sampling at two different (nested) temporal scales, twice before and twice after an environmental disturbance (indicated by the arrow) to detect an impact that causes changed temporal variation, but no change in mean abundance.

suggest that pulse disturbances and large press disturbances should be detectable for many populations with only two or three control locations, sampled four to six times before and after the disturbance, with three to five replicate samples at each time in each location. What matters most is to allocate effort in the most effective and interpretable manner. Otherwise, all the effort (and budget) is expended to no purpose at all!

Independent sampling in rivers

A major problem with biological sampling in rivers is that abundances in any location are not likely to be independent of the data in samples upstream. There are many processes that can cause correlations in the abundances of a population from one place to another. In the case of environmental perturbations, for example effluents from a point source, there may be large-scale impacts, causing correlated changes in abundance at numerous locations downstream. This is well known and explains the widespread advocacy of using an area upstream of an outfall as a control location for determining any impact on populations downstream (reviewed by Green 1979). It is explicitly recognized in this procedure that no control location could be identified downstream because it is likely that any impact would probably extend a long way from the outfall (see, for example, Cuffney *et al* 1990).

What does not seem to be so widely recognized is the great potential that always exists for non-independence between two areas of a river because they are linked by the flow of water. For example, downstream drift of stream invertebrates (e.g. Cuffney *et al* 1990; review by Brittain & Eikeland 1988) will presumably link the abundances of a species in lower reaches of the stream with those in the source populations upstream. The abundances of many organisms in an upstream and a downstream location would be positively correlated.

Independence of samples, within and between groups, is a fundamental requirement of most statistical procedures (e.g. Fisher 1925; Snedecor & Cochran 1967; Winer 1971; Sokal & Rohlf 1981). It is impossible to discuss here all of the problems caused by non-independence of data.

The abundances of organisms in two locations will be positively correlated if, for example, a similar proportion of any population drifts downstream to another location. Whatever the abundance upstream, the abundance downstream will be related to it. If upstream/downstream differences are being examined in several rivers, there will be problems if the samples from each upstream and each downstream location are considered independent when they are, in fact, positively correlated.

Under these circumstances, the probability of rejecting the null hypothesis (that there is no difference in mean abundance between upstream and downstream locations) is not that given in tables for such statistics as t, F, various rank-order or binomial tests. The probability of Type II error (retaining the null hypothesis when it is, in fact, false) is enhanced (Cochran 1947).

The solution to the problem is to divide the rivers randomly into two groups. The upstream data are then taken from one half of the rivers (one group) and the downstream data from the other half. The data for the two conditions are completely independent of each other (they come from separate rivers). Alternatively, the data could be treated as pairs, so that the difference (upstream minus downstream) can be tested against the null hypothesis that the mean difference is zero (i.e. the upstream and downstream locations in each river have the same abundance, on average over several rivers).

Non-parametric, binomial and t-tests are available for either stratagem. Which of the two approaches is better depends on various factors. The second (paired) approach requires less rivers to be sampled for the same power of test. Each of n rivers furnishes upstream and downstream data. In the first approach, to obtain n replicate upstream and n replicate downstream sets of data requires $2n$ rivers to be visited (although only one or other type of data is taken from each). Apart from this, the decision about whether to use paired data rests on the degree to which the abundances in the two locations in each river are actually correlated and the variances among the replicate samples in each location. An excellent account of how to make the decision is given by Snedecor and Cochran (1967).

If the purpose of sampling is to identify in a particular river any difference between upstream and downstream that might be associated with an environmental disturbance, several control locations are needed. The task then becomes one of deciding whether the difference (upstream minus downstream) in the putatively impacted river is more or less than would be expected by chance in a population of such differences. Such a population of differences has, of course, been sampled as the control rivers.

Theoretically, upstream/downstream data could be taken in other, similar, higher stretches of the same river (they cannot be downstream in case the impact is extensive and widespread). This may, however, still result in non-independence of the data; abundances of organisms in any downstream section of a river may be correlated with those higher up.

It seems that more research is needed to determine the degree to which upstream and downstream localities do, in fact, have correlated abundances of various types of organisms. Samples from numerous upstream and downstream locations at different spatial scales apart need to be examined for positive or negative correlation. Some types of animals and plants are less likely to be correlated than others (e.g. they do not drift). At some distances apart, upstream and downstream locations are less likely to be correlated. Once it can be established that there are some species and some spatial scales along a river that will provide independent data, this information should be used in planning the sampling for assessment of potential environmental impact (or any experimental field programme requiring upstream and downstream locations to be sampled).

11.3 BASELINE DATA

Many types of disturbance are unpredictable and there are many difficulties with identifying human-induced changes to populations that have large temporal fluctuations or spatial differences. As a result, much assessment of environmental impact must be done with limited 'before' data. For accidental disturbances, there is no planned period 'before'. In the case of planned developments, there is, at best, a limited period of possible investigations before the development begins.

So, assessment of the effects of disturbances must often depend on comparisons among locations after the putative impact has occurred (see particularly Green 1979). Many useful features of the sampling designs discussed previously still apply, but the focus of the problem has, of course, shifted. There is no method for addressing the question of whether there has been a *change* in abundance in the disturbed location, different from that in control locations and coincident or following from the disturbance. The issue is now to determine whether there is some *difference* between the abundance in the disturbed location and that in the controls, or whether there is a different time-course of abundance in the disturbed location compared with that in the controls. These questions are far less indicative of an impact than can be demonstrated when data are also available from before the disturbance. There may always have been a measurable difference in the mean abundance, or in the temporal trajectory of mean abundance, between the single disturbed locations and the controls. This can never be established.

It would therefore be worth considering procedures which would allow some estimation of what might have been happening before the disturbance. By and large, there are two research programmes (Lakatos 1974) that will help. First is the general class of monitoring or baseline studies, which could be restructured to test hypotheses about the degree of spatial and temporal variability in natural, undisturbed populations (i.e. like those in control locations).

Second are intrusive or manipulative experimental programmes that seek to test hypotheses about the nature, magnitude and rates of responses to disturbance, so that better predictions can be made about the likely effects of different human activities. These will be considered later.

Estimation of background variances

It would be very informative to know the ranges and patterns of temporal and spatial variation for species with different sorts of life histories in a variety of riverine habitats. Sampling to determine these variances would, if done properly, allow general assessments of effects of disturbances in other similar habitats.

The need to assess spatial patchiness, by replicated sampling at different spatial scales, was identified earlier. If this is done in a set of undisturbed localities, it is obviously equivalent to data before disturbance in those habitats. If the spatial patterns are examined at several times (different seasons, different years), they can form a background assessment of spatial variance that should represent any similar habitat. The mean abundance of a species of mayfly in areas of hard substratum in stretches of a river of a certain range of speed of water flow, pH, oxygen concentration, etc. is, itself, a variate from a distribution (an unknown frequency distribution) of such mean abundances over all possible similar habitats. If the mean abundance is sampled in say, five independent, representative stretches of this habitat, the variation among the habitats provides a measure of the variance of the entire population of similar habitats. This is a familiar consequence of the theory of unbiased, representative sampling (Fisher 1925; Feller 1968; Johnson & Kotz 1969).

To ensure that the sample of localities examined is representative of the entire possible population of localities, they must be chosen as a 'random factor', in the terminology of analysis of variance (Scheffe 1959; Winer 1971; Underwood 1981). Once the sort of habitat being examined has been defined (i.e. the ranges of depth and speed of water, the substratum, etc., have been decided), a random sample of places that fall within the definition can be sampled.

The places must not be chosen on the basis of any particular feature that is not part of the definition of the habitat. Thus, a particular location that happens to be the nearest to a main road, or that is locally reputed to contain very large trout, etc. should not be included in the sample because the investigator thinks it would be informative to attempt to investigate the result of being near a road (or of having large trout nearby). All possible locations that fit the defined conditions should have an equal chance of being sampled.

If abundances are estimated in this sample of locations, the variation among the locations provides an estimate of the variance among all the locations in the defined distribution of localities in the defined habitat. Therefore, the variation from location to location in the sample is an unbiased estimate of the variation among locations in any other set of representative localities. Thus, once this variation has been estimated, it is known for other sets of the defined habitat — including any set of locations chosen as controls for some putatively impacted location. Thus, a properly sampled set of representative locations will provide the 'before' data for any localities of that habitat. So, it is not impossible to use properly documented estimates of variation in abundance among representative locations instead of

controls for a potential impact in a particular location.

Of course, nothing is ever quite as simple as just described. The differences among locations are not constant from time to time. Consequently, the sampling just described must be repeated at several time-scales, chosen because of known time-courses of the life history of the sampled organism(s). These samples provide unbiased estimates of the temporal variation of abundances in this type of habitat. The temporal variance is, anyway, required for control locations in a study to detect environmental impact (just as the spatial differences must be known).

A temporal series of estimates of abundance in a representative set of locations of a particular habitat also provides a reliable estimate of the interactions between time and space that must be analysed for undisturbed sites in order to detect an environmental impact (Table 11.6). So, once this is sampled properly, the estimates should be reliable to use as control, before and after data for any disturbance that might affect another 'impacted' location.

The validity of using these estimates where

Table 11.6 Calculation of variances for temporal and spatial patterns of abundance of a population, using the Cornfield–Tukey calculations of mean squares estimates. The analysis is of four randomly-chosen locations (l), each sampled three times (t) in each of 2 years (y). The locations could not be sampled at the same times (hence, times are nested in the combinations of year and location). There were $n = 6$ replicate samples at each time in each location. σ^2_Y is variance between years; σ^2_L is variance among locations; σ^2_{YXL} is variation associated with the interaction between years and locations; $\sigma^2_{T(YXL)}$ is variance among times of sampling in each location and year. These data correspond to 'before', control data for any other locations that come from the habitat represented by the locations sampled here. Confidence intervals for these variance components can also be calculated (see Winer 1971 for details)

Source of variation	Df	Mean square estimates	Data from analysis
Between years	1	$\sigma^2_R + n\sigma^2_{T(YL)} + tn\sigma^2_{YL} + ltn\sigma^2_Y$	268
Among locations	3	$\sigma^2_R + n\sigma^2_{T(YL)} + tn\sigma^2_{YL} + ytn\sigma^2_L$	273
Years × locations	3	$\sigma^2_R + n\sigma^2_{T(YL)} + tn\sigma^2_{YL}$	181
Among times (years × locations)	16	$\sigma^2_R + n\sigma^2_{T(YL)}$	107
Residual	120	σ^2_R	80

Calculated estimates of variance components:

$\sigma^2_R \quad = \qquad\qquad 80.0$

$\sigma^2_{T(YL)} = (107 - 80)/6 \quad = 4.50$

$\sigma^2_{YL} \quad = (181 - 107)/18 = 4.11$

$\sigma^2_L \quad = (273 - 181)/36 = 2.55$

$\sigma^2_L \quad = (268 - 181)/72 = 1.21$

'before' data are not available can be checked by collecting 'after' data in some control locations after the particular disturbance has occurred. All other things being correct (i.e. the current locations are from the same frequency distribution or population of localities as previously sampled), the estimates of spatial and temporal variances and their interaction in the previous, general sampling should be similar to those in the 'after' samples collected now. This proposition can be tested by analysing to compare the general data with the new 'after' data. If the proposition is reasonable, the previously gathered, general data can be used to replace the unavailable 'before' data from the not-yet-impacted and control localities.

The calculation of the appropriate variances is dependent on the number of replicate samples, the number of times sampled and the number of localities examined. For any size of sampling, the estimates of variance can be calculated from analyses of variance, using the Cornfield–Tukey formulae for estimated mean squares (Cornfield & Tukey 1956; Scheffe 1959; Winer 1971; Underwood 1981). This is illustrated in Table 11.6.

11.4 EXPERIMENTAL PROGRAMMES TO INCREASE PREDICTIVE CAPABILITY

Inertia, resilience and stability

To be able to predict the potential consequences of some disturbance to a habitat obviously requires knowledge of several attributes of the populations that might be affected. In an idealized view of populations, these attributes can be divided into three main features – the inertia, resilience and stability of the abundance of a population (although the terminology is a minefield; Underwood 1989).

Inertia is the property of a population not to respond to a disturbance (Murdoch 1970; Orians 1974). An inert population does not change in abundance when a pollutant arrives in its habitat. A less inert population declines in abundance (Fig. 11.14a). A population will be inert if, for example, the animals have behavioural adaptations to move away from excessively polluted parts of their habitat, biochemical adaptations to detoxify

Fig. 11.14 Attributes of idealized, model, equilibrial populations. (a, b) Inertia. Population (a) is inert to a small (thin arrow) and a large (thick arrow) disturbance. Population (b) is less inert and shows a response to the larger disturbance. (c, d) Resilience. Population (c) is resilient and recovers from a small and a large disturbance. Population (d) is less resilient and cannot recover from the larger disturbance. (e, f) Stability. Population (e) is very stable and recovers quickly from two disturbances. Population (f) is less stable and takes longer to recover from either a small or a large environmental perturbation causing an impact. See text for reality.

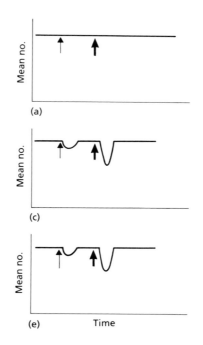

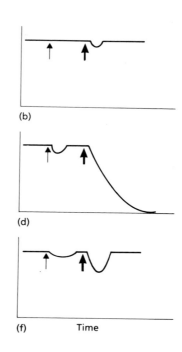

their bodies so that pollutants do not become deleteriously concentrated, or cellular tolerances to the pollutant so that it does not interfere with any vital functions. Inertia is measurable in terms of the smallest magnitude of disturbance that elicits a response. If the inertias of populations were known, precise predictions could be made about whether a particular form and magnitude of disturbance would have any effect on abundances.

Resilience, in contrast, is the capacity to recover from a disturbance if it is large enough to cause a change (although there have been competing definitions and uses of the term: Holling 1973; Orians 1974), reviewed by Underwood (1989). A resilient population will recover from a disturbance (Fig. 11.14b). An idealized population will return to equilibrial abundance. In the real world, its abundance will converge with that of control, undisturbed populations (Underwood 1989). A less resilient population will not recover and its abundance will be permanently altered (including possibly to extinction).

Resilience is thus measured as the maximal departure from undisturbed abundances from which the populations can recover. Clearly, knowing this would allow precise prediction about the outcome of a disturbance causing a change in abundance. Alleviation and remedial action are urgently required for less resilient populations. Resilient populations will recover from the effects of disturbance (but see the consequences of instability, below).

Stability is the rate at which abundance of a population recovers from the effects of a disturbance. Other terms have been used for this (Boesch 1974; Connell & Sousa 1983). Recovery, again, can be defined in terms of idealized responses of equilibrial systems (Fig. 11.14c) or, realistically, as returning to the range of values of undisturbed controls. Knowledge of the stability of a population, which must be measured in relation to disturbances of particular magnitudes, is crucial for predicting the consequences of environmental impacts. In a stable population, recovery (if the disturbance has not moved the abundance beyond the resiliences of the population) will be rapid. Repeated disturbances will be similar. In an unstable population, subsequent disturbances will

arrive before recovery from a previous one; there will then be quite different consequences.

How much perturbation can a system stand?

It follows from the previous discussion that estimates of inertia, resilience and stability of populations in relation to natural patterns of temporal and spatial variability would be extraordinarily useful in environmental assessment. The former will assist in predicting the consequences and the latter in detecting the magnitude of environmental disturbances. The determination and interpretation of these attributes is, of course, the whole point of modern ecology (e.g. Krebs 1978). So, ecology as a discipline and its application to environmental assessment can move even closer together.

Experimental perturbations will be necessary to create the stresses from which the responses of populations can be estimated and to unconfound natural variability (e.g. Underwood 1989). Intrusive, manipulative experiments have been very successful in unravelling complex biological interactions in very variable marine environments (Connell 1972, 1975; Underwood 1985, 1986). Experimental analyses of environmental disturbances in rivers and streams have an equally long and healthy history. They range from microcosmal studies of diatoms (Patrick 1975) to responses to changes in entire ecosystems (Likens *et al* 1970; Bormann *et al* 1974). Manipulations of streams (e.g. Bernard *et al* 1990) have revealed a great deal about toxins. Experimental diversions of streams (e.g. Hopkins *et al* 1989) or artificial, experimental streams (e.g. Clements *et al* 1988) have been successfully used to create replicated arrays of treatments to determine the effects of various disturbances. There should be many more such efforts.

Finally, the outcome of environmental disturbances can be examined using planned or previous cases of the disturbance. More widespread use could be made of the fact that many planned disturbances in natural systems are repeated in space and time. Thus, there are many outfalls into rivers from pulp mills or other industries. There are many industrial plants using freshwater for cooling. There are numerous weirs, dams, irrigation programmes, etc. It is appropriate to consider these as parts of large-scale experiments (Hilborn & Walters 1981). Planning appropriate experiment is not simple, but there are immense possibilities (Underwood 1989).

Choice of species

As a final comment on detection and interpretation of environmental disturbances, considerable thought must be given to appropriate species or groups of species to sample. It has been argued that abundant, widespread species are the most useful (e.g. Lewis 1976). These are, however, probably the most inert, resilient and stable — which is why they persist abundantly in numerous locations. They are therefore unlikely to be sensitive to many types of environmental disturbance.

Other authors have argued for attention to be on 'middle abundance' species that show responses to a range of disturbances (Gray & Pearson 1982; Gray 1989). There are numerous other considerations and strategies (e.g. Underwood & Peterson 1988), including the efficiency and ease of sampling, taxonomic reliability, role in structuring assemblages, or in energy transfer through food webs, etc.

To add to the list of possible criteria, the temporal variance of abundance of populations should be considered. Are relatively invariant numbers a sign of inertia (the population is not responding to the numerous local natural disturbances that beset more variable populations)? Or is it a sign of great stability (the populations are disturbed but recover so rapidly that sampling fails to reveal this)? Are populations that show great temporal variability the ones that have small inertia (they are always being perturbed), yet massive resilience (they keep bouncing back)? Experimental analyses to ascertain which is an appropriate interpretation will be very helpful. Organisms with different patterns of temporal variance may be shown by experiments to have different classes of inertia, resilience, stability or interactions among these attributes. If so, it may prove possible to discover the different features of life histories, sizes, rates

of growth, position in food webs, phylogenies, etc. that are correlated with these attributes. This would be very important because it should enable predictions to be made about the effects of disturbances on populations for which there is sufficient knowledge of natural history to classify the species into appropriate groupings of inertia, stability and resilience, but for which there are insufficient quantitative data (and no time) before a disturbance begins. Such a classification would enable predictions about the effects of a disturbance even though no quantitative data are available about the population. The development of better theory relating life history to disturbance is only going to be possible through better experimental intrusions into natural populations.

11.5 CONCLUSIONS

In conclusion, the need for improved scientific input into environmental decision-making is large and urgent. Much more thought is required about the processes by which detection, interpretation and prediction of environmental threats can be improved. Considerable care is needed, but is too infrequently included, in environmental programmes of sampling (Green 1979; Hurlbert 1984; Stewart-Oaten *et al* 1986; Underwood 1981, 1986, 1991, 1992). Searches of the relevant literature in preparation of this review did not reveal many good case histories. For freshwater research, they were, perhaps, not found or not published, rather than not done. There are some interesting examples of pilot experiments on the methods to be used, their replication and sources of variability caused by their use (e.g. Furse *et al* 1981). The review by Clark (1989) considered a number of approaches to evaluations of contamination in field sites and Elliot (1977) remains the standard text.

The intellectual challenge is to design realistic field experimental perturbations to measure effects of possible impacts and to understand the requirements for management, reconstruction of habitat and rehabilitation of species. Without this, public pressure, environmentalists' emotional biases and the random outcomes of legal processes will be the only components of environmental protection. It is a collective responsibility for environmental scientists to do better science, to avoid the total demise of a rational, objective understanding of how best to conserve species in natural habitats subject to human influences. If this discussion provokes any thought about current problems of logic, design of sampling and interpretation of data and reliability of conclusions, it will have achieved some purpose.

ACKNOWLEDGEMENTS

The preparation of this chapter was supported by grants from the Australian Research Council and the Institute of Marine Ecology, University of Sydney. I am grateful for the advice from and discussions with Drs M.G. Chapman, P.G. Fairweather, K.A. McGuinness and P.A. Underwood and to K.L. Astles for considerable help in the preparation of the paper.

REFERENCES

Andrew NL, Mapstone BD. (1987) Sampling and the description of spatial pattern in marine ecology. *Annual Review of Oceanography and Marine Biology* **25**: 39–90. [11.2]

Arthur JW, Zischke JA, Erickson GL. (1982) Effect of elevated water temperature on macroinvertebrate communities in outdoor experimental channels. *Water Research* **16**: 1465–77. [11.2]

Bender EA, Case TJ, Gilpin ME. (1984) Perturbation experiments in community ecology: theory and practice. *Ecology* **65**: 1–13. [11.1]

Bernard DP, Neill WE, Rowe L. (1990) Impact of mild experimental acidification on short term invertebrate drift in a sensitive British Columbia stream. *Hydrobiologia* **203**: 63–72. [11.4]

Bernstein BB, Zalinski J. (1983) An optimum sampling design and power tests for environmental biologists. *Journal of Environmental Management* **16**: 35–43. [11.2]

Boesch DF. (1974) Diversity, stability and response to human disturbance in estuarine ecosystems. *Proceeding First International Congress of Ecology* **1**: 109–14. [11.4]

Bormann FH, Likens GE, Siccama TG, Pierce RS, Eaton JS. (1974) The export of nutrients and recovery of stable conditions following deforestation at Hubbard Brook. *Ecological Monographs* **44**: 255–77. [11.4]

Brittain JE, Eikeland TJ. (1988) Invertebrate drift – a review. *Hydrobiologia* **166**: 77–93. [11.2]

Clark JR. (1989) Field studies in estuarine ecosystems: a review of approaches for assessing contaminant effects. In: Cowgill UM, Williams LR (eds) *Aquatic Toxicology and Hazard Assessment*, vol. 12, pp. 120–33. ASTM, Philadelphia. [11.5]

Clarke KR. (1993) Non-parametric multivariate analyses of changes in community structure. *Australian Journal of Ecology* **18**: 117–43. [11.1]

Clarke KR, Green RH. (1988) Statistical design and analysis for a 'biological effects' study. *Marine Ecology Progress Series* **46**: 213–26. [11.1]

Clements WH, Cherry DS, Cairns J. (1988) Structural alterations in aquatic insect communities exposed to copper in laboratory streams. *Environmental Toxicology and Chemistry* **7**: 715–22. [11.4]

Clifford HF. (1982) Effects of periodically disturbing a small area of substratum in a brown-water stream of Alberta, Canada. *Freshwater Invertebrate Biology* **2**: 39–47. [11.1]

Cochran WG. (1947) Some consequences when the assumptions for the analysis of variance are not satisfied. *Biometrics* **3**: 22–38. [11.2]

Cochran WG, Cox G. (1957) *Experimental Designs*, 2nd edn. John Wiley, New York. [11.2]

Connell JH. (1972) Community interactions on marine rocky intertidal shores. *Annual Review of Ecology and Systematics* **3**: 169–92. [11.4]

Connell JH. (1975) Some mechanisms producing structure in natural communities: a model and evidence from field experiments. In: Cody MS, Diamond JM (eds) *Ecology and Evolution of Communities*, pp. 460–90. Harvard University Press, Cambridge, Massachusetts. [11.1, 11.4]

Connell JH, Sousa WP. (1983) On the evidence needed to judge ecological stability or persistence. *American Naturalist* **121**: 789–824. [11.1, 11.4]

Connor EF, Simberloff D. (1986) Competition, scientific method and null models in ecology. *American Scientist* **75**: 155–62. [11.1]

Cornfield J, Tukey JW. (1956) Average values of mean squares in factorials. *Annals of Mathematical Statistics* **27**: 907–49. [11.3]

Cox G. (1958) *The Planning of Experiments*. Wiley, New York. [11.2]

Cuffney TF, Wallace JB, Lugthart GJ. (1990) Experimental evidence quantifying the role of benthic invertebrates in organic matter dynamics of headwater streams. *Freshwater Biology* **23**: 281–99. [11.2]

Dayton PK. (1971) Competition, disturbance and community organization: the provision and subsequent utilization of space in a rocky intertidal community. *Ecological Monographs* **41**: 351–89. [11.1]

Den Boer PJ. (1979) The significance of dispersal power for the survival of species, with special reference to the Carabid beetles in a cultivated countryside. *Fortschritte Zoologie* **25**: 79–94. [11.1]

Den Boer PJ. (1981) On the survival of populations in a heterogeneous and variable environment. *Oecologia* (Berlin), **50**: 39–53. [11.1]

Elliott JM. (1977) *Methods for the Analyses of Samples of Benthic Invertebrates.* Freshwater Biological Association Scientific Publication No. 25, Reading. [11.2, 11.5]

Feller W. (1968) *An Introduction to Probability Theory and its Applications.* Wiley, New York. [11.3]

Fisher RA. (1925) *Statistical Methods for Research Workers.* Oliver & Boyd, London. [11.2, 11.3]

Frank PW. (1981) A condition for a sessile strategy. *American Naturalist* **118**: 288–90. [11.1]

Furse MT, Wright JF, Armitage PD, Moss D. (1981) An appraisal of pond-net samples for biological monitoring of lotic macro-invertebrates. *Water Research* **15**: 679–89. [11.5]

Gray JS. (1989) Effects of environmental stress on species rich assemblages. *Biological Journal of the Linnaean Society* **37**: 19–32. [11.4]

Gray JS, Pearson TH. (1982) Objective selection of sensitive species indicative of pollution-induced changes in benthic communities. I. Comparative methodology. *Marine Ecology Progress Series* **9**: 11–21. [11.4]

Green RH. (1979) *Sampling Design and Statistical Methods for Environmental Biologists.* Wiley, Chichester. [11.1, 11.2, 11.3, 11.5]

Green RH, Hobson KD. (1970) Spatial and temporal structure in a temperate intertidal community, with special emphasis on *Gemma gemma* (Pelecypoda: Mollusca). *Ecology* **51**: 999–1011. [11.2]

Hilborn R, Walters CJ. (1981) Pitfalls of environmental baseline and process studies. *Environmental Impact Assessment Review* **2**: 265–78. [11.4]

Holling CS. (1973) Resilience and stability of ecological systems. *Annual Review of Ecology and Systematics* **4**: 1–23. [11.4]

Hopkins PS, Kratz KW, Cooper SD. (1989) Effects of an experimental acid pulse on invertebrates in a high altitude Sierra Nevada stream. *Hydrobiologia* **171**: 45–58. [11.4]

Hurlbert SJ. (1984) Pseudoreplication and the design of ecological field experiments. *Ecological Monographs* **54**: 187–211. [11.1, 11.2, 11.5]

Johnson NL, Kotz S. (1969) *Distributions in Statistics: Discrete Distributions.* Wiley, New York. [11.3]

Kennelly SJ, Underwood AJ. (1984) Underwater microscopic sampling of a sublittoral kelp community. *Journal of Experimental Marine Biology and Ecology* **76**: 67–78. [11.2]

Kennelly SJ, Underwood AJ. (1985) Sampling of small invertebrates on natural hard substrata in a sublittoral kelp forest. *Journal of Experimental Marine Biology and Ecology* **89**: 55–67. [11.2]

Krebs CJ. (1978) *Ecology: the Experimental Analysis of Distribution and Abundance.* Harper & Row, New York. [11.4]

Lakatos I. (1974) Falsification and the methodology of scientific research programmes. In: Lakatos I, Musgrave AE (eds) *Criticism and the Growth of Knowledge,* pp. 91–6. Cambridge University Press, Cambridge. [11.3]

Lewis JR. (1976) Long-term ecological surveillance: practical realities in the rocky littoral. *Annual Review of Oceanography and Marine Biology* **14**: 371–90. [11.4]

Likens GE, Bormann FH, Johnson NM, Fisher DW, Pierce RS. (1970) Effects of forest cutting and herbicide treatment on nutrient budgets in the Hubbard Brook watershed-ecosystem. *Ecological Monographs* **40**: 23–47. [11.4]

Murdoch WW. (1970) Population regulation and population inertia. *Ecology* **51**: 497–502. [11.4]

Norris *et al.* (1994) The sampling problem. In: Calow P, Petts GE (eds) *The Rivers Handbook*, Vol. 1, pp. 282–306. Blackwell Scientific Publications, Oxford. [11.1]

Orians GH. (1974) Diversity, stability and maturity in natural ecosystems. In: van Dobben WH, Lowe-McConnell RH (eds) *Unifying Concepts in Ecology,* pp. 139–50. W. Junk, The Hague. [11.4]

Patrick R. (1975) Structure in stream communities. In: Cody MS, Diamond JM (eds) *Ecology and Evolution of Communities,* pp. 445–59. Harvard University Press, Cambridge, Massachusetts. [11.4]

Pielou EC. (1969) *An Introduction to Mathematical Ecology.* Wiley, New York. [11.1, 11.2]

Scheffe H. (1959) *The Analysis of Variance.* Wiley, New York. [11.3]

Snedecor GW, Cochran WG. (1967) *Statistical Methods,* 6th edn. University of Iowa Press, Ames. [11.2]

Sokal RR, Rohlf FJ. (1981) *Biometry,* 2nd edn. Freeman, New York. [11.2]

Stewart-Oaten A, Murdoch WM, Parker KR. (1986) Environmental impact assessment: 'pseudoreplication' in time? *Ecology* **67**: 929–40. [11.2, 11.5]

Underwood AJ. (1978) An experimental evaluation of competition between three species of intertidal prosobranch gastropods. *Oecologia* **33**: 185–208. [11.2]

Underwood AJ. (1981) Techniques of analysis of variance in experimental marine biology and ecology. *Annual Reviews of Oceanography and Marine Biology* **19**: 513–605. [11.1, 11.2, 11.3, 11.5]

Underwood AJ. (1984) Vertical and seasonal patterns in competition for microalgae between intertidal gastropods. *Oecologia* **64**: 211–22. [11.2]

Underwood AJ. (1985) Physical factors and biological interactions: the necessity and nature of ecological experiments. In: Moore PG, Seed R (eds) *The Ecology of Rocky Coasts,* pp. 371–90. Hodder & Stoughton, London. [11.4]

Underwood AJ. (1986) The analysis of competition by field experiments. In: Kikkawa J, Anderson DJ (eds) *Community Ecology: Pattern and Process,* pp. 240–68. Blackwells, Melbourne. [11.1, 11.2, 11.4, 11.5]

Underwood AJ. (1989) The analysis of stress in natural populations. *Biological Journal of the Linnaean Society* **37**: 51–78. [11.1, 11.2, 11.4]

Underwood AJ. (1990) Experiments in ecology and management: their logics, functions and interpretations. *Australian Journal of Ecology* **15**: 365–89. [11.1]

Underwood AJ. (1991) Beyond BACI: experimental designs for detecting human environmental impacts on temporal variations in natural populations. *Australian Journal of Marine and Freshwater Research* **42**: 569–87. [11.1, 11.2, 11.5]

Underwood AJ. (1992) Beyond BACI: the detection of environmental impact on populations in the real, but variable, world. *Journal of Experimental Marine Biology and Ecology* **161**, 145–78. [11.2, 11.5]

Underwood AJ. (1993) The mechanics of spatially repli-cated sampling programmes to detect environmental impacts in a variable world. *Australian Journal of Ecology* **18**, 99–116. [11.2]

Underwood AJ, Peterson CH. (1988) Towards an ecological framework for investigating pollution. *Marine Ecology Progress Series* **46**: 227–34. [11.1, 11.4]

Warwick RM. (1993) Environmental impact studies on marine communities: pragmatical considerations. *Australian Journal of Ecology* **18**: 63–80. [11.1]

Winer BJ. (1971) *Statistical Principles in Experimental Design*, 2nd edn. McGraw-Hill Kogakusha, Tokyo. [11.2, 11.3]

12: System Recovery

A. M. MILNER

12.1 INTRODUCTION

This concluding chapter focuses on the ways in which biotic communities in river systems recover following disturbance. Five key aspects of recovery are reviewed: recovery pathways; indicator end-points used to determine recovery; the role of succession in recovery processes; recovery mechanisms of the biota; and factors affecting recovery rates. Some examples of recovery times following specific disturbances are included. In certain cases the extent to which recovery rates may be enhanced through restoration practices is indicated.

A brief set of definitions is presented here with specific reference to fluvial systems, but the reader is also referred to Chapter 11. Some of the principal problems in the field of recovery concern misinterpretation of terms through differing definitions. The term *disturbance* has suffered this problem due to its frequent use in a great variety of contexts (Rykiel 1985; Peters 1988). Disturbance in general terms is considered 'any relatively discrete event in time that disrupts ecosystem, community or population structure and changes resources, substrate availability or the physical environment' (White & Pickett 1985). Sousa's (1984) definition of disturbance is a discrete removal of organisms that are subsequently replaced by reproduction of resident survivors or by immigration. A key problem of defining disturbance by its effects is that disturbances may not be detected if they occur at a small spatial scale of low intensity and the rate of recovery is rapid, even with regular site monitoring (Lake 1990). In rivers, Resh *et al* (1988) narrow the scope of a disturbance to in-clude only those physical and biological events that occur outside the normal range of predictable frequencies, severities or intensities for that system. For example, an annual spate that causes severe scour and bed material transport in a stream system would not constitute a disturbance within this definition (Gore & Milner 1990), unless its timing or magnitude was 'atypical' (Sparks *et al* 1990). The rationale is that riverine communities are adapted to the annual flood as a predictable event and have evolved various behavioural and reproductive strategies to ensure rapid recovery. In contrast, a 50-year flood in the same stream is unpredictable and would constitute a disturbance.

One practical problem with this definition of disturbance is determining what is the 'normal' or 'typical' range of predictable frequencies, severities or intensities; it may be impossible to determine whether an event is a disturbance without a long-term database for the system under examination (Gore *et al* 1990). This definition of disturbance also requires that recovery must be examined against these constant fluctuations, replacements and processes within the biotic communities in response to 'non-disturbance' events, for example an annual flood. Poff (1992) suggests that organisms are not necessarily pre-adapted to predictable environments; potential adaptation to disturbance predictability is itself dependent upon other attributes of the disturbance regime as some components are interactive. Most of the discussion surrounding disturbances in rivers concerns the effects of altered flow regimes. However, variations in discharge represent only one form (albeit one of the most important) of disturbance affecting riverine communities; other events, particularly those of anthropogenic origin, are unlikely to be predictable and hence will constitute a disturbance under any definition.

Recovery is defined by Davis *et al* (1984) as the process of species returning to 'normal' population levels after an impact. Again how is 'normal' defined? In many cases no or negligible pre-disturbance data exist to determine what 'normal' populations are in rivers and, in addition, over various temporal scales, freshwater communities are continually adjusting to biotic and abiotic factors within the ecosystem (see Section 12.2 below). Recovery is probably best viewed as a return to an ecosystem which closely resembles unstressed surrounding areas or source areas (Gore 1985) or to an unstressed condition (Kelly & Harwell 1990). Recovery is thus a natural process and is distinct from restoration, enhancement or rehabilitation.

Restoration is a process that involves management decisions and manipulation to enhance the rate of recovery (after Davis *et al* 1984). Consequently Gore (1985) defines river restoration as 'recovery enhancement' and considers it a technique to enable disturbed river ecosystems to stabilize at a much higher rate than through the natural physical and biological recovery processes of habitat development and colonization. *Enhancement* refers to improving the current

state of the ecosystem without reference to its initial state, while *rehabilitation* is probably a mixture of enhancement and restoration (Magnuson *et al* 1980).

Resistance is the ability of a community to initially resist a disturbance while *resilience* refers to the ability of a disturbed community to recover to a state existing before the disturbance (*sensu* Webster *et al* 1975). Relative to other ecosystems riverine communities are considered to have a low resistance to disturbance (Reice 1985; Doeg *et al* 1989a) but a high resilience (Gurtz & Wallace 1984; Lake & Barmuta 1986; Lake *et al* 1989). High resilience is attributed to the relatively short life cycles of riverine species. The more resilient the fauna then the faster will be the recovery rates of biotic communities in rivers.

12.2 RECOVERY PATHWAYS

Figure 12.1 illustrates recovery pathways that may occur following disturbance to a community whereby recovery may result in different endpoints (A or B) rather than a return to the pre-disturbance community. The pre-disturbance community may only result by implementing restoration procedures. Depending upon the timescale necessary for recovery, the structure of the pre-disturbed community may, in any event, have changed through development and successional

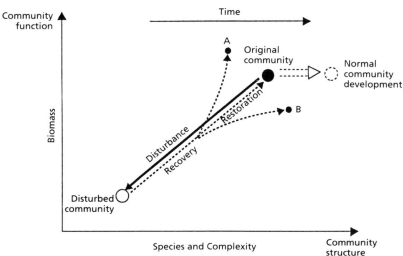

Fig. 12.1 Recovery pathways of a disturbed community (see text) (after Bradshaw 1988).

processes in response to the natural physico-chemical environment and habitat changes. Hence, if a pre-disturbance situation is to be achieved, restoration and recovery may require mimicking the presumed successional stage had the system been permitted to continue normal community processes (Cairns 1990); this is a difficult scenario for a river manager to achieve.

12.3 INDICATOR END-POINTS OF SYSTEM RECOVERY

What indicator or set of indicators constitutes a suitable end-point to recovery that is acceptable to such parties as the river manager, the developer, the polluter and the general public? The establishment of acceptable end-points to recovery is a complex issue and a criterion of immense importance in the management of rivers recovering from disturbances.

In attempting to characterize the initial and long-term recovery patterns of river ecosystems in terms of single, multiple, acute, chronic or cumulative disturbance events, one must select from a number of indicator end-points which reflect some characteristic of the system at some spatio-temporal scale of observation (Kelly & Harwell 1990). The end-points of recovery are potentially different according to the nature of the disturbance (Cairns 1990; Gore et al 1990).

The common end-points used in assessing the recovery of river systems are divided into either biotic or abiotic (Fig. 12.2). Biotic recovery is examined principally at the community level. A community can be defined as an assemblage of species populations which occur together in space and time. Although an ecosystem is generally regarded to represent a community together with its abiotic environment, it is impossible to consider a community in isolation from the environment in which it exists (Begon et al 1990). At the community level there are both structural and functional end-points to recovery.

Structural end-points cover the make-up of community assemblages in terms of such attributes as density, number of species, species diversity, etc. and typically involve comparison with the pre-disturbance or a reference com-

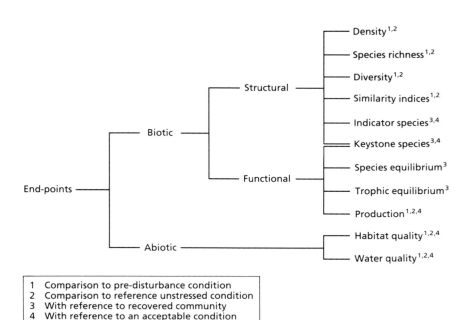

Density[1,2]

Species richness[1,2]

Diversity[1,2]

Structural — Similarity indices[1,2]

Indicator species[3,4]

Keystone species[3,4]

Biotic — Species equilibrium[3]

Functional — Trophic equilibrium[3]

Production[1,2,4]

End-points — Habitat quality[1,2,4]

Abiotic — Water quality[1,2,4]

1 Comparison to pre-disturbance condition
2 Comparison to reference unstressed condition
3 With reference to recovered community
4 With reference to an acceptable condition

Fig. 12.2 Possible end-points that can be used to determine recovery success.

munity. Similarity indices such as Jaccard's Index (Southwood 1978) can be used to compare the structure of a recovered community with a reference community, as shown by Townsend *et al* (1987) and Gore (1979), who compared the persistence of communities several years apart. Indicator species are individual species selected for their ability to provide an indication of the well-being of the habitat or water quality within a river following recovery, e.g. stoneflies or salmonids. Keystone (or gold star) species can be defined as species which are of special significance to the structure and function of the riverine community and may have important commercial, recreational or conservation value. Examples would be the recovery of recreationally or commercially valuable fish species, such as trout and salmon, or species of conservation value such as the otter. A species could potentially be both an indicator and a keystone, for example salmonid species.

Functional end-points refer to the functioning of the community, for example species equilibrium, and may be evaluated independently of a reference community. It may be that functional end-points are more important when a particular purpose is attempting to be fulfilled (Kelly & Harwell 1900); Another potential indicator of recovery is trophic structure of the macroinvertebrate functional feeding groups (see Cummins 1994 for definitions). Predators are typically the last trophic group to arrive during the recovery process (Gore 1982), and Minshall *et al* (1983) found that trophic structure by functional group was not attained at the end of 3½ years after a flood-induced disturbance. Production is a further possible recovery end-point but has rarely been used in recovery studies due to the intensive sampling and analysis needed for its measurement. However, it is potentially a very important recovery end-point and recent techniques make its calculation considerably easier.

Abiotic end-points to recovery are considered to be such parameters as physical habitat quality or water quality and are assessed independently of the community present. Depending upon the disturbance involved, some examples of physical habitat quality might include percentage of fine sediment among the gravels/cobbles and heterogeneity of the substrate. Water-quality end-points might include such parameters as dissolved oxygen, pH, total suspended sediment or heavy metal concentration and typically reflect performance standards set by a regulatory body.

Most recovery studies have reported density, species richness or a combination of the two through a diversity index as end-points. These structural end-points can, however, indicate the completeness of recovery before it has actually occurred and thus may prove misleading (Shaw & Minshall 1980; Minshall *et al* 1983). Maximum densities may ignore the dominance or species replacement by disturbance-tolerant forms (Gore & Milner 1990). For example, as shown by Krumholz and Minckley (1984), an equilibrium of pollution-tolerant species at densities comparable to pre-disturbance levels can be expected under situations of chronic organic loading (sewage outfalls). Species equilibrium (where rate of immigration of colonizing species is equal to the rate of extinction) frequently lags behind maximum density because of a period of dynamic adjustment before equilibrium. For example Minshall *et al* (1983) reported that following a major flood macroinvertebrates took 400 days to reach maximum densities but between 600 and 650 days to achieve species equilibrium.

However, certain communities may never attain species equilibrium due to constant successional adjustments to abiotic events or disturbances. Some river systems are believed to maximize species diversity by being maintained in a non-equilibrium state reducing competitive hierarchies through intermediate disturbances (Ward & Stanford 1983). Reice (1985) suggests that the intermediate disturbance hypothesis probably does not apply to streams and rivers because competitive hierarchies have not been widely demonstrated. The dynamic equilibrium model (Huston 1979) is proposed by Reice *et al* (1990) as the most appropriate for rivers. This model suggests that the recurrence interval of disturbance events is shorter than the time necessary for competitive or predator–prey interactions to cause the elimination of species. Hence species equilibrium within riverine communities may be an unattainable end-point; this subject creates much debate among river ecologists.

Another important question regarding end-points is whether the structural and functional end-points of a recovered or restored community can be maintained without constant management. Cairns (1990) considers that unless a self-sustaining community based on natural reproduction, succession and adaptation is attained then system recovery has not been achieved.

12.4 RECOVERY AND SUCCESSION

Succession is most simply defined as community changes that occur at a site following a disturbance (after Fisher 1990). Statzner and Higler (1985) suggest that if disturbances cause losses and gains of species, then it would be expected that the biological community in rivers is re-established by means of succession and therefore river systems cannot be viewed independent of time. One of the problems is that successional changes are superimposed and confounded by diel, seasonal and long-term schedules which also produce changes in the community (Fisher 1990).

Primary succession occurs after a disturbance that is so intense that no trace of the previous community exists (Fisher 1990) or where a new channel is formed. Secondary succession can be viewed as community change at sites that have been structured physically and chemically by previous resident assemblages and where organic matter remains to support initial colonizers (after Gore & Milner 1990). It is a rare disturbance in lotic systems that eliminates all organisms from a stretch of river and thus there are a limited number of examples of recovery through primary succession (see Section 12.7 below). Except in the severest of floods and droughts, organisms can obtain refuge in the hyporheic zone and act as a colonizing source within the stream section as pre-disturbance conditions return; hence this is not primary succession (Fisher 1990). The colonization of artificial substrates placed in rivers could be considered an example of primary succession. However, because the scale is so small substrates are likely to be overwhelmed by continued rapid colonization from adjacent communities so that there is no opportunity for distinct successional communities to exist.

Therefore, the difference between primary and secondary succession is probably only discernible at scales that limit colonizers. In rivers this scale probably reaches 10^3–10^4 m in length (Fisher 1990). Exceptions to this scale have been demonstrated by McCormick and Stevenson (1991), who found distinct successional algal communities on tiles placed in a stream.

12.5 MECHANISMS OF RECOVERY

Good dispersal abilities, high production rates, short generation times and flexible life history strategies typically enable periphyton species to recover rapidly following disturbances (Steinman & McIntire 1990). Recovery times may be considerably longer if propagule sources upstream from the disturbance area are impacted (Resh *et al* 1988).

Four principal migration sources and mechanisms for stream benthos have been identified: (i) downstream migration or drift; (ii) upstream migration; (iii) vertical migration from within the substrate (the hyporheic zone); and (iv) aerial sources (Williams & Hynes 1976; Williams 1981). Depending upon the disturbance, some or all of these sources may be available in river systems recovering from disturbances. For an artificial stream in Canada where upstream sources of colonizers were present, Williams and Hynes (1976) concluded that the order of importance for recovery in June was drift > aerial sources > movement from the hyporheic zone > upstream movement. Where present, downstream drift is typically the most important recovery mechanism of the benthos (Niemi *et al* 1990) although this is not always the case. Doeg *et al* (1989b) found that for gravel and stones, crawling across the substratum was the most common method of colonization although the scale was small.

For certain major disturbances (e.g. elimination of fauna along an entire channel without upstream sources of drift) aerial colonization represents the major, if not only, source for recovery. Chironomids (Diptera) have a high dispersal ability, being small winged and relatively light (Brundin 1967). Generally most Ephemeroptera (mayflies), Trichoptera (caddisflies), and many

Plecoptera (stoneflies) are considered weak fliers, while Odonata (dragonflies and damselflies), some Coleoptera (beetles) and Hemiptera (bugs) are good fliers (Williams 1981). Even if adult insects are able to invade a drainage there is no certainty that they will colonize the stream. Five years after the Mount St Helens eruption, caddis flies, which were relatively abundant as adults in the impacted drainages, were either absent or at low abundances in the streams (Anderson & Wisseman 1987). Molluscs are typically one of the last taxa to recover following disturbances (Wallace 1990), presumably as a result of poor dispersal mechanisms.

Mechanisms of recovery in fish include redispersal of surviving adults within the watershed and increased recruitment of young through various age classes. In severe disturbances where fish are completely eliminated, fish must colonize from other streams or via the straying of anadromous adults returning to spawn.

12.6 FACTORS AFFECTING RECOVERY RATES

This section overviews the principal factors that influence recovery rates for any particular disturbance. Some attempt is made to prioritize these factors according to their overall influence, beginning with those factors having the most effect on recovery rates. The effects of these factors are summarized in Table 12.1. The scale in this table is arbitrary and relative; a factor of 0 has little effect while a factor of −3 or +3 has the greatest effect, either retarding or enhancing recovery rates respectively.

Physical habitat

Disturbances that impact physical habitat probably exert some of the greatest influences on system recovery. Physical habitat impacts include the introduction of fine sediment onto the river bed from road construction and logging, the removal of large woody debris from rivers, the loss of heterogeneity of the river bed substrate and the lack of diversified flow patterns through channelization and the loss of cover through

removal of riparian vegetation These impacts severely influence colonization processes by the biota, frequently resulting in long recovery times. For example, sediment accumulation between the bed cobbles may restrict access to the underside of stones for invertebrates and may eliminate or significantly modify the hyporheic habitat (Campbell & Doeg 1989). For this factor management assistance through restoration may then be needed if recovery rates are not to be greatly retarded.

Recovery of terrestrial and riparian vegetation

River communities are closely linked to terrestrial plant conditions in the surrounding watershed (Cummins & Klug 1979; Vannote *et al* 1980). Hence the recovery of trophic functional groups within the invertebrate community may, in certain disturbances, be long term and dependent upon the recovery of terrestrial vegetation. Fish recovery may also depend on the suitable regrowth of riparian vegetation. For example, redevelopment of riparian habitat was a major factor in the recovery of coho stocks in an impacted drainage following the Mount St Helens eruption in western Washington, USA (Martin *et al* 1986) and of trout populations following a catastrophic debris flow in an Oregon stream (Lamberti *et al* 1991).

Size of disturbed area/upstream sources of drift

Spatial scales are very important in determining recovery rates. The larger the area affected by the disturbance then the greater the distance to colonizing sources, particularly in the case of major disturbances. Source distance effects described by Gore (1979, 1982) are then significant and will determine the immigration rates of colonizing species (see Section 12.7, 'Channel modifications'). Another major factor governing the immigration of invertebrate colonizers following disturbances is whether upstream sources of drift are present. As discussed previously under recovery mechanisms, drift is a major source for colonization and where present significantly increases recovery rates.

Table 12.1 Factors that can potentially influence recovery rates of the biota (the solid bar equals definite + or − to end of that range where the broken bar means variable over that range)

Factor	Influence of factor	Level at which factor influences recovery	Lower recovery rate −3	−2	−1	0	Increased recovery rate +1	+2	+3
Physical habitat	Alteration influences colonization processes	Severe alteration		▬	▬				
		Minor alteration			▬				
Recovery of terrestrial and riparian vegetation	Affects recovery of certain trophic groups and fish populations	Vegetation growth frequently long-term process		▬	▬				
Size of disturbed area/ source of drift	Affects immigration of colonizers	Large/no upstream sources of drift	▬	▬	▬				
		Small/sources of drift present					▬	▬	▬
Continued disturbances	Arrests succession and recovery	Frequent/large		▬	▬				
		Infrequent/small			▬				
Previous disturbances	History of events in system	Similar to present disturbance					▬	▬	
		Dissimilar to present disturbance					▬		
	No history—relatively stable physical/ chemical environment				▬				
Presence and proximity of refugia	Provides colonizing source	Present/close					▬	▬	▬
		Absent/far	▬	▬	▬				
Flushing capacity	Affects persistence of disturbance	High					▬	▬	▬
		Low	▬	▬	▬				
Land use/basin characteristics	Affects water quality	Enhanced contaminant input and toxicity		▬	▬				
		Reduced contaminant input and toxicity					▬	▬	▬
Time of year/life cycle stage	Affects availability of colonizers and community resilience	High latitudes — ice-covered season		▬	▬				
		Low latitudes					▬	▬	▬
Nutrient input and turnover time	Low nutrient inputs and slow turnover reduces system resilience	Slow turnover			▬				
		Rapid turnover					▬		
Location of disturbance	Lower in river system	Increases diversity of food resources					▬		

Continued disturbances

Continued disturbances will arrest the successional pathways and hold recovery in an early successional stage, thereby increasing recovery times. This continuance of the disturbance parallels the difference between a *pulse disturbance* and a *press disturbance* as defined by Bender *et al* (1984). A pulse disturbance is a disturbance of limited and easily definable duration whereas press disturbances are longer and frequently involve changes in the watershed or the river channel. Examples of pulse disturbances are floods or inputs of non-persistent pollutants while press disturbances include logging, mining, persistent toxic chemicals and stream channelization.

History of previous disturbances

Colonization by biotic communities will probably occur more rapidly in river systems with
a history of episodic disturbances due to the
potential selection for species within the community that can rapidly recolonize following displacement. Hence a community that experiences
regular and frequent floods will likely recover
more rapidly to similar type events than a community in a more stable physical environment. It
is probable that these communities will also recover more rapidly to dissimilar events such as
point- or non-point-source inputs of pollutants.
This more rapid recovery is principally due to the
adaptive strategies of species within the community for coping with frequent disturbance
by selecting for opportunistic species with high
vagility, high fecundity and early maturation.
Communities living in a more stable physical/
chemical environment are likely to be less
adapted to respond rapidly when disturbed. For
example, unpredictable droughts in normally permanent streams may result in invertebrate recovery rates in excess of 1 year (Ladle & Bass
1981) but in regions with seasonally predictable
dewatering, recovery may occur in less than 2
months (Sagar 1983). In addition in many rivers
stressed by pollution, the pre-disturbance fauna is
made up of pollution-tolerant species which are
likely to recover quicker than a diverse pristine
fauna.

Presence and proximity of refugia

There are many types of refugia within a river
system including localized microhabitats and/
or zones within the channel, unique reaches,
riparian vegetation, floodplains and groundwaters
(Sedell *et al* 1990). In many cases refugia may be
inhabited by biota that are different or transient
in comparison to the communities that typically
occur in the channel. Nevertheless these refugia
function as source areas for recolonization of
rivers following disturbances that reduce biomass
or diversity (Sedell *et al* 1990). If the disturbed
river section is far from available refugia, then the
vagility of adults, generation times and fecundity
of the colonizers assume more importance in
dictating recovery rates (Niemi *et al* 1990).

Flushing capacity/persistence of disturbance

The persistence of a disturbance will have a
major influence on the ability of a river system to
recover. Where flushing capacities (i.e. the ability
of a river to flush out contaminants or sediments)
are high the persistence of certain disturbances
will be reduced and recovery rates enhanced. This
persistence is particularly the case with point-
and non-point-source chemical pollutants, particularly where the pollutants become incorporated
into the sediments, and with disturbances that
influence the structural habitat of the river. For
example, sediment inputs from highway construction or logging can severely impact benthic
organisms and survival of juvenile fish (Everest *et
al* 1987). Sand deposition on river substrate has
been shown to hinder upstream movements
of aquatic insects (Luedtke & Brusven 1976).
Deposited sediment may be difficult to remove
without substantial flushing flows.

Land use/basin characteristics

Land use within a catchment will influence the
transport of contaminants to a river and affects
the magnitude and frequency of disturbances. For
example, poor management of drainage patterns
on agricultural land without riparian vegetation
may increase the runoff of sediment and other
potential contaminants into the river. This may
result in continued disturbances and retard recovery times. Basin geology influences the ability
of a watershed to buffer water-quality degradation
within a river, which in turn influences the toxicity and persistence of various chemical pollutants and thereby affects recovery rates. For
example, metal toxicity will be greater at lower
hardness levels, which could contribute to longer
recovery rates.

Time of year of disturbance and
life cycles of the biota

The time of year that a disturbance occurs
may significantly affect the ability of certain
species to follow dispersal routes for colonization,
especially in the case of aquatic insects. This
is particularly evident at higher latitudes
where macroinvertebrates have long seasonal life

cycles compared to more milder climes where life cycles are frequently aseasonal (Wallace 1990). For example, some multivoltine taxa (e.g. Chironomidae) may pass from the egg through adult stages in under 2 weeks in warm-water streams (Fisher & Gray 1983). At higher latitudes many species are univoltine (one generation a year) while in some taxa (e.g. Plecoptera) certain species have one generation every 2 or 3 years (Oswood *et al* 1995). Hence aerial colonization by aquatic insects following disturbances at these higher latitudes can only occur at certain times during the ice-free season and in certain species with long life cycles potentially only once every 2 or 3 years.

Even in more temperate latitudes, the timing of the disturbance during the year may significantly influence recovery rates. An atypical summer flood in an Irish river caused longer recovery times to summer invertebrate assemblages than a comparable more common flood in the winter (Giller *et al* 1991) while colonization in natural gravel patches has been shown to be more rapid in summer than winter in an Australian river (Doeg *et al* 1989a). The time of the year also determines which life stage of an organism is present following a disturbance; for example, during drought some animals survive as eggs which enhances recovery when suitable conditions return (Morrison 1990).

Thus the sequence of colonization, succession and possible end-point community may be significantly influenced by which species are able to become part of the colonizing pool at the time following the disturbance.

Nutrient input and recycling

Disturbances which affect autotrophic production or the allochthonous inputs to a river will influence recovery rates of benthic organisms and fish (DeAngelis *et al* 1990). Productivity in some streams has been shown to be nutrient limited (e.g. Peterson *et al* 1985) indicating that disturbances which alter the nutrient loading to, and recycling within, a river channel will also influence the system's ability to recover. Where nutrient inputs are low and there is a low turnover and cycling of nutrients, resilience will con-

sequently be low (Webster *et al* 1975) and thus recovery times will be longer (DeAngelis *et al* 1990). In rivers there is the further complicating factor of flow, which tends to move allochthonous nutrients downstream. Webster and Patten (1979) suggested the term 'nutrient spiralling' to describe the coupled process of nutrient cycling and transport, and the 'tightness' of the spirals is an indication of the retention and reutilization of a nutrient. Retention devices, such as fallen trees, will increase the tightness of the spirals, and, if retention efficiency is disturbed, recovery times will likely be increased. Restoration techniques in rivers sometimes involve increasing retention efficiency.

Location of disturbance in stream course and stream order

The farther downstream a disturbance occurs then the greater the upstream source of colonizers (particularly for colonization by drift) and, in light of the river continuum concept (Vannote *et al* 1980), the greater the availability of different types of food resources due to upstream processing (Gore & Milner 1990). Higher stream orders (larger rivers with many tributary inputs) may thus potentially recover more rapidly.

12.7 RECOVERY RATES

Levels of disturbance

From the foregoing, it is evident that many factors influence recovery rates, which consequently can be extremely variable. Recovery rates also depend upon the end-point selected. Nevertheless some general conclusions are drawn here about the ranges of recovery rates for any particular disturbance. Most of the recovery times given here refer to time to attain maximum densities, biomass or taxa richness unless otherwise stated. In the case of macroinvertebrates, 90% of the cases reviewed by Niemi *et al* (1990) indicated recovery times within a year. This section covers only a small percentage of the recovery studies reported, more to provide a range and indicate circumstances where recovery is longer than is typical for any particular disturbance. These ranges are

Table 12.2 Range of recovery times for macroinvertebrates and fish following various disturbances (the broken bar equals tentative range)

Disturbance		Level	Recovery time in years (approx. range read from bars)
Watershed disturbances	Logging	3 and 4	macroinvertebrates ~10–20
	Mining	2, 3 and 4	macroinvertebrates ~15 to >20
	Fires	3	macroinvertebrates ~5–10 (tentative)
	Volcanic activity	1	~5 to >20 (tentative) ?
Channel modifications	New channel (no upstream colonizers)	1	macroinvertebrates ~10–15
	New channel (upstream colonizers present)	2	macroinvertebrates ~0.6–2.0; fish ~2.0–10
Floods	Adapted fauna	1B and 3	macroinvertebrates ~0–0.4
	Non-adapted fauna	1A(?) and 3	macroinvertebrates ~0.4–2.0; fish ~2.0–3.0
Drought	Adapted fauna	2 and 3	macroinvertebrates ~0–0.2
	Non-adapted fauna	2 and 3	macroinvertebrates ~0.8–1.0
Pesticides	Indirect application	2 and 3	macroinvertebrates ~1.0–2.0; fish
	Direct application	2	macroinvertebrates ~0.6–4.0
Chemical spills and toxic pollutants	Persistent	2 and 3	macroinvertebrates ~3.0–5.0
	Non-persistent and flushed-out	2 and 3	macroinvertebrates ~0.6–1.0; fish
Organic pollutants		3	macroinvertebrates ~0.6–1.0

Recovery-time column scale (years): 0 0.2 0.4 0.6 0.8 1.0 2.0 3.0 4.0 5.0 10.0 15.0 20.0 >20.0

▬▬▬ Macroinvertebrates; ••••• Fish

summarized in Table 12.2. The reader is directed to excellent reviews by Yount and Niemi (1990) and Niemi *et al* (1990) for a more detailed treatment of this aspect of recovery.

To aid in determining likely recovery times from disturbances, Gore and Milner (1990) suggest that disturbance first be categorized at a number of different levels.

Level 1A

Disturbance completely destroys communities along the entire stream length leaving no upstream or downstream sources to colonize and may result in a new stream channel. This level of disturbance leads to recovery through primary successional processes. Examples include volcanic deposits and ice movements.

Level 1B

Disturbance completely destroys surface communities along the entire stream length leaving no upstream or downstream sources to colonize; but there remains a remnant hyporheic component or near-surface source of eggs and smaller instars. Such disturbance probably leads to recovery via secondary succession. Examples are floods in low-order streams with no confluence with a downstream source (e.g. some small desert streams and coastal streams that empty directly into the ocean) and some forms of drought.

Level 2A

Disturbance completely destroys communities in a reach of stream but upstream and downstream colonization sources remain, leading to recovery through primary succession. Examples are chemical spills, reclaimed or diverted river channels, and surface mining effects.

Level 2B

As 2A, but the hyporheic zone is not destroyed, leading to secondary succession. Examples are application of insecticides, some chemical spills and some types of dewatering.

Level 3

This level of disturbance results in reduction of species abundance and diversity from pre-disturbance levels in a section of stream but does not completely eliminate the benthos, leading to secondary succession recovery processes. Examples include floods and chronic non-point- and point-source pollutants.

Level 4

Disturbances of this level result in reduction of species abundance and/or diversity or loss of benthos compared to pre-disturbance levels in discrete patches within a stream section but such that proximal patches are unaffected. Recovery is by secondary succession. As previously pointed out, if these patches represent too small a scale, then succession does not take place. Examples are sediment inputs from highway construction and logging.

Watershed disturbances

One of the principal watershed disturbance effects on rivers arises from timber harvest through the effects of clear-cutting, road construction and in certain areas planting (levels 3 and 4). Commercial logging and associated road building may cause a variety of effects on stream communities, including increased sediment deposition (Everest *et al* 1987), increased discharge, increased stream temperatures (Beschta *et al* 1987), alterations in the quantity, quality and timing of allochthonous matter, and increases in autochthonous primary production (Webster *et al* 1983; Duncan & Brus-

ven 1985a,b). Clear-cutting of a watershed is a large-scale, low-frequency, anthropogenic disturbance and the stream biota have not evolved appropriate adaptations to such disturbances (Gurtz & Wallace 1984), hence recovery can be lengthy.

This type of disturbance illustrates the problems of determining recovery rates where cumulative effects influence riverine communities. Cumulative effects result from environmental change due to the accumulation and interaction of localized or small impacts which increases the effect on the resource (Burns 1991). For example, increased sediment delivery to a river channel from logging practices, combined with altered sediment transport and storage downstream due to changed large woody debris inputs, may cause stream-bed aggradation, channel widening and degradation of the physical habitat (Smith 1989). Cumulative effects are not always synergistic in their action and may be antagonistic. Increases in streamflow may moderate the effects of increased stream temperatures that result from the removal of stream vegetation (Chamberlain *et al* 1991). In logged watersheds of the southern Appalachian Mountains, USA, there was a significant shift in energy base to autochthonous production (Webster *et al* 1992) accompanied by an associated shift in benthic invertebrates dominated by scrapers and collectors (Gurtz & Wallace 1984; Wallace *et al* 1988). Wallace and Gurtz (1986) found that the invertebrate taxa (*Baetis* and chironomids) that increased possess short generation times and respond rapidly. A similar increase in primary production was observed in low-order streams of southeast Alaska (Duncan & Brusven 1985a) although no significant alteration in the ratio of functional groups was apparent (Duncan & Brusven 1985b). In addition responses by invertebrates to major watershed disturbances like logging are frequently substrate mediated with more taxa recovering in larger substrates (Gurtz & Wallace 1984).

Thus potentially after the deleterious effects of sediment from timber harvest and road construction have been flushed out, the invertebrate densities and biomass in the clear-cut area could be considered acceptable when compared to the predisturbance condition. However, the trophic structure of the benthic community (particularly the shredders) could take considerably longer to recover and be dependent upon riparian zone development to supply allochthonous leaf input (Haeffner & Wallace 1981; Wallace *et al* 1988). These results again indicate the problems for a river manager in determining what is an acceptable end-point to community recovery.

The increased invertebrate biomass may be considered of value for it will potentially lead to increased growth and abundance of fish. Although this effect has been reported in a number of logged southeastern Alaskan streams, increases in juvenile salmon growth and densities may be nullified by a shortage of essential winter habitat (Heifetz *et al* 1986; Murphy *et al* 1986), leading to increased overwintering mortality. Hence the manager of a river in a watershed disturbed by logging may decide that the best end-point may be a keystone species, for example the abundance and production of salmon. Physical habitat quality may have an extremely long recovery time for river channels in watersheds disturbed by logging, particularly in certain geographical areas. Large woody debris (material >10 cm in diameter and >1 m long – see Murphy & Koski 1989) is an important structural part of salmon habitat in stream orders 1–4 in forests of the Pacific Northwest in the USA. A model developed by Murphy and Koski (1989) predicts that 90 years after logging, a 70% reduction in large woody debris would occur and recovery to pre-logging levels would take at least 250 years. Four case histories of the effects of logging on the response and recovery of stream channel habitat indicated that channel recovery ranged from 5 to 60 years and recovery of riparian vegetation ranged from 100 to 200 years (Sullivan *et al* 1987).

Strip mining (level 2 and 3 disturbances) within a watershed also causes long recovery times of the benthos due to the regrowth of vegetation, with estimates of 20–25 years to reach pre-disturbance densities and species composition (Tolbert & Vaughan 1979).

Fires are an integral part of many ecosystems and constitute a significant watershed disturbance (level 3). Fires alter large woody debris, sediment suspension, nutrient cycling and leaf litter input. Heavy accumulations of fine sediment diminish invertebrate standing crops and

cause recovery to be delayed until the sediments are flushed out. Following the 1988 fires in Yellowstone National Park, USA, Minshall *et al* (1989) estimated that benthic invertebrates would take at least 3 years to recover.

The Mount St Helens eruption in May 1980 also provided an opportunity to study the recovery of stream communities after a major disturbance to the watershed. In most watersheds near the blast zone, riparian vegetation was eliminated and ash deposits of a few millimetres to over 5 cm were reported (Cook *et al* 1981). Rushforth *et al* (1986) reported that within 15 months or less of the eruption, algal communities were established in streams throughout the blast zone although due to continued disturbances some of these communities remained in an early successional stage (principally diatoms). Two years after the eruption, few aquatic insect species had reinvaded the denuded streams, and Wilzbach *et al* (1983) suggested that it may be 100 years for complete recovery in some streams due to the instability of channel banks and substrates which lead to continued disturbances at successive high-flow events. Recovery is proceeding more rapidly in watersheds where some or all of the forest remained intact compared to watersheds where the forest was completely destroyed (Hawkins & Sedell 1990). Restoration measures have been employed in a number of drainages to enhance recovery but these have caused a number of controversies (see Franklin *et al* 1988).

Channel modifications

Channel relocation and reconstruction projects are relatively rare but provide an indication of recovery times where a major physical modification of the river channel occurs. These cases are not recovery *per se* as there is no original condition with which to compare but provide information on colonization and community development within a primary successional framework with reference areas used for comparison. These projects represent level 2 disturbances as there is typically an upstream source of colonizers. However, channelization of rivers can lead to long recovery times for both fish and macroinvertebrate communities (Niemi *et al* 1990), particularly where upstream sources are absent and where the physical habitat is impaired.

In a colonization study of a newly formed channel in the Tongue River, Wyoming, USA, maximum densities of macroinvertebrates were obtained in less than 90 days with equilibrium levels reached in about 200 days when source areas were less than 200 m upstream (Gore 1979, 1982). Recovery times increased proportionally according to distance from source areas of colonizers. Macroinvertebrate recovery was dependent upon accumulation of organic detritus and establishment of periphyton populations for the invasion of grazers and detritivores. Predators were the last trophic group to arrive and trophic equilibrium was attained after taxa equilibrium. For a new stream channel associated with the Ponesk Burn in the uplands of Scotland, Doughty and Turner (1991) reported maximum diversity and similarity to a reference site after 80–100 days of invertebrate colonization, and taxa equilibrium at one site was reached after 140–150 days. Trophic equilibrium was reached at this site after 476 days. Equilibrium was not attained at the other two sites. Source distance effects on colonization rates were also observed in this study. Aquatic insects took 5.5 years to achieve similarity to control areas after a channel relocation project in Wisconsin, USA; the long recovery rate being attributed to sandy substrates and lack of coarse particulate organic matter (Narf 1985). In contrast, Malmqvist *et al* (1991) found that invertebrate diversity in a man-made channel (1.5 km long) was similar to that in reference lake-outlet streams within 1 year.

Overall, where channelization reduces substrate heterogeneity and stability, it is likely to reduce the abundance and species richness of the colonizing invertebrate communities (Hortle & Lake 1982). Resident fish populations (mostly Centrachidae) were not established in the new channel of the Tongue River 2 years after colonization had commenced despite the placement of cover structures and boulders to diversify flow patterns and enhance recovery (Gore & Johnson 1980). Similarly in the new channel associated with the Ponesk Burn, brown trout populations had not reached the levels of the reference site after 2 years although recovery was retarded by further disturbances (Doughty & Turner 1991). One of the longest recovery times in the literature relates to a channelized section of the Luxapalila River, Mississippi, USA, where fish populations were considered not to have recovered after 52 years (Arner *et al* 1976).

A recently formed stream following glacial recession permits a unique opportunity to examine the colonization of a new stream channel along its entire length without upstream source areas (equivalent of level I disturbance). After approximately 25 years of development, species equilibrium and maximum diversity have not yet been reached and no non-insect forms have colonized (Milner 1987 and unpublished). However, maximum densities were attained some 14 years earlier. This study illustrates that colonization (and hence recovery) is a long-term process when there are no upstream source areas for drift and refugia areas are distant.

Floods

Floods are rarely of sufficient magnitude to remove the entire stream biota (Minshall *et al* 1983) and so typically fall under level 3 disturbances. Nevertheless floods constitute significant and common disturbances to community structure and function, and recovery times can be relatively long, particularly where there is no or little history of floods in the system. During floods, scour and redistribution of sediment can influence the physical habitat and thereby restrict the ability of macroinvertebrates and attached algae to colonize.

Frequent floods can truncate algal successional sequences and favour well-attached resistant taxa or taxa with recolonization and growth rages high enough to accumulate biomass between floods (Power & Stewart 1987). These authors found that following a flood the filamentous alga *Rhizoclonium* (with specialized basal attachment cells) was reduced four-fold in occurrence whereas *Spirogyra* (usually unbranched and free-floating) decreased by a factor of 20. The distributional pattern of these algae was restored after 26 days. Although filamentous forms of algae are more susceptible to scour during flood events, habitats colonized by certain filamentous forms are frequently characterized by high light and nutrient levels, thereby enhancing faster growth and recovery rates (Steinman & McIntire 1990). In lowland desert streams, gross primary production has been shown to exceed respiration after 5 days following flash flooding (Fisher *et al* 1982).

As mentioned previously, Minshall *et al* (1983) reported recovery times of 650 days for macro-invertebrates to attain species equilibrium after a major flood on the Teton River, Idaho, USA (possibly level 1 leading to primary succession) although maximum densities were reached significantly earlier. After a flood, which had reduced densities to 5% of pre-flood levels in a small Irish river, macroinvertebrates only reached 50% of previous densities after 2 years (Giller *et al* 1991). However, there was no apparent effect on the resident salmonid populations. Molles (1985) reported that biomass and diversity of invertebrates was similar within 1 year of a flash flood on a northern New Mexico stream although differences in community structure remained after 2 years.

In contrast, recovery rates are typically more rapid in rivers where the fauna are adapted to frequent floods. In an unstable, braided river in New Zealand, where flows were highly variable and floods common, numbers and densities of the invertebrate fauna had recovered to pre-flood levels within 132 days following a major flood (Scrimgeour *et al* 1988). In Arizona desert streams in the USA, invertebrate densities recovered within 21 days after flash floods (Fisher *et al* 1982) and within 6 weeks after a 100-year magnitude flood (Collins *et al* 1981).

Matthews (1986) reported fish similarity to have recovered in 8 months following a catastrophic flood in an Arkansas stream (USA), while Meffe and Minckley (1987) showed rapid recovery of fish in desert streams due to behavioural responses during flooding which allowed the native fish to persist. Rainbow trout recolonized a 1-mile stretch of a Californian river within 4 years following the complete elimination of the resident population (Lambert 1988).

Drought

In contrast to floods, drying of stream channels normally occurs gradually and thus many species have evolved life history or behavioural adaptations for rapid recovery when flow returns.

Most studies report macroinvertebrate communities recovered within 1 year (e.g. Larimore *et al* 1959; Ladle & Bass 1981, Griswold *et al* 1982; Morrison 1990) and within 3 months where the community has a history of similar droughts (e.g. Harrison 1966; Sagar 1983). Fish were also shown by Larimore *et al* (1959) to have recovered within 1 year.

Pesticides

Pesticides cover a wide range of toxic chemicals used to control or eradicate undesirable organisms and include insecticides and herbicides. Pesticides can affect waterbodies either indirectly from application to or within the watershed or directly to the river. Recovery times can vary from <1 month to >25 years depending upon the magnitude, toxicity and continued use of the pesticide and its overall persistence (Wallace 1990). This disturbance together with chemical discharges and spills probably causes the greatest variability in recovery times. This topic has been reviewed extensively by Muirhead-Thomson (1987).

Indirect forest spraying with pesticides typically results in recovery times for invertebrates of less than 3 years (Hoffman & Drooz 1953; Dimond 1967; Kreutzweiser & Kingsbury 1987). Similar recovery times have been reported for trout and Atlantic salmon fry and parr (Keenleyside 1967; Warner & Fenderson 1962). Pesticide application frequently induces post-spray drift of invertebrates (Morrison 1977), which thereby become susceptible to predation and physical damage (Kreutzweiser & Kingsbury 1987).

Most direct applications of pesticides have been the result of experimental additions. An acute experimental spill with the insecticide parathion showed macroinvertebrate diversity recovered within 3 months (Ghetti & Gorbi 1985), while Morrison (1977), using experimental treatments with rotenone in three Scottish hill streams, documented densities of invertebrate fauna recovered within 1 year. The rotenone treatment caused increased drift and some mortality of invertebrates. Cook and Moore (1969) reported aquatic insect taxa returned to pre-disturbance levels within 3 months (except Plecoptera – 6 months) following rotenone treatment of a Californian stream. Densities and species diversity of invertebrates took 17 months to recover after an intended point-source introduction of DDT into a Montana stream (Schoenthal 1963). However, in a Nigerian stream, macroinvertebrates had recovered within 3 months after an accidental input of the insecticide, Gammalin-20 (Victor & Ogbeidu 1986). Experimental additions of the insecticide methoxychlor to a small headwater stream in western North Carolina eliminated most insect taxa apart from a few long-lived forms. No upstream sources of colonizers were present and although trophic recovery was complete in 2 years, taxonomic recovery required 5 years (Wallace *et al* 1991). This study highlights the apparent stochastic element to recovery depending upon the timing of the treatment and the flight period of the ovipositing adults when no upstream sources of colonizers are present.

Chemical spills and toxic pollutants

This disturbance is similar to pesticides in causing some of the most variable recovery times, depending upon the initial scale of mortality to the river fauna and the continued persistence of the chemical after the spillage has occurred. Chemical spills typically come under level 2 and 3 disturbances depending upon the impact to the faunas. Edwards (1987) and Yount and Niemi (1990) in their review quote recovery times of nearly instantaneous to >10 years for these types of disturbances.

A fire in a chemical storehouse near Basel, Switzerland in November 1986 (the 'Sandoz Accident') caused what was categorized at the time as 'one of the worst chemical spills ever' into the River Rhine (see Capel *et al* 1988). The spill caused a massive mortality of benthic organisms and fish. Nevertheless within 1 year the benthos had recovered to pre-disturbance levels (Capel *et al* 1988) and within 2 years 40 of the 47 indigenous fish species present before the spill had recolonized (Lelek & Kohler 1990). However, the pre-accident benthos was not highly diversified for it was already affected by chronic chemical contamination. This case again illustrates rapid recovery where the fauna is adapted to previous

disturbances and stresses and where there is a lack of persistence of the chemicals at the affected areas.

The recovery times of periphyton communities exposed to heavy metals may be longer than other disturbances, particularly where the metals adsorb to the sediments or become sequestered inside the cells of the periphytic organisms (Steinman & McIntire 1990). The potential long-term recovery rates of benthic communities completely eliminated by metal pollutants were shown by Chadwick *et al* (1986) in a headwater stream in Montana that had been affected by copper mining and domestic wastes for over 100 years. Invertebrates did not colonize until 3 years after the water quality improved, and after 10 years only partial recovery had been recorded when compared to reference areas. The slow recovery time was attributed to possible continued leaching of metals from streambanks and the lack of an upstream source of colonizers. The continued input of toxic material from abandoned waste lagoons was cited by Hill *et al* (1975) as the principal reason that 2 years after the cessation of pollutant inputs from a chemical plant, aquatic insects had only partially recovered. Where flushing flows remove the persistence of the chemical and there is no residual toxicity, Smith and Distler (1981) reported benthic communities recovered within 6–9 months after being destroyed by a toxic chemical discharge.

Pollution control measures on the River Ebbw Fawr in Wales, UK, improved the water quality of an effluent from a steelworks, and fish, particularly brown trout, began to colonize rapidly (Turnpenny & Williams 1981). At Sixteenmile Creek in Montana, USA, brook and brown trout populations required 3 years to recover after a large quantity of toxaphene-based cattle dip was dumped into the creek (Workman 1981). Recovery was a function of reproductive success and survival of the fish and because the physical habitat had not been significantly altered. Similar recovery times were reported by Johnston and Cheverie (1980) for brook and brown trout populations following the poisoning of a stream in northern Canada with an accidental spill of the insecticide endosulfan, and by Valdez *et al* (1977) for Dolly Varden charr after a massive spill of drilling muds (an aqueous suspension of oils, phenols, bentonite, lignite and ferrochrome lignosulphonate) in a maritime tundra stream in Alaska. In each of these studies sufficient time was necessary for juvenile trout and the charr to move through three age classes to replace the older fish that had been lost. Faster recovery times of 1 year were documented for fish in streams after kills of warm-water species (Gunning & Berra 1969; Olmstead & Cloutman 1974).

Organic pollutants

In most cases recovery from organic pollutants that are biodegradable is more rapid than recovery from chemical or toxic pollutants as typically the pollutants are less persistent, providing there are no further inputs. Given the short generation times of periphyton and their dispersal and colonization abilities, periphyton recovery should only take weeks or months following the cessation of organic pollutant input (Steinman & McIntire 1990).

In the Big River in Ireland, benthic invertebrates had recovered in similarity to upstream reference areas after 8 months following the cessation of organic wastes input from a factory (Douglas & McCreanor 1990). Within 1 year of the improvement of water quality from gross organic pollution in the River Derwent, UK, Brinkhurst (1965) observed a diverse fauna of invertebrates, including molluscs and oxygen-sensitive taxa. Probably one of the most dramatic cases of recovery following organic pollution occurred in the River Thames estuary in England as documented by Gameson and Wheeler (1977). Although a grossly polluted river from the first half of the 19th century, improvements in sewage works effluents since 1955 have dramatically improved the river and no hydrogen sulphide has been present in the water since 1965. A rapid recovery by fish has followed and by 1967, 62 species had been found which represented more than a single capture.

Restoration

With reference to Table 12.1 the factors which cause a −3 on the recovery scale are candidates

for the application of restoration techniques to enhance recovery rates. These include disturbances where the physical habitat is altered, terrestrial and riparian vegetation are significantly affected, there are large disturbed areas far from colonizing sources and where there are continued disturbances arresting recovery.

12.8 CONCLUSIONS

From this overview the following eight key points can be made to summarize the principal conclusions regarding recovery of biotic communities from disturbance that is important to the river manager.

1 The most common forms of anthropogenic disturbances to rivers reported in the literature are DDT insecticide applications in forest sprayings, logging activity, dredging/channelization, and rotenone applications. The most common form of natural disturbance is floods.

2 Recovery end-points most commonly used in studies are total density, total biomass and taxa richness, although they typically occur earlier than other potential end-points such as taxa equilibrium, keystone species recovery, production and physical habitat recovery. The most suitable end-point is system and disturbance specific and the river manager must decide which is the most appropriate under the circumstances. It may not always be in a manager's best interests for a river system to return exactly to the pre-disturbance community which, in any event with the passing of time, may be difficult to define. Also in many cases of disturbance, no pre-disturbance data are available and thus reference areas are necessary for comparison.

3 For most disturbances, macroinvertebrate total density, total biomass and taxa richness typically recover within 1 year (see Fig. 12.3). Where upstream sources of drift are absent and refugia are distant, recovery times of macroinvertebrates can be significantly longer. At the order level, time to recovery for the major riverine insect groups are ranked: Diptera < Ephemeroptera < Trichoptera < Plecoptera (see Fig. 12.4).

4 Fish population recovery is generally longer than macroinvertebrates and in many cases

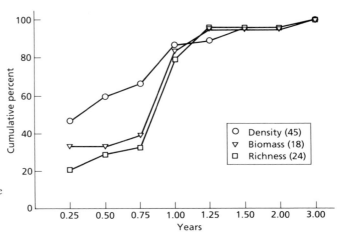

Fig. 12.3 Recovery times of macroinvertebrate total density, total biomass and taxa richness following disturbances (from Niemi *et al* 1990).

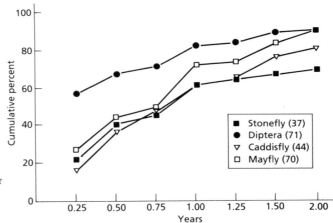

Fig. 12.4 Cumulative percentage over time for recovery end-points for four macroinvertebrate orders (from Niemi *et al* 1990).

requires juveniles to pass through yearly age classes before recovery is complete.

5 Macroinvertebrate communities, with species assemblages that are opportunistic with short life cycles selected as a result of a history of previous disturbances, will recover more rapidly to future similar disturbances when compared to a community in a relatively stable environment. It is also likely the former communities will also recover more rapidly to dissimilar disturbances.

6 Level 3 and 4 disturbances typically result in relatively rapid recovery times compared to level 1 and 2, except where the watershed or the physical habitat is significantly disturbed. Watershed disturbance (e.g. mining and logging) and channel modifications which alter the physical habitat result in the longest recovery times of the biotic communities. These types of disturbances frequently necessitate restoration techniques.

7 Pesticides, chemical spills and toxic pollutant disturbances typically result in the most variable recovery times depending upon the persistence of the toxicant and the flushing capacity of the system. Recovery in a number of systems has been delayed by the continued leaching of toxi-

cants after the initial disturbance had ceased. **8** Recovery from organic pollutants is typically more rapid than chemical and toxic pollutants.

ACKNOWLEDGEMENTS

I am extremely grateful to Ross Doughty, Paul Giller, David Gilvear, Jim Gore, Sam Lake and Bruce Wallace for their constructive comments on an earlier version of this manuscript. Thanks to Geoff Petts and an anonymous reviewer for additional comments and to Maureen Milner for preparing the figures and tables.

REFERENCES

Anderson NH, Wisseman RW. (1987) Recovery of the Trichoptera fauna near Mt. St. Helens five years after the 1980 eruption. In: Bournaud M, Tachet H (eds) *Proceedings of the 5th International Symposium on Trichoptera*, pp. 367–73. W. Junk, Dordrecht. [12.5]

Arner DH, Robinette HR, Frasier JE, Gray MH. (1976) *Effects of Channelization of the Luxapalila River on Fish, Aquatic Invertebrates, Water Quality, and Furbearers*. Office of Biological Sciences, US Department of Interior, Fish and Wildlife Service, Washington, DC. [12.7]

Begon M, Harper JL, Townsend CR. (1990) *Ecology: Individuals, Populations and Communities*, 2nd edn. Blackwell Scientific Publications, Oxford. [12.3]

Bender EA, Case TJ, Gilpin ME. (1984) Perturbation experiments in community ecology: theory and practice. *Ecology* **65**: 1–13. [12.6]

Beschta RL, Bilby RE, Brown GW, Holtby LB, Hofstra TD. (1987) Stream temperature and aquatic habitat: fisheries and forestry interactions. In: Salo EO, Cundy TW (eds) *Streamside Management: Forestry and Fishery Interactions*, pp. 191–232. Forestry Resources Contribution no. 57, University of Washington, Seattle. [12.7]

Bradshaw AD. (1988) Alternative endpoints for reclamation. In: Cairns JJ (ed.) *Rehabilitating Damaged Ecosystems*, Vol. II, pp. 69–85. CRC Press, Boca Raton. [12.2]

Brinkhurst RO. (1965) Observations on the recovery of a British river from gross organic pollution. *Hydrobiologia* **25**: 9–51. [12.7]

Brundin L. (1967) Insects and the problem of austral disjunctive distribution. *Annual Review of Entomology* **12**: 149–68. [12.5]

Burns DC. (1991) Cumulative effects of small modifications to habitat. *Fisheries* **16**: 12–17. [12.7]

Cairns JJ Jr. (1990) Lack of theoretical basis for predicting rate and pathways of recovery. *Environmental Management* **14**: 517–26. [12.2, 12.3]

Campbell IC, Doeg TJ. (1989) Impact of timber harvesting and production on streams: a review. *Australian Journal of Marine and Freshwater Sciences* **40**: 519–39. [12.6]

Capel PD, Giger W, Reichert R, Wanner O. (1988) Accidental input of pesticides into the Rhine River. *Environmental Science and Technology* **22**: 992–7. [12.7]

Chadwick JW, Canton SP, Dent RL. (1986) Recovery of benthic invertebrate communities in Silver Bow Creek, Montana, following improved metal mine wastwater treatment. *Water, Air and Soil Pollution* **28**: 427–38. [12.7]

Chamberlain TW, Harr RD, Everest FH. (1991) Timber harvesting, silviculture, and watershed processes. In: *Influences of Forest and Rangeland Management on Salmonid Habitat*, pp. 181–205. American Fisheries Society Special Publication. American Fisheries Society, Betscheda. [12.7]

Collins JP, Young G, Howell J, Minckley WL. (1981) Impact of flooding in a Sonoran desert stream, including elimination of an endangered fish population (*Poeciliopsis O. occidentadlis*, Poeciliidae). *Southwestern Naturalist* **26**: 415–23. [12.7]

Cook RJ, Barron JC, Rapendick RI, Williams GJ. (1981) Impact on agriculture of the Mount St. Helens eruptions. *Science* **211**: 16–22. [12.7]

Cook SF, Moore RL. (1969) The effect of a rotenone treatment on the insect fauna of a Californian stream. *Transactions of the American Fisheries Society* **98**: 539–44. [12.7]

Cummins KW. (1994) Invertebrates. In: Calow P, Petts GE (eds) *The Rivers Handbook*, Vol. 1, pp. 234–50. Blackwell Scientific Publications, Oxford. [12.3]

Cummins KW, Klug MJ. (1979) Feeding ecology of stream invertebrates. *Annual Review of Ecology and Systematics* **10**: 147–72. [12.6]

Davis WP, Hoss DE, Scott GI, Sheridan PF. (1984) Fisheries resource impacts from spills of oil or hazardous substances. In: Cairns J Jr, Buikema AL Jr (eds) *Restoration of Habitats Impacted by Oil Spills*, pp. 157–72. Butterworth, Boston. [12.1]

DeAngelis DL, Mulholland PJ, Elwood JW, Palumbo AV, Steinman AD. (1990) Biochemical cycling constraints on stream ecosystem recovery. *Environmental Management* **14**: 685–97. [12.6]

Dimond J. (1967) Pesticides and stream insects. *Maine Forest Service Bulletin* No. 23, pp. 1–21. [12.7]

Doeg TJ, Lake PS, Marchant R. (1989a) Colonization of experimentally disturbed patches by stream macroinvertebrates in the Acheron River, Victoria. *Australian Journal of Ecology* **14**: 207–20. [12.1, 12.6]

Doeg TJ, Marchant R, Douglas M, Lake PS. (1989b) Experimental colonization of sand, gravel and stones by macroinvertebrates in the Acheron River, southeastern Australia. *Freshwater Biology* **22**: 57–64. [12.5]

Doughty CR, Turner MJ. (1991) *The Ponesk Burn Diversion: Colonization by Benthic Invertebrates and Fish.* Technical Report No. 98. Clyde River Purification Board, East Kilbride. [12.7]

Douglas DJ, McCreanor J. (1990) The Big River, Co. Louth, Ireland: a case study in recovery. *Annals of Limnology* **26**: 73–9. [12.7]

Duncan WFA, Brusven MA. (1985a) Energy dynamics of three low-order southeast Alaska streams: allochthonous processes. *Journal of Freshwater Ecology* **3**: 233–48. [12.7]

Duncan WFA, Brusven MA. (1985b) Energy dynamics of three low-order southeast Alaska streams: autochthonous production. *Journal of Freshwater Ecology* **3**: 155–66. [12.7]

Edwards RW. (1987) Ecological assessment of the degradation and recovery of rivers from pollution. In: Ravera O (ed.) *Ecological Assessment of Environmental Degradation, Pollution and Recovery*, pp. 159–94. Elsevier Press, Amsterdam. [12.7]

Everest FH, Beschta RL, Scrivener JC, Koski KV, Sedell JR, Cederholm CJ. (1987) Fine sediment and salmonid production: a paradox. In: Salo EO, Cundy TW (eds) *Streamside Management: Forestry and Fishery Interactions*, pp. 98–142. Forestry Resources Contribution No. 57, University of Washington, Seattle. [12.6, 12.7]

Fisher SG. (1990) Recovery processes in lotic ecosystems: limits of successional theory. *Environmental Management* **14**: 725–36. [12.4]

Fisher SG, Gray LJ. (1983) Secondary production and organic matter processing by collector macroinvertebrates in a desert stream. *Ecology* **64**: 1217–24. [12.6]

Fisher SG, Gray LG, Grimm NB, Busch DE. (1982) Temporal succession in a desert stream ecosystem following flash flooding. *Ecological Monographs* **52**: 93–110. [12.7]

Franklin JF, Frenzen PM, Swanson FJ. (1988) Re-creation of ecosystems at Mount St. Helens: Contrasts in artificial and natural approaches. In: Cairns J Jr (ed) *Rehabilitating Damaged Ecosystems*, vol. II pp. 1–34. CRC Press, Boca Raton. [12.7]

Gameson ALH, Wheeler A. (1977) Restoration and recovery of the Thames estuary. In: Cairns J Jr, Dickson KL, Herricks EE (eds) *Recovery and Restoration of Damaged Ecosystems*, pp. 72–101. University of Virginia Press, Charlottesville. [12.7]

Ghetti PF, Gorbi G. (1985) Effects of acute pollution on macroinvertebrates in a stream. *Verhandlungen Internationale Vereinigung für Theoretische und Angewandte Limnologie* **22**: 2426–31. [12.7]

Giller PS, Sangpradub N, Twomey H. (1991) Catastrophic flooding and macroinvertebrate community structure. *Verhandlungen Internationale Vereinigung für Theoretische und Angewandte*

Limnologie **24**: 1724–9. [12.6, 12.7]

Gore JA. (1979) Patterns of initial benthic recolonization of a reclaimed coal strip-mined river channel. *Canadian Journal of Zoology* **57**: 2429–39. [12.3, 12.6, 12.7]

Gore JA. (1982) Benthic invertebrate colonization: source distance effects on community composition. *Hydrobiologia* **94**: 183–93. [12.3, 12.6, 12.7]

Gore JA. (1985) Mechanisms of colonization and habitat enhancement for benthic macroinvertebrates in restored river channels. In: Gore JA (ed) *The Restoration of Rivers and Streams*, pp. 81–101. Butterworths, Boston. [12.1]

Gore JA, Johnson LS. (1980) *Establishment of Biotic and Hydrologic Stability in a Reclaimed Coal Strip-Mined River Channel.* Institute of Energy and Environment, University of Wyoming, Laramie. [12.7]

Gore JA, Milner AM. (1990) Island biogeographic theory: can it be used to predict lotic recovery rates? *Environmental Management* **14**: 737–54. [12.1, 12.3, 12.4, 12.6, 12.7]

Gore JA, Kelly JR, Yount DJ. (1990) Application of ecological theory to determining recovery potential of disturbed lotic ecosystems: research needs and priorities. *Environmental Management* **14**: 755–62. [12.1, 12.3]

Griswold BL, Edwards CJ, Woods LC III. (1982) Recolonization of Macroinvertebrates and fish in a channelized stream after drought. *Ohio Journal of Science* **82**: 96–102. [12.7]

Gunning GE, Berra TM. (1969) Fish repopulation of experimentally decimated segments in the headwaters of the two streams. *Transactions of the American Fisheries Society* **98**: 305–8. [12.7]

Gurtz ME, Wallace JB. (1984) Substrate-mediated responses of stream invertebrates to disturbance. *Ecology* **65**: 1556–69. [12.1, 12.7]

Haefner JD, Wallace JB. (1981) Shifts in aquatic insect populations in first-order Appalachian stream following a decade of old field succession. *Canadian Journal of Fisheries and Aquatic Sciences* **38**: 353–9. [12.7]

Harrison AD. (1966) Recolonization of a Rhodesian stream after drought. *Archiv für Hydrobiologie* **62**: 405–21. [12.7]

Hawkins CP, Sedell JR. (1990) The role of refugia in the recolonization of streams devastated by the 1980 eruption of Mount St. Helens. *Northwest Science* **64**: 271–4. [12.7]

Heifetz J, Murphy ML, Koski K. (1986) Effects of logging on winter habitat of juvenile salmonids in Alaskan streams. *North American Journal of Fisheries Management* **6**: 52–8. [12.7]

Hill DM, Taylor EA, Saylor CF. (1975) Status of faunal recovery in the north fork Houlston River, Tennessee and Virginia. *Proceedings of the Southeastern Associ-*

ation of Game and Fish Commissioners **28**: 398–413. [12.7]

Hoffman CH, Drooz AT. (1953) Effects of a C-47 airplane application of DDT on fish-food organisms in two Pennsylvania watersheds. *American Midland Naturalist* **50**: 172–88. [12.7]

Hortle KG, Lake PS. (1982) Macroinvertebrate assemblages in channelized and unchannelized sections of the Bunyip River, Victoria. *Australian Journal of Marine and Freshwater Research* **33**: 1071–82. [12.7]

Huston M. (1979) A general hypothesis of species diversity. *American Naturalist* **113**: 81–101. [12.3]

Johnston CE, Cheverie JC. (1980) Repopulation of a coastal stream by brook trout and rainbow trout after Endosulfan poisoning. *Progressive Fish Culturist* **42**: 107–10. [12.7]

Keenleyside MHA. (1967) Effects of forest spraying with DDT in New Brunswick on food of young Atlantic salmon. *Journal of the Fisheries Research Board of Canada* **24**: 807–22. [12.7]

Kelly JR, Harwell MA. (1990) Indicators of ecosystem recovery. *Environmental Management* **14**: 527–45. [12.1, 12.3]

Kreutzweiser DP, Kingsbury PD. (1987) Permethrin treatments in Canadian forests. Part 2: Impact on stream invertebrates. *Pesticide Science* **19**: 49–60. [12.7]

Krumholz LA, Minckley WL. (1984) Changes in a fish population in the upper Ohio River following temporary pollution abatement. *Transactions of the American Fisheries Society* **93**: 1–6. [12.3]

Ladle M, Bass JAB. (1981) The ecology of a small chalk stream and its responses to drying during drought conditions. *Archiv für Hydrobiologie* **90**: 448–66. [12.6, 12.7]

Lake PS. (1990) Disturbing hard and soft bottom communities: A comparison of marine and freshwater environments. *Australian Journal of Ecology* **15**: 477–88. [12.1]

Lake PS, Barmuta LA. (1986) Stream benthic communities: persistent presumptions and current speculations. In: DeDecker P, Williams WD (eds) *Limnology in Australia*, pp. 263–76. Dr W. Junk, Dordrecht. [12.1]

Lake PS, Doeg TJ, Marchant R. (1989) Effects of multiple disturbance on macroinvertebrate communities in the Acheron River, Victoria. *Australian Journal of Ecology* **14**: 507–14. [12.1]

Lambert TR. (1988) Recolonization of a small stream by rainbow trout following a flood event. In: *68th Annual Conference of the Western Association of Wildlife Agencies*, pp. 258–64. Western Division, American Fisheries Society, Albuquerque. [12.7]

Lamberti GA, Gregory SV, Ashkenas LR, Wildman RC, Moore KMS. (1991) Stream ecosystem recovery following a catastrophic debris flow. *Canadian Journal*

of Fisheries and Aquatic Sciences **48**: 196–208. [12.6]

Larimore RW, Childers WF, Heckrotte C. (1959) Destruction and re-establishment of stream fish and invertebrates affected by drought. *Transactions of the American Fisheries Society* **88**: 261–85. [12.7]

Lelek A, Kohler C. (1990) Restoration of fish communities of the Rhine River two years after a heavy pollution wave. *Regulated Rivers: Research and Management* **5**: 57–66. [12.7]

Luedtke RJ, Brusven MA. (1976) Effects of sand sedimentation on colonization of stream insects. *Journal of the Fisheries Research Board of Canada* **33**: 1881–6. [12.6]

McCormick PV, Stevenson JR. (1991) Mechanisms of benthic algal succession in lotic environments. *Ecology* **72**: 1835–48. [12.4]

Magnuson JJ, Reiger HA, Christie WJ, Sonzogni WC. (1980) To rehabilitate and restore great lake ecosystems. In: Cairns J Jr (ed) *The Recovery Process in Damaged Ecosystems*, pp. 95–112. Ann Arbor Science Publishers, Ann Arbor. [12.1]

Malmqvist B, Rundle S, Brönmark C, Erlandson A. (1991) Invertebrate colonization of a new, man-made stream in southern Sweden. *Freshwater Biology* **26**: 307–24. [12.7]

Martin DJ, Wasserman LJ, Dale VH. (1986) Influence of riparian vegetation of posteruption survival of coho salmon fingerlings on the westside streams of Mount St. Helens, Washington. *North American Journal of Fisheries Management* **6**: 1–18. [12.6]

Matthews WJ. (1986) Fish faunal structure in an Ozark stream: stability, persistence and a catastrophic flood. *Copeia*, pp. 388–97. [12.7]

Meffe GK, Minckley WL. (1987) Persistence and stability of fish and invertebrate assemblages in a repeatedly disturbed Sonoran Desert stream. *American Midland Naturalist* **117**: 177–91. [12.7]

Milner AM. (1987) Colonization and ecological development of new streams in Glacier Bay National Park, Alaska. *Freshwater Biology* **18**: 53–70. [12.7]

Minshall GW, Andrews DA, Manuel-Faler CY. (1983) Application of island biogeographic theory to streams: macroinvertebrate recolonization of the Teton River, Idaho. In: Barnes JR, Minshall GW (eds) *Stream Ecology: Application and Testing of General Ecological Theory*, pp. 279–97. Plenum Press, New York. [12.3, 12.7]

Minshall GW, Brock JT, Varley JD. (1989) Wildfire and Yellowstone's stream ecosystems. *BioScience* **39**: 707–15. [12.7]

Molles MC Jr. (1985) Recovery of a stream invertebrate community from a flash flood in Tesuque Creek, New Mexico. *The Southwestern Naturalist* **30**: 279–87. [12.7]

Morrison BR. (1977) The effects of rotenone on the invertebrate fauna of three hill streams in Scotland.

Fisheries Management **8**: 128–38. [12.7]

Morrison BR. (1990) Recolonisation of four small streams in central Scotland following drought conditions in 1984. *Hydrobiologia* **208**: 261–67. [12.6, 12.7]

Muirhead-Thomson RC. (1987) *Pesticide Impact on Stream Fauna with Special Reference to Macroinvertebrates*. Cambridge University Press, Cambridge. [12.7]

Murphy ML, Koski K. (1989) Input and depletion of woody debris in Alaska streams and implications for streamside management. *North American Journal of Fishery Management* **9**: 427–36. [12.7]

Murphy ML, Heifetz J, Johnson SW, Koski KV, Thedinga J. (1986) Effects of clear-cut logging with and without buffer strips on juvenile salmonids in Alaskan streams. *Canadian Journal of Fisheries and Aquatic Sciences* **43**: 1521–33. [12.7]

Narf RP. (1985) Aquatic insect colonization and substrate changes in a relocated stream segment. *The Great Lakes Entomologist* **18**: 83–92. [12.7]

Niemi GJ, DeVore P, Detenbeck N, Taylor D, Yount JD, Lima A, Pastor J, Naiman RJ. (1990) Overview of case studies on recovery of aquatic systems from disturbance. *Environmental Management* **14**: 571–88. [12.5, 12.6, 12.7, 12.8]

Olmstead LL, Cloutman DG. (1974) Repopulation after a fish kill in Mud Creek, Washington County, Arkansas, following pesticide pollution. *Transactions of the American Fisheries Society* **103**: 79–87. [12.7]

Oswood MW, Irons JG, Milner AM. (1995) Alaska. In: Cushing CE, Minshall GW, Cummins KW (eds) *River and Stream Ecosystems*. Elsevier Press, Amsterdam. pp. 9–32 [12.6]

Peters RH. (1988) Some general problems for ecology illustrated by food web theory. *Ecology* **69**: 1673–6. [12.1]

Peterson BJ, Hobbie JE, Hersey AE, Lock MA, Ford TE, Vestal JR, McKinley VL, Hullar MAJ, Miller MC, Ventullo RM, Volk GS. (1985) Transformation of a tundra river from heterotrophy to autotrophy by addition of phosphorus. *Science* **229**: 1383–6. [12.6]

Poff NL. (1992) Why disturbance can be predictable: a perspective on the definition of disturbance in streams. *Journal of the North American Benthological Association* **11**: 86–92. [12.1]

Power ME, Stewart AJ. (1987) Disturbance and recovery of an algal assemblage following flooding in an Oklahoma stream. *American Midland Naturalist* **117**: 333–45. [12.7]

Reice SR. (1985) Experimental disturbance and the maintenance of species diversity in a stream community. *Oecologia* **67**: 90–7. [12.1, 12.3]

Reice SR, Wissmar RC, Naiman RJ. (1990) Disturbance regimes, resilience, and recovery of animal communities and habitats in lotic ecosystems. *Environ-*

mental Management **14**: 647–59. [12.3]

Resh VH, Brown AV, Covich AP, Gurtz ME, Li HW, Minshall GW, Reice SR, Sheldon AL, Wallace JB, Wissmar RC. (1988) The role of disturbance theory in stream ecology. *Journal of the North American Benthological Society* **7**: 433–55. [12.1, 12.5]

Rushforth SR, Squires LE, Cushing CE. (1986) Algal communities of springs and streams in the Mt. St. Helens region, Washington, U.S.A. following the May 1980 eruption. *Journal of Phycology* **22**: 129–37. [12.7]

Rykiel EJ. (1985) Towards a definition of ecological disturbance. *Australian Journal of Ecology* **10**: 361–6. [12.1]

Sagar PM. (1983) Invertebrate recolonization of previously dry channels in the Rakaia River. *New Zealand Journal of Marine and Freshwater Research* **17**: 377–86. [12.6, 12.7]

Schoenthal ND. (1963) Some effects of DDT on cold water fish and fish-food organisms. PhD Thesis. Montana State College, Bozeman. [12.7]

Scrimgeour GJ, Davidson RJ, Davidson JM. (1988) Recovery of benthic macroinvertebrates and epilithic communities following a large flood, in an unstable, braided, New Zealand river. *New Zealand Journal of Marine and Freshwater Research* **22**: 337–44. [12.7]

Sedell JR, Reeves GH, Hauer FR, Stanford JA, Hawkins CP. (1990) Role of refugia in recovery from disturbances: Modern fragmented and disconnected river systems. *Environmental Management* **14**: 711–24. [12.6]

Shaw DW, Minshall GW. (1980) Colonization of an introduced substrate by stream macroinvertebrates. *Oikos* **34**: 259–71. [12.3]

Smith DL, Distler DA. (1981) Recovery of a benthic macroinvertebrate community following a toxic chemical discharge in a sandy plains stream. *Southwestern Naturalist* **25**: 547–51. [12.7]

Smith RD. (1989) Current research investigating channel unit distribution in streams of southeast Alaska. In: Alexander EB (ed) *Watershed 89: Proceedings of a Conference on the Stewardship of Soil, Air and Water Resources*. Alaska Region R-10-MB-77, U.S. Forest Service, Juneau. [12.7]

Sousa WP. (1984) The role of disturbance in natural communities. *Annual Review of Ecology and Systematics* **15**: 353–91. [12.1]

Southwood TR. (1978) *Ecological Methods with Particular Reference to the Study of Insect Populations*. Chapman & Hall, London. [12.3]

Sparks RE, Bayley PB, Kohler SL, Osbourne LL. (1990) Disturbance and recovery of large floodplain rivers. *Environmental Management* **14**: 699–709. [12.1]

Statzner B, Higler B. (1985) Questions and comments on the river continuum concept. *Canadian Journal of Fisheries and Aquatic Sciences* **42**: 1038–44. [12.4]

Steinman AD, McIntire CD. (1990) Recovery of lotic

periphyton communities after disturbance. *Environmental Management* **14**: 589–604. [12.5, 12.7]

Sullivan K, Lisle TE, Dolloff CA. (1987) Stream channels: the link between Forests and fishes. In: Salo EO, Cundy TW (eds) *Streamside Management: Forestry and Fishery Interactions*, pp. 39–97. Forestry Resources Contribution No. 57, University of Washington, Seattle. [12.7]

Tolbert VR, Vaughan GL. (1979) Stripmining as it relates to benthic insect communities and their recovery. *West Virginia Academy of Science* **51**: 168–81. [12.7]

Townsend CR, Hildrew AL, Schofield K. (1987) Persistence of stream invertebrate communities in relation to the environmental variability. *Journal of Animal Ecology* **56**: 597–613. [12.3]

Turnpenny AWH, Williams R. (1981) Factors affecting the recovery of fish populations in an industrial river. *Environmental Pollution (Series A)* **26**: 39–58. [12.7]

Valdez RA, Helm WT, Neuhold JM. (1977) Aquatic ecology. In: Merritt ML, Fuller RG (eds) *The Environment of Amchitka Island*, pp. 287–313. Technical Information Center, ERDA, Washington DC. [12.7]

Vannote RL, Minshall GW, Cummins KW, Sedell JR, Cushing CE. (1980) The river continuum concept. *Canadian Journal of Fisheries and Aquatic Sciences* **37**: 130–7. [12.6]

Victor R, Ogbeidu AE. (1986) Recolonisation of macrobenthic invertebrates in a Nigerian stream after pesticide treatment and associated disruption. *Environmental Pollution (Series A)* **41**: 125–37. [12.7]

Wallace JB. (1990) Recovery of lotic macroinvertebrate communities from disturbance. *Environmental Management* **14**: 605–20. [12.5, 12.6, 12.7]

Wallace JB, Gurtz ME. (1986) Response of *Baetis* mayflies (Ephemeroptera) to catchment logging. *American Midland Naturalist* **115**: 25–41. [12.7]

Wallace JB, Gurtz ME, Smith-Cuffney F. (1988) Long-term comparisons of insect abundances in disturbed and undisturbed Appalachian headwater streams. *Verhandlungen Internationale Vereinigung für Theoretische und Angewandte Limnologie* **23**: 1224–31. [12.7]

Wallace JB, Huryn AD, Lugthart GJ. (1990) Colonization of a headwater stream during three years of seasonal insecticide applications. *Hydrobiologia* **211**: 65–76. [12.5, 12.7]

Ward JV, Stanford JA. (1983) The intermediate disturbance hypothesis: an explanation for biotic diversity patterns in lotic ecosystems. In: Fontaine TD, Bartell SM (eds) *Dynamics of Lotic Ecosystems*, pp. 347–56.

Ann Arbor Science Publishers, Ann Arbor. [12.3]

Warner K, Fenderson OC. (1962) Effects of DDT spraying for forest insects on Maine trout streams. *Journal of Wildlife Management* **26**: 86–93. [12.7]

Webster JR, Patten BC. (1979) Effects of watershed perturbation on stream potassium and calcium dynamics. *Ecological Monographs* **49**: 51–72. [12.6]

Webster JR, Waide JB, Patten BC. (1975) Nutrient recycling and the stability of ecosystems. In: Howell FG, Gentry JB, Smith MH (eds) *Mineral Cycling in Southeastern Ecosystems*, pp. 1–27. US Energy Research and Development Administration (CONF-740513). [12.1, 12.6]

Webster JR, Gurtz ME, Hains JJ, Meyer JL, Swank WT, Waide JB, Wallace JB. (1983) Stability of stream ecosystems. In: Barnes JR, Minshall GW (eds) *Stream Ecology: Application and Testing of General Ecological Theory*, pp. 355–95. Plenum Press, New York. [12.7]

Webster JR, Golladay SW, Benfield EF, Meyer JL, Swank WT, Wallace JB. (1992) Catchment disturbance and stream response: An overview of stream research at Coweeta Hydrological Laboratory. In: Boon PJ, Calow P, Petts GE (eds) *River Conservation and Management*, pp. 231–53. John Wiley & Sons, Chichester. [12.7]

White PS, Pickett STA. (1985) Natural disturbance and patch dynamics: an introduction. In: White PS, Pickett STA (eds) *The ecology of natural disturbance and patch dynamics*, pp. 3–13. Academic Press, New York. [12.1]

Williams DD. (1981) Migrations and distributions of stream benthos. In: Lock MA, Williams DD (eds) *Perspectives in Running Water Ecology*, pp. 155–207. Plenum Press, New York. [12.5]

Williams DD, Hynes HBN. (1976) The recolonization mechanisms of stream benthos. *Oikos* **27**: 265–72. [12.5]

Wilzbach P, Dudley TH, Hall JD. (1983) *Recovery Patterns in Stream Communities Impacted by the Mt. St. Helens Eruption*. Water Resources Research Institute Report No. WRRI-83. Oregon State University, Corvallis. [12.7]

Workman DL. (1981) Recovery of rainbow trout and brown trout populations following chemical poisoning in Sixteenmile Creek, Montana. *North American Journal of Fisheries Management* **1**: 144–50. [12.7]

Yount JD, Niemi GJ. (1990) Recovery of lotic communities and ecosystems from disturbance — a narrative review of case studies. *Environmental Management* **14**: 547–69. [12.7]

Index